THE KING'S CUSTOMS

THE KING'S CUSTOMS

VOL. II

AN ACCOUNT OF MARITIME REVENUE,
CONTRABAND TRAFFIC, THE INTRO-
DUCTION OF FREE TRADE, AND THE
ABOLITION OF THE NAVIGATION AND
CORN LAWS, FROM 1801 TO 1855

BY HENRY ATTON & HENRY HURST HOLLAND

WITH A PREFACE BY F. S. PARRY, C.B.
DEPUTY-CHAIRMAN OF THE BOARD OF CUSTOMS AND EXCISE

LONDON
JOHN MURRAY, ALBEMARLE STREET, W.
1910

CHARLES W. PEACH, A.L.S.

Frontispiece.

PREFACE

IN the history of the British Customs, as perhaps in the history of civilized Europe, the end of the eighteenth century may be said to mark 'the passing away of old things.' Our authors' first volume described a Britain in which the consumer was in a way at the mercy of the producer, the labourer defenceless against the employer. The consumer's only remedy lay in smuggling, the labourer's in riot. Almost every article of import was dutiable ; the income tax was unknown.

The present volume describes a period during which it might have been truly said, ' Lo, all things are becoming new.' The navigation and corn laws disappeared, the slave trade and slavery were extinguished, the copyright laws were remodelled, the ancient levies of 4½ per cent., prisage, butlerage, and many of the old import prohibitions and restrictions, were abolished. Labour organized its forces ; indeed, the evolutionary methods of trade unionism interwove themselves so closely with those of free trade that their results have been often confounded. The Colonies, with the precedent of the American Revolt to guide them, asserted with success their fiscal independence, the home Government meanwhile gracefully doing its best to disprove Burke's acrid maxim that ' to tax and to please, no more than to love and to be wise, is not given to man.'

Administratively speaking, the period at which this second volume appears is scarcely less important than that described at pp. 88-92, when the separate Customs Boards of the three kingdoms were centralized in Thames

Street, for it is little more than a year ago that the
amalgamation of the services of Customs and Excise gave
to one Board full control of the indirect taxation of the
United Kingdom.   Our authors have not hesitated to
emphasize the popular objections to Customs and Excise
duties ; still, the joint establishment may be allowed to
secure comforting assurance against any fears of imminent
dissolution, by contemplating the equally obvious objections to direct taxation.

Customs history, properly studied, may be found fruitful
of striking lessons.   Possibly the most novel of these is
the vital importance of discriminating clearly between
names and things.   To mention an instance that is near
to all of us : the terms ' Free Trade ' and ' Protection '
existed a century ago, but whether they meant the same
as they mean to-day is a question worth deep individual
consideration.   It is as a welcome help towards closer
thinking on such matters, and not merely as a picturesque
account of old days, old commerce, old taxes, old evasions,
and the struggles of the old legislative mind, that this
work deserves the attention of the reading public, both
here and in the Colonies.

F. S. PARRY.

INTRODUCTION

THIS treatise deals with that memorable period during which the British Customs system was gradually moulded into the form suggested by Adam Smith. The sources of authority and quotation have been found in departmental records—accounts of the practical working of the revenue, navigation, slave, corn, fishery, and copyright laws, preserved in a room at the Custom House, London. These are by no means so numerous as they might have been, had half the care in custody which now obtains been practised in the past. It is evident that many documents have become dispersed or been destroyed—documents which might have been of great use to future historical students—students who may be more desirous to understand their ancestors' habits and doings than to study battles, dates, and coronations.

One tolerably good ' find ' has been made quite recently. The ' Plantation Papers,' relating to colonial Customs matters from 1814 (the date of the burning of the Custom House) to the termination of the British Customs Board's control of colonial revenue, have been discovered in the cellars of the King's Warehouse. Among these are many documents highly illustrative of Customs and commercial proceedings in the colonies, and we have taken the opportunity of quoting from them at considerable length.

The practice pursued in vol. i. of blending revenue and departmental history in the first part of each chapter, and preventive laws and smuggling incidents in the second, has been followed in this volume. The list of ' Illustrative Documents ' has been made retrospective, and much more extensive than the previous one, many readers having expressed a desire in that direction.

Great care has been taken in selection and quotation, yet the documents used have been so numerous and complicated that it is possible we may here and there have committed slight blunders; but we think that these, if they exist at all, will merely take the form of unimportant errors of detail. The labour has been arduous, and the exigencies of duty and locality have compelled us to work separately and confer by correspondence.

We beg to express our sincere thanks to their Honours the Commissioners of Customs and Excise for allowing access during unofficial hours to their recently collected old books and manuscripts, and to the Marquis of Londonderry for the use of his library at Wynyard Park, also to the editors of the *Athenæum*, *Vanity Fair*, the *Annual Register*, and the *Times*, for their kind permission to use certain material.

THE AUTHORS.

CONTENTS

	PAGE
PREFACE	V
INTRODUCTION	vii
CHAPTER	
I. HUNGER AND CONSOLIDATIONS	I
II. THE PERIOD OF GRADUAL RELAXATIONS	135
III. TOWARDS FREE TRADE	285
IV. CUSTOMS LITERATI	394
APPENDIX, SHOWING ILLUSTRATIVE DOCUMENTS	406
INDEX	493

ix

LIST OF ILLUSTRATIONS

CHARLES JAMES PEACH - - - - *Frontispiece*

SIR FRANCIS HASTINGS DOYLE - - - *To face p.* 122

REVENUE CRUISER 'VIGILANT,' WITH BARGE
    'ALFRED' IN TOW - - - - ,, 234

BOARD-ROOM, CUSTOM HOUSE, LONDON - - ,, 286

REVENUE CRUISER CHASING SMUGGLER BY
    NIGHT ON THE KENTISH COAST - - ,, 340

SPECIMEN PAGES FROM REGISTER KEPT BY
    HUMPHREY READ, DEPUTY-CONTROLLER,
    PARKGATE - - - - *Between pp.* 406-7

FACSIMILE OF REPORT OF THE 'JOHN,' OF
    DUMFRIES. JOHN PAUL ('PAUL JONES'),
    MASTER (1769). - - - - *To face p.* 439

ERRATA

Page 68, line 2, *for* 'island' *read* 'colony.'
Page 136, line 28, *for* 'square-rigged' *read* 'fore-and-aft.'

THE KING'S CUSTOMS

CHAPTER I

HUNGER AND CONSOLIDATIONS

1801—1825

BEFORE entering upon the purely fiscal history of the first half of the nineteenth century, it is necessary to deal with a matter of even greater importance. Nothing is so momentous as the question of physical sustenance, and at no period of English history has the question assumed so ugly and daunting an aspect as in the year 1801. To a certain extent this was caused by alterations in the laws affecting the importation of corn. Be it borne in mind that the enforcement of those venerable statutes lay with the Customs.

There is much misconception at the present day as to the structure and tendency of the old Corn Laws. Most people think that protection of English agriculture was a measure adopted during the first forty years of the nineteenth century, and that the dearness of bread then prevailing was due to Protection only. This is a fallacy. The supply of corn had for hundreds of years been an important subject of consideration with English legislators, and many thoughtful people believed that a sliding scale was the best method of insuring cheap bread, and at the same time safeguarding the interests of agriculture and the landed gentry. It is necessary to examine into this. Yet, before displaying cold figures, it must be repeated that at the beginning of the nineteenth century the ogre of starvation was firmly installed in Great Britain. No matter of a famine price for a month or two, as occasionally of old, to fall as soon as the golden bounty of a full harvest glistened in the sunlight. Certainly, for the first time in English history, there was prospect of *permanent* dearness of bread.

A recapitulation of the ancient laws governing the importation and exportation of corn is necessary. By the Old Subsidy of 1660 the poundage *value* for imported wheat was fixed at £2 a quarter when the market price of wheat did not exceed 44s. When it exceeded that price, the poundage value was 6s. 8d. Proportional ' regulating prices ' were fixed for barley, rye, oats, etc. The outward poundage value was £1 a quarter, irrespective of price (see below).

MARKET PRICE NOT EXCEEDING 44s.

	Poundage Value.	Duty.*
	£ s. d.	£ s. d.
Wheat, imported, per quarter ..	2 0 0	0 2 0

MARKET PRICE EXCEEDING 44s.

	Poundage Value.	Duty.
	£ s. d.	£ s. d.
Wheat, imported, per quarter ..	0 6 8	0 0 4

	Poundage Value.	Duty.
	£ s. d.	£ s. d.
Wheat, exported, per quarter (irrespective of price)	1 0 0	0 1 0

The first important alteration was effected by the Act of 1670, ' for encouragement of Tillage.' The poundage

* The duty was 5 per cent. of the ' value.'

on imported corn was abolished, and the duty made as below :

MARKET PRICE NOT EXCEEDING 53s. 4d.

	£	s.	d.
Wheat, imported, per quarter	0	16	0

MARKET PRICE EXCEEDING 53s. 4d. AND NOT EXCEEDING £4.

	£	s.	d.
Wheat, imported, per quarter	0	8	0

MARKET PRICE EXCEEDING £4.

	£	s.	d.
Wheat, imported, per quarter	0	0	4

The Corn Bounty Act of 1689 prescribed an export bounty at the rate of 5s. a quarter whenever the price of wheat did not exceed 48s. All export *duties* on corn were abolished in 1700.

The above scale for regulating duty by prices remained in force till 1773, but it must be understood that as each additional Subsidy was levied on merchandise the *duty* payable on wheat was increased. The *net* duties (fractions rejected and discounts deducted) payable in 1770 were :

PRICE NOT EXCEEDING 44s. A QUARTER.

	£	s.	d.
Wheat, imported, per quarter	1	1	9

PRICE EXCEEDING 44s. AND NOT EXCEEDING 53s. 4d.

	£	s.	d.
Wheat, imported, per quarter	0	16	11

PRICE EXCEEDING 53s. 4d. AND NOT EXCEEDING £4.

	£	s.	d.
Wheat, imported, per quarter	0	8	11

PRICE EXCEEDING £4.

	£	s.	d.
Wheat, imported, per quarter	0	1	3

During the years extending from 1696 to 1773 statistics of English imports, exports, and prices were compiled in the office of the Inspector-General of Imports and Exports, Custom House, London.* Through those seventy-eight years, *according to the official returns*, wheat was rarely at what would now be deemed a high price. So well accustomed were the lower classes to what we should call cheap bread that during the reign of George II. there were riots to prevent the exportation of corn from England, and to resent the price of foodstuffs, when, according to the statistics, the *average* price of wheat did not exceed £2 a quarter. The average price of wheat during the period from 1696 to 1764 was 33s. 3d. a quarter.

It appears that prices were mounting in 1765, so exportation of corn, etc., was prohibited, and foreign corn admitted duty-free, during a period of several years. It is apparent that from 1696 to 1764, inclusive, low prices had been maintained though the high scale of duty must have been leviable. The prices were not really high even from 1765 to 1773. The average was about 45s.

It should be observed that the inefficiency of the home-grown supply to meet the demand was contemporaneous with the full operation of the Enclosure Acts, the effacement of cottage industries, the expansion of the factory system, and the consequent commencement of the efflux from country to town. An element of obfuscation intrudes here. It may be asked : ' Were not the Enclosure Acts supposed to have increased the acreage of arable ? And was not the system of cultivation steadily improving ? And say you not that the import duties were removed for a space ? Then how can you explain the rise in prices ?' A straight cord runs through all the apparent intricacies of the question. It is a homely fact that when the peasant has a pig, a cow, and a share in common land, he is not confined to a bread diet. When many thousands of such peasants are seduced or driven into the cities, the land becomes less *useful*, despite scientific farming and

* Charles Davenant and Horace Walpole held the patent of this office at various periods.

enclosures of common. When the number of people who can with ease produce *their own* food grows less, when the cities become crowded, when, in addition to these circumstances, the importation of fruit, meat, and fish is limited by primitive methods of traffic and repeated wars, most of the poor have to fall back upon bread alone. Up goes the price of corn. As misery increases the poor become more prolific : it has ever been thus. The streets are full of puny, squalid children ; the sweater has his way. Up goes the price of corn.

In 1773, in order that the slow rise in price should not proceed too far, the regulating figures were altered. The duty then stood thus :

PRICE NOT EXCEEDING 44s.

	£	s.	d.
Wheat, imported, per quarter	1	1	9

PRICE EXCEEDING 44s. AND NOT EXCEEDING 48s.

	£	s.	d.
Wheat, imported, per quarter	0	16	11

PRICE EXCEEDING 48s.

	£	s.	d.
Wheat, imported, per quarter	0	0	6

But this had no effect. The unfavourable conditions were being slowly intensified. Factories were rising in localities hitherto immune, the urban population was increasing at an ominous rate. Busy people still strove to stave off the evil day when it should depend upon foreign supplies as to whether the poor should starve or be filled. Much waste land was reclaimed in the maritime counties, and in the sylvan parts of England the axe resounded in the woodlands. The rise, though resistless, was gradual. The average price for the twenty years succeeding 1773 was about 44s. a quarter—greatly in excess of 33s. 3d. ; still, not intolerable.

It will now be seen that for nearly one hundred years the *average* price of wheat in England was so low that the high duty on foreign corn must have been leviable during most of the period.* We are confronted with the spectacle of a plenteous supply of cheap bread while a bounty was paid on the exportation of home-grown corn and a high duty levied on foreign.

The 'imposts on proceeds,' and the alterations under the Consolidation Act, left the duties immediately after 1787 as follow :

PRICE UNDER 48s.

	£	s.	d.
Wheat, imported, per quarter	1	4	3

PRICE AT OR ABOVE 48s.

	£	s.	d.
Wheat, imported, per quarter	0	0	6

In 1791 the duties stood thus :

PRICE UNDER 50s.

	£	s.	d.
Wheat, imported, per quarter	1	4	3

PRICE 50s. OR UNDER 54s.

	£	s.	d.
Wheat, imported, per quarter	0	2	6

PRICE 54s. OR ABOVE.

	£	s.	d.
Wheat, imported, per quarter	0	0	6

Soon it became apparent that no sliding scale could prevent dearness, and that the scale last adopted had worked as a factor in raising prices. The imposts of 1796 and 1797 increased the corn duties. In 1800 they stood thus :

	High Duty.			First Low Duty.			Second Low Duty.		
	£	s.	d.	£	s.	d.	£	s.	d.
Wheat, imported, per quarter	1	6	$8\frac{2}{20}$	0	2	9	0	0	$6\frac{12}{20}$

During the concluding years of the century, despite the danger to commerce by the widespread European wars, the importation of corn into Great Britain had increased

* Not at every port, for the prices occasionally varied much in different counties ; but it is evident that, with such low average prices, corn could rarely have been dear, even in the districts most unproductive.

rapidly. Still the price had kept on climbing, climbing. From 1696 to 1773 the exports of corn had always exceeded the imports; the import duties had been high, and the prices extremely low. From 1774 to 1794 the imports slightly exceeded the exports ; the import duties were higher than of yore : the prices had increased, yet were reasonable. During the last few years of the century the imports greatly exceeded the exports, the duties mounted, the prices gradually became tremendous. It is therefore clear that dearness of bread is not always a direct result of high corn duties. One may find it necessary to burn all the time-honoured reference-books ere a correct conclusion on this matter may be achieved. When economics fail to enlighten, a judicious blend of ethics and common sense may avail. It would seem to be inevitable that, when the poor are driven from the land, the poor will in the end have to bear the suffering entailed by deprivation.

One undeniable cause of high corn prices must not be overlooked. The old restraints upon engrossing had been swept away in 1791. Their abolition was due to the teachings of that incorrigible doctrinaire, Adam Smith. For forty years subsequent to 1791 the engrossing of corn became a popular branch of speculation.* Rents grew higher as prices went up ; even in counties remote as Wilts and Somerset the rent of an ordinary farm rose from 15s. per acre to £3. It was as though a great curse had fallen upon the home territories. The manly sports and exercises, for which rural England in particular had long been famous, began to fall into disuse. The physique of the agricultural labourers deteriorated ; child labour and adult slavery were fast removing even the signs of humanity from the toilers of the great industrial towns. There is no part of English history so terrible as that of the years from 1790 to 1830.

Below is a return of the average prices of wheat in

* When corn was at its highest, the ports were often crowded with corn-laden ships, discharge being purposely delayed.

England from 1792 to 1800, and of the quantities imported and exported.

			Average Prices.		Quarters Wheat Imported.	Quarters Wheat Exported.
			s.	d.		
1792 ..	..	..	42	11	20,201	250,982
1793 ..	..	..	48	11	429,350	44,866
1794 ..	..	..	51	8	324,637	116,273
1795 ..	..	..	74	2	287,930	677
1796 ..	..	..	77	1	820,381	677
1797 ..	..	..	53	1	456,903	23,076
1798 ..	..	..	50	3	394,407	22,138
1799 ..	..	..	67	6	445,047	16,960
1800 ..	..	..	113	7	1,174,654	7,866

Below is an account of the average prices of wheat at Dublin market (per barrel of 280 pounds = $\frac{5}{9}$ of an English quarter).

PRICES IN IRISH CURRENCY.

			s.	d.					s.	d.
1792 ..	..	..	23	4	1797 ..	..	..		26	7
1793 ..	..	..	28	0	1798 ..	..	..		28	3
1794 ..	..	..	32	4	1799 ..	..	..		38	4
1795 ..	..	..	38	1	1800 ..	..	..		62	0
1796 ..	..	..	37	11						

Thus the average price of a quarter of wheat in England during the nine years quoted may be stated roughly as a little over 64s., and the average price per English quarter of wheat in Ireland may be expressed as a little over 58s. in *English* currency. The British shortage raised prices in Ireland. Great Britain became compelled to buy oversea : Ireland, especially in time of war, was the market most convenient to buy in. Ireland *had* to sell. In England the price of corn usually regulated rents ; in Ireland the middleman had fostered subletting, especially in the southern counties.* (The

* Extract from evidence given before a Commission of Inquiry held early in the nineteenth century : ' The noblemen and gentlemen in the south of Ireland, in a greater degree than those in the north, let their lands to a class of people called middlemen. These in some instances keep large tracts in their own hands, in other instances they underlet tracts of considerable extent to

cotters in Ireland, be it remembered, had no such privileges as the cottagers and commoners of England, prior to the Enclosure Acts, had enjoyed.)

Readers of our first volume may remember that the concluding portion contained a short review of the condition of the British Customs towards the end of the eighteenth century, and a brief history of Irish revenue. As the fiscal contingencies of the Union of Great Britain and Ireland now present themselves for enumeration, we cannot do better than preface the account with another review of the condition of both the British and Irish departments.

To commence with England. In spite of the Act of 1798, there remained an imposing list of Customs sinecures, the total yearly emoluments amounting to about £25,000. The Customs revenue had increased considerably, partly through the duties being higher, partly through the growth of commerce.

The Scottish contributions to the revenue of Great Britain were still unimportant. The proportions of the Customs returns (gross) in the two countries may be stated as about 20 in England to 1 in Scotland. The Scottish list was packed with sinecurists and pensioners. Among the latter were no fewer than four Cockburns and eleven Hays.

The Irish revenue business was carried on in a very slack way ; the British method, bad as it was, appears in comparison exactness itself. Whenever Commis-

---

other tenants under them. And sometimes that second class of tenants underlet again to others, till at last the property comes to be divided into lots of an acre or half an acre, and sometimes still less than that.'

Here was a numerous class of small holders, deprived by the middleman system of everything that tends to make division of land beneficial. (The witness was no local agitator, but a Scotsman acting as steward and valuer in Ireland.)

sioners of Inquiry were sent across channel to overhaul
matters, most amazing anomalies were recorded.   Huge
defalcations were dragged into publicity, and the system
of accounts shown to be especially blamable.   The old
Revenue Board had been rearranged towards the close
of the eighteenth century, the number of Commissioners
being reduced to nine—four sitting for Customs, two for
Excise, and the other three as Commissioners of both
Customs and Excise.   The scope of the work to be performed by each set was not exactly definable ; indeed, so
jumbled was the control that certain Commissioners of
an Inquiry held soon after the Union declared themselves
unable to state which set was responsible for any particular branch of the duties.

Fees were charged at an exorbitant rate—as means
towards official emolument—and many of these were unsanctioned except ' by usage.'   The scale had been fixed
by statute shortly after the Restoration, but it had been
increased in 1695, and the increase sanctioned by the
Irish Parliament.   Soon the scale came to be altered ' by
usage,' and always in the direction of increase.   At the
end of the eighteenth century there were no two Irish ports
at which similar fees were charged.   If a merchant complained to the Board, the latter directed the officer concerned to comply with the 1695 scale, but took no steps
to enforce compliance unless the merchant complained
again and again.*

* The following letter, sent by the collector of Dundalk in
answer to a query as to his emoluments, illustrates the vagarious-
ness of the Irish system of fees :
' I am under the necessity of informing you that I am utterly
ignorant of the nature or amount of the fees of the patentee
officers, and no trace of them ' (no trace of an authorized scale)
' can be discovered in this office, nor any clue which can enable
me to comply with the order in question.   The employments of
the patentee officers have degenerated into sinecures from time
immemorial, and, my predecessor having constantly contracted
to receive the fees of those officers for a much longer period than
I can possibly learn the date of, the patentees' fees have become
blended with those of the collector, and from ancient usage no
separate charge is ever made.   I found things in this state on
being appointed, and made no alteration, except having the

Most of the Irish foreign trade was transacted at Dublin. The collector of that port, when accounting for his net receipts, always kept a large sum in hand. The outport collectors were supposed to remit monthly, but this was rarely done, whence many defalcations.*

---

deputation of the patentees made to my first clerk instead of myself, who, however, has no emolument thereby.'

(The explanation of this is that, having no authorized scale to go by, and the patentees being non-resident, the collector had ordered his clerk to levy, as best he could, fees on foreign and coastwise traffic, at the highest rate the merchants would endure. Then the collector divided the spoil into three equal portions— one portion for himself, one for each of the patentees. Each portion amounted in the year under question to £662 16s. The collector's hours of employment were ten till three, and he was a captain in the yeomanry.)

* Below is an extract from the Irish Exchequer Memoranda, showing proceedings taken and pending against various collectors of customs and hearth-money, their sureties, etc., towards the end of the eighteenth century :

'His Majesty against William Doyle, heir of Charles Doyle. Also against the heir and tertenants ' (actual occupiers of landed property) ' of Thomas Bunbury. Also against Francis Vernon Wilson. Also against Samuel Wilkinson.' (Charles Doyle, Bunbury, Wilson, and Wilkinson were sureties for George Martin, late collector of Dublin, whose defalcations amounted to over £9,000. The sheriff of Carlow returned Wilson ' not to be found.')

' Same against Meredith Workman, formerly collector of Dundalk, with John Bond and the Rev. James Smith, his sureties.'

' Same against George Parker, late collector of Wexford, with Admiral Parker and Captain Parker, his sureties.' (Defalcation £4,998.)

' Same against James Cavendish, late collector of Dundalk, with Sir Henry Cavendish and Guy Moore Coote, his sureties.' (Defalcation £2,569.)

' Same against Simon Marshall, formerly collector of Galway, with Richard French and John Eyre, his sureties.

' Same against Joseph Matthews, late collector of Kilkenny, with Arthur Webb, senior, and Arthur Webb, junior, his sureties.' (Defalcation £2,768.)

' Same against John Dalton, late collector of Athlone, with the Hon. Peter Brown-Kelly and Sir Patrick Bellew, his sureties.' (Defalcation £1,939.)

' Same against William Ormsby, late collector of Sligo, with George Ormsby and Robert French, his sureties.' (Defalcation £5,155.)

' Same against Sir Edward Newenham, formerly collector of Dublin, with Alicia O'Callaghan and Jane Pierce, his sureties.' (Debt £1,395.)

There was much circumlocution in dealing with ships and goods, and this was enforced solely with a view towards multiplying fees. When a shipmaster reported a cargo inwards, not only the collector, but the patent customer, the controller, the surveyor-general, and the searcher (or their deputies for them), insisted on initialling the report, though they never examined either it or the goods to which it related. This was done so that each might charge a fee. When a ship cleared outward double fees were charged, one scale by the patentee searcher, one by his deputy. The patentee was always absent, so could check nothing. The deputy was always present (in his office, to collect the patentee's fees and his own), but he checked neither clearance nor goods.

Every entry for goods which were duty-paid at landing was quintupled, so as to secure five sets of fees. The documents were supposed to be subjected to a circuitous system of check, yet inaccuracies slipped through by the hundred. Even then, during six years the number of surcharges and rebates in the port of Dublin was over 17,000.

The privilege of landing goods *ad visum* (popularly known as ' by bill of view,' in England called ' on sight ') was scandalously abused. The system had been originally intended to act as an occasional indulgence. For instance, if a merchant's imports were not fully advised on his invoices, he might depose to that effect, and request permission to ' view ' the goods on landing, and then ' perfect

---

(Thus it appears that two successive collectors of Dublin were being prosecuted at the same time.)

Besides the above, proceedings were taken against the persons and sureties of twenty-six collectors of hearth-money. In three cases the sheriffs concerned reported, ' No bodies, goods, chattels, iands, or tenements '; and in eight cases, ' No goods, chattels, lands, or tenements.' In the case of a collector named Sankey, the sheriff of Tipperary returned, ' No goods, and both sureties dead,' and in the case of one Burrows the sheriff of Wexford returned, ' One surety dead, the other surety and the principal not to be found.'

the entry ' within seven days.   The goods were put into
the King's Warehouse for safety till the transaction was
completed.   This reasonable regulation had been extended and relaxed ' by usage ' till at each port the
King's Warehouse had been converted into a kind of
' duty-free warehouse,' unsecured, so far as the merchants
were concerned, by bond.   The King's Warehouse in
Dublin being crammed with ' Bill of View ' articles, the
authorities hired several private warehouses, which were
soon filled with similar goods.   Often the articles remained there for months, the entries meanwhile unper-
fected and the duties unpaid.   Then certain merchants
were allowed to take ' Bill of View ' goods to their own
warehouses, and keep them there as long as they chose,
nor were the doors fitted with Customs locks.   This loose
system was extended gradually so as to apply to the
greater part of the foreign goods landed in Dublin.   The
landing-officers' examination of goods was extremely inaccurate, especially with regard to spirits, the gauging
being random, and the hydrometer used in testing quite
an imperfect instrument.   The most inexperienced reader
will perceive that when goods thus erratically examined
were at once handed over to the owners, and left in their
charge, unsecured by bond, till they thought fit to pay
the duties involved, many opportunities must have arisen
for collusion between merchants and officers.   That collusion of the grossest kind took place is evident from the
official statement that in 1800 it had become apparent
that goods landed upon Bill of View had passed into consumption without duty being paid on them to an extent
representing a loss to the Revenue of £200,000.   Yet so
muddled were the accounts that proceedings could not be
taken.*

* An attempt at stock-taking was made in Dublin, but so little
reliance could be placed on the accounts that it was decided not
to essay anything in the nature of a complete check, but merely
to count the packages !   The original account of goods landed on
bill of view (goods that had been duty-paid being, of course,
deducted) showed 29,972 packages.   The indoor ' jerque ' account

There were great frauds in the exportation of Irish-made spirits, the goods being tampered with while in transit from distillery to export ship. The account of moneys received as proceeds of fines and forfeitures was terribly inexact. And it should be mentioned, as an exemplification of the assiduity with which the average man will persevere in collecting, for his own benefit, trifling sums of public money, that certain high officials and wealthy noblemen were in receipt of a few pounds each per year, as commutations of the old exemptions from wine duty granted during Elizabeth's reign.*

The victualling of the revenue cruisers was in the hands of two Dublin merchants, and the prices charged did by no means correspond with the market rates. These worthy burghers paid the Inspector of Cruisers a handsome commission upon all stores and provisions ordered by him.

The Customs hours (' all round ') were nine to three in summer, and ten to three in winter.

Thus we have made it plain that Revenue matters in Ireland were pervaded by that happy spirit of irresponsibility, and conducted with that utter disregard of routine and precision, so characteristic of Celtic financial procedure. To some this statement may appear unfair, for at the time official departments in England and Scotland were not above suspicion, and, indeed, it is evident from the nomenclature that most of the revenue officials in Ireland were of English descent. But the most Irish person in existence is your Irishman whose ancestry has been typically English, and, when every possible allowance has been made, it remains undeniable that in the record of Irish revenue lapses there is some-

---

showed 31,023. Comparison was then made with another indoor account kept by ' The Clerk of the Check.' This showed 44,859. When the computers went to the warehouses and counted the stock, they found only 8,369. The investigation lapsed.

* See vol. i., p. 426. (The original grant had been broken up into many portions.)

thing racy of the soil, a touch of the utterly and genially picaresque, that does not appertain to the English and Scottish depredations.

By Cap. 67 of 40 Geo. III. the British Parliament enacted that the Union of Great Britain and Ireland should take place on January 1, 1801, and the respective countries be thenceforth called ' The United Kingdom of Great Britain and Ireland.'   They were to be represented in one and the same Parliament, and their inhabitants were to be placed on the same footing as regarded trade and navigation. All commercial prohibitions and bounties in force between them, except those referring to corn, flour, etc., were to be repealed, and, with certain exceptions, commerce between them was to be duty-free.   Below is a summary of the new fiscal arrangements.

The following goods were liable to *ad valorem* duties of 10 per cent., on importation from either country to the other : Apparel, wrought brass, cabinet ware, carriages, wrought copper, cottons, glass, haberdashery, hats, wrought iron and hardware, gold and silver lace, thread, and bullion, millinery, stained paper, pottery, manufactured leather, silk manufactures, and tin plates. These duties were to exist for twenty years.

Certain goods, being products or manufactures of, and liable to excise duty in, the respective countries, were made liable to countervailing duties on importation from one country to the other.   Parliament might rearrange the said countervailing duties, or impose others.   Goods thus liable were entitled to a drawback on shipment, equal to the countervailing duty demanded in the country to which they were exported.

The woollen manufactures known from ancient times as ' old draperies ' and ' new draperies ' were to pay, on importation from either country into the other, the duties previously payable in Ireland.   The duty on Irish coal

brought into Great Britain was to be the previous British
duty, and no more.   The duty on salt brought into Ireland
from Great Britain was to be the previous Irish duty, and
no more.

Calicoes and muslins, imported from either country
into the other, were to pay the amount of the previous
Irish duty, and no more, till 1808 ; thenceforth the rate
was to be reduced annually so as to reach 10 per cent.
on the value in 1816, and to remain at that rate till 1821.
Cotton yarn and twist, imported from either country into
the other, were to pay the amount of the previous Irish
duty, and no more, till 1808 ; thenceforth the rate was
to be reduced annually so as to expire in 1816.

If goods liable to duty on export from Great Britain
to foreign parts, but duty-free if exported to Ireland,
were shipped in Great Britain for foreign, and passed in
transit through an Irish port, that, of course, did not
exempt the goods from the British export duty.   The
same rule applied to Irish goods exported through Great
Britain to foreign ports ; they paid the Irish export duty
when shipped in Ireland.

If foreign or colonial goods paid duty in either country,
and were then shipped to the other, the import duties
paid were to be drawn back, or they might be placed
to the credit of the country to which the goods were
exported.

For twenty years subsequent to date of Union the
respective contributions towards the united expenditure
were to be in the proportions of fifteen from Great Britain
and two from Ireland. This arrangement was to be
revised at the end of the period by—

Comparison of values of imports and exports during
a given period ; or

Comparison of values of beer, sugar, wine, spirits,
tobacco, tea, and malt consumed ; or

Comparison of national incomes.

The scale was to be afterwards revised at periods of
not less than seven and not more than twenty years,

unless the United Parliament should decide that expenditure should be defrayed by equal taxation on commodities in both countries.

The Irish revenues were to be funded, and charged with the interest on the Irish debt, and with the reduction of the said debt by means of a sinking fund. The residue was to go towards defraying the expenditure of the United Kingdom. If any surplus then remained, it was to be applied to reducing Irish taxes, or to other Irish purposes.

In regulating subsequent taxation, no article imported into Ireland was to be charged with a duty higher than that payable on the said article in England.

Any loan raised after the Union for the United Kingdom was to be a joint debt, and borne in the proportions above mentioned ; but this provision might be altered by the United Parliament. The Parliament was also authorized to formulate new devices if at any future period either country's debt were liquidated (quite an unnecessary proviso).

All revenue derived from colonial possessions was to be applied to the benefit of each country in proportion to the country's contribution towards the united expenditure.

Thus each country had its own scale of duties on foreign and colonial goods imported ; certain articles carried between the two countries were subject to various. duties and restrictions, and the rest of the trade across the Irish Channel was duty-free. Between the date of Union and the operation of Cap. 72, 4 Geo. IV., an immense number of variations were made in the above arrangement. A full account of these would mystify and disgust readers, and serve no useful purpose, so we shall merely mention, as we proceed, certain striking acts of alteration. Only genuinely *historical* statutes, affecting the Customs in either country, will receive full notice.

The Act brought about a considerable reduction in

the Irish Customs establishment. In the list of compensations for offices vacated the following are worth notice :

Office.	Compensating Grant (Annual).		
	£	s.	d.
One Exchequer Baron	2,000	0	0
Auditor of Imprest (office held by Earl of Westmeath for self and Countess) (each)	1,000	0	0
One Customs Solicitor	716	14	4
One Deputy-Paymaster of Corn Premiums ..	670	0	0
Another	286	19	4
Four clerks of port permits (in all)	397	15	5½

Amongst the compensations granted for loss of fees on account of the new arrangements appear :

Office.	Compensating Grant (Annual).		
	£	s.	d.
One Assistant-Examiner of Customs	600	0	0
A collector	305	5	9
Another	168	17	0
A jerquer's clerk	326	5	9
Another	163	2	10
A clerk of debentures	163	1	11
A clerk of minutes	59	4	10

The *British* Quarantine Acts were consolidated by Cap. 80, 40 Geo. III. Certain tonnage duties were placed on vessels that performed quarantine in Great Britain, and these were applied to the erection of a lazaret on Chetney Hill, Kent. It was provided that if a customs officer performing duty as a quarantine official deserted his post, or knowingly permitted goods, ships, or persons to escape from quarantine, he should suffer death. Persons who escaped from quarantine were made liable to the same penalty.*

* Alarmists were never wanting. Some urged the Government to strengthen the smuggling laws in the interests of public health. ' The wisest and severest laws that can possibly be enacted will never sufficiently secure us against the secret and subtile infection of the plague, so long as there is a single smuggler on our

The Thames police force was instituted by Cap. 87, 40 Geo. III., ' for the more effectual prevention of depredations on the cargoes, stores, and materials of vessels.' In the Act of institution appeared this sentence : ' Whereas divers ill-disposed and suspected persons and reported thieves frequent the said river, its quays, warehouses, and the avenues leading thereto.'

Cap. 107, 41 Geo. III., amended the Copyright Act, providing that the authors of all books composed in the United Kingdom, but not printed or published prior to July 2, 1801, and of all books subsequently composed in the United Kingdom, were to have the sole right of printing and reprinting the same for fourteen years from date of first publication. (They might assign this privilege.) Contraveners, including importers of pirated books, were to forfeit to the proprietor of copyright the books dealt with, and he was to have them made into waste. The offenders were to forfeit 3d. a sheet, half to go to the Crown, half to the informer concerned. This Act reaffirmed the existing provisions against the importation of books first produced in the United Kingdom, and printed or reprinted elsewhere. As of old, customs officers were to be rewarded for seizing pirated books.

In December, 1802, the following notice was posted at the London Custom House, and copies were sent to the outport collectors, who were instructed to secure publication thereof in the local papers : ' Whereas advertisements have at different times appeared in the newspapers, offering sums of money for the procuring of places or situations in the Customs, etc.' The notice then referred to the Statute of 5 and 6 Edw. VI., which disabled purchasers of offices, and rendered forfeitable the offices of such as assisted in the sale. A reward of

extensive coasts. This is a point of most awful consideration, and calls for the immediate deliberation of the Legislature.'— *Letter from Abbott, of the Levant Company, to Lord Grenville, November* 20, 1800 (*Dropmore Collection*).

£100 was offered for satisfactory evidence of the trading of offices in the Customs.

The provisions of the Act of 1782, disqualifying British customs officers from voting at Parliamentary elections, were extended by Cap. 25, 43 Geo. III., so as to include the Irish Customs.

Cap. 56, 43 Geo. III., regulated the Plantation passenger traffic. Said the preamble : ' Persons have been seduced to leave their native country under false representations, and have suffered great hardships on shipboard for want of water and provisions.' It was enacted that no British vessel might take passengers from the United Kingdom to the Plantations in a greater number than one to each two tons burden. The parts of the ship that were occupied with cargo were not to count in estimating burden, and the crew were to be counted as passengers. Before the vessel sailed, a magistrate and the customs officers of the port were to attend, muster the crew and passengers, and allow any passenger to leave who was desirous of doing so. Passengers were only to be taken on board at places where customs officers were stationed. A certified copy of the muster-roll was to be given to the master. If the vessel carried fifty or more, she was also to carry a certificated surgeon and a proper medicine-chest. Both master and doctor were to keep journals, and on return produce them to the Customs. (Foreign vessels might only carry passengers in the proportion of one to each five tons burden.) Bond was to be given to the Customs as to seaworthiness of ship. Ships of war and revenue cruisers might board and search during voyage, and check the muster-roll. An abstract of the Act was to be displayed in every custom-house in the United Kingdom.* (It is illustrative of the extreme tenderness with which the humanitarians of the day regarded the negro, and of their callousness as to the sufferings of their own countrymen, that similar

* Later the Act was amended, the magistrate's attendance being declared unnecessary.

provisions had been applied to the slave trade *in 1788*.
Yet the horrors of Plantation passenger traffic had been
exemplified thousands of times during the previous two
hundred years.)

The Customs tariff of Great Britain was re-consolidated
by Cap. 68, 43 Geo. III. The Act stated that many
new duties and separate accounts had been instituted
since the Consolidation of 1787, and that the computa-
tion of duties had 'again become complicated and
intricate.' Many of the duties were increased. The
produce of the additional duties was estimated at
£250,000. Even foreign wool, which, to stimulate the
woollen manufactures, had previously been kept free of
all imposts except the convoy duty, was made liable to
a slight duty under this Act. The excise duty on tea,
which under the Act of 1787 had been £12 10s. per £100
value, was made 50 per cent.

Now appeared those terrible imposts, the so-called
'temporary' war duties, increases upon the consolidated
rates, amounting in most cases to 12½ per cent. (Cap. 70,
43 Geo. III.).

What is known as the 'First Warehousing Act,'
Cap. 132, 43 Geo. III., was the next important revenue
measure. This has been frequently referred to as the
first step towards 'bonding' dutiable goods, but the
designation is absurd. Postponing payment by entering
into bond for the amount of duty involved was an ancient
practice ; indeed, it would be difficult to state the precise
period at which the system commenced. There can be
no doubt that from time immemorial it had been a practice
to forbear in certain instances the prompt collection of
duty, but in such cases the merchant was liable for the
full duty as payable on landing, no matter to what
extent his goods might diminish by natural waste before
he cleared them. This explains the old Customs discounts,
granted to merchants who paid duty on their goods *at
time of landing*. The East India Company had for a long
period enjoyed what amounted to bonding privileges,

the duties on their goods being forborne till after sale. In 1714 tobacco had been allowed to be warehoused on the merchants' own premises, they paying a small portion of the inward duty, and completing payment when the goods were sold, or drawing back their partial deposit if the goods were exported. This system continued till 1789 (see the Tobacco Act of that year, in vol. i., p. 385), and many, many cases there were, according to the Receiver-General's books, in which the transaction was never consummated, the merchant selling his goods and then failing, or the sureties levanting, or some outrageous claim being made on the authorities' clemency on account of loss by decay, fire, etc. In 1742 Plantation rum was allowed to be warehoused without payment of the excise duty (see vol. i., pp. 206, 207), and in 1765 it was provided that rice might be warehoused at certain ports on payment of a small portion of the import charge. (In 1797 it was allowed to be warehoused duty-free.) In 1767 coffee and cocoa were allowed warehousing privileges—only part of the import duty to be paid, and the rest at clearance (drawback if exported). All these facilities had been intended to favour *export* trade, to relieve the merchant from paying duty on goods which might ultimately be sold in foreign markets.

But the Act of 1803 went considerably farther. It allowed cotton, ginger, indigo, mahogany, molasses, pimento, and rum from the West Indies, and cocoa, sugar, and coffee from any place, to be bonded at the West India Docks, London ; and rice, tobacco, wine and spirits, other than from the West Indies, to be bonded at the newly-constructed London Docks, Wapping. Many other classes of goods might be bonded at such places as the Treasury might appoint. The Act was in a way experimental, it being provided that the Treasury, by Order in Council, might extend the privileges to other goods and other ports. (In 1805 special authorization was granted to the Treasury in this respect, there being a host of applications from various ports for permission to share in the benefits conferred by the Act.)*

The goods warehoused were to be secured under locks, in most cases the joint locks of Crown and warehouse proprietor. When required for home consumption, they were to be liable to the duties then leviable, upon the quantities ascertained at delivery. They might be exported from warehouse on payment of the temporary war duties only, but a certificate of landing at the place of destination was required. Goods not cleared within fifteen months were to be sold. If they failed to realize a price covering the duty they were to be destroyed. If they realized more than the duty, the Crown was to be satisfied and the overplus to go to the proprietor. Goods liable to excise duties were to be entered with the Excise as well as with the Customs, and the excise officers were to be present on delivery. (The provisions of this statute were extended considerably by Cap. 126, 48 Geo. III. ; Cap. 142, 52 Geo. III., etc.)

It appears from Cap. 156, 43 Geo. III., that at this period the Prisage and Butlerage of England were assigned to—

The King, on all liable wines brought into the ports of Lancashire ; the Prince of Wales, on all liable wines brought into the ports of Cornwall and Plymouth ; the duke of Beaufort, on all liable wines brought into the ports of Swansea and Chepstow ; the marquis of Bute,

---

* It might have been to the public advantage if, prior to making a compact with the London dock companies in 1907, inquiry had been made into the old methods of fostering London trade. From time immemorial up to the beginning of the nineteenth century the great city enjoyed remarkable commercial privileges, the desire of legislators being to centralize trade as far as possible, and thus facilitate the collection of Customs revenue. The official with the inkhorn and tuckstick was the active agent in more than one stupendous change. The independence of the United States, and the present dropsical condition of the British metropolis, are due to him and his mentors. (London's preponderance in trade began to decline directly her privileges were withdrawn.)

on all liable wines brought into the ports of Cardiff ;
the duke of Grafton, on all liable wines brought
into the remaining ports of England.

(Prisage and Butlerage were not leviable in Scotland.
See vol. i., pp. 166-167.)

Various committees of inquiry had recommended that
these ancient impositions should be re-vested in the
Crown. The Treasury were accordingly empowered to
treat with the grantees for surrender, on consideration of
annuities, to be granted by Parliament out of the Consolidated Fund.

By Cap. 124 (local and personal), 43 Geo. III., the
Treasury were authorized to advance £100,000 out of
the Consolidated Fund, to repair and extend the moorings
in the Thames, and to improve the Thames navigation,*
the loan to be repaid out of the proceeds of additional
tonnage rates. They were also empowered to buy the
London ' legal quays ' — viz., the string of landing-
places, approved under the Acts of Elizabeth and
Charles II., extending from London Bridge to the Tower
Dock, at which, previous to the construction of docks
in London, all foreign merchandise had been landed,
and from which all goods for exportation to foreign parts
had been shipped or water-borne for shipment, except
certain rough goods and occasional cargoes, allowed
special privileges under ' sufferances ' or Treasury
warrants.   (Some of these quays, notably ' Brewers '
and the ' Wool Quay,' were extremely ancient.   Most
of the East India Company's goods were lightered from
and to the ships, and discharged at or water-borne from
a quay called ' Somers and Lyons ' near the Custom
House.)   Billingsgate Dock, and the piece of ground
adjacent, then known as ' Room Land,' were exempted
from the provisions of this Act, and it was provided that
the Fish Market and its appurtenances should not be
interfered with. The purchase was to be completed

* Another instance of the fostering of London's commercial
interests.

within three years, but this period was repeatedly extended.*

The building of the East India Docks was authorized by Cap. 126 (local and personal), 43 Geo. III. The preamble ran : ' Whereas the ships in the employ of the East India Company are of a larger size than other vessels employed by merchants in trade, and many of them nearly equal in bulk to ships of the line in the Royal Navy.'

A Treasury warrant, worded thus, reached the Board of Customs : ' Having considered your Secretary's letter aforegoing, these are to authorize you to cause articles, the produce of New South Wales and Norfolk Island, to be admitted to entry on payment of duty, as if the produce of, and imported from, any British Plantation in America ; also that articles exported to New South Wales and Norfolk Island should be subject to such duties and drawbacks as on exportation to the British colonies.' This would appear to mark the initiation of important trade with the Antipodes.

A rather curious trial took place in the Exchequer during the year under survey. A ship from Virginia arrived in the tier off Wapping Old Stairs, having on board a quantity of staves and 524 casks of leaf tobacco. By the letter of the law regulating the importation of tobacco the minimum ' legal weight ' at which packages of tobacco might be imported was 450 pounds net. (This regulation was a device to prevent smuggling. See vol. i., pp. 143 and 385.) Tide-surveyor Haskings went on board as soon as unlading commenced, and found that

---

* It is evident that purchase was soon initiated, for we find that in 1805 Mr. Dutton, the occupier of Brewers Quay, was paying £1,500 a year as rent to the Treasury. On January 8, 1806, the Customs Secretary applied to the East India Company as to Somers and Lyons Quay. The directors replied that the Customs Solicitor had offered them, pro forma, £100 as a Crown tender for the quay, but they would take £40,000 if the Treasury would grant them legal quays for their goods at Cock Hill and Stone Stairs, Ratcliff. (In 1831 the Treasury, fearing that the quay trade would fall off, proceeded to dispose of their purchases.)

two of the packages were rather badly broken, and on weighing them net he discovered that one was 70 and the other 107 pounds short of the legal weight. The damage had been caused by ' avaricious stowage,' the casks having been ' screw-jacked ' at lading, so as to squeeze them into as small a space as possible. Other casks had been cracked by the use of the screw-jack, and these, with the two packages found to be defective, were detained by the officer. It appears there was no suspicion of fraud, but the letter of the law had been violated. The importer of the goods was exchequered, and many packages of tobacco, landed in similar condition from other American ships, were detained pending result of the trial. The case went before a jury, and a verdict was given for the defendant. The Crown sought and obtained a new trial. It is matter of regret that the records do not supply the result, although they consist of many pages, mainly devoted to the most persistent and abominable wrangling and hair-splitting. It is amazing that such a case should be taken up by an Attorney-General, for it is quite evident that it was merely a matter of crowded stowage. The Crown lawyer stuck valiantly to his case, defining the Crown's attitude towards the merchant thus : ' You shall not use such machinery as shall damage the packages, and cause them to arrive in a prohibited condition.' (But why, in the name of equity, should the *importer*, an Englishman resident in London, be prosecuted for the act of a Virginian stevedore ?)

Arbitrary as some of the Customs prosecutions were, they were not so harsh as certain actions entered by the Excise. Baron Macdonald, the Exchequer judge who presided during the above case, quoted an extraordinary suit preferred by the latter department. An immense quantity of coffee, taken as prize from French and Spanish vessels, had been shipped from the West Indies to London. Owing to the vastness of the consignments, proper casks could not in all instances be obtained, and many of the packages, when landed at Custom - house Quay, were found to be under the legal net. The customs officers overlooked this unimportant informality, and the prize agents paid duty on the goods. Then the excise officers intervened, seized every cask which was in the slightest degree under weight, and secured condemnation of the goods in the Exchequer, thus casting upon the Customs the responsibility of refunding the duties on the seized casks, or of contesting the unfortunate agents' claim for rebate. ' I was obliged,' said Baron Macdonald, ' to declare it was a matter of positive regulations. . . . A very distressing case.' (Readers may be inclined to wonder why regulations should not altogether supersede judges, if a judge were justified in thus conniving at an injustice, through allowing himself to be overridden by the bare letter of the law. Law thus used becomes a mere engine of criminality. An irresponsible despot would be a better adjudicator than a devotee of formula like Baron Macdonald. It is certain that if such a case had been brought to the decision of a savage chief, justice would have been done, the prize agents would have got their coffee, and there would have been an instant reduction in the Excise establishment.)

The commanders and mates of the revenue cruisers became dissatisfied with their full-dress uniform, and asked the Board of Customs' permission to enhance its glories at their own expense. The decorations suggested were : commanders, a silver epaulet, buttonholes bound with silver twist, side-arms, and cocked hats with cockades ; buttons on coat to be set three and three, the breeches and waistcoat as usual. Mates : lapels, buttons set two and two, cocked hats with cockades. Minute : ' Allowed, except epaulets.'

Certain provisions of the Act of 1791, regulating the Corn duties, were repealed by Cap. 109, 44 Geo. III., and fresh regulations provided, to the effect that wheat might not be exported if the price exceeded 54s. a quarter, and, if exported when the price was at or under 48s., should be

bountied at the rate of 5s. a quarter. The ' high duty '
on imported wheat was to obtain when the price was
under 63s. a quarter, the ' first low duty ' when it was at
63s. or under 66s., the ' second low duty ' when it was
at 66s. or above. Proportionate regulating prices were
fixed for other kinds of corn. The North American
colonies were treated preferentially. The regulating
prices were to be fixed by striking an average of the prices
in all the various districts.   The return below will indicate
that the second low duty of 6d. a quarter on wheat was
payable during the greater part of the first twelve years
of the century.

AVERAGE PRICE OF WHEAT, PER QUARTER, IN ENGLAND AND
WALES.

			£	s.	d.				£	s.	d.
1801	..	..	5	18	3	1807	..	..	3	13	3
1802	..	..	3	7	5	1808	..	..	3	19	0
1803	..	..	2	16	6	1809	..	..	4	15	7
1804	..	..	3	0	1	1810	..	..	5	6	2
1805	..	..	4	7	10	1811	..	..	4	14	6
1806	..	..	3	19	0	1812	..	..	6	5	5

By indenture dated March 26, 1806, an agreement was
entered into between the duke of Grafton and the
Treasury, by which the former relinquished his interest
in the Prisage and Butlerage of England, in consideration
of an annuity of £6,870, payable by quarterly instal-
ments to him during life, and afterwards to the
heirs male of his great-grandfather, Henry Fitzroy, a
nobleman who had been quartered on the Prisage and
Butlerage by letters patent of 24 Chas. II. (Cap. 79,
46 Geo. III.).

The Customs holidays in London were restricted by
Cap. 82, 46 Geo. III., to Christmas, Good Friday, Restoration Day, Coronation Day, the king's, queen's, and
Prince of Wales's birthdays, and the public fasts. The
hours of employment of the outdoor men were stated
as nine to four from November 10 to May 9 inclusive,
eight to four for the rest of the year ; but this did not
affect the officers at the West India, East India, and

London Docks.   The fees previously charged by surveyors, warehouse-keepers, landing-waiters, gaugers, inspectors, searchers, tide-waiters, clerks, messengers, etc.,
were abolished, and salaries granted instead.   (The only
' patentees ' affected by this alteration were two of the
patent searchers.)   The prescribed hours of employment
might be exceeded if the Board thought it necessary for
the public service.

Cap. 97 of 46 Geo. III. provided for free trade in corn,
without duty or bounty, between Great Britain and
Ireland.   Cap. 150 dictated the procedure of the English
Customs Receiver-General.   Moneys received by him
were to be paid into the Bank of England on day of receipt,
and the Bank was to keep a separate account.   He might
retain not exceeding £1,000 to meet casual demands, or
the Board might authorize him to hold back a larger sum
not exceeding £5,000.   He might also retain moneys received as tax on salaries, as contributions to the Superannuation Fund, and on account of repairs to Dover
Harbour.   If at any time the Receiver-General had not
sufficient money in hand to discharge drawbacks, etc.,
he might draw on the Bank.

We find that in 1806 the net proceeds of the sales of
goods collected in Barbados and the Leeward Islands as
' 4½ per cent. duties ' (see vol. i., p. 146) amounted to
£25,400 0s. 6d.   The goods collected were sugar, ginger,
and aloes.   Thirty-five pensioners were quartered upon
the account, and the disposal of proceeds was as
below :

	£	s.	d.
To pay salaries of customs collectors and con-trollers in Barbados, St. Kitts, Nevis, Antigua, and Tortola	2,476	2	4
Retained as balance in hand by the ' Husband ' of the 4½ per cent.	33	16	6
Paid to thirty-five pensioners	19,793	16	8
Paid to Customs Receiver-General, to be trans-mitted to Exchequer	3,096	5	0
	25,400	0	6

ᶠ· It appears that the Irish revenue had risen at a great rate during the latter part of the eighteenth century and the beginning of the nineteenth.   Thus :

	£
Irish revenue (of Customs and Import-Excise only) in 1781	548,389
Irish revenue (of Customs and Import-Excise only) in 1786	928,258
Irish revenue (of Customs and Import-Excise only) in 1791	1,006,069
Irish revenue (of Customs and Import-Excise only) in 1796	1,113,680
Irish revenue (of Customs and Import-Excise only) in 1801	1,787,024
Irish revenue (of Customs and Import-Excise only) in 1806	1,989,684

(In 1811 it reached £2,206,301, and in 1816 £2,653,880.)

By Cap. 12 of 47 Geo. III. it was provided that the patent customers' offices at Baltimore, Belfast, Cork, Donaghadee, Drogheda, Dundalk, Galway, Killibeg, Kinsale, Larne, Limerick, Londonderry, Newry, Ross, Tralee, Waterford, Wexford, Wicklow, and Youghal, and the patent searchers' offices at Dublin, Belfast, Cork, Donaghadee, Drogheda, Dundalk, Galway, Kinsale, Larne, Limerick, Londonderry, Newry, Ross, Strangford, Waterford, and Youghal, the office of surveyor-general of Ireland, and the office of Irish Taster of Wines and Surveyor of the Outs (see vol. i., p. 428), should be abolished as they became vacant.   The patentees already enjoying the offices and pocketing the unearned fees were not to be compelled to give attendance.   The offices of craner and wharfinger of Dublin, customers (actual) of Dublin, clerk of the ships' entries of Dublin, coast clerk of Dublin, Irish Comptroller and Accountant-General, Irish Examiner of customs, Registrar-General of Irish shipping, and the offices of the controllers at all the Irish ports, were not to be granted in future, unless the Board thought such grant necessary, and then each appointment was to be approved by the Treasury, the Lord-Lieutenant, and Parliament.

Cap. 36, 47 Geo. III., abolished the slave trade.   Vessels

contravening might be seized by officers of customs and excise, as well as by those of the army or navy.* By Cap. 51 the provisions of the Act of 1806, abolishing most of the Customs fees in London, and regulating Customs hours, were extended to the British outports. From the list of officers it appears that registrars of tide-waiters, ' sitters ' (commanders) of preventive galleys, riding officers, preventive officers, quarantine officers, gatekeepers, and customs coopers, had been in the habit of collecting fees. (From whom, under Heaven, could such fees have been extorted ?)

Cap. 26 of 48 Geo. III. increased the duties on most foreign goods exported from Great Britain, and a later Act extended the provisions to Ireland. The preamble of the British Act is worth quoting : ' Whereas measures which have been taken by powers at war with your Majesty, prohibiting in violation of the law of nations all intercourse with this kingdom, and all trade in any articles of its growth or manufacture, have rendered it necessary for your Majesty to issue orders in Council to counteract the disadvantages which were thereby imposed upon the trade of your Majesty's subjects, and to retaliate upon the enemy the evils which he intended to inflict upon this kingdom.'

The Irish Customs fees were abolished by Cap. 56, 48 Geo. III. (from January 1, 1809). Tables were pre-

---

* Humane laws may sometimes cause inhuman actions. On June 4, 1811, the Portuguese brig *Falcon* was captured off St. Domingo by H.M. brig *Liberty*, and found to have 384 Africans on board. The Vice-Admiralty Court at Tortola decided that she had been wrongfully seized. Her captors appealed against the decision, and, as the captain could not furnish security to answer judgment, the vessel was detained at St. Thomas's. Her provisions ran out, and, as the judge made no order pending trial of appeal for subsisting the slaves, the latter were soon in a pitiable condition. The captors gave no assistance ; they merely ' hung on ' to the vessel. Her condemnation ' with tackle ' was all that interested them. Between the date of capture and June 23, 1812, 112 of the wretched negroes perished from disease and starvation, in spite of the efforts of the customs collector of St. Thomas's, who did his very best to provide them occasionally with food and water.

pared, showing the amounts received as fees by the various
officers during the three years ending January 1, 1804.
An average was struck, and the Lord-Lieutenant then
prescribed the amounts which should be granted as compensation.*   By this Act the Irish Customs holidays and
hours of attendance were made much the same as the
British.

A curious complication occurred in Jamaica. The
controller of Montego Bay seized the *Bella Americana* for
contravening the navigation laws.   The vessel was
afterwards released, and he was cast in damages by the
Grand Court of the island, even although his counsel
pleaded in defence that Cap. 22 of 7 and 8 Wm. III. provided that Plantation officers, if sued for any error committed in the execution of their duty, might plead the
general issue, and thus claim the exemption enjoyed by
customs officers in England.   A similar case occurred in
1811.   The collector of Falmouth, Jamaica, seized the
Two Brothers, for landing goods without having entered
them on the ship's report.   Action was taken against
him at the Cornwall Assizes, Jamaica.   The seizure was
declared illegal, and he was cast in damages in a subsequent action for trespass, the judge declaring that the
British laws were inefficient when opposed to enactments
made by the Legislature of Jamaica.   This in spite of
there being statutes on the British rolls making void all
Plantation revenue laws that were repugnant to imperial
Acts.   All the collectors and controllers of Jamaica signed

---

* There were a great many pensioners on the Irish Customs
establishment, some of them receiving large benefits. One,
Bernard Shaw, ex-collector of Cork, was listed for a pension of
£700 and an item of £2,579 19s. 7d. (whether this last was an
annual pension or a lump sum is not clear).   Jonas Harrison,
export-surveyor of Cork, was listed for £2,600 (evidently an
annual pension) and a pension of £50 in right of his wife.   (It is
probable that Mrs. Harrison had been ' female searcher ' at the
port in question.)

Lord Avonmore was one of the patentees compensated under
the above Act.   He had been patent searcher of Cork.   He died
in 1870, having drawn his pension during sixty-one years.   The
aggregate amount paid him figures out at £41,470 11s. 11d.

a printed memorial, asking the Board to protect them. The English Solicitor-General's opinion was taken, and he advised that the matter should be dropped, but it is clear that he was influenced by the extremely arbitrary nature of the seizure. As will be seen later, the officers, both in the Plantations and the United Kingdom, frequently strained the regulations with a view to profiting by rewards.

From the commencement of the century to the period last reviewed several Acts had been passed repealing the remnants of the old laws against regrating (buying to turn over). It is evident that Adam Smith's teaching was responsible for these doubtful proceedings, as well as for the previous abolition of the laws against engrossing. The newly-sanctioned engrossing and regrating of foodstuffs worked blithely with the tremendous war taxes in raising the prices of commodities.

Another re-consolidation of the Customs was enacted on June 10, 1809, by Cap. 98, 49 Geo. III., to come into operation on July 5. It did not affect the duties on goods passing between Great Britain and Ireland. It continued the temporary war duties, and in many cases increased the other rates upon goods.

The provisions of Edward VI.'s Act against the trading of public offices, which had previously extended to the offices of Administration of Justice ; King's rents, treasures, and revenues ; Customs ; wardenships of fortresses ; and clerkships of Record in England, were amplified by Cap. 126 so as to include the departments under the Treasury, Secretary of State, Admiralty, Ordnance, Commander-in-Chief, Secretary for War, Paymaster of Forces, India Commissioners, Excise, and many others in the United Kingdom and Plantations, including the East India Company. Certain appointments in the royal household, and army commissions, were specially excepted. The Chancery officials in Ireland might trade their offices until death or vacation.

Cap. 64, 50 Geo. III., provided that dutiable goods

II.   3

warehoused under bond might be removed from the port of warehousing (by sea or inland navigation only) to any other port that enjoyed bonding privileges, but only for exportation from the port to which removed. If the owner, after removal, desired to clear his goods for home consumption, he had to pay *the duties as due at landing*, without any allowance for shrinkage while in warehouse.

On July 12, 1810, the Attorney-General proceeded in the Exchequer against Johan Olkhausen, master of a Dutch galliot ' lying off St. Katherine's near the Tower.' Probably this was the last important case in which proceedings were taken under the old Acts that forbade the exportation of coin of the realm. The prosecuting counsel opened thus : ' Against a foreigner, importing that he was detected in the act of endeavouring to export from this country the coin of the country, against the King's licence. You know very well, gentlemen of the jury, how important it is to prevent that practice if possible. The country is already drained of its coin very much by this practice. Our gold coin sells in another country to a great advantage, and it has been the practice to buy up the coin by giving 22s. for a guinea, and carrying it to a foreign country as merchandise. There are repeated Acts upon this subject, and those of a very ancient date, one so long ago as the reign of Richard II. It is easy to apply for the King's licence, which would not be withheld in a proper case, but to attempt to do it without the King's licence is contrary to law, and the coin is forfeited.'

William James, tide-surveyor of customs, then stated that he went on board the defendant's ship on December 13, 1809, and asked him what money he had. Defendant produced several banknotes and ten guineas in gold, which last he stated were ' for his expenses.' ' I suffered him,' said James, ' to return them to his pocket.' James afterwards found in the defendant's berth two sealed bags, one containing 200 guineas, the other 40.

It was urged in defence that the wisest writers on com-

mercial policy had stated that merchandising coin was
not prejudicial to the interests of the realm, also that the
action was taken under a statute of Henry IV., which
provided that if any king's searcher found gold or silver,
in coin or in mass, *passing out of the realm* without licence,
such gold or silver should be forfeited ; and that no proof
had been furnished that this Dutch shipmaster was passing out of the realm.   He was the manager of the vessel ;
she had no supercargo ; the ship was his domicile.   It had
been stated that he might have banked the money.   True,
but there would have been some risk—witness a recent
huge failure in Lombard Street ; indeed, so perilous had
banking become that the Dutchman's guineas might be
safer even in the clutches of the customs officer who
seized them, etc., etc.

Here the judge intervened, and declared the defending
counsel to be in error.   The ship had been cleared outwards by the Customs, and it had always been held that
when a ship had been cleared outwards she was on her
outward voyage.   Verdict for the Crown.

By indenture made between the Irish Treasury and the
trustees of the earl of Ormond, the Prisage and Butlerage
of Ireland were surrendered to the Crown,* but these
duties within the port of Cork were claimed by the Cork
Corporation ; therefore it was expressed in the indenture
that the claim might be tried in the King's Bench,
Common Pleas, or Exchequer (Ireland), so as to be determined prior to January 1, 1812.   The amount to be
paid to the trustees of the earl (if the Corporation failed
to establish claim to a portion of it) was £216,000.†

It was enacted (Cap. 117, 50 Geo. III.) that a statement
of the increase or diminution in public salaries, allowances, and superannuations, should be laid before both
Houses annually.   Compensations and superannuations
were to be sanctioned by at least three Treasury Com-

---

* See Cap. 101, 50 Geo. III.
† The collection of Prisage and Butlerage in Ireland ceased on
July 1, 1811.

missioners, and authorized by Treasury warrant or letter. The conditions under which superannuation pay might be granted were set out thus :

	Proportion of Annual Pay and Emoluments.
Claimant under sixty, with ten years' good service, and infirm of mind or body ..	One-third.
Claimant under sixty, with more than ten and not exceeding twenty years' good service, and infirm of mind or body	One-half.
Claimant under sixty, with above twenty years' good service, and infirm of mind or body ..	Two-thirds.
Claimant sixty or more, with fifteen years' good service, and irrespective of mental or bodily condition	Two-thirds.
Claimant sixty-five or more, with forty years' good service, and irrespective of mental or bodily condition	Three-quarters.
Claimant sixty-five or more, with fifty years' good service, and irrespective of mental or bodily condition	All.

By Cap. 207 (local and personal), 50 Geo. III., Parliament authorized the building of the Commercial Docks, London (really an extension of the dock previously used by whalers, and known as the ' Greenland Dock ').

To illustrate the abuses existing in the Plantation Customs, we quote a few extracts from certain evidence forthcoming. It appears that in 1810 the net emoluments (mostly fees) of the three higher customs officials of the port of Halifax, Nova Scotia, were as follow :

Collector, £1,453 ;* controller, £590 ; surveyor, £561. Yet immense smuggling was carried on with impunity between the adjacent colonies and the United States. Nearly all the tea, three-fourths of the wine, nine-tenths of the spirits, seven-eighths of the soap and candles, most of the indigo, starch, mustard, tobacco, East India cottons, and bandanas, and all the nankeens, sail-cloth, cordage, and anchors, imported into New Brunswick, were smuggled thither by Americans. Many of the inhabitants were patriotically inclined, and would have

* These and the emoluments subsequently quoted are stated in sterling, not in currency.

preferred dealing with the mother country, but for fear
of being ruined by illicit competition.

The American Government, to discourage smuggling
from the United States to Nova Scotia and New Brunswick, allowed no drawback on American goods shipped
thither, but the subtle American smugglers and corrupt
American officials easily evaded this provision. The
American customs officers accepted delusive manifests,
setting forth that the cargoes were for other places, and
the smugglers produced on return forged certificates
of landing, which the American Customs passed as satisfactory, and on the strength of which drawback was
claimed and paid. Meanwhile the goods had been run
into Nova Scotia or New Brunswick, where the dilatory
and inept Plantation officials sat at their desks, charging
fees on clearances, entries, etc., fees no doubt gladly
paid by the smugglers, and regarded as warrants of
impunity.

The collector stationed at New Brunswick was seventy-
six years old—old enough to have learned better methods.
The net emoluments of his office in 1810 were £871 ; the
controller gained £541 ; the surveyor £464. And, while
audacious and deliberate smuggling went on all around
them, the preventive officers gained respectively £602
and £302, much higher emoluments than fell to the lot
of preventive men of similar rank in England.

The port of Bridgetown, Barbados, was still more
profitable to officials. See the return for 1810 : Collector,
£3,556 (£3,376 of this had been taken in fees) ; controller,
£1,473 ; searchers, £722 each ; landing-waiters, £502
each.

Cap. 55, 51 Geo. III., abolished the Customs Superannuation Fund (see vol. i., p. 166), as rendered unnecessary
by Cap. 117 of the previous year. No more official contributions to the fund were to be taken, and the moneys
in hand, which the Board had invested, were appropriated
by the Receiver-General, and paid into the Exchequer
to the account of Consolidated Customs, an account from

which all subsequent Customs superannuations and allowances were to be met.*   (The Scottish Customs Superannuation Fund was dealt with similarly, under Cap. 60, 52 Geo. III.)

Most of the English Customs sinecurists, whose offices were to become vacant at death of holders (see vol. i., pp. 405-407), were still alive, and punctual in attendance at the pay-seat. Cap. 71, 51 Geo. III., provided that their offices should be abolished on January 5, 1812, they to receive compensation, and all Customs fees in London were to be abolished, except as below expressed :

1. The Customs Solicitors might still charge. 2. The Long Room clerks might still make out entries for the merchants, if the latter were willing, and receive the customary fees. 3. The receivers and collectors might continue to pocket ' the odd pence ' superfluous on payment of duties, if the merchants were willing (see vol. i., p. 367). 4. Certain Long Room officials might continue to charge fees for delivering warrants at times other than the usual hours of attendance. 5. The cocket-writers might still charge fees, the merchants to have power to choose which cocket-writer they would honour with their custom. All officials who had taken illegal fees were indemnified, and it was provided that the Treasury might extend the Act to outports on giving notice in the *London Gazette*.

We furnish an account of the emoluments, etc., of various Plantation officers during 1811 (shillings and pence rejected). (See pp. 40-41.)

It should be noted that the amounts shown as ' duty

---

* The stock of the English Superannuation Fund stood as below :

	£	s.	d.
Arising from official contributions :			
Invested in 3 per cent. Consols	178,459	8	10
Invested in reduced annuities	12,500	0	0
Arising from patentees' fees which had been appropriated :			
Invested in 3 per cent. Consols	63,018	0	0
	253,977	8	10

taken ' in Antigua and St. Kitts do not include the
comparatively important duties of 4½ per cent., which
were realized in London.   Nearly all the ' emoluments '
consisted of fees, to a great extent levied on coasting
traffic, the victims being the masters and owners of the
little ' drogers ' that plied between island and island.
The salaries were nominal : the collector's salary at an
important station rarely exceeded £100.

The average annual ' ordinary duty ' taken at Chris-
tianstadt, St. Croix, was £740 ; ' the special duty,' taken
on American produce and tonnage by Order in Council
of 1809, was £4,017 : total, £4,757—quite an important
sum, and the collector took as emoluments £3,362 ; the
controller £1,211 ; and the landing-waiter £613.   At
Frederikstadt, St. Croix, the ordinary duty amounted to
£18, and the special to £1,860, the collector pocketing as
emoluments £2,813 ; the controller £935 ; and the landing-
waiter £785.   At Quebec the Plantation duties amounted
to £1,900, against which there was a charge of £598 as
' incidents.'   The officers collected certain inland duties
as well, which were applied to local purposes, and produced about £50,000 per annum.   On this they received
a commission.   Their total emoluments appear to have
been : Collector, £2,760 ; controller, £1,626.

A curious kind of fraud was practised in connection
with the ' rum and lumber trade ' between Quebec and
the West Indies.   If a cargo of lumber, provisions, or
cattle were shipped—say from Quebec to Barbados—
a certificate obtained from the Barbadian customs
officers that the goods were landed, and then a cargo of
rum were laden at Barbados (value of said rum not exceeding value of the cargo landed), the rum might be
delivered duty-free in Quebec.   This was a device to
encourage intercolonial trade, but mark how, by the
ineptitude of officials, the system had become a vehicle
of fraud.   The principal articles of lumber shipped at
Quebec were hoops and staves.   The rate of value fixed
per 1,000 feet had for years been applied to every 1,000

Port.	Emoluments.	Hours.	Amount taken as Duty.	Remarks.
St. Lucia	Collector, £2,414 Controller, £834 Landing-waiters, £463 (each)	9 to 1	Not shown	
Kingston (St. Vincent)	Collector, £1,896 Controller, £636 Searcher, £493 Landing-waiter, £293	9 to 2	Not shown	—
Roseau (Dominica)	Collector, £1,182 Controller, £424	9 to noon	Not shown	Trade may have dwindled. In the previous year the collector had taken nearly £1,800
Fort Royal and Trinite (Martinique)	Collector, £1,480 Controller, £635	9 to 1	Not shown	—
St. Pierre (Martinique)	Collector, £3,656 Controller, £1,705	9 to 1	Not shown	—
Pointe à Petre (Guadaloupe)	Collector, £3,025 Controller, £1,173	Not shown	About £86	—
Basseterre (Guadaloupe)	Collector, £1,876 Controller, £814	Not shown	About £55	—
St. John's (Antigua)	Collector, £1,320 Controller, £392	Not shown	About £585	—

Basseterre (St. Kitts)	Collector, £1,904 Controller, £545 Searcher, £450 Landing-waiter, £435	Not shown	About £463	A charge of £212 for 'incidents' against the duty. Collector on leave in England. Landing-waiters proceeding to England
Marigot (St. Martin's)	Collector, £613	Not shown	About £23	Charge of £210 for 'incidents' against duty
Phillipsburgh (St. Martin's)*				
St. Thomas's	Collector, £3,685 Controller, £1,140 Landing-waiter, £571	Not shown	£740	A charge of £228 as 'incidents' against duty
Sandy Point (St. Kitts)	Collector, £3,363 Controller, £85	Not shown	Nil	The collector resided on his estate in Antigua. The controller had been absent for a year. The landing-waiter collected their fees for them. (Charge of £293 as 'incidents.')
Tortola	Collector, £717	Not shown	Not shown	Collector so infirm as to be able to do nothing except collect his fees. Controller on leave in England. Landing-waiter appointed to the port in 1807, but had not arrived. A 'resident,' who acted in his stead, was the only official who did any work

* No accounts forthcoming, but there is a statement that the collector had only visited the office once during three months.

hoops, and thus the total value of every cargo of lumber
had been hugely overstated. On the other hand, the
value of the rum shipped in the West Indies had been
understated, and thus nearly all the rum that reached
Quebec passed duty-free. This was good for West
Indian distillers, and pleased the thirsty Canadian
lumbermen, but it was decidedly against the Plantation
revenue.

The nature of Canadian outward traffic may be judged
from the following annual list of exports from New
Carlisle :

17,000 quintals dry codfish.	1,650 tons white pine.
1,000 quintals wet codfish.	160 tons black birch.
1,050 barrels pickled herrings.	16,839 feet pine plank and
300 barrels pickled salmon.	boards.
20 tuns cod-oil.	70 cords lathwood.
100 hogsheads cod-oil.	39 spars.
80 barrels cod-oil.	240 handspikes.

The trade from this port was principally to Portugal.
The goods were exchanged at Lisbon and Oporto for wine
and fruit. The wine and fruit were taken to England,
where the vessels loaded woollens, linen, hardware,
tobacco, and salt, which they took to New Carlisle.

The London Custom House was in a dilapidated condition, and Parliament, by Cap. 49, 52 Geo. III., issued
directions to the Treasury to purchase land in the vicinity
of Lower Thames Street, so that a new custom-house
might be erected.

The Revenue claims on flotsam, jetsam, lagan, and
wreck were recited by Parliament.* When the goods
consisted of spirits or tobacco, the finder was enjoined to

* By an order of December 24, 1803, the Customs Board, on
the strength of a decision given by high legal officers, had directed
that in future no duty should be charged on derelict goods, thus
reversing their decision of 1729 (see vol. i., p. 205). In an order
of August 15, 1811, they had quoted the Attorney-General's
opinion as to manorial rights. If the officers found the goods,
the lord of the manor could not recover them until after a year
and a day, except by process under Cap. 4, 3 Edward I. ; if the
lord of the manor found the goods, the officers could not claim
them until a similar period had elapsed.

apprise the Customs or Excise within twenty-four hours. The officers apprised were to demand the duty payable, and put the goods under lock if payment were refused. The manorial rights over wreck, etc., were reaffirmed, the lord of the manor being allowed to keep the goods if he gave bond for the duties payable. Duties to be paid within a year and a day, otherwise the goods were to be taken by the Revenue department concerned (Cap. 159, 52 Geo. III.).

It may be instructive to quote the British duties payable in 1812 upon wine.

Wine per gallon (fractions of a penny disregarded in totals). The gallon used was a little over seven-eighths of the modern measure.

	Imported in a British Ship.			Imported in a Foreign Ship.		
	£	s.	d.	£	s.	d.
French wine :						
Customs duty	0	5	2½	0	5	6½
Excise duty	0	6	2½	0	6	2½
	0	11	5	0	11	9
Rhenish, German, and Hungarian wine :						
Customs duty	0	5	2	0	5	6
Excise duty	0	4	2	0	4	2
	0	9	4	0	9	8
Madeira wine :						
Customs duty	0	3	6	0	3	9
Excise duty	0	4	2	0	4	2
	0	7	8	0	7	11
Spanish red wine :						
Customs duty	0	4	4	0	4	7
Excise duty	0	4	2	0	4	2
	0	8	6	0	8	9
All other wine :						
Customs duty	0	3	5	0	3	8
Excise duty	0	4	2	0	4	2
	0	7	7	0	7	10

It was provided by Cap. 21, 53 Geo. III., that the Board might grant money towards the subsistence in prison of needy persons who were confined for offences against the Revenue.

Vengeful duties were levied by Cap. 33, 53 Geo. III., on many kinds of French goods, as below :

On French or French territorial products, except wine and silk : An additional temporary Customs duty, amounting to two-thirds of the previous *permanent* duties.

On all French or French territorial silk, except raw silk : An additional Customs duty, described as ' permanent,' amounting to 25 per cent. of the previous permanent duties.

On all French or French territorial goods, except wine, raw silk, sugar, tea, and raw cotton : An additional permanent Customs duty, amounting to 25 per cent. of the previous permanent duties.

The first and second of these duties were repealed by Cap. 65, 54 Geo. III. (Napoleon abdicated in April, 1814).

This Act also laid an additional 50 per cent. on the temporary duties previously levied on exported goods, and a temporary duty of 9s. 4d. a cwt. on all foreign ' hides in the hair ' exported to France or French territories.

Additional excises were put on foreign tobacco by Cap. 34, 53 Geo. III., and an additional excise of £63 a tun on French wine, imported or exported. This made the total duty payable on a gallon of French wine—

		In a British Ship.			In a Foreign Ship.	
		£	s.	d.	£	s.	d.
Customs duty	..	..	0	5	2½	0	5	6¼
Excise duty	..	..	0	11	2½	0	11	2½
			0	16	5	0	16	9

An Order in Council dated May 20, 1813, provided that British ships clearing out for Africa might take arms and ammunition, to traffic with on the coast, to the extent of 10 guns, 10 brace of pistols, and 1 barrel of gunpowder, to every 10 tons of measurement.

On December 10, 1813, the Scottish Board issued

a schedule of missing certificates of ships' registry, from which it appeared that within a limited period ninety-three Scottish vessels had been captured by the French.

On December 23, the Secretary to the Treasury sent the following letter to the Board : ' Gentlemen, I am commanded by the Lords, etc., to desire you will issue the necessary orders for the delivery to Lord Valentia, duty-free, of certain masses of the Rock of Gibraltar, which have been brought home for his Lordship by Captain Turner, of H.M. store-ship *Weymouth*.'

About 6 a.m., February 12, 1814, Mr. Lingham of Thames Street, owner of the vaults which still bear his name, observed a strong light near the river, and found that the Custom House was on fire. This, of course, was long before business hours, and the place was occupied only by the customs watchmen ; a lady named Kelly, who acted as housekeeper ; her brother, General Kelly ; several other relatives ; and the domestic servants who looked after the establishment. On the quay, close to the building, were many casks of oil and turpentine. Mr. Lingham gave the alarm, and a number of people assembled, some of whom exerted themselves manfully in the saving of life and property. Captain Richbell, of the Impress service, with the crew of H.M.S. *Enterprise*, worked wonders in this direction, being ably helped by the Aberdeenshire militia and a company of artillerymen, who came from their quarters in the Tower to render assistance. The East India Company also sent a body of their soldiers to help, but in spite of these laudable efforts the building was reduced to ashes, together with several adjacent warehouses and dwellings.*

(The fire broke out in the bedroom occupied by General Kelly, but the cause is not clear. It appears that Miss

* The landlord of the ' Yorkshire Grey' (a sign still displayed in Thames Street) stated in evidence at the subsequent inquiry that he broke into the Solicitors' room, and rescued an iron chest and a number of books. Then he found that his own house was on fire, and ' went to attend to it.'

Kelly, the housekeeper, spent the previous evening in Aldermanbury. She returned early on the morning of the fire, and interviewed her brother before he retired. He was in failing health, and had to keep a light in his room, but this can scarcely have caused the fire, as she stated it was merely a rushlight, ' kept in an earthenware pan.' The General's deposition was to the effect that the fire broke out in a closet near his bed.)

Some of the spectators and employés behaved with conspicuous heroism. A young lighterman named Drinkald got the casks of oil and turpentine on board a vessel moored at the quay, then broke into the searcher's office and saved many valuable documents, then attempted to break into the armoury and magazine, where a quantity of gunpowder was stored, and, failing in this, headed a sally into the Long Room, and cleared it of most of its contents. While this last work was proceeding the magazine exploded, wounding several of his assistants, but he escaped without a scratch.

A labourer named Carlisle, who was going to his work when the fire was discovered, distinguished himself greatly. General Kelly, who had been badly burned, had got partly out of a window, and hung there in a hopeless condition. A ladder was procured, but it was much too short. Carlisle managed to place a van alongside the building, put the ladder on top of the van, mounted through the flames and smoke, took the General in his arms, and brought him safely down. He also procured the keys of the engine-house from one of the watchmen, broke in—the room being in flames—and brought out the engine. He found the man who looked after the magazine, and asked him to show him the place, so that he might enter and remove the gunpowder, but the man refused to go with him, and this no doubt was wise, for the place blew up immediately afterwards. Carlisle was badly hurt, and had to go into hospital.*

* Miss Kelly gave Carlisle £20 for saving her brother, and the Board made him a ' customs weigher.'

The son of the customs blacksmith made desperate attempts to save the building, and sustained severe burns and bruises. Two maidservants who slept in an upper room perished in the flames. General Kelly died a few days after the event. The newspaper accounts of the fire state that an elderly official displayed great temerity in attempting to reach his offices in the centre of the burning structure, and that after the fire he was observed searching amid the smoking ruins. The bystanders attributed this exhibition of official heroism to a desire to rescue the documents in his charge. They went to his assistance, and succeeded in finding an iron safe. The old gentleman unlocked the safe, took out a bag full of guineas, counted his treasure, and retired precipitately, without uttering a word of thanks.

On March 18, 1814, the Board made a provisional report to the Treasury. They blamed none for the fire, admitting that it was impossible to state with certainty the cause of the disaster.

Immense stores of official records, many of which might now be of great historical value, were destroyed. Yet many volumes survived. Some of these are not connected with Customs matters, yet they are of value, and indicate that at the beginning of the century the Commissioners possessed an extensive *private* library, and that many of the volumes therein were bound and furbished in sumptuous style. At this time the Board kept a private stock of wine in vaults beneath the Custom House. Shortly after the fire an official salvor furnished an account of the wines 'gott out of the ruins of the Comishiners Sellers,' stating them as 1 full butt, 2 full hogsheads, 1 ullaged hogshead, 437 full bottles, 56 ullaged bottles, and 1,134 empty bottles. He also rendered account of 'a quantity of copper coyne, two peecis of silver, and a sixpence,' found in the same shadowed receptacles. The salvors, or some of them, must have been honest folk, for on the day of the fire certain persons who had busied themselves in saving property handed over to the Customs Secretary five bags containing gold and silver coin.

The Board tried to hire Bakers' Hall, but, there being some delay, an attempt was made to secure Ironmongers' Hall instead. The Ironmongers' Company held a meeting on the matter, and their master Warden curtly informed the Customs that his fellow-guildsmen were not disposed to acquiesce. So the Customs business was transacted temporarily at the Commercial Chambers, Mincing Lane.*   On April 14, 1814, the Privy Council

* The designing and rebuilding of the new Custom House were entrusted to Mr. David Laing, the Customs ' Surveyor of Buildings.' Competition was not invited ; the matter was a close job. Mr. Laing's estimate was £228,000, and the actual cost was £255,000. It can scarcely be claimed that his efforts were praiseworthy, although he afterwards published a rather pompous tome in commemoration of his performance. He produced a formal and intensely sombre structure, which owes whatever picturesqueness it may possess to its outlook upon the crowded river. That there were people, even in Mr. Laing's time, who thought little of his architectural abilities, is evident from a report made in 1819 by several able officials, who stated that better results might have been obtained had the authorities invited competition, and selected such plans as combined ' beauty of design with fitness.' The report contained this telling remark : ' To trust to the person who happens to be Surveyor of the Establishment is not to take the best means of procuring magnificence of elevation or utility of arrangement.'

Though Mr. Laing was not exactly an architectural genius, he was a good business man. His salary as Surveyor of Customs Buildings (£400 a year, with travelling expenses at the rate of £1 a day and 1s. 8d. a mile when visiting the outports) ran on while he was engaged in his new work, so he charged the new work as ' extra service.' Below is his bill :

	£
For making surveys of premises in Lower Thames Street belonging to the Crown ..	100
Plans and drawings for the new Custom House	100
Two sets of working drawings and specifications	150
Commission at 5s. per cent. on estimate (£228, 000)	570
Commission at £5 per cent. on actual cost (£255,000)	12,750
	£13,670

The last item seems a monstrous imposition. The Treasury referred Mr. Laing to the Board of Works, who disallowed the third item. Thus he received, beside his salary and allowances, directed that British vessels and vessels of friendly powers might be allowed by the Customs to clear for such French ports as had hoisted the white flag and declared for Louis XVIII. The Customs Board thereupon asked at which ports this had been done. The Council were unable to enlighten them, and rescinded the order, except as regarded Bordeaux.

On May 19, 1814, the Treasury gave instructions that foreign persons of distinction arriving in the United Kingdom, and bringing pictures or images ' for purposes of devotion,' might have the articles duty-free.

During the latter part of 1813 Mr. Pellew, the customs collector of Falmouth, had contrived to bring about the seizure of four Prussian ships—the *Teutrauwen, Vrow Maria, Hendrik,* and *Theophilus*—which had each brought French cargoes under licence. The pretext for seizure was that these vessels had arrived at periods much later than those on which their licences expired, and that the vessels themselves did not fully correspond in build, tonnage, ownership, etc., with the particulars furnished in the licences. The collector sent the seized ships to London, and they were moored in the London Docks, pending the usual formalities attending forfeiture.

£13,520 for three years' work, and a year or two later the Treasury were apprised that in future he intended to charge commission upon the actual cost of any Customs building that might be repaired or erected under his supervision, if said cost exceeded £5,000. The officials who referred this astounding announcement to the Treasury intimated that if Mr. Laing were allowed to do the like he should at least be prevented from basing the rate of commission upon the precedent created in the case of the new Custom House.

Later the building was found to be insecure, and the Crown took proceedings in the Exchequer against the contractor (Mr. Peto), it being alleged that he had not performed the piling properly, and that the spandrels of the arches had been filled with rubbish. The contractor threw the blame on Mr. Laing, and the contractor's counsel, in referring to a recent Parliamentary debate on the matter, declared that the Government had prosecuted the wrong man. The Attorney-General stated that Laing would probably be prosecuted afterwards, the Custom House being scarcely reared before it fell to the ground. Verdict for defendant.

II.   4

On February 16, 1814, another Prussian vessel—the *Lucia Margarita*—arrived with a French cargo at Falmouth, and the captain produced his licence to Mr. Pellew. The period covered by the document and an additional period prescribed by the Treasury as a concession had expired—in short, the vessel was over two months in excess of her grants. Mr. Pellew seized her. The ship's agent then approached the Treasury, pleading that the original licence had been issued on September 26, 1812, for four months ; that the vessel had gone to France and taken in a cargo, completing her lading on January 14, 1813 ; that while coming down the Gironde she was damaged and had to be unladen and repaired ; that she reloaded ; and then her master had news of several seizures made in England of ships with overdue licences, and that this caused him to remain in port till news reached him of the Treasury's above-mentioned concession ; that contrary winds prevented him from sailing ; and then he was taken ill, and another master had to be procured. The vessel sailed, and reached Falmouth too late to profit by the extension. Then, continued the agent, the collector seized the ship, and at once started to land her cargo under a writ of appraisement. The agent prayed the Treasury to put a stop to Mr. Pellew's highhanded proceedings, and allow the *Lucia Margarita*, with her valuable cargo (rendered doubly valuable by the immense duties then leviable on French goods), to proceed under British convoy to Bremen or some other port ' not in the enemy's possession.'

The Treasury Commissioners at once took a reasonable view of matters, and desired the Board of Customs to direct the collector to release the vessel at once ; warrant to follow. The Board complied. Meanwhile the Treasury had enjoined that the cargoes of the four ships seized and sent to London should be admitted to entry. But neither Board nor Treasury were as yet thoroughly acquainted with Mr. Pellew, collector of Falmouth ; his infernal ingenuity in interpreting in his own favour

passages of the complicated laws of navigation and
revenue ; his mulish stubbornness ; his superhuman
self-confidence ; and his bandit-like determination in
prey. (Readers must bear in mind that the condemnation of the five vessels and their highly taxed cargoes
would have meant a huge pecuniary award to him.)
There began one of the most extraordinary official conflicts in history : one subtle, determined customs officer
pitted against the legal advisers of two powerful departments—against reason, common sense, and the *spirit* of
the law as well.

On March 8, 1814, Mr. Pellew apprised the Board that,
in his humble opinion, the four ships in the London Docks
were liable to forfeiture, and that he was about to take
steps to secure their condemnation. His attorney would
be pleased to wait upon the Secretary of Customs, and
meantime Mr. Pellew delicately reminded the Board that
he had previously asked to be allowed to prosecute at
his own risk and expense.

On March 19 the Treasury referred to their previous
order, and desired the Board to authorize the Customs
Solicitor to call for the issue of writs of delivery out of
the Court of Exchequer, on payment by the ship's agent
of the usual law costs. On the top of this arrived another
letter from Mr. Pellew, referring to previous reports of
his, which he feared might have perished in the fire that
consumed the Custom House. The five vessels, Mr.
Pellew opined, were justly liable to condemnation. He
had already on his own responsibility directed legal proceedings. Here he interjected a startling item, which
seems to have been news to both Board and Treasury.
*He had already succeeded in getting the ' Lucia Margarita '
condemned in the Exchequer !* (This was confirmed soon
after by a piteous letter from the ship's agent, stating :
' Very hasty proceedings have been taken by Mr. Pellew
in the Court of Exchequer, unknown to me.')

The Treasury sought the aid of the King's Proctor, they
having meanwhile received an expression of opinion from

the Privy Council that the cargoes of the four ships in
the London Docks were available for entry. Thus a
third great department had declared against Pellew, yet
he was not at all dismayed.

The King's Proctor suggested tripping Pellew by
means of formalities. The learned gentleman had conferred with the Advocate-General, and they were of
opinion that Pellew would not be able to proceed in the
High Court of Admiralty as on a ' prize seizure.' As
to the contemplated proceedings in Exchequer, they
thought that sections 13 and 14 of Cap. 77, 26 Geo. III.,
would enable the Attorney-General to enter a *nolle
prosequi*. Yet there might be other circumstances
worth considering, and they submitted that a reference
be made to the Attorney-General.

On March 26 the Customs Surveyors at the London
Docks asked the Board for instructions as to the four
vessels, as they had been informed that, though the
Board had directed release, the seizing officer still held
on. About this time Mr. Pellew wrote the Customs
Secretary from an inn in London. He had left his port
in charge of his clerk, for whose good conduct he was prepared to be responsible. The journey had made Mr.
Pellew ill, but he hoped that in a few days he would be
well enough to wait upon Mr. Delavaud (the Secretary).
He wished the Board to be apprised that he had served the
Exchequer writs of appraisement for the seized vessels
and their cargoes, and he expected their Honours to
assist him in carrying the law into effect. Three days
later he informed the Board that the officers at the docks
had made several seizures on board the vessels—seizures
which tended to confirm his action—and he urged the
Board to have the cargoes landed and put in a secure
place. The Board did not comply with this audacious
invitation, but called on him to furnish full particulars
of the cargoes seized by him. This was a dexterous move,
for how could he furnish full particulars of mixed cargoes,
only part of which had been landed ? But there lay the

request, suggested by a cunning official connected with
the King's Warehouse, who had made a report on the
matter, and intimated that the seizing officer was ' the
party most competent to render an account of what he
himself has done.' But it needed a more subtle sleight
than that, to trip Mr. Pellew. He coolly replied that,
being an outport officer, he was ignorant of the London
method of taking goods to account, and requested instruction from the Board on that point. Had the Board
given him instruction they would have assisted towards
confirming his seizure, so the matter was dropped.

The Commissioners of Appraisement approached the
Board, asking instructions. The writs had reached them
in an unusual course, being served by Pellew's lawyer
instead of by the Customs Solicitor. They had no account
of the goods, so could not proceed. *That* matter was
allowed to stand over.

On March 31 the Treasury directed the Board to
carry out the previous order and release the ships, and
if they received any more letters from Pellew they were
to forward them to Whitehall at once. The message
stated that Pellew had not only been guilty of insubordination, but had violated the law. He was warned accordingly, but the warning had no effect. He wrote the
Board, informing them that 130 barrels of wine, part of
the cargo of one of the vessels, had been delivered for
exportation, and he requested that the officers might be
ordered to see that these goods were at once relanded
and secured. The Board, probably fearing that the wine
might leave the country before the matter was finally
settled, felt themselves bound to comply, meanwhile
appealing to the Treasury. The Treasury directed that
the wine should be released, and the vessels at once freed
from detention.

But Pellew had another card up his sleeve. On board
one of the ships—the *Vrow Maria*—were certain packages
of brandy, as to which he had entered proceedings at
Falmouth, charging the crew with having conspired with

a resident of that town to run the goods ashore. (These proceedings had been based on the evidence of an informer, a person described by several responsible inhabitants of Falmouth as a disreputable character.) This, of course, delayed release of the *Vrow Maria*. Then Pellew played his last card. He informed the Board that he had discovered that the *Lucia Margarita* was not a Prussian, but a French vessel, manned and owned by ' the king's enemies,' and travelling with mere imitations of Prussian documents. In support of this he produced the ship's papers, and a written opinion upon them, furnished by an expert. Though there is every evidence that Pellew in all his previous proceedings had acted in the manner of a brigand, and that the charge of smuggling made against the crew of the *Vrow Maria* was a rascally fabrication, assisted in by one of the greatest rogues in Falmouth, there is little reason to doubt that the charge of forgery was justifiable. But the Board and the Treasury had gone too far to withdraw. They could not allow the *Lucia Margarita* to be condemned on a side issue, foster a glaring precedent in encouragement of insubordination, and cause serious international complications, merely because Mr. Pellew's grimy fingers had unearthed one legitimate reason for seizure. The Customs Solicitor was accordingly instructed to apprise all concerned that there could be no condemnation. Pellew then warned him by letter that if he persisted he would be sued for the seizing officer's share of the *Lucia Margarita* and her cargo. It appears that the letter alarmed the lawyer, and the Treasury were asked to state how this contumacious rogue should be dealt with.

The writ of delivery so precipitately granted in the Exchequer against the *Lucia Margarita* was withdrawn by special order of one of the Exchequer judges, and it might appear that the ships were free. But the case was down for trial, so they could not be released, and, just to show his mettle, Pellew formally reseized the *Vrow Maria* on the Falmouth smuggling charge.

The case was tried on May 14, 1814, and it was decided that the Board of Customs had power to restore seizures, when convinced that there had been no real intention of fraud.   Pellew contended that in such cases the Board were compelled to cause the owner of the goods to compensate the seizing officer.   This contention the Exchequer barons recommended to the consideration of the Board, stating that it was not binding.   The writs of appraisement might not be quashed, but the Court stayed all proceedings under them.   Thus the ships, with their cargoes, might be delivered, except the *Vrow Maria*.   She was to be detained under the charge of smuggling.

This charge was heard soon after, and the Court reaffirmed the opinion that the Board had power to restore seizures, and stated that Pellew had violated the law. Thus the *Vrow Maria* was at last freed.

It appears that Pellew got his costs.*   The whole proceeding forms a remarkable illustration of the ferocity with which some of the revenue officers attempted to enforce seizures.   Such men were really revenue lawyers rather than officers, and the revenue Acts, badly drafted and unutterably complicated, afforded every facility for enterprises of the kind.†

* It does not appear that he was punished.   We find his signature years later as collector of Falmouth.

† The expert's opinion upon the *Lucia Margarita's* papers is worth reproduction.   No doubt the statements are correct. Many curious devices were practised at the time to evade the navigation laws :

No. 1. A bill brief, or builder's certificate, purporting to be granted at Stettin May 27, 1806.

Remark : ' The originals are never made out on parchment, but on particular hot-pressed card-paper.   The above, therefore, is evidently simulated.'

No. 2. A certificate of property, purporting that the *Lucia Margarita* belongs to Captain Jacob Daene and co-partners.

Remark : ' The paper and stamps do not appear to be genuine. The usual form of such certificates is a printed one in German type, and the particulars filled in in writing.   This certificate is made like those they grant for cargoes, and not for ships.'

No. 3. A certificate of the ship's measurement, purporting to be granted at Stettin May 19, 1806.

On August 11, 1814, the Treasury sent a letter to the Board of Customs, referring to many unjust detentions of ships and goods. ' In some of these cases,' said my Lords, ' the precise letter of Acts of Parliament, framed

---

Remark : ' The stamps, type, and paper are so different from any originals as to admit of no doubt of their being very awkwardly simulated.'

No. 4. A certificate from the Prussian consul at Bordeaux, stating that Captain Daene has left his ship on account of ill-health (the gout), and appointed P. Lett in his stead.   Dated Bordeaux, November 13, 1813.

Remark : ' This document may be genuine, but does not prove the fact it pretends, being made in France.'

No. 5. A bill of sale for one-third and one-fourth of the ship, from William Stark to Peter Daene.

Remark : ' This paper bears evident marks of simulation.   The legend on the wafer seal is badly imitated.   The inscription under the notarial seal (in red wax), so far as it is legible, is, strange to tell, composed of French words instead of German and Latin. The witness who has attested it, although he has altered the handwriting from that in the body of the document, was not able to make a German capital G of a different shape.'

The expert deals in the same manner with the muster-roll, the ' Protest against the Sea,' the manifest, etc.   He displays great powers of research and combination, and winds up as below :

' From these papers it appears that a fallacious attempt has been made to account for the delay of nearly a whole twelve-month by pretended damages at sea, and the captain's ridiculous story of the gout, while in reality, from the casks being perfectly new, it is quite incredible that they should have remained (as the story goes) confined in the ship's hold for nearly twelve months in a hot climate, without fermenting and bursting the casks. From which I conclude, considering all circumstances combined, that the intention must have been to make use of an expired licence, granted to another captain, and probably to another ship (as the tonnage does not agree with that stated on the licence), and this for the nefarious purpose of imposing upon Government, in return for its indulgence of two months' extension of licences.

' There is no burger-brief belonging to the captain, whereas at Stettin captains ought to carry along with them, and produce when required, a German printed burger-brief accompanied by a printed affidavit in German.

' The foregoing is what I have extracted from and remarked upon the papers produced to me of the *Lucia Margarita*.

' FREDK. JAS. ALBERS,
' Commercial Agent, and translator of Languages.

' LONDON,
' *May* 10, 1814.'

many years ago, in time of peace and circumscribed commerce, has been rigorously applied amid all the difficulties incidental to war, and against the manifest spirit of the Acts themselves.' Special mention was made of a case at Bristol, where the officers had detained a consignment of sugar, the marks on the goods being ' R. S.,' and shown on the entry as ' RS ' (merely minus the dots). For this informality in miniature the goods were put under stop, and the official vultures concerned refused to release them except on payment of ' a satisfaction ' at the rate of a guinea per cask. In another case an officer had detained certain hogsheads of sugar for being ' in excess of ship's report,' and it was found on investigation that the goods were reported correctly, but he had made a mistake in counting the packages. In another case part of a cargo had been seized because the marks on the goods did not exactly agree with those furnished on the report. These were Bristol cases, but a worse case had occurred in London. A vessel arrived with a cargo which by the letter of the law might not be landed. The importers applied for special permission to land these goods and warehouse them for exportation. The officers construed this action into ' evidence of intent to land goods illegally,' and actually seized both ship and cargo while the Board were considering the request. Said my Lords to the Board, in conclusion : ' You may confidently rely, without reference to us, upon our full support in whatever measures may be necessary for the punishment of oppressive and contumacious officers.'

During 1814 the Board issued orders to the Plantation Customs to the effect that the officers were to obey the various colonial governors, make public all the revenue Acts applying to the Plantations, refrain from making out manifests of cargoes under compact with the shipmasters, etc., etc. Another order may be regarded as a notable pronouncement on Plantation Customs tactics. It directed that the waterside officers, instead of, as before, confining their attention to dutiable goods, were also to examine goods entered as duty-free. It is evident that this had not been done previously, which may account for a portion of the smuggling that prevailed.

The old wool Acts, which had been eased by Cap. 55 of 20 Geo. III., were relaxed to a still greater extent by Cap. 78, 54 Geo. III. Cap. 156 extended the duration of copyright to twenty-eight years (or as long as the author's life endured). Cap. 171 extended to the Treasury the powers previously possessed by the Board of Customs of restoring seized vessels and goods. (It followed, therefore, that though the Customs Commissioners retained their powers, the Treasury might intervene, and remit, restore, or mitigate, in cases where seizures were made or penalties inflicted, whether under the laws of Customs, Excise, Navigation, or Trade. Undoubtedly this Act was passed because it had been made apparent during the trial of Pellew's case that the Board held powers superior to those possessed by the Treasury.)

During 1814 the Treasury apprised the Board that Liverpool might be admitted to the full privileges of the East India trade, as soon as proper accommodation could be provided for the East India goods likely to be imported there.

The proprietors of the theatres at Drury Lane and Covent Garden applied to the Treasury for exemption from the ' painted and stained linen ' duties (Excise) on their stage scenes and decorations. My Lords refused.

On October 26, 1814, the Secretary to the Treasury wrote the Customs Board :

' GENTLEMEN,
        ' It being represented to the Lords, etc., that your officers are in the constant habit of opening a bottle of the cases of wine, etc., brought to this country for H.R.H. the Prince Regent, I am commanded to desire that this practice may immediately cease, and that such packages be invariably delivered without such examination. I

am also commanded to enclose a memo. of five chests cordials, landed from the *Hibernia* from Bordeaux for H.R.H., and to desire that they may be delivered without examination and without delay.'

By Cap. 26, 55 Geo. III., the corn duties and corn laws were again 'amended.' When the average price of British wheat was 80s. a quarter or more, foreign wheat might be imported duty-free. The rule was applied to the other kinds of corn, thus : rye, beans, and peas, 53s.; barley, 40s. ; oats, 27s. If the average price of any particular kind were less, the article might not be imported for home consumption, nor might it, if previously landed and warehoused, be taken out of warehouse for home consumption. Preferential terms were extended to the North American colonies, the prohibitive prices for their corn being : wheat, less than 67s. ; rye, etc., less than 44s. ; barley, less than 33s. ; oats, less than 22s. This arrangement, and the increase (subsequently quoted) in the duties on foreign butter and cheese, resulted from the deliberations of a Commission which sat during 1804-1812, to investigate ' Agricultural Distress.'

The duke of Manchester, governor of Jamaica, applied to the Treasury for his portion of the proceeds of seizures in that island from 1810 to date. The application was referred to the Board, and they reminded the Treasury of a deficiency in Customs moneys at Jamaica in 1810 —a deficiency as yet unexplained—in consequence of which all payments of the kind referred to by the duke had been suspended. ' We submit that no further payment can be made to the governor of Jamaica at present.' (The amount due to the duke was stated as £2,051 18s. 3¼d.)

On the return of the duke of Wellington from France, Mr. Eales, assistant-surveyor at the King's Warehouse, attended at the duke's residence, to examine ' upwards of 200 packages of baggage,' and the duchess gave him ' a remuneration ' for his trouble. The Customs Secretary came to know, and apprised the Treasury. The Treasury's reply ran as follows : ' The acceptance by your officers of any remuneration of the nature alluded to is illegal and improper.   Instruct Mr. Eales to return in the most respectful manner the money received from the duchess of Wellington, informing her Grace that the acceptance of it would be contrary to law and his official duty.'

Many Plantation collectors were superannuated in 1815, probably in consequence of an inquiry previously held.   Among these was Sir John Bontein, collector of St. Thomas's.   That gentleman wrote an effusive letter to the Board, thanking them for their services in securing him an ample retiring allowance.   His letter commenced : ' Having been nominated to a pension of a thousand a year . . . owing to the very handsome recommendation [of me] you have been kind enough to make, permit me to offer your Honours my warmest thanks for your kindness, which I shall ever remember with the deepest sense of gratitude, etc.'   (Sir John's baptismal certificate is appended to the letter.   It appears that he was ' retired ' at the age of sixty-two, and had served twenty-five years in the colonial Customs.)

In 1815 appeared Mr. Jickling's celebrated ' Digest,' a recapitulation of the provisions of all the Customs laws actually in force.   It appears that in 1786 one Mr. Frewin (afterwards made a Commissioner of Customs) had submitted to Mr. Pitt a scheme for repealing the obsolete Customs Acts then on the Statute Book.   The scheme was frustrated by the breaking out of war with France.   Meanwhile Mr. Jickling compiled his treatise, a tome of 1,375 pages in large quarto.   On May 15, 1814, the Treasury directed Frewin to proceed with his measure, and named Jickling as his assistant.   (Both these gentlemen were rewarded on a munificent scale.*   Mr. Frewin's literary exertions secured him a Commissionership, a grant of £2,000 on May 11, 1813, and five subsequent

* See ' Gatley's Memoranda.'

grants, making in all £6,500. Mr. Jickling received
£3,000 for his 'Digest' in 1816, and £1,000 in 1818. In
1820 he received £2,000 for acting as Mr. Frewin's
assistant—in all, £6,000. It is not too much to state
that any zealous worker with a gift towards literary
condensation could do all in two years that was performed by these well-paid and highly-rewarded gentlemen.)

In October, 1815, the collector of Antigua forwarded a
list of 512 negroes, captured in the French slaver *La Belle*
by H.M.S. *Barbados* and *Columbia*. The list makes
curious reading, especially as regards the names of the
negroes—names probably bestowed by the officers of
the vessels that captured the slaver. In the list of males
appear 'Marquis Drogheda,' 'Earl Carhampton,' 'Earl
Harcourt,' 'Nesbit Balfour,' 'Earl Cathcart,' 'Lord
Harris,' 'Eyre Coote,' 'Earl Elgin,' 'Baron Alten,'
'Viscount Lake,' 'Lord Probyn,' 'Patrick St. Clair,' and
'Edward O'Toole.' Amongst the older females are
'Dulcinea Grenville,' 'Lucy Manners,' 'Prudence Dar-
ling,' 'Dolly Fuller,' 'Lovely Tarrant,' 'Nelly Brown,'
and 'Bab Bland.' Among the girls are 'Virgin,' 'Vestal,'
'Venus,' 'Niobe,' 'Melpomene,' 'Dido,' 'Cleopatra,'
'Charmian,' 'Amoret,' 'Celia,' 'Sukey,' 'Sal,' 'Fatty,'
and 'Wowsky.' Ages : males, twenty-six to seven ;
females, twenty-three to thirteen. The return shows
that they were of rather short stature, only eight males
being above 5 feet 7 inches. Against each there appears
in the 'column of description' the words, 'very fine
negro.'

It was provided by Cap. 23, 56 Geo. III., that during
Napoleon's stay at St. Helena there should be no trade
to that colony except by the East India Company's
ships, or other vessels licensed by the king or the
governor of the island. (St. Helena belonged to the
East India Company ; it was not made a Crown colony
until 1833.)

By Caps. 25 and 26, 56 Geo. III., new duties were laid

upon foreign butter and cheese imported into Great
Britain.   Below is a comparison :

PREVIOUS DUTIES.				DUTIES AS UNDER THE NEW ACT.			
	£	s.	d.		£	s.	d.
Butter, per cwt. ..	o	3	3	In a British ship ..	1	o	o
Temporary war duty	o	1	1	In a foreign ship ..	1	5	o
	o	4	4				
Cheese, per cwt. ..	o	2	9	In a British ship ..	o	10	6
Temporary war duty	o	o	11	In a foreign ship ..	o	13	o
	o	3	8				

On May 28, 1816, a complaint from the collector of
Shelburne, Nova Scotia, reached the Board, that American
fishermen had been in the habit of coming within the
limits prescribed by the Treaty of Paris, and taking fish
and bait in defiance of the authorities, and that when they
wanted food or stores they took them by force from the
Nova Scotian settlers.   He had written to Captain
Wilson, commander of H.M.S. *Portia*, acquainting him
that the Americans, to the number of ' 160 stout men,'
were ' parading about ' at Cape Negro, ' bidding defiance
to the revenue officers.'   Captain Wilson captured eight
of the encroaching vessels, took them to Halifax, and
consulted the Nova Scotian Attorney-General, who was
of opinion that the fishermen should be at once released.
Released they were, but the collector had not done with
them.   ' We,' he wrote, ' having observed their thankless
and insolent demeanour, exacted from them the usual
fees of report (17s. 6d. each), and the provincial officers
charged them fees of light dues.'
    On September 2, 1816, a person named Kershaw wrote
from Boston, Mass., to Mr. Croker, Secretary to the Admiralty, furnishing a statement as to immense smuggling
from the U.S.A. into the British North American Plantations.   He also stated that many vessels owned by
Americans were trading under British licences.   ' The
law,' said he, ' is evaded through the depravity of some

English subjects, who for a small remuneration procure
the official documents, and then sign demonstrations of
trust in favour of the real owners.' He then offered his
services as a spy. ' I will serve you with integrity and
at a reasonable rate. I should think with travelling
charges never exceeding three dollars per diem . . . I am
young, active, bred to the law, and possessed of some
little penetration, besides a great desire to see the vaunt-
ings of these people [the Americans] effectually checked.'

A quotation from the opening part of the letter
may exemplify this cheap rogue's character : ' Born
and brought up in London, and cheered by prospects highly advantageous, that accursed failing which
has ruined many proved too fatal to me, and an unfortunate acquaintance with one of the other sex having
exposed me to very serious charges, I adopted the resolution to visit this part of the world, until, by my exertions in favour of my own country, I should in some
degree merit the royal clemency.' Whether he got his
three dollars per diem does not appear, but his statements
as to smuggling were communicated to the various
collectors.

Although peace had been secured, the ghastly effects of
years of war were but the more apparent. Bread was
dear, the rent of land had risen enormously, the fiscal
experts were still busy—riveting upon commerce the
ancient imposts, and devising new ones. Public lotteries
were still being run. The nation had entered upon the
second and worst phase of the worst period ever endured
in England. The factory system was at its very vilest.
The industrial eminence of Great Britain was sustained
by the wholesale sacrifice of the children of the poor.
Yet a few slight concessions had been made to humanity
and common sense. The punishment of the pillory, and
the disembowelling and quartering of criminals convicted of high treason, had been recently abolished.
Tenderness to the negro was preached everywhere, and
in many instances by people who had grown rich out of

the proceeds of white slavery. There appeared no likelihood of lighter taxation, yet high officials were not wanting to recommend cleaner, cheaper, and more sensible methods of collection. Some of these, as before observed, had cast impatient glances upon the crowded Statute Book, and desired to sweep away hundreds of the stuttering, bewildering revenue enactments.

The various ' temporary ' war duties, granted since 1803 upon goods imported into and exported from Great Britain, were made ' perpetual ' by Cap. 29, 56 Geo. III. Loans amounting to over £38,000,000 had been charged upon these and the temporary excise war duties. It is evident this had been a futile appropriation, for the Act provided that the duties by it made perpetual should pass into the Consolidated Fund, and *go towards* defraying the *interest* on the said loans.

Several Acts had been passed since 1800, authorizing the exportation of machinery to erect mints in various foreign countries, and relaxing incidentally the laws forbidding emigration of artificers. By Cap. 92, 56 Geo. III., similar provision was made as to machinery and artificers for erecting a mint in the United States (to take effect on January 5, 1817).

It was provided by Cap. 98 that the revenues of Great Britain and Ireland should be brought into one fund, called ' The Consolidated Fund of the United Kingdom,' and that this should be charged with the interest of the national debts of the two countries, the whole of their Civil List charges, and all other charges payable out of the previous funds. The separate Exchequers were maintained, but there was to be only one High Treasurer, with Treasury Commissioners for the United Kingdom, though a Vice-Treasurer *might* be appointed for Ireland. Issues by the Irish Exchequer were to be authorized by the Lord-Lieutenant, and recorded by the Auditor-General of the British Exchequer. Annual accounts of income, expenditure, produce of taxes, arrears, debts, exports, imports, shipping, and application of moneys issued for the national service, were to be laid before Parliament.

The instrument* used by the revenue officers in trying the strength of spirits (Clarke's Hydrometer) had long been deemed unsatisfactory. Cap. 140, 56 Geo. III., provided that an instrument called 'Sikes' Hydrometer' should be introduced on January 5, 1817, an instrument which, said the Act, 'hath with great care been completed, and hath by proper experiment, made for that purpose, been ascertained to denote as proof spirit that which at the temperature of 51 degrees by Fahrenheit's thermometer weighs exactly $\frac{12}{13}$ths of an equal measure of distilled water, and also to determine the strengths of all other spirits in proportion to the quantity of such proof spirit which is contained in them, or which can be made from them, with a degree of accuracy never before obtained.' A 'Table of Strengths' accompanied the instrument, and sliding-rules for casting proof quantities. (The instrument and tables are still in use.)

Cap. 73 (local and personal), 56 Geo. III., authorized the establishment of a 'Benevolent Fund' for the widows, children, and relatives of officers or persons belonging to the *English* Customs. Such officers and clerks of the Port of London as were willing to contribute

* The ancient methods of testing spirits were by oil and deflagration. The oil test was simply to mix spirit with oil. If of a tolerable strength, the spirit floated. The other system was burning the spirit in a brass jar. After the alcohol had been consumed, the residue was measured. 'If it measured more than half, the spirit needed further rectification ; if less than half, it was strong ; if no residue appeared, the spirit was deemed pure' (Basil Valentine, 1420, quoted in Scarisbrick's 'Spirit Assaying'). Then came the 'proof' test (mixing with gunpowder and burning). 'Clarke's Hydrometer' came into use early in the eighteenth century. Although an imperfect instrument, principally through not being adjusted to fit definite thermometrical indications, it displays evidence of considerable ingenuity. The invention of the instrument now in use is attributed to Bartholomew Sikes, Secretary of Excise.

This Act was confirmed by Cap. 28 of 1818, and it was provided that spirits sweetened so as to defeat the action of the hydrometer should be forfeitable, foreign cordials, British brandy, and British compounds excepted.

II.   5

were to appoint twelve of the principal officials to act as a committee of formation, and to issue rules. The rules, being ratified by a judge of King's Bench or Common Pleas, or a baron of the Exchequer, were to apply as though specified in the Act. Contributions to the Fund were to be deducted from the salaries of the contributors (2d. in the £ quarterly for eight quarters, then 1d.). Membership not compulsory. Nominees might benefit, though not related. Directors might be sued in the name of their secretary. Profits to go to the benefit of the Fund only. Subscribers to be furnished with a report of the accounts on September 1 in each year.*

The Fund benefited otherwise. There was a patent in existence entitling its holder to the profits of the ' Bill of Entry ' (an official return of commercial transactions connected with shipping, issued in the Custom House, London). Half the proceeds of the patent were to go to the Benevolent Fund, the patentee to retain the balance.

The Board of Customs consulted the Crown lawyers on the matter of oysters, and the decision was made public on October 29, 1816. It was to the effect that British-taken oysters brought in British ships were duty-free, and that foreign-taken oysters were dutiable but not prohibited. It seems that there had been some error in the Customs measurement of oysters for duty. At certain ports the officers had measured by the Billingsgate bushel instead of the Winchester bushel. (The Billingsgate measure was twice as large as the Winchester.)

The staff employed at the Custom House in the collection of statistics consisted of an inspector-general, one assistant-inspector, one chief clerk, and fifteen ordinary clerks. Total annual cost, £3,895. (In 1908 there were in the same department 1 principal, 1 deputy, 7 senior clerks, 20 junior clerks, 8 minor clerks, 187 assistant-clerks, 34 boy clerks, 2 typists, and a lithographer. Total cost, exclusive of overtime pay, about £30,321.)

* The Fund is still flourishing.

There had been considerable ill-feeling between the good people of Newcastle and of North Shields, the latter having tried to induce the Treasury to sanction the establishment of a custom-house at their port, and the Newcastle folk being averse to any diminution of their own exceptional privileges. It appeared at first that the Shields men would gain their end, but the influence of the Novocastrians predominated, and the application was refused. The contest gave to the world a Newcastle dialect poet, author of the 'Quayside Ditty,' quoted below :

'Ah, what's yor news th' day, Mr. Mayor ?
Ah, what's yor news th' day, Mr. Mayor ?
The folk o' Sheels, they say,
Want wor Custom-house away,
An' ye canna say them nay, Mr. Mayor.

'But dinna let it gan, Mr. Mayor,
Or ye'll ruin us tiv a man, Mr. Mayor :
They say *a Branch* 'll dee,
But next they'll tak the Tree,
An' smash wor bonny Kee,* Mr. Mayor.'

On February 13, 1817, the collector of Montserrat reported that he had seized twelve mules, value £540 currency, for being imported in a foreign ship, contrary to the Navigation laws. The importing vessel escaped, the adjacent fort being so defective that fire could not be opened on her. 'The batteries at the out-bays,' stated the collector, 'being totally dismantled, affords a perfect freedom for the ingress and egress of all vessels disposed to the violation of the laws.' (Report referred to the Secretary of State for the Colonies, March 15, 1817.)

On May 1, 1817, the collector of St. John, New Brunswick, reported to the Board that the legal importations of tobacco into the island during the past seventeen years were 65,203 pounds, and that of this quantity 59,988 pounds had been exported since, leaving only 5,215 pounds duty-paid. He estimated the *annual*

* 'Kee '=quay.

consumption as 100,000 pounds. Thus 100,000 × 17 —
5,215 = say, 1,694,000 pounds, smuggled into the island
from the U.S.A. in seventeen years. He also stated that
a number of British and colonial vessels, captured during
the American War, were being used as American traders.
He quoted a return furnished by Lloyd's, from which it
appeared that from June 12, 1812, to December 24, 1814,
the Americans captured 1,172 British and colonial ships,
and that only 383 of these were re-taken or given up.

Early in 1817 the *Montague* postal packet arrived from
the West Indies. Five of her crew had died of yellow
fever during the voyage, and eighteen others were down
with the same complaint. The captain did not hoist the
quarantine flag at Dartmouth, as he should have done,
and, strange to tell, the Customs did not visit the vessel
there, as they were supposed to do. But quite a number
of Dartmouth people went aboard, and some of the ship's
company, including the doctor and one of the sick men,
went ashore. When the vessel reached Falmouth the
master, on being questioned in the usual way by the Customs
as to health of company during voyage, made many misleading statements. The ship's papers were forwarded
to the Privy Council by the officers, there being doubt as
to the master's *bona-fides*, and when it was discovered later
that there was yellow fever on board it was too late to
recall the papers for fumigation. This raised ugly con-
siderations, for by the law both transmitters and recipients
were liable to quarantine. But it seems that the authorities decided to relax the regulations with a view to their
own convenience, and this may have been the reason
why the master, doctor, and customs men concerned
escaped with a caution.

Cap. 10, 57 Geo. III. provided that no passenger ship
should sail from the United Kingdom to Canada, Nova
Scotia, New Brunswick, Cape Breton, or Prince Edward's
Island, unless the master entered into bond not to take
more than one adult passenger, or three children under
fourteen, for every $1\frac{1}{2}$ tons burden of ship (cargo space

excluded). The diet and water supplies were specified, and the administration of the Act left, as usual, with the Customs. (There had been many villainous transactions in connection with the passenger traffic. One method of evading the regulations had been to ship the regulated number of passengers at an English port, and then hover on the coast of Ireland, picking up at a cheap rate numbers of unfortunate people, who joined the vessel by stealing off in boats during the night.)

The Navigation laws were relaxed by Cap. 36, so as to grant to all the king's subjects more extensive powers of trade in the parts (except China) within the scope of the East India Company's charter, but the carrying of tea was still left an exclusive privilege of the Company. Asiatic seamen might be employed in ships trading in the latitudes affected, under licences granted by the governors of ports, but only when British seamen could not be obtained.

Many reforms were effected in public offices.* It was provided that, ' on termination of existing interests,' the offices in the English Exchequer of King's Remembrancer, Clerk of Pleas, Clerk of Pipe, Comptroller of Pipe, Marshal, Foreign Apposer, Surveyor and Receiver-General of Greenwax, Lord Treasurer's Remembrancer, Clerk of Foreign Estreats, Clerk of Nichells, and Comptroller of Firstfruits, should be executed in person, instead of by deputy. The same rule was applied to the three Commissioners' offices, the two entering clerks', and the Receiver-Generals' in the Alienation Office, and to the offices of Master in Chancery and Exchequer Solicitor. The fees in vogue were to continue, and their proceeds to be applied to the furnishing of salaries, residue to go to the Consolidated Fund. A number of useless offices in Ireland were abolished, and others deprived of much profit. Among these were the Customs offices of Pratique Master of the port of Dublin, and Customs storekeepers of Dublin. The salaries of certain Scottish

* Cap. 60, 62, 64, 84, 57 Geo. III.

officials were to be pruned ' on termination,' and other offices were ordered to be performed in person.   Among the latter were those of Auditor of Exchequer, King's and Lord Treasurer's Remembrancers, and Presenter of Signatures.   Others were to be abolished.   These included the offices of the Clerk of the Pipe and Controller-General of Customs.   The offices of Auditors, Tellers, and Clerks of Pells in England and Ireland were to be performed in person.

The old Irish aulnage laws (Acts relating to the measurement of cloth) were abolished by Cap. 109.   The patent office of Aulnager of Ireland was held by Lord Blaquiere, under a grant of 1797.   He was compensated by a pension of £500 per annum, payable to him or his heirs till expiration of patent.

The ' winter ' hours for shipping goods in the port of London had been defined by Elizabeth's Act as 7 a.m. to 4 p.m., from September to February inclusive.   These were in a way extended by Cap. 116, 57 Geo. III., it being provided that goods which had been sent from the quays during the ' legal hours,' to be shipped in the river, might be taken on board up to the time of sunset.

On January 31, 1818, the collector of Deal informed the Board that on the previous night the officers had stopped a postchaise which was entering the town, and found in it several cases containing gold coin of the realm, but that under the circumstances they did not feel justified in seizing the goods.   In reply the Board quoted the opinion of the Attorney-General that coin merely found in transit for exportation was not seizable, and advised the collector to release the goods and keep an eye upon them, so that they might be seized when actually ' passing out of the realm.'   The Board's letter ended thus : ' We inform you that a person of the name of John Atkins of Deal is now in the practice of exporting the coin of this country to France, and has very lately been in town for the purpose of purchasing coin to a considerable amount.'

By a patent of June 20, 18 Edw. IV., the power of

appointing the City gauger had been vested in the Mayor and Commonalty of London, in discharge of a debt of £7,000 contracted by the king. The City worthies made a practice of granting this office to some esteemed acquaintance. It seems that in olden times it had been lucrative, but since the establishment of the West India and London Docks the profits of the office had fallen off, most of the gaugeable goods being landed in the docks, instead of at the legal quays within the City. The grantee made claim in the Court of King's Bench in 1807 to levy on goods gauged within the docks. The dock companies disputed his claim, but he succeeded in establishing it, only to find the decision upset on a new trial. In 1817 Parliament allowed him to be compensated, the moneys to be obtained by means of extra charges on fees levied by City brokers.

About the middle of the year a strange circumstance occurred. Captain Stirling, of H.M.S. *Brazen*, captured a foreign vessel called the *Tigress* within three miles of the coast of Trinidad, took her into Port of Spain, and ' libelled ' her in the Vice-Admiralty Court for contravening the Navigation laws. He did not hand her over to the collector of customs, as required by law, but held her in charge until she was condemned. Then, under the advice of the Attorney-General for the island,* and with the concurrence of the Judge of Vice-Admiralty, he effected a compromise with the owners of the vessel. They paid him £738 17s. 8d. sterling, and also paid the costs (of course, as monstrous as usual). Captain Stirling then restored the vessel, and divided the proceeds of compromise, taking £128 as his own share, and distributing the balance among his officers and crew.

The proceedings were in two points illegal. The gallant captain should have placed the vessel in charge of the Customs, and when the compromise was effected he

---

* Henry Fuller, Esq. This learned gentleman's name figures in connection with many strange legal transactions. See Illustrative Documents, No. 35.

should have handed half the proceeds to the Customs, to be placed in the king's chest for subsequent remittance to the Receiver-General, as the ' Crown's share.' It is certain that the Trinidad Customs men were cognizant of the transaction, for a seizure and trial of the kind could not escape their notice, yet they made no report of these illegal proceedings.

(It will be well to trace the matter through all its subsequent ramifications. The London Customs lawyers were informed—by whom does not appear—in 1820, and a letter was sent to Captain Stirling—then resident in England—calling on him to pay promptly to the Receiver-General £64 out of his own share, and then to make arrangements for refunding half the sum he had paid to his officers and crew. He wrote back, admitting his liability, promising to pay the £64 at once, and asking relief in respect of the rest. He urged that he had acted under presumably competent advice, tendered by the Attorney-General of Trinidad. ' I beg the Board will consider an officer of the navy has in such cases no guides but the Crown lawyers, and that his situation is indeed deplorable if, after having been employed, there is no time of his life in which he may hope to consider himself safe from the responsibility of errors in law.' The Board replied that they could grant no relief. Meanwhile they censured the Trinidad collector for not reporting the matter, and hinted that they had at first been inclined to surcharge him with the amount of the Crown's share.

It seems that somehow the matter passed temporarily out of ken. In 1823 the Board found that Stirling had not paid the money, so he was written to a second time. He replied, blandly admitting liability. ' I ought not in justice to keep the £64, nor do I intend to do so.' But he pleaded that it would be too bad to make him pay the other £305 odd. The Board ordered prompt payment of the £64, and told him they would ask the Treasury's directions as to the rest.

No reply was received till about a year later, when

Stirling wrote, stating that he had just returned from abroad, and had found the Board's letter awaiting him. He would be happy to pay the £64 at once, and hoped he might be relieved from the other burden.

Again the matter dropped out of official ken, and, candid and ready in acknowledgment as Stirling had been, he took no steps to revive cognizance. It is evident that he had altered his mind, since that far time when he wrote, 'I ought not in justice,' etc., for not a penny did he tender, and the papers remained pigeonholed *till 1833*, when some inquisitive person dusted and inspected them, and the Board received a memo. from the same, to the effect that Captain Stirling had not up to the present paid in His Majesty's share. Again he was written to. Then he began to show his hand. He answered that he was willing, and extremely desirous, to pay the £64, but feared that such payment might be held to render him fully liable for the remainder.

The Board were in a quandary. If they brought the matter to the notice of the Treasury they would in a way impeach the efficiency of their own department. In the first place, a vessel had been seized, condemned, and released on payment of a sum of money, the Crown had been hindered of its share of proceeds, and the Board had heard nothing of this from the responsible officers. Then the Board had allowed themselves to be trifled with by Stirling, and the papers had been overlooked on one occasion for a year, and again for nine years. The lawyer's opinion was taken. He stated that there was little likelihood of success if legal proceedings were taken against Stirling for either sum. Thereupon a very bland and polite note was sent to the rollicking sea-dog, telling him that if he paid the £64 the Board would waive claim of the rest.

After conducting his own defence during fourteen years with such marked ability, Stirling broke down in the end. Had he but declared that on further consideration he had come to the conclusion that he was not liable even

for the £64, it is likely he would have heard no more of
the matter. But he failed thus to crown his edifice of
evasion. Still, he was not precipitate. He wrote,
stating that he had instructed his agent, Sir F. Ommaney,
to pay the £64 to the Receiver-General, but the old year
went and the new year came, and Sir F. Ommaney did
not darken the doors of the office in Thames Street.
Then a letter was sent to the agent, and in March, 1834,
nearly seventeen years after the seizure of the *Tigress*,
and nearly fourteen years after Captain Stirling first
promised to refund His Majesty's share informally appropriated, the smaller portion of the debt was discharged.
Then fresh trouble arose. The Receiver-General, no
doubt alive to the peculiar nature of the whole transaction, took the £64, but declined to give a receipt. Sir
F. Ommaney wrote the Board a letter of complaint, *the
Board* sent a receipt, and thus this extremely remarkable
transaction was adjusted.)

On August 13, 1818, the Secretary to the Postmaster-
General requested the Board of Customs to direct their
officers to be vigilant in preventing the smuggling of letters
outward, the Post-office authorities having come to know
that a vast number of letters were carried to Rotterdam
and other Dutch ports, to the great detriment of the
postal revenue.

On November 20, 1818, the Treasury apprised the
Board that a fraudulent scheme had been set afoot by
certain speculators. It appears these gentlemen had
imported a large quantity of foreign hops, and obtained
remission of most of the duty on the plea that the goods
were ' sea-damaged.' Then they formed a design to
export them and claim the full drawback, as though all
the duty had been paid on landing.

The British Customs duties were again consolidated
by Cap. 52, 59 Geo. III., it being provided that they should
cease on July 5, and be replaced by a new scale. (The
Act announced that foreign goods, imported into and then
exported from Great Britain, were liable to duty if re-

imported.)   The duties were in many instances increased.
The corn regulations were not affected by the Act.   Some
of the more important duties, and one or two of the
quainter kind, are quoted below :

Anchovies and botargo, 1s. per pound ; caviare, 12s.
per cwt. ; eels, £13 1s. 3d. the ship-load. (The importation of eels was exclusively in the hands of the Worcum
traders, even as now.   The vessels used were all of one
type, and of about the same tonnage.)   Oysters, 1s. 6d.
per Winchester bushel ; stock-fish, 5s. per 120 ; sturgeon,
7s. 6d. the keg. Lobsters and turbots were duty-free.
Fresh fish, British-taken and brought in British ships,
were duty-free ; so were British-taken-and-cured fish.

Glass manufactures, not being bottles, window, flint,
or plate glass, paid 80 per cent. on the value, and an excise
duty of six guineas per cwt.   Wrought iron paid 50 per
cent. on the value ; leather manufactures, 75 per cent. ;
foreign-made sails, whether in use or as merchandise,
paid at the rate of £104 9s. 2d. for every £100 value.
Lemons in a British-built ship paid £1 5s. per 1,000 ;
in a foreign-built ship, £1 7s. 6d. per 1,000 ; eggs paid 10d.
per 120 ; truffles, 5s. 6d. per pound.

The difficulties attendant on assessment and calcula-
tion are evinced by the number of ' divisions of articles,'
each chargeable with a specific duty.   There were 24
different rates of duty on the various kinds of stone,
53 on oils, 81 on skins, 104 on linen, and 183 on wood.

Tea, coffee, and cocoa were duty-free as regarded
customs, but they were subjected to crushing excise duties
on delivery from warehouse.

The duties outward stood thus : Coals were liable to a
special export duty (besides the duty of 10s. in the £100
value, which was levied on all exported British goods,
except corn, flour, linen, and cotton manufactures, woollen
manufactures exported to places within the East India
Company's charter, refined sugar, molasses, and articles
intended for use in the Plantation fisheries, all which
excepted goods were free from export duties).

The tonnage rates on ships endured.   The only coastwise duties leviable were upon coal, slate, and stone.

During 1818 the controller at Falmouth, Jamaica, had died, and appointed Robert Gilpin, the collector, as his executor.   The governor of the island appointed one Joseph Wood, a resident, as controller, pending the Board's dealing with the vacancy.   Wood entered into bond in the usual way, but Gilpin, by various excuses, evaded handing over to him the controller's key of the money-chest.   After a time a new controller arrived from England, and had scarcely taken up his duties ere Wood died.   Gilpin evaded the new controller's request for the key for some time, and then was taken ill, and his spirit went to join those of the two departed controllers. The new controller, after Gilpin's death, succeeded in obtaining possession of both the collector's and controller's keys, and opened the chest, which, according to the books, should have contained about £5,000 in currency. States the report on the matter : ' Only one piece of money, of very small amount, was found therein.'   Action was taken against Gilpin's executor, Wood's surety, and the new controller and his surety, at the assizes at Cornwall, Jamaica, in November, 1822, and judgment was obtained against all the defendants.   Afterwards the Board released all the defendants, except Gilpin's executor, from the penalties, on condition of their paying the costs incidental.

On March 26, 1819, the Board reported on a letter which had been sent, through Rear-Admiral Harvey, to the Treasury, by Captain Elliott of H.M.S. *Scamander,* stationed at Barbados.   The gallant captain stated that smuggling was carried on extensively between Martinique and St. Vincent ; that French goods were publicly exposed for sale in the latter island ; that he seized an English schooner laden with contraband goods from Martinique, another vessel which had loaded without a permit, and a vessel called the *Bellona ;* that the last-mentioned vessel was restored by the Vice-Admiralty Court of

Trinidad ; that he seized a brig called the *Problem*, and she was also restored to her owners ; and that he received for his trouble, in the last two instances, merely trifling sums as 'satisfactions.' He seized two other vessels, which were condemned, but he had not as yet been paid even the expenses of seizure. He then seized the *Harmony*, and secured her condemnation, which cost him £400 currency in law expenses, and he had not as yet received his share of the proceeds. This letter was sent to the Board, and they stated that, with a view to prevent improper and vexatious detentions, it had been their practice to insist that the responsibility for all seizures should rest upon the officers who made them, and that seized vessels were never released unless with a provision that the owners paid all reasonable expenses incurred.

On August 3, 1819, the Privy Council for Trade reminded the Customs Board that though, under the Act of 1815, the importation of foreign corn had been prohibited except when the British price reached a certain figure, the said Act did not apply to the Isle of Man, and that the Manx legislators had refused to alter their code in the way of assimilation ; therefore it was possible for foreign corn to be imported free into the island when the price was low, and then carried to Great Britain as Manx corn. It is curious to fall across such an instance of obstinacy on the part of local legislators, and still more curious that the Council should have thought it necessary to apprise the Board of a contingency of which the Board must have been aware.

On October 8, 1819, proclamations were issued by the Governor of the Leeward Islands that, on account of destruction wrought by the late dreadful hurricane, the Navigation laws might be relaxed for six months, to permit provisions and lumber to be imported into Tortola, Nevis, and St. Kitt's, in vessels of any nationality, and sugar, rum, and molasses to be exported in said vessels up to the value of the import cargo. The Privy Council for Trade desired the Board of Customs to direct their solicitor to draft a bill of indemnity to cover the governor's action—said bill to be laid before Parliament (the usual proceeding in such cases).

A letter dated December 30, 1819, reached the London Board from St. Kitt's, stating that extensive smuggling was carried on from Antigua into St. Eustatia. The Board referred this to the collector of Antigua, and that official made answer that he knew nothing of the traffic referred to. He also stated that by his great zeal in protecting the revenue he had incurred the animosity of the members of the Antigua House of Assembly, and hinted that the information might have been prompted by them. It appears they had attacked him on the matter of fees, alleging that the Customs and naval charges ' had given a formidable and repulsive aspect to the trade of the town of St. John's' (Antigua), ' and acted as a terror to all his Majesty's liege subjects engaged in lawful traffic.'

In a report sent by the collector of Halifax, Nova Scotia, it was stated that the coal-mines at Sydney, Cape Breton, were leased to one Leaver, who paid the Crown 6s. 4d. a chaldron on all coals shipped, and that the lease would expire on December 31, 1820 ; also that the mines were still being worked by horse-power, as none would erect a steam-engine unless a longer lease were granted.

A review of the condition of the Customs at the end of George III.'s reign becomes necessary. The revenue had swollen since the Act of Union, partly through augmentation of trade—especially export trade—partly through increase in the rates of duty. The values of imports and exports were stated as below :

		Imports (Foreign and Colonial).	Exports to Foreign Countries and the Colonies.
		£	£
1817	.. ..	30,805,655	50,379,629
1818	.. ..	36,900,681	53,559,710

The net produce of the Customs in England, Scotland, and Ireland, for the year ending January 5, 1819, appears to have been :

					£
England	..	..	..	..	10,176,794
Scotland	..	..	..	..	760,926
Ireland	..	..	..	..	1,860,089
Total		..	..	..	12,797,809

(By ' net produce ' is signified the sum remaining after drawbacks and expenses of management had been paid. The expenses of management amounted to over 9 per cent. of the *gross* proceeds in England, and over 16 per cent. of the gross in Scotland and Ireland.)

The whole of the net was not paid into the Exchequer. Large sums were deducted, and applied as bounties towards certain public undertakings. These amounted to :

					£
In England	..	..	..	..	189,924
In Scotland	..	..	..	..	85,149
In Ireland	..	..	..	..	147,556

The balances kept back by the various collectors amounted to :

				£
In England	..	..	..	38,380
In Scotland	..	..	..	47,393
In Ireland	..	..	..	17,104

Out of the English moneys £62,512 went towards building the new Custom House at London. Out of the Scottish £71,332 went towards the support of the Scottish Civil Government. In each of the three countries a sum was withheld because, though collected during the years under survey, it was not due till the following year. Thus the actual payments into the Exchequer were :

				£
From England	..	..	..	9,601,903
From Scotland	..	..	..	432,845
From Ireland ..	..	..	..	1,635,470
Total	..	..	..	11,670,218

(The Irish returns are expressed in British currency.)

The annual accounts of seizures show that the preventive men were kept busy. From 1816 to 1818 the records of total values on condemnation (in England alone) stood thus :

					£
1816	..	..	..	..	182,774
1817	..	..	..	..	76,116
1818	..	..	..	..	117,776

Yet the amounts recovered in fines and penalties were only—

					£
1816	..	..	..	..	24,989
1817	..	..	..	..	28,808
1818	..	..	..	..	21,360

The gradual extension of the bonding system had proved a great boon to merchants, but they still complained of the restrictions placed upon trade by the system of calling for unnecessary bonds on many trifling transactions. (Great relief had been afforded to the coastwise trade in this respect, but foreign traffic was still hampered.) The annual stamp duty realized on Customs bonds reached the huge sum of £40,000.

The building of the West India, East India, London, and Commercial Docks, had effected great improvement in the trade of the Port of London, but the lessees of the various legal quays and uptown warehouses complained that their business suffered through the system of granting special warehousing privileges to the dock companies.* A commission of 1819 reported in favour of the complainers, urging that ' care should be taken not to grant such exclusive privileges to any one of the dock companies as might operate to prevent that spirit of competition which secures to the merchant a moderate charge for the warehouse rent of his merchandise.'

* It is curious to note that, in spite of special privileges of this kind, the London dock companies have recently been compelled in a way to solicit the public to relieve them of their responsibilities, while the legal quays are able to hold their own. Much coddling, though it may foster for a time, destroys efficiency in the end.

Circumlocution was still rampant in the Revenue departments. Trifling Customs transactions were made subjects of petitions to the Board, the result being much waste of time and paper, for the method of dealing with such applications was horribly imperfect. (It may be mentioned, as an illustration of this, that when cattle, sheep, etc., intended as food for passengers, arrived in or were shipped by the East India Company's vessels, fodder might not be taken on board for their support until special written application had been made to the Customs. The document was referred for the reports of certain officials—men by no means inclined to hurry—and considerable time elapsed before the transaction was *formally* ' allowed.' Meantime the animals were on short commons, unless the landing-officers of customs thought fit to wink at an evasion of formality.) On March 1, 1817, a number of important shipowners had memorialized the Treasury, complaining bitterly of the delay experienced in obtaining answers to applications—applications which the high customs officials persisted in demanding, in many instances without any apparent reason.

The Port of London was overstaffed, but a reduction had been recommended. Abolition of the following offices was suggested : 1 surveyor of searchers, 5 searchers, 13 landing-waiters, 4 ' extra ' landing-waiters, 35 ' occasional ' landing-waiters, 1 gauger, and 2 ' occasional ' gaugers, and the reduction of the jerquers from 5 to 2, and of the jerquer's clerks from 7 to 2 (certainly an instructive suggestion). The ' piazza-men '—preferential tide-waiters, fifty in number, who were employed on the Customs quay or in guarding during transit from warehouse to exporting ship the goods which had been sold by the East India Company to various merchants for exportation—were quite unworthy. Wholesale fraud took place during the conveyance of the above-mentioned goods, and it was recommended that the services of the fifty ' preferentials ' should be dispensed with, and the

II.   6

goods sent in charge of licensed lightermen.* It was a common practice with dishonest traders to buy high-duty goods which had been warehoused by the Company for exportation, enter them for shipment (exportation being, of course, allowed without payment of duty), and then convey them inland, producing for shipment a consignment of non-dutiable goods in packages similar to those entered. The Customs examination at shipment was imperfect, and the profitable game went merrily on till discovered (probably by accident). A favourite trick was to buy pepper, a commodity highly rated, and ship oats instead of the odorous berries. As the piazza-men were put in charge of the pepper at the door of the Company's warehouse, and were supposed not to leave their charge till the goods were shipped, it seems that they must have been bribed, or else that they did some tolerably sound sleeping on the way from the legal quays to the East Indiamen's mooring-place.

The emoluments of the Customs Solicitors were still on an extravagant scale. The solicitor for the London district received during the year ending January 5, 1819, as salary £500 ; other emoluments, £4,163. The solicitor for the northern ports of England took as salary £300 ; other emoluments, £1,232. The solicitor for bonds and criminal prosecutions took as salary £500 ; other emoluments, £1,277. The unlucky solicitor for coast bonds took as salary £150. He had no other emoluments, and, needless to state, he had little to do.

Liverpool had become an important trading centre, especially as regarded exports. No fewer than 164 bonded warehouses had been established at this port. The Liverpool Customs business was conducted in an unsatisfactory way. The guard of ships was eminently defective, the tide-waiters who performed that duty being beyond control. Many of them were in collusion with smugglers and waterside thieves. The following statement appears in an official report : ' There is scarcely a robbery com-

* See vol. i., p. 167.

mitted about the docks without a tide-waiter being implicated in it, either as principal or receiver.' Once a
system of nightly visits of ships on which tide-waiters
were boarded was instituted suddenly. Three visits were
paid, and 226 tide-waiters found to be absent.

Below is an account of the chief Scottish trading ports,
and their yield of Customs (gross) revenue :

	£		£
Greenock ..	338,599	Dundee	22,799
Leith ..	230,987	Glasgow	8,384
Port Glasgow ..	202,210	Perth	6,314
Grangemouth ..	39,684	Montrose	6,213
Aberdeen	23,747		

The yield of the remaining Scottish ports averaged
just over £1,000 a port, and the charges of management
nearly £1,400.

So unsatisfactory were Scottish revenue matters that
certain Commissioners of Inquiry actually interjected in
their report a sly censure of the Scottish Board, which
evoked a passionate protest from the high officials affected.
The Board, in their appeal to the Treasury, claimed reference to the opinion of the mercantile community in Scotland, ' to the numerous persons who have occasion to
communicate with us on subjects connected with the
revenue of Customs, to the members of the other departments of the public service, and to the different public
bodies of this city ' (Edinburgh), ' and to your Lordships,'
etc., etc.

At many of the Irish outports the expenses of management were much in excess of the takings. It should be
observed that one inevitable evil of a high tariff is the
necessity of maintaining preventive officers at remote
places where little or no legitimate trade is done. Still,
the pay of Baltimore's preventive guard could scarcely
have been responsible for the condition of affairs at that
port, where the average annual amount of duty collected
was £420, and the expenses of management were £8,365.

One cause of the apparent smallness of the Irish net

return was the system of defraying the cost of building
and maintaining public docks and warehouses out of the
Customs moneys.   It appears that private capital was
not forthcoming.   The system might have furnished an
encouraging precedent, but for the easy methods pursued
by the directing officials, under which merchants were
charged such absurdly small dues that there was next to
no recompense for the outlay.

' Retrenchment all round ' was the cry, but this was
not so much an outcome of logical thought as an explo-
sion of dismay at the state of affairs.   The country had
been at peace for nearly five years, yet most of the taxes
were higher than at any previous period.   The condition
of the poor was appalling.   Social anomalies and political
disabilities had existed in olden days, but then they had
not been found so grievous.   There had been many
avenues of escape, since blocked ; many havens of immunity, since closed.

The accession of George IV. was contemporaneous with
the commencement of a series of official reforms.   The
first Act in this direction (Cap. 7, 1 Geo. IV.) abolished a
number of useless bonds and oaths previously required
by the Customs in connection with bounties, export
transactions, etc.   It announced that ' many evil-dis-
posed ' officers continued to collect fees, although by law
forbidden.   It enjoined that persons *tendering* such fees
should be liable to a fine of £500.   The duties on wood
were rearranged by Cap. 37, 1 and 2 Geo. IV., many
alterations being made in the system of measurement for
duty, and many substantial reductions of duty.   The
Navigation laws were again amended by Cap. 65, further
privileges being granted as regarded trade by the king's
subjects with the places within the East India Company's
charter.   (The Company still retained the exclusive right
of carrying tea and trading with China.)   The registration of wool carried coastwise in the United Kingdom was
abolished.

In 1820 the governor of Trinidad suggested to the Privy Council for Trade that the bonds taken of ship-masters in the Plantation trade to land their cargoes at the ports for which they cleared should be dispensed with. ' It must,' he stated, ' be for the common interest that the cargo should be disposed of at the place which will give the best price for it.' He adverted to the injustice of compelling masters, when carrying colonial goods to Europe, to land and reship them in the United Kingdom, a process ' attended with delay and expense, and in the article of cocoa ' (a product of Trinidad) ' very often with damage.' It is instructive to find that, though the Customs Solicitors and high officials who reported on this proposal were against any alteration of the Navigation laws, one or two of them hinted that the said laws were in some cases oppressive ; indeed, the Customs controller-general stated boldly that they were ' generally allowed to be a clog on commerce.' The Board, in a report which contained a fine précis of the Navigation laws, declined to recommend conformity with the sugges-tion. (If the governor's scheme had been adopted, the Navigation Act would have become practically a dead-letter.)

On July 31, 1821, the Board dealt with a complaint made by the House of Assembly, Nova Scotia, in 1820, as to excessive fees taken by the colonial customs officers. The Board were of opinion that in most instances the fees charged were legal, and stated that at some of the Planta-tions the colonial Houses of Assembly had established scales of fees, which the officers had accepted. It was suggested that the whole system of colonial Customs fees should be revised. ' This,' stated the Board, ' might put an end to the complaints and dissensions which have so long and generally prevailed.'

On August 16, 1821, the following case was tried at the Maidstone Assizes : A vessel called the *Limerick Trader* had been quarantined at Standgate Creek, and her cargo removed to the *Courageux* lazaret hulk for disinfection.

It was found that the goods had been tampered with, and a search of the quarantine officers' berths was directed, a man being also stationed to watch the outside of the vessel. Soon the sentinel saw a number of pieces of silk passing into the creek through one of the ports. This resulted in a charge against one Plucknell, tide-waiter. The defendant's counsel, Mr. Adolphus, raised many quibbles, one being that the indictment was informal, the *Limerick Trader* being named therein as a ship bound to ' the Port of London.' Mr. Adolphus held that no proof of this had been furnished, and that at the time of the alleged offence she was beyond the limits of the port ; but it was decided that in getting into Standgate Creek she had passed across the extreme eastern limit. Verdict for the Crown against Plucknell, but judgment stayed, and a new trial ordered (with what result does not appear).

On August 18, 1821, a rather remarkable case was tried at the Dorchester Assizes. A customs officer named Power, stationed at Weymouth, had become unpopular, and one morning, as he was proceeding homeward, a fellow named Brinsley followed him along the street, repeatedly challenging him to fight. It should be mentioned that Power had been made town constable, and his appointment in that capacity seems to have been unwise, for it is evident that he was an excitable person. He lost his temper, entered his house, took down his staff of office, and then went out and menaced Brinsley with it. Brinsley, who had only one arm, thereupon struck him with his fist. Power knocked him down with the truncheon, and then beat him over the head till the weapon broke in two. A young fellow named Davis intervened, and challenged Power to fistic combat, which the latter declined. Both Brinsley and Davis were charged with threatening and assaulting Power in the discharge of his duty, and the former was also charged with a common assault. The case against Davis was abandoned, the principal count against Brinsley withdrawn, and he was found guilty of a common assault only. The minutes of the trial certainly *read* against Power, and it seems strange that both cases were not dismissed. It appeared in cross-examination that he had been deprived of his office as constable since the date of the assault, for 'firing at some boys, and wounding one of them.'

Cap. 41, 3 Geo. IV. commenced : ' Whereas several statutes and Acts of Parliament or certain parts thereof, respectively relating to the importation of goods . . . made and passed at various times before the twelfth year of the reign of King Charles the Second, remain unrepealed, although the same are inconsistent with or rendered unnecessary by the Acts made since that time.' It proceeded in repeal of an immense number of hoary edicts relating to wool, cloth, gauging, places for landing and shipping goods, alien and denizen traders, prohibitions, customs officers, and exportation of coin, and between seventy and eighty Acts relating to the Staple. (The Stapling Acts had been obsolete for over 200 years.) The period affected extended from the commencement of the reign of Edward III. to the date of the Old Subsidy (1660).* The next Act of the Session swept away numerous sections and several complete Acts of the old Navigation laws, and the next consolidated the remainder.

On March 16, 1822, the Board informed all the Cornish collectors that a person named Jones had entered Cornwall from France, for the purpose of enticing workers in iron and tin to leave their native country and settle in France. The news was also sent to Rochester, Faversham, Sandwich, and Deal, so it appears that the artificers were to embark at one of the Kentish ports.

About this time the Treasury and Board were pestered by letters from various amateur fiscalists, propounding schemes of taxation, reform, etc., and usually containing explicit avowals of the authors' mercenary motives.

* See reference to Jickling's 'Digest' at p. 60.

Below is a copy of a letter from the Customs Secretary, addressed to one of these unwelcome correspondents :

' *To Mr. Thomas Ivey, No.* 1, *Lisbon Place, Halloway, Bath, Somerset.*

' SIR,

'   The Commissioners having read your letter of the 10th instant, in which you state that you can suggest a plan whereby the revenue would be greatly augmented, I have it in command to acquaint you that you are at liberty to submit the plan alluded to for the Board's consideration, that they cannot enter into any stipulation with you, but that, should the revenue be benefited in consequence of any communication which you may make, you will be paid such reward as your services may appear to entitle you to.

'   G. DELAVAUD.

' *September* 21, 1822.'

On the night of July 24, 1822, the custom-house at Castries, St. Lucia, was robbed of 3,564 dollars. The collector reported : ' We can entertain no doubt but that this outrage has been in a great measure instigated by the futility of the late proceedings against certain inhabitants for smuggling, and the hatred consequently excited against us.' (The papers dealing with the case refer to similar robberies at Harwich and Portsmouth.)

Cap. 23, 4 Geo. IV., provided that the king might appoint one Board of Customs and one Board of Excise for the United Kingdom ; neither Board to have more than thirteen members, and that he might also appoint Assistant Commissioners of Customs and Assistant Commissioners of Excise (not exceeding four of each) to transact current business in Scotland and Ireland, under the control of the central Boards at London. Both Customs and Excise Commissioners were to be under the control of the Treasury. Previously there had been nine Commissioners of Customs in England, five in Scotland, and

four in Ireland.   Under the new arrangement there were
thirteen Commissioners for the United Kingdom.   Eleven
of these sat in London, one at Dublin, and one at Edinburgh, and each of the two last-mentioned had two
resident Assistant or Local Commissioners under him.
Any of the Local Commissioners might be directed to
remove from Scotland to Ireland, or from Ireland to Scotland, if necessary.   The Commissioners who retired under
this new arrangement were compensated according to the
following scale :

Having served less than twenty years, two-thirds of
salary per annum.

Having served a longer period, three-quarters of salary
per annum.

(One of the retiring Commissioners was granted compensation at his full rate of salary, on account of length
of service.)

The Commissioners who had acted as Chairmen of the
previous Scottish and Irish Boards had received salaries
larger than they became entitled to as members of the
new Consolidated Board.   The excess of salary was
continued to them.

The Irish Customs takings were still to be remitted to
Dublin, and paid into the Irish Exchequer, but the
Scottish collectors were to remit direct to London.   As
soon as the patent for the Consolidated Board was issued,
a General Order was sent from the Custom House,
London, dated October 16, 1823, apprising all the customs
officers of the United Kingdom as to the new Board's
jurisdiction, and the liability of officers to be called upon
to serve in any part of the United Kingdom.   The
Treasury enjoined periodical inspection of ports by
members of the new Board, and half-yearly reports of
the condition, receipts, and expenditure of the Customs
establishment.   The duties of the Commissioners were
allotted as below :

One Commissioner to act as Chairman.

One Commissioner to deal with matters connected with

the King's Warehouse, up-town warehouses, and London Docks.

One Commissioner to deal with matters connected with the other docks in London.

One Commissioner to deal with matters connected with the sufferance wharves.

One Commissioner to deal with matters connected with the coasting business.

One Commissioner to deal with matters connected with the waterside work, except at the docks.

One Commissioner to deal with matters connected with the waterguard.

One Commissioner to deal with matters connected with East India goods.

One Commissioner to deal with the solicitors, Accountant of Petty Receipts, and Receiver of Fines and Forfeitures.

One Commissioner to deal with all other indoor work, including the Long Room.

One Commissioner to deal with tradesmen's bills, and the repair and alteration of Customs buildings.

(All the above sat in London.)

One Commissioner to sit at Edinburgh (with two Assistant or Local Commissioners for Scotland under him).

One Commissioner to sit at Dublin (with two Assistant or Local Commissioners for Ireland under him).

The previous Acts relating to the warehousing of bonded goods were repealed, except as regarded the approval of ports and warehouses, and a new Act was issued (Cap. 24, 4 Geo. IV.).

Cap. 69, passed on July 11, 1823, repealed the duties on certain imported goods, and provided new duties— some higher, some lower. It contained the first specimen of a special duty on cigars, which were rated at 12s. a pound. (There was an excise duty as well.) It repealed the prohibition of manufactured cocoa, which had endured since 1722, and of cocoa shells and husks, which had endured since 1731, but the repeal only affected manufactured cocoa, etc., from the Plantations.* The duties on oil and blubber were still highly preferential with regard to British takers and importers. See below :

*The Tun of
252 Gallons.*

	£	s.	d.
Blubber, caught by the king's subjects, and brought from British colonies ..	0	13	4
Blubber, of foreign fishing ..	22	3	4
Train oil, spermaceti, etc., caught by the king's subjects, and brought direct from British colonies ..	1	0	0
Train oil, spermaceti, etc., of foreign fishing ..	33	5	0
Whale-fins, caught by the king's subjects, and brought direct from British colonies ..	3	3	4
Whale-fins, of foreign fishing ..	95	0	0

The above alterations of duties did not affect Ireland.

A most important alteration was effected by the Act, it being provided that in future certain duties should not be managed partly by the Customs and partly by the Excise, but should be apportioned by Order in Council, it being advisable that all import duties should be under the Customs Board.†

* During the period of prohibition all cocoa legally imported had been in the ' nib,' and this was called for revenue purposes ' cocoa-nuts.' Students of the old rate-books will do well to bear this in mind.

† The Order in Council was issued on February 2, 1825. It transferred to the Customs the management of the duties previously collected by the Excise on imported coffee, cocoa, tobacco, snuff, pepper, spirits, wine, and all high-duty goods except tea. The change took place on April 5, 1825, and caused a considerable increase in the Customs staff, many officers being transferred thither from the Excise. The instructions issued by the Customs Board in consequence of the change directed that the customs officers were to take an acocunt, in presence of the excise officers, of all the goods, previously under Excise bond, which were brought under Customs management, and to give a receipt for them. The Excise locks were to be removed, and all Excise offices vacated were to be surrendered to the Customs. All bonds entered into for exportation of wine and manufactured tobacco from merchants' stock for drawback were to become Customs bonds, but bonds for the exportation of British-made excisable commodities for drawback were to remain Excise. When tea was landed, the customs men were to deliver it into Excise custody.

This transfer was due to the reports made by a Commission of

The duties on nearly all foreign goods imported into or exported from Ireland were made similar to the British rates by Cap. 72, 4 Geo. IV., and the ' countervailing duties ' were abolished. It was provided that the Treasury might fix a date on which all traffic between Great Britain and Ireland was to be deemed coastwise traffic. All Irish duties were to be paid in British currency, and assessed according to British weights and measures.

Cap. 77 provided that the king might by Order in Council assimilate the duties upon goods brought in British and foreign ships, but that this should not apply

---

Inquiry (1818). There had been many complaints by merchants, who had to pay separate duties on the one article. Cases had even occurred in which seizures were apportioned to two departments, the Customs seizing the ship and the Excise the goods.

On June 7, 1819, Mr. Brougham had stated in Parliament that the charge for collecting the Customs was 13 per cent., and for collecting the Excise only just over 5 per cent., and that a saving of half a million might be effected by abolishing the Customs Boards, and empowering the Excise to collect all the revenue on imports and exports. It appears that this statement was made without balancing the facts. The whole charge of the preventive *boat* service, of the administration of quarantine, of the riding officers, and of the Plantation revenue staff, was paid out of the Customs. There was no such ' pull ' on the Excise, and the latter department's great return was due to the fact that it collected duty at much higher rates than the Customs did, on the articles most extensively consumed. See below :

	Customs Duty.			Excise Duty.		
Tea (British ship)	6 per cent. on value.			90 per cent. on value.		
	£	s.	d.	£	s.	d.
Tobacco (British ship), per pound..	0	1	0	0	2	2
French wine, Rhenish, etc. (British ship), per tun	65	13	0	78	4	0
Madeira wine (British ship), per tun	44	3	0	52	10	0
Port, etc. (British ship), per tun ..	43	1	0	52	10	0
Plantation rum (British ship), per gallon	0	1	$2\frac{1}{4}$	0	10	$4\frac{1}{2}$
Cordials, double (British ship), per gallon	0	5	$6\frac{1}{2}$	1	13	$3\frac{3}{4}$
Cordials, single (British ship), per gallon	0	5	$6\frac{1}{2}$	0	17	0
Brandy, geneva, etc. (British ship), per gallon	0	1	9	0	17	0

to goods carried by vessels belonging to countries in
which British traders were not granted 'equal' privileges. The pilotage regulations for British and foreign
vessels were made similar.

From 1817 to 1824 repeated complaints were made by
the Council of New Brunswick that the collector of
customs was in the habit of levying extortionate fees.
An investigation was held, and the collector was censured
by the Treasury, and ordered to pay the costs of the
inquiry (£250). Even after this arrangement the Council
continued to protest against this enterprising official's
extortions, accusing him of authorizing the preventive
officers at the Bay of Fundy and the Gulf of St. Lawrence
to collect outrageous fees, and then appropriating half
of the sums collected, and dividing that portion with the
naval officer and the controller. It was stated that in
one year he had by this method succeeded in pocketing
£2,900.*

Cap. 65, 5 Geo. IV., provided that the abominable salt
duties should be abolished after January 5, 1825, and
Cap. 79 exempted public officials from taking the oath of
supremacy.

Cap. 97 repealed the laws forbidding the emigration,
without special licence, of British artificers. It will be
seen that the legislators were knocking off the old shackles
at an alarming rate.

A uniform system of weights and measures for England
had been prescribed by Magna Charta, yet many varying
systems prevailed. The injunction had been reaffirmed
by the Act of Union between Great Britain and Scotland,
apparently with little effect. By Cap. 74, 5 Geo. IV.,
Parliament dictated a standard of lineal measure, a standard of troy weight, and standards of capacity—liquid

* The documents connected with the Plantation Customs
contain many similar statements. The colonial administrators
were continually complaining of the extortion practised by the
customs officers, and the officers retaliating by charging their
detractors with favouring contraband dealing. No doubt much
that was true was uttered by both sides, much also that was
outrageously false or partial.

and dry. The yard was defined as the measure of the straight line between the centres of the two points in the gold studs in the straight brass rod (then in the custody of the Clerk of the House of Commons, and marked ' Standard yard, 1760 '), when the temperature of the rod was 62° F. If the standard rod were lost or defaced, it might be reconstructed by comparison with ' a pendulum vibrating seconds of mean time, London latitude, in a vacuum at the level of the sea.'

The standard troy weight was declared to be the standard measure of all weight, and defined as the brass weight held in same custody; date of construction, 1758. This might at any time be reconstructed by comparison with a cubic inch of distilled water, weighed in air by brass weights at 62° F., barometer at 30 inches.

A new gallon measure, much larger than the old wine measure, was prescribed, the standard to contain 10 pounds avoirdupois of distilled water at 62° F., barometer at 30 inches. The gallon for dry measure was the same. The bushel for dry goods which were sold by *heaped* measure was to contain 8 such liquid gallons.

The customs and excise officers were to be supplied with accurate tables, based upon the measures prescribed. (The Act came into force on January 1, 1826.) This statute repealed a great number of laws and parts of laws, extending from the date of the ancient ' Assisa Panis et Cervisiæ ' to 1803.

Prior to 1765 the Manx revenue had been a perquisite of the Athol family, and when the Treasury bought the island the family were compensated by an annuity (amounting to one-fourth of the gross Customs proceeds). In 1825 it was directed that the family should be bought out (Cap. 34, 6 Geo. IV.).

Several ports in the Plantations, previously exempted from the ordinary Plantation restrictions as regarded

* On November 25, 1825, the Customs Board directed that all the ' Exchequer weights,' by which the Customs weights at the various ports were adjusted, should be sent to London, so that they might be readjusted and restamped.

certain kinds of Plantation trade, were granted ware-housing privileges. The ports affected were Kingston, Halifax, Quebec, St. John in New Brunswick, and Bridge Town in Barbados (Cap. 73, 6 Geo. IV.).

Although a consolidation of the Customs laws and a consequent revision and alteration of duties had been arranged to come into effect on July 5, 1826, certain Customs duties were repealed by Cap. 104, 6 Geo. IV. (July 5, 1825), and other temporary duties granted. A table was included in the statute, expressing the duties which would be payable on goods affected by the new measures of capacity. In this, for the first time, the duties on wine were specified per gallon instead of per tun.

An account of the more important preventive laws, and of certain incidents connected with smuggling, during the period extending from 1801 to 1825, will be informative at this juncture. Choice of the latter is difficult, simply on account of the enormous amount of second-hand material available.

The character of contraband traffic underwent some alteration. The extensive employment of the military and navy in prevention checked the old gallant system under which the smuggling craft 'carried guns and fought their way.' Smugglers, in choosing and preparing their vessels, came to rely more upon speed and less upon armament. Swift-sailing craft, laden with kegs, ready slung, and having 'sinkers' handy, so that the goods could be thrown overboard and submerged if the chase became hot, were much used between the Continent and the southern and eastern coasts of England. The running inland was not to the same extent conducted in the old daring fashion, when troops of horsemen, armed to the teeth, went clanking along the Kentish and Sussex by-roads, their hardy little nags loaded with contraband, debouched at night into the main roads near London, and carried their 'truck' into the suburbs, often past the very noses of the cowering ' land-carriage-men ' who were deputed to watch the turnpikes. The goods were more frequently sent inland in fish-baskets, in packs of wool, in bales of hops, and by many other methods of secret stowage. Caves were dug along the coast, in which large quantities of goods were placed, and left till suitable sale could be effected. Concealments on board trading vessels became common, and some of the devices used were extremely ingenious.

Frequent allusions may be found in the records as to immense smuggling on the southern and western coasts of Ireland during the period from 1810 to 1819. Little definite information is forthcoming ; still, it is evident that the Irish revenue was extensively defrauded, principally by Americans, huge runs being made, and the goods conveyed inland, with the full cognizance of thousands of people. The Irish Customs men were either powerless or hopelessly corrupt. The chief article smuggled was tobacco. When the coastguard was established vast seizures were made, the Irish record of seized tobacco for 1820 amounting to nearly 400 tons !

Stringent as the laws had been, they were gradually strengthened. In 1802 the limit within which ' hovering ' entailed forfeiture of vessel was made eight leagues from the coast, except between Beachy Head and the North Foreland. If at trial of case the distance were not clearly established, a verdict might still be given for the Crown if it could be proved that the ship had *prohibited* goods on board. Persons found signalling from the shore to smugglers were made liable to a fine of £100. Rewards on a most consoling scale were promised to informers. This Act (Cap. 82, 42 Geo. III.) applied to Great Britain only.

On March 4, 1804, the customs officers seized at a house in South Molton Street, London, a quantity of lace, which they held to be smuggled French goods, the pieces not being stamped by the Customs as duty-paid. When the case came on in the Exchequer it was contended in defence that the goods were English-made, and that the English manufacturers of lace had become so expert that it was next to impossible to tell English lace from French. The matter of the goods not being stamped did not affect the case much, for it was shown in evidence that the retailers usually removed the stamps. (The judge, Baron Macdonald, delivered himself solemnly upon this proven infringement of the statute, stating that the stamps should remain, and adding : ' The bread of thousands of women and children in this country, who manufacture the article, depends upon it.') A deadly wrangle took place over the question of opinion as to country of manu-facture. Several dealers were called as witnesses for the defence, and they declared that none could tell. Yet the Crown secured a verdict.

On February 25, 1805, the *Tartar* cutter (Customs) and the *Lively* cutter (Excise) chased a lugger into Dungeness Bay. The smugglers ran their vessel aground, and escaped. The revenue men boarded her, and found in her hold 665 casks brandy, 237 casks geneva, 118 casks rum, 119 bags tobacco, 6 packages wine, and 43 pounds tea. The people of Lydd and Dungeness mustered, and attempted a rescue. A company of the Lancashire militia, quartered hard by, advanced upon the rioters, cleared the beach, and enabled the revenue men to carry the goods to a safe place. *Nine years later* two men, named Jeremiah Maxtell and Thomas Gilbert, were arrested, removed to London, and charged at the Old Bailey, as participators in the attempted rescue. The case against them was remarkably defective, and it is a matter of wonder that they were arrested at all on such flimsy evidence. Verdict for defendants.

Cap. 121, 45 Geo. III. opened thus : ' Whereas in de-fiance of the several laws of Customs and Excise great quantities of goods are illegally imported into and landed in the United Kingdom, as well by clandestine means as by open force,' and proceeded to extend the provisions rendering forfeitable any vessel that had on board spirits, obacco, or tea in illegal packages. The extension applied to vessels not square-rigged, and a startling extension it was, for any such vessel owned or part owned by the king's subjects, or having on board a crew more than half of whom were the king's subjects, was made forfeitable if found with the above-named illegal goods within *100 leagues* of the British or Irish coasts. No vessel of less than 100 tons might bring spirits or tobacco as cargo. The preventive powers previously vested in officers of customs and excise were granted also to all commissioned officers in the army, navy, or marines. Convicted smugglers might escape the ordinary penalties by volunteering to serve five years in the army, navy, or marines.

It appears that in certain localities the collection of inland revenue was an occupation almost as dangerous as the prevention of smuggling. On the night of February 6, 1806, the excise collector of Carmarthen, accompanied by twenty-two other excise officers, went (all mounted and armed) to the village of Llansantfroid, to search for illicit malt. A quantity of malt was found, but a crowd of people assembled and effected rescue of the goods. The officers were driven into the village of Llanor, and they took refuge in a public-house. Soon the place became too hot to hold them, and they retired with their horses to an adjacent field. It appears this was not exactly with good judgment, for the collector, in his report of the affair, described the field as ' the most stony ground I ever knew.' The mob surrounded the officers, and stoned them in barbarous fashion, injuring several of them severely, and maiming some of the horses. In the end the officers drew their pistols, and fired upon their persecutors, dispersing them at once. ' Some of the rioters,' reported the collector, ' are privates in the volunteers. I look upon the greater part of the regiment to be either smugglers or the friends of smugglers. The captain of one company, Mr. Strike, is well known to be the greatest smuggler in Wales.'

On May 24, 1806, the Board of Customs received a

letter from the Treasury on the suppression of smuggling. One paragraph was truly remarkable : ' Their Lordships being aware that, if the measures pursued by Government for the effectual suppression of smuggling should meet with the success which the Legislature had in view, the emoluments of several of the officers of this Revenue will be materially diminished, and in many cases nearly annihilated, are pleased to desire that the Commissioners will report to their Lordships what steps it may be proper to take for rewarding such officers in a manner suited to the importance of their zealous and successful efforts, and the beneficial effects which they will in that case produce on the revenue, the fair and legitimate commerce, and the morals, of this nation.' (Thus it would seem that the extension of legitimate trade, the prosperity of the revenue, and the moral condition of the British people, depended in a great measure upon the efforts of officials, some of whom obtained remuneration in its most ample and assured form by making occasional large seizures and winking at general smuggling.)

On May 25, 1806, Captain Haddock, of the *Stag* cutter, stationed in the Downs, reported that on the night of the 23rd he sent two six-oared boats to intercept several luggers which were standing in towards Deal. One boat succeeded in getting alongside a lugger, and was at once saluted with a volley of small-arms. Several of the boat's crew were badly wounded. All the luggers ran ashore, and about 300 natives of Deal at once assembled and conveyed the cargoes into that ancient and eminently law-abiding town. The weather being very rough, the wounded men were unable to get their boat back to the cutter, and she drifted ashore. The smugglers surrounded and disarmed the sailors, and, stated Captain Haddock, ' kicked and beat them in a most shameful manner.' The hardened wretches then stove in the boat, and stole the oars and rigging. (One of the wounded men died shortly afterwards.)

Cap. 66, 47 Geo. III., provided that any lugger ex-

ceeding 50 tons, built in the United Kingdom, should be
forfeitable. All vessels not exceeding 50 tons were to
carry licences. Boats of the United Kingdom rowed with
more than six oars were made forfeitable if found without licence within 100 leagues of the coast (whale-boats,
ship's boats, lifeboats, revenue boats, excepted). Vessels
of the United Kingdom found with contrivances for
sinking, slinging, or smuggling goods within 100 leagues
of the coast, were made forfeitable, and foreign vessels
were made similarly liable if within the smaller limit
(8 leagues, or 4 leagues between Beachy Head and the
North Foreland). No vessel of the United Kingdom was
to load spirits, tobacco, or snuff, in a foreign port, without
licence from the Privy Council, Admiralty, or Secretary
of State. It was also provided that the Board of Customs
might grant special rewards to officers who detained
persons found on forfeitable vessels, and secured their impressment for the army or navy. The power of granting
licences to ships, boats, etc., which by an Act of 1784 had
been vested in the Admiralty, was transferred to the
Customs.

A Treasury order was issued, granting the following
scale of awards :*

To the commander of the revenue cruiser by which, in the
    year ending October 1, 1808, the greatest number of
    smugglers should be captured, and delivered for service   £
    in the navy   500
To the commander, etc., capturing and delivering the second
    greatest number 300
To the commander, etc., capturing and delivering the third
    greatest number 200

In 1808 the pensions allowed to the widows of certain
higher preventive officers who had been killed by

* This was continued through several succeeding years. The
results were not remarkable. In 1810 the first prize was taken
with a record of only thirteen smugglers. Then it was directed
that only two prizes should be given, and they only when the
first winning captain could quote a bag of at least twenty
smugglers, and the second of at least fifteen. In 1813 it was
decided that the rewards, when payable, should be divided
amongst the ships' companies.

smugglers were increased, the widows of ordinary mariners thus killed being left on the old scale. Only six widows benefited by this increase, the relicts of the commander of the cutter stationed at Cowes, of the mates of the cutters stationed at Dover and St. Ives, of the commander and mate of the cutter at Yarmouth, and of a Southampton riding-officer.

In 1809 it was enacted that any person, not a passenger, found on a British vessel from which goods had been thrown overboard to prevent seizure, should forfeit £100. Persons detecting spirits which had been sunk for smuggling purposes were made entitled to one-half the value of the goods (Cap. 52, 49 Geo. III.).

In 1810 most of the provisions of the British preventive Acts were extended to the Isle of Man. The governor of the island, the deputy governor, or any one of the 'deemsters,' might enforce the penalties incidental (Cap. 62, 50 Geo. III.).

On July 7, 1810, the case of Williams v. Burgess was tried in the Court of Common Pleas. The defendant, an officer of customs, had searched the premises occupied by the plaintiff, a Wapping pawnbroker. No smuggled goods were found, and Williams claimed redress for the unnecessary invasion. The jury granted him damages at the rate of £1 a minute for the period occupied in searching, but the Court held that his case had failed owing to an informality in the wording of the plea.

A new system of landguard for England was devised. The coast was divided into three districts, one extending from London to Penzance, another from Penzance to Carlisle, another from Berwick to London. There were 120 riding-officers in all, and it is evident that some of them had other means of employment, for the order setting out the districts warned the officers to confine themselves to the performance of their preventive duties.

A case curiously illustrative of the complexities of revenue proceedings was tried in the Exchequer on

December 2, 1811. It appeared that on November 8, 1810, two officers of customs and one exciseman searched a coachmaker's premises in Worship Street, City. They found a large quantity of foreign silks, bandanas, gloves, and silk stockings, and 485 ' pieces ' of foreign cambrics. A firm of linen-drapers in Cannon Street claimed the cambrics, stating they had taken them in satisfaction of a debt due from a certain Hebrew merchant. This gentleman appeared in court, and swore that he had bought the goods from a firm of importers of cambrics, which firm had paid duty on them. It was found from the Customs books that the last-mentioned firm had paid duty, in 1809, upon several thousand pieces, and though the Israelite could not produce one scrap of paper in support of his statement, a stubborn defence was based upon it. There was not the slightest proof that the Jew had bought goods from the firm that paid the duty ; the goods had not been found on his premises, or on the premises of the firm quoted as sellers, but in the possession of a coachmaker who had long been suspected of dealing with the Kentish smugglers. They were found along with silks, etc., that were admitted to be prohibited goods, and they were actually in what was known as ' smuggling packages '—viz., small bales packed between boards, so as to be carried in panniers on the horses ridden by the contrabandists. It is likely that several startling feats of perjury were performed during this trial. Verdict for the Crown.

On June 19, 1812, one Mrs. Selth, of Deal, was charged in the Exchequer with harbouring smuggled or prohibited goods, and with being a wholesale smuggler who employed others to go about and sell her wares. A witness named Sturt stated that in 1810 she was asked by Mrs. Selth to sell smuggled silks, shawls, etc. Sturt declined, but introduced one Mrs. Bishop, who accepted the offer. A reserve price was put upon the goods, and the hawker might keep all obtained in excess. Mrs. Bishop commenced a trade with silks, shawls, cornelian beads, and gloves. The customs officers seized a large quantity of these goods in her house at Dover, and her husband was sentenced to six months' imprisonment. Both she and Sturt went frequently to Mrs. Selth and asked her for money, as Bishop's family were starving. Mrs. Selth refused—whence the information.

It was pleaded in defence that the charge was the result of conspiracy, also that the defendant had a husband alive, though not living with her, and that if anyone was responsible it was he.* The judge held that even if Mrs. Selth's husband were living with her he might not be responsible. Verdict for the Crown.

Certain customs officers charged the Marchioness of Wellesley with attempting to smuggle silks. We quote the letter written to the Board on the matter by the Secretary to the Treasury:

' GENTLEMEN,
    ' Having laid before the Lords of the Treasury your report of the 5th inst., on the application of the Marchioness of Wellesley, requesting to be relieved from a prosecution, I am commanded by my Lords to acquaint you that, the information upon which your officers proceeded in the case in question appearing to be groundless as to the silks charged to be in Lady Wellesley's possession, and the allegations that her Ladyship is in the habit of dealing with smugglers being unsupported by any sort of proof, their Lordships do not think this a case proper to be vigorously insisted on, and are disposed to wish such a compromise to be made as may mitigate the loss of the party, without at the same time affecting the interest of the seizing officers.

' R. WHARTON.
' 12th May, 1813.'

A letter was sent on the same day, relative to certain pictures seized by the officers at Penzance in the baggage

* See vol. i., p. 355.

brought by Lord Fife on his arrival from Cadiz, directing
that the pictures should be given up to his Lordship on
payment of the proper duties.

During the same year the officers seized at the Ship
Inn Waggon Office, Borough, a case. containing apparel,
sent from India by Lady Hood to Countess Spencer. The
Treasury directed that such of the seized articles as were
prohibited should be warehoused for exportation, and the
rest admitted to duty. The Countess was to compensate the seizing officers (amount of ' satisfaction,' ten
guineas).

During May and June, 1814, information reached the
English Board that several notorious ' smuggling merchants ' had left Alderney for Cherbourg, an establishment for smuggling having been formed at the latter
place since the declaration of peace, and that a number
of smuggling vessels from Lyme, Portland, and the Isle
of Wight had gone to Cherbourg, also that vast numbers
of ' tubs ' were stored on the Cherbourg quays, and many
coopers were busily occupied in making others. It was
stated that a ' smuggling concern ' had been established
at Treguier, the members being certain renowned
smugglers who had previously been in the habit of
running goods into Cornwall, and that a company
was being formed in Guernsey for the purpose of
smuggling from France into various places on the Cornish
coast.

On May 24 and 27, 1814, no fewer than fifteen revenue
cases were dealt with in the Exchequer, the defendant in
each case submitting to a verdict for the Crown. On
June 30, 1814, fifteen other cases were disposed of, all
undefended.

No doubt the many inducements held out to revenue
informers tended to encourage vindictive and truthless
information, and there is good ground for suspicion that
occasionally the informer was a mere *agent provocateur*.
The case of the Attorney-General *v*. Mary Gamwell
appears to reveal black business.

It was tried in the Exchequer on July 1, 1814. The defendant, a haberdasher of Aldersgate Street, was charged with having harboured French gloves, being therefore liable to a penalty of £200, and treble the value of the goods. The informer—one Brown, a hawker—stated that he became acquainted with the defendant in 1812, and that in 1813, at her request, he sold a number of pairs of French gloves, she charging him 3s. a pair—he, of course, charging as much as he could get—that he began to owe her money, that she sued him, that he was imprisoned for debt, and while in the spunging-house laid information against her. This scoundrel had to admit threatening to inform upon Mrs. Gamwell if she did not take him out of the clutches of the sheriff's officer, and the sheriff's officer swore that Brown told him he would ruin the widow if she did not agree to his request. ('Revenge,' said Brown, 'will be sweet.') Verdict for defendant.

On April 18, 1815, the Treasury desired the Board to direct the officers to be vigilant in preventing the clandestine exportation of arms to France. (Lord Sidmouth had received information that this traffic was persistently encouraged by the French Government.)

On July 25, 1815, the Board issued to the officers of revenue cruisers a set of instructions in the method of using the tourniquet, and a list of medicines which were to be supplied for use on board. The medicines were of the good old searching type : vomiting-powders, purging-powders, sweating-powders, calomel pills, laudanum, cough-drops, stomach tincture, scurvy-drops, friars' balsam, mercurial ointment, blistering ointment, etc., etc.

Cap. 104, 56 Geo. III., provided that customs officers should have full powers of search, seizure, prosecution, etc., under the Excise laws, and excise officers full powers under the Customs laws. The powers, previously vested in justices of the peace, to determine Customs cases where the penalty was not more than £50, were extended, and justices were made competent to determine any Customs case, irrespective of amount of penalty. Proceedings were only to be taken on the Board's special order, unless they were in the name of the Attorney-General. This Act reaffirmed many of the old restrictions.

During the latter part of the year much information as to smuggling from France reached the authorities. It was stated that cambrics had been cut into handkerchiefs, and in that form smuggled extensively into Great Britain, and that concealed contraband goods came over in the French egg and fruit smacks, and were run into the southern ports. One of these vessels was found to have double bulk-heads between her cabin and hold, the space within being filled with spirits, wines, and plums. Another was found to have a similar contrivance, stuffed with silk handkerchiefs, between hold and forepeak. Another brought a consignment of cases containing plaster figures. The figures were found to be hollow, and filled with clock movements, bronzes, porcelain articles, and small pictures.

It is apparent that there was much smuggling into the Plantations, for some of the seizure records are quite remarkable, and it is certain that at most not more than one-twentieth of the contraband goods were captured. We submit a few quotations from the Jamaica list :

' *July* 12, 1816.—Spanish schooner *El Carmen*, with wine and oil, seized by Captain Roberts, of H.M.S. *Jay*.

' *July* 16, 1816.—Spanish schooner *Fortuna*, with wine and gin, seized by Captain McKellar, of H.M.S. *Salisbury*.

' *July* 22, 1816.—Spanish schooner *Eugenie*, with wine, brandy, and vinegar, seized by the customs officers of Kingston.

' *July* 27, 1816.—British schooner *Fickle*, with tobacco, seized by Captain Tait, of H.M.S. *La Pique*, and a seizure of 300 bushels of corn by the land officers.

' *October* 2, 1816.—Spanish sloop *Hoppa*, with brandy, gin, wine, and pickles, seized by the customs officers of Kingston.'

In 1817 the penalties and restrictions as to boats with more than the legal number of rowlocks, and vessels fitted for swift sailing and for smuggling, were made still more comprehensive and severe (Cap. 87, 57 Geo. III.).

An officer at one of the outports was about to weigh some cases of bound books from France, so as to assess the duty. (The duty on books was assessed according to weight ; those on prints, maps, and drawings, unaccompanied by descriptive letterpress, were special duties.)* He examined some of the volumes, and found that each contained ' a vast number ' of valuable coloured prints, with a little letterpress which did not appertain. A further examination revealed that the covers were hollow, and that these contained many valuable prints and drawings.

On March 27, 1817, Messrs. Peate and Newton, midshipmen of H.M.S. *Ganymede*, discovered five ' smuggling caves ' in the Sandhills between Deal and Sandwich. These were simply large square holes dug in the ground, surrounded and roofed with two-inch planking, the roofs being covered with deep beds of shingle. Entrance was obtained through traps in the roofs, the traps being covered with iron troughs hidden by shingle.

On June 28, 1817, tidings were sent to the western English ports that six vessels belonging to Cardigan were about to leave for Ireland, where it was intended they should ship salt for running on the western coast of England.

On August 30, 1817, the Board sent information to all the western ports as follows : ' The sloop *British Fair*, of Folkestone, Mark Watt master, about 70 tons, running bowsprit, a quarter-deck, bound from Holland to Ireland with a cargo of tobacco, principally concealed, the vessel having a false bottom '; and on September 4 to all the eastern ports relative to the *Dart*, 110 tons, clench built,

* Books, bound, per cwt., £5 9s. 4d. ; unbound, £4 2s. Coloured prints, 50 per cent. of the value ; maps and charts, the piece, 1s.

under foreign papers, with an English captain named Marsh, from Holland, with a full cargo of spirits and tobacco, to run at Robin Hood's Bay ; and on September 19 to all western ports as to the cutter *Jane*, 200 tons (foreign papers), with an English commander named Matthews, having a cargo of tobacco and spirits for Ireland.

On October 16, 1817, they sent word to Dublin of the cutter *Earl Spencer*, 140 tons (foreign papers), with an English captain named Whittingham, and carrying a full cargo, also for Ireland.

On October 21, 1817, the Customs Secretary sent the following confidential note to a person named G. Mackay, residing at 24, Princes Street, Westminster :

' In reply to your letter of the 27th ultimo, stating that two persons of the names of the Count de Beaumont and Monsieur Cariat are in the practice of smuggling, I have it in command to acquaint you that officers have been directed to keep a strict watch on the houses of the above-mentioned persons.

' G. DELAVAUD.'

On December 12, 1817, the Secretary penned the following significant missive :

' *To Mr. Pelham, Controller at Brighton.*
' SIR,
' The Commissioners having had before them certain examinations of Louis Anthony Losser, a prisoner in the Fleet, as to sundry smuggling transactions at Brighton, in which it appears you are implicated, I have it in command to transmit you extracts thereof, and to direct you to answer the same for the Board's further consideration, and to return your report confidentially under cover to me, marked " Private."

' G. DELAVAUD.'

Early in 1818 the following information was sent to various stations :

Dates when Sent.	Particulars.
Jan, 6, 1818.	To Inspector of River, Gravesend, to look out for *Marquis of Anglesey*, which left Ostend on January 4 with a quantity of goods. To search the crew, they having playing-cards concealed on their persons.
Jan. 6, 1818.	To certain southern ports, that a look-out be kept for the *Ox*, of Folkestone—a long and narrow vessel with a running bow-sprit, about to smuggle from Boulogne to Rye.
Jan. 7, 1818.	To collector at Lyme, to prosecute eleven persons detected in carrying smuggled goods, and four others known as receivers.
Feb. 6 and 7, 1818.	To the Admiralty and seventy-five outports. To look out for the *Jane*, 200 tons, forty-four men, sixteen guns, which left Flushing January 24 with tobacco, tea, and 5,000 bandanas ; also the *Idas*, 135 tons, thirty men, not armed, which left Bremershaven with tobacco and tea. (Both the above expected to run in the north of Ireland.) Also the *Unicorn*, ready to sail, with tobacco stowed in her false bottom and false sides. (' May run in the north of Ireland, or at any intermediate port.') Also the *Dart*, 120 tons, which left Flushing February 2, with 500 ankers of spirits for Redhead, Scotland. Also a long and narrow cutter called the *Renard*, 70 tons, under foreign colours, which sailed from Flushing February 4, laden with rum, geneva, and tobacco.
Feb. 16, 1818.	To the Admiralty and outports. To look out for a cutter (crew mostly foreigners) which went ashore in a fog near Calais on 12th. (She was got off, and proceeded down Channel.) She had previously left Flushing laden with small kegs of spirits, nominally for Rio de Janeiro, ' but was bound, it is conjectured, for the coast of Ireland.'

(At this time there was much information as to clandestine shipment of arms and volunteers at Deal* for the use and assistance of ' the insurgents in Spanish South America.')

* See footnote, p. 110.

In 1818 the penalties applicable to such of the king's subjects (not being passengers) as were found aboard smuggling or ' hovering ' vessels were made to apply to foreigners when the vessels carried spirits as cargo. The penalties on illegal unshipment of tea were made frightfully severe (£10 for each pound of tea unshipped or £100 on the total quantity, at the choice of the prosecuting officer.)

In February, 1818, a large quantity of China crape and silk was seized at Deal, concealed among shingle in the ballast-bags of the *Fame* lugger.*

At this period many small parties of cavalry were stationed along the coast to assist the preventive officers. It is doubtful whether these were reliable unless under strict supervision. The 7th Hussars landed at Calais from Dover on April 12, 1818, and, by arrangement with their commander, were searched by the French douaniers. Many of the troopers were discovered to have English lace concealed upon their persons. It appears that a sutler of the 52nd Regiment had paid them to smuggle these goods into France for his profit. The *Benevolent* transport arrived at Calais, with British troops on board, on the 13th. That very night her captain was caught conveying a quantity of smuggled goods into the town. The ship was searched. More smuggled goods were discovered, and many packages were found sunk in the harbour near her. On the return of the transports to Dover several of the masters were caught smuggling by the English Customs officers.

* From the earliest records down to those of the end of the nineteenth century there are mountains of evidence as to the smuggling propensities of the inhabitants of Deal. The peculiar position of the town, and the skill and nefarious energy of its seafaring population, made it a place of resort for shippers of wool and coin, criminals eager to escape the law, and importers of contraband. If we were asked to state which, in our opinion, were the two seaside towns of the United Kingdom that in olden times contained the greatest proportion of daring and violent smugglers, we should without hesitation name Deal and Chichester.

In May, 1818, a boat was seized at Plymouth containing a number of large 'boxes' filled with spirits. The boxes were of hard wood, tapering slightly from the middle, hooped strongly at the ends, and fitted with bungholes and with lines and gear for sinking.

In December, 1818, a vessel was seized at Weymouth. She had reported 'in ballast,' but on removing the ballast the officers found a platform fitted on either side the keelson, extending nearly the length of the vessel. Underneath this were kegs of spirits.

On April 7, 1819, a customs officer stationed at Erith boarded a lugger that was sailing up the Thames, and proceeded to search her. There were but two men on board, and one of these, named Henry Hart, protested against the search. Finding protest of no avail, he caught the officer up in his arms, dashed him violently upon the deck, and then beat him with a stick, winding up by throwing him into the Customs boat and sailing off in triumph. The lugger, which belonged to Rye, was afterwards captured, and found to have a large quantity of contraband goods on board intended for London. Hart was tried at the Maidstone Assizes in August, 1819, and sentenced to nine months' imprisonment.

A number of barrels, entered as containing pitch, were examined at one of the outports, and found to contain plate-glass and East India goods, pitch having been run in at the bungholes so as to conceal the contents.

On July 15, 1819, proceedings were taken in the King's Bench against one Scurrah. This person had become indebted to a London merchant named Laing (amount £200) and, failing to pay, had been imprisoned in the Fleet. His fellow-lodger there was one Hickman, imprisoned at the suit of a Mr. Whalley of Gloucester. Scurrah succeeded in inducing a customs officer named Steel to accept information against Mr. Whalley, to the effect that the latter had sold smuggled goods to Scurrah in 1815, and against Mr. Laing as a subsequent dealer in the goods (amount of duty involved stated as £2,000).

This information had been trumped up by the two debtors. Scurrah was convicted of perjury.

Information was received in August, 1819, that large quantities of French jewellery were smuggled in raised pies, loaves of bread, etc., and in November, 1819, that many tubs of smuggled spirits had been carried inland packed in bags of wool.

The rewards to seizing officers were increased,* and it was provided that land might be acquired on the coasts for the erection of Customs watch-houses. Preventive officers were empowered to haul their vessels ashore anywhere below high-water mark, provided that any part of the crew resided on board (gardens, pleasure-grounds, and bathing-places exempted). The power, previously vested in magistrates, of mitigating the penalty of £100 for being found on board a smuggling-vessel, was taken away. The Treasury still had power to mitigate. It was provided that masters of ships should be compelled to furnish the customs officers boarded on their vessels with sleeping-places under the deck.

During 1820 a seizure was made of casks of spirits fastened to the bottom of a ship by a rope passed through the keel, both ends being rove through holes in the ship's bottom on either side the keel. The casks were fixed head to head in rows, and made fast to the rope. They were carried on deck till danger appeared, then thrown overboard, and drawn by means of the rope under the ship's bottom. Tobacco was seized, rolled up in balls, each ball covered with a skin and 'clayed,' so as to resemble a potato. Three boats were seized having hollow spare foremasts and outriggers, stuffed with contraband. A large seizure was made at Shoreham of contraband goods, concealed in hollow pieces of iron which were used as ballast. A hawser was seized, the inner strands of which were made of tobacco.

From a report made in 1820 it appears that the preventive work in England was arranged thus : Part was

* Cap. 43, 1 Geo. IV.

performed by naval cruisers, under command of the admirals at Plymouth, Portsmouth, and Sheerness ; part by the ' Coast Blockade,' a force under Admiralty control, with Captain McCullock (at Deal) as immediate commander, and stationed from the North Foreland to Newhaven ; part by the ' revenue cruisers,' originally under the Boards of Customs and Excise, but lately placed under the Admiralty ; part by ' preventive boats,' formerly under Customs, lately placed under Treasury (immediate commander, the ' Preventive Controller-General ') ; part by riding-officers, still under the Customs, and assisted by small bodies of soldiers ; and part by a few of the old preventive ' smacks,' which still did duty at the mouth of the Thames and at several outports. The three branches last mentioned were paid out of the Customs. States the author of the report : ' Various seizures have been made since the rewards were augmented, collusively, or under circumstances of strong suspicion of collusion. Several instances of glaring collusion have been proved, and the officers dismissed. Whenever a seizure of considerable quantities of spirits is made near the shore, and no men are taken, that of itself is, to my mind, a presumptive case of suspicion.'

Mr. Lundy Dickenson, a midshipman holding a Customs commission, had made himself unpopular with those incorrigible smugglers, the good people of Radnor Street, Folkestone. In November, 1821, he, with his crew, conveyed three smugglers to the Town Hall, Folkestone, for trial. The sailors composing the escort were then sent back, Dickenson remaining to protect the Crown witnesses. When the case was over he left the court, and was at once surrounded by furious longshoremen. A fellow named Wigden challenged Dickenson to fight, and followed him along the street, the mob howling approval. Dickenson drew his sword and turned upon his tormentors, who at once bespattered him from head to foot with the scourings of the Folkestone gutters. Brandishing a sword in one hand and a cocked pistol in the other, he managed to work his way back to the Town Hall. The constable on duty, one Burton, was drunk. He prevented Dickenson from taking shelter in the building, and even pushed him back among the rioters. Other constables arrived, and actually threatened to take Dickenson into custody for ' breaking the peace '! He then made a dash for ' The Battery,' the mob pursuing him, and stoning him right into his quarters.

Burton was charged at Maidstone with ' obstructing,' etc., and convicted. (During proceedings reference was made to a previous riot at Deal, in which several smugglers were rescued by the mob.)

In the journal kept by Lieutenant Lilley of the Coast Blockade appear the following laconic memoranda, curiously mixed up with the ordinary records as to visiting, creeping for tubs, etc. :

' *Tuesday, April 24th*, 1821.—Rode to the village of Herne Bay, in consequence of firing observed in that direction. Found that Mr. Snow had been dangerously wounded by an arm'd gang of smugglers.

' *Thursday, April 26th.*—Visited Herne Bay, and went into the interior of the country to endeavour at discovering the people concerned. Repeated and vivid flashes of lightning round the horizon.

' *Friday, 27th.*—At 10.20 departed this life Sydenham Snow, who had received 1 musquet-ball thro' the thigh and another thro' the body. Went to Canterbury, and arranged with the coroner.

' *Monday, 30th.*—Conveying the body in military procession to the churchyard at the village of Herne Street. The funeral service perform'd and the corpse interr'd. At the funeral were Capt. McCulloch, Lieuts. Elphick, Dove, Grandy, Barton, Graham, Fayreman, and Byne, 8 midshipmen, and 47 men.'

As a specimen of the work thrown upon judges and juries by the Customs laws, we quote the list of revenue cases at Lewes Assizes, August, 1821 :

Collusion.—Several customs officers stationed at Rye arranged a collusive seizure. A smuggler named Heath went to Boulogne, and brought back in his lugger 250 tubs spirits, a quantity of tea and tobacco, and a parcel of bandanas. The lugger ' hovered,' and the goods were put into boats and landed by night at a place called ' The Mullet Pound,' in Rye Harbour, *directly opposite the Customs watch-house.* It appears that a division was contemplated, the smugglers to take part of the goods, and the officers to seize the rest ; but a few man-of-war's-men who happened to be in the neighbourhood intruded, and gave unwelcome assistance. Thus the officers were compelled to seize the whole cargo. This enraged the smugglers, and information of collusion was tendered. Several officers were prosecuted, and two of them convicted.

Conspiracy to Corrupt.—Several smugglers were charged with attempting to bribe a preventive man. They arranged with him that a cargo was to be run while he was on watch, and that he was to afford every facility. The goods were run, and the officer was presented with four bank-notes. But he had informed his superior, who arrived with a strong force just as the carriers were about to travel inland. Away went the horsemen, leaving a few tubs, which the officers seized. The watchman handed the rustling ' flimsies ' to his chief, and it was found that they were only £1 notes, instead of £5 notes as agreed on. Defendants convicted.

Again.—Two men were charged with trying to corrupt an officer at Bexhill. Convicted.

Warning Smugglers.—Twelve defendants were charged with ' using a device to warn smugglers.' The offence was stated to have taken place in ' The Haddocks,' near Fairlight. Certain officers deposed that, seeing a boat put in at night, and a crowd go down to the beach to meet her, they signalled for assistance by firing their pistols, on which the crowd dispersed, crying, ' Keep off ! keep off !' and the boat went out to sea, its occupants

shouting derisively, ' You haven't got us yet !'   Defendants discharged on their own recognizances.

Rescue of Goods.—A riding officer, stationed at Chichester, while going his rounds, met between Selsey and Sidles-
ham two men carrying a tub slung on a pole.   He
stopped them, and announced seizure.   They dropped
their burden, pulled him from his horse, and clubbed him
savagely ; then they took up the keg and went away.
Both charged and convicted.

In 1821 a boat was seized at Folkestone for having on
board six large hollow stones containing tin cases full of
spirits.   A quantity of silk was seized at Newhaven concealed in hams from Dieppe.   The meat and bones had
been scooped out, except at the ends, the silk had been
wrapped in oiled silk, and then in paper, and fixed inside,
the orifices neatly closed, and the whole covered with
dirt and sawdust.

By Treasury Minute of February 15, 1822, the whole
of the preventive forces, except the Coast Blockade
and the naval ships employed (see p. 113), were consolidated, and placed under control of the Customs
Board.

In November, 1821, the English Board made their final
pronouncement upon a squabble between Customs and
Administration in the colony of Demerara.   The officers
had seized two sloops and a quantity of contraband goods,
and placed the vessels in charge of a negro guard.   The
owner, a notorious smuggler named West, boarded one
of the vessels in the night, accompanied by several armed
men, and carried her to sea, taking the informer, who was
on board, as well.   The officers, in their report, blamed
the governor and the military for being slack in pursuit
of the culprits.   This produced a long letter from Major-
General Murray, the governor, in which it was made to
appear that the officers had not taken proper precautions
with regard to the custody of their prize.   The Board

took sides with the governor, and censured the seizing officer.

Early in 1822 a vessel called the *Fame*, bound to Cork, was wrecked near Bristol. Amongst her cargo was found a cask containing 106 'instruments of iron, apparently well fitted to be fixed at the top of poles, sufficiently long to be managed with effect at a greater distance than a bayonet at the end of a musket.' The Board directed the collector of Bristol to keep a watch upon anyone who might apply for the goods.

On January 26, 1822, the collector of St. John, New Brunswick, reported to the Board that two notorious smugglers named Dunham and Johnston went to the residence of a tide-waiter who had made himself obnoxious to them, and produced a chest, stating that it contained tea. The tide-waiter found it to be empty. He expressed annoyance at this, upon which Dunham took him by the throat, and drove his head through the window. The tide-waiter gasped : ' Do you mean to murder me ?' ' Yes !' thundered Dunham, ' we'll have your life before we go !' They then maltreated him further. They were charged in the Supreme Court of the island. Johnston was acquitted, Dunham convicted, but for some reason difficult to divine he was allowed to remain at large.

This showed that New Brunswick was not a pleasant place for strict officials, as was proved further on Valentine's night during the following year. Four officers who were on watch near Carlton Ferry, St. John, stopped a sled loaded with tea. In charge of the sled were ' five stout smugglers,' one of them being the redoubtable Dunham. They overpowered the officers, and drove off with the tea.

On the following night the officers took up position at the same place, accompanied by a squad of the 74th Regiment. Along came two sleds containing, not tea, but smugglers armed with boathooks and bludgeons, and accompanied by some of ' the peace officers ' of the town.

These attacked the customs men, but the military kept
them off.   Dunham was present, and extremely busy
both with tongue and bludgeon.   Among the ' peace
officers ' who assisted him were ' Nolan, calling himself
deputy sheriff, though only a head constable and keeper
of the gaol ; Featherly, also a high constable ; and Lawrence Strivers, a constable.'   ' Nolan and Featherly,'
said Mr. Kelly, the customs surveyor, in his report, ' were
particularly violent, threatening to drive my teeth down
my throat.'

It appears that by this time Dunham had paid a £20
fine for his first offence.   He was not captured on account
of the last till 1825, when he was brought up for trial with
two of his accomplices.   The judge of the Vice-Admiralty
Court, who was a practising lawyer, obtained leave from
the governor to defend the smugglers.   He urged that
the officers had no right to be patrolling in search of
seizures, as they were officials who had been appointed
locally, and had not as yet been commissioned by the
Board of Customs.   This plea secured acquittal.

On February 16, 1822, the American schooner *Peru*,
from New York with a cargo of tobacco, was seized in
the harbour of Kinsale.   (It appears she ran aground
at Cove.)   She had a crew of thirty-one men, and the
Customs had to obtain assistance from the garrison at
Charles Fort.   When the crew were charged, the plea
was put forward in defence that the vessel was ' driven
in by necessity,' and the case against them was dismissed.
Afterwards the master admitted that he had attempted
to run his cargo at Glandore, in the Baltimore district.
One of the preventive water-guard officers* had given

---

* The following additional particulars are furnished merely to
illustrate the pertinacity with which claims for seizure awards
were pursued :
One Dillon (evidently the preventive officer referred to above)
put in a claim for special participation in the proceeds of the
Peru and her cargo.   It appears that he was granted £150, but
this did not satisfy him, and he seems to have devoted a considerable portion of the following twenty-seven years to attempting to secure a larger grant.   Allusion to his case appears among

notice of this attempted run, stating that the vessel carried guns. The Kinsale collector stated in his report that she had no guns, while admitting that she was fitted with gun-ports, and that she might have thrown her guns overboard when she was driven in. He also stated that gun-matches were found on board, and a bag of bullets. The Customs then entered proceedings against ship and cargo. Meanwhile, the vessel's agent served the collector with notices of action on behalf of the master and the owners.

Later two of the crew came forward to prove that the *Peru* was a smuggling vessel, and that it had been intended to run her cargo on the Irish coast. (Various attempts were made to tamper with the informers, and

---

the records of 1849. Annexed to the papers is a copy of a petition intended to be presented to the House of Commons by Feargus O'Connor. This document states that the armed American brig *Peru*, manned by forty-three determined smugglers, and freighted with 2,053 bales of leaf and 1,090 pounds of manufactured tobacco, appeared off the Irish coast in 1822 ; that Dillon, with eleven men in two open boats, prevented her from landing her cargo at Tralong Cove, County Cork, where 400 smugglers were waiting to receive it ; and that he chased her into Kinsale river, expending during the action 187 shot, four rockets, and two blue lights, and leaving his boat-hook in her fore rigging ; and that she was then captured by Mr. Martin, the Kinsale surveyor. It goes on to state that Dillon received a letter of thanks from the Treasury, that £53,252 accrued to the public by the vessel's condemnation, and that afterwards the Treasury, influenced by ' most unfounded reports,' refused to allow him to participate to the extent warranted by his exertions, and accused him of cowardice because he did not board the vessel at sea ; that he then laid his case before Admiral Codrington, who brought it to the notice of Parliament, but the Chancellor of the Exchequer overruled the Admiral's representations. Attached to this remarkable statement are an affidavit made by Dillon's chief boatman, a reference to certain papers relative to the departure of the *Peru* from New York, and a request that the Board of Customs may recommend Dillon's case, so that he may obtain fitting compensation for the great expense he has been put to in prosecuting his claims.

It appears that the authorities had much difficulty in shaking him off. There is a letter from him to the Customs Secretary, accusing the Board of acting unjustly, and incidentally begging the Secretary to befriend him in the matter, and another in which he refers the Board to ' Robinson's Admiralty Reports and Pope's

one of them was maltreated.)   The vessel and her cargo
were condemned in April, 1822.   The only official account
of the cargo that can be gathered from the papers to hand
states that it consisted of ' 2,500 to 3,000 bales tobacco
of 50 to 60 pounds each.'   Some of the tobacco was found
to be damaged, and was destroyed.   (Dillon's correspondence, see p. 119, puts the amount of cargo at 2,053
bales leaf and 1,090 pounds manufactured, but it is likely
he means the sound part, which would be the chief factor
in assessing his claim of award.)   So it seems that the
cargo, as originally shipped, amounted to nearly 70 tons
—quite an enterprising venture in contraband.

On March 15, 1822, an officer of the Coast Blockade

Revenue Laws.'   The reply is : ' The Board have not the power
to allow any expenses of the nature alluded to.   They cannot
recommend the same to their Lordships.'   Dillon returns to the
charge, referring to tidings, transmitted to him in the thirties,
that Mr. Spring Rice ' malignantly invented and represented to
William IV.' that objection lay against Dillon's claim because
the latter had displayed cowardice, and stating that Dillon has
since received letters from Mr. Spring Rice of different purport,
which leave him in bewilderment as to how that gentleman can
have previously misrepresented him.   He reminds the Board
that he has lately been to New York, and hunted out, at great
expense, fresh information about the *Peru*, which information he
has submitted.   He opines the Board cannot be so destitute of
honour as not to be aware that a charge of cowardice is the most
deadly aspersion that can be cast upon the character of an officer.
The Board, he declares, have ruined his reputation, his professional prospects, and his private fortune, and prejudiced all his
friends against him.   He has expended £5,000 in prosecuting his
claim, and received only £150.   Minute : ' The Board can only
repeat that they have not the power to comply.'

Then appears a letter from Dillon to Sir Thomas Fremantle,
the Chairman, and an address to the Commissioners, in which it
is asked if anything more could in reason be required by ' an
honest Board, governed by truth and justice,' than the proofs
already furnished.   Minute : ' The Board do not consider any
further order necessary.'

In another letter, bearing date 1850, he approaches the Customs
Secretary, announcing that he will present another petition to
the House of Commons, and declaring that the Treasury and the
Board have been misled by the statements of an officer who, on
the night of the action, was five miles away, and who, on hearing
Dillon's ' heavy firing,' was afraid to venture out to his assistance.
(Nothing more concerning the matter has been found.)

stationed at Folkestone seized a boat called the *Wig Box*. Her oars, masts, bowsprit, and ' bumpkin ' contained tin tubes full of spirits. The tide-surveyor at Rye seized a lugger called the *Fox*. Her bed cabins had double bottoms, and in the spaces thus created were bales of bandanas. The same officer found on the smack *Isis*, also of Rye, a concealment under the ballast, entrance to which was obtained by removing a panel in the bulkhead of the forehold. The tide-surveyor at Sandwich seized the smack *Albion*, of London, for not being licensed. On rummaging her afterwards at his leisure, he found her to be fitted with most elaborate smuggling contrivances (false bows and a complete false stern).

During May, 1822, the *Badajos*, of London, was rummaged at Kilrush, Ireland, and found to be fitted up for concealments in an extraordinary fashion. The seizing officer stated in his report : ' I cannot more fully describe the vessel than by stating she is two vessels, completely one within the other. The contrivance to admit into the concealment is the most ingenious possible. The crew of this vessel managed their concerns so completely that they had not a boy belonging to the vessel, for fear his youth may lead him to disclose the secret ; all hands were stout, trusty fellows. From a memorandum-book found in the master's cabin, it appears this vessel had one or two similar cargoes in her before the present,' etc. (The goods found were tobacco.) The seizing officer's report was flamboyant as well as ungrammatical. He seems to have been inclined to leave nothing unsaid that could redound to his credit as a searcher, therefore it may be as well to state that the seizure was made solely by information supplied through the collector and controller of Dover.

During this year the Board made a tour of inspection, and it appears from their report that they considered the most likely part of the coast for smuggling was from Seaford west to Plymouth. (It will be remembered that eastward to the Medway the shores were protected by the Coast Blockade.) They had reason to think that the smuggling of spirits was carried on with great success. They found that the preventive men, the riding officers, the dragoons, and the officers of the cruisers, did not work together amicably. The boatmen were ' very fine men.' Some parts were difficult to guard, notably the Wight, where, from the indented nature of the coast, the patrol had to travel 100 miles in guarding 20 miles of sea. The riding-officers were of little use, many of them being old and ' locally connected.' There was a tendency to make collusive seizures. In the Brighton district collusion was apparent, there being many suspicious seizures and few men captured ; while in the Chichester district many smugglers were taken, the inspecting commander, Captain Boxer, being very daring and energetic. The smugglers had lately begun to build fast rowing-boats, which they used to run goods from ' hoverers.' The system of selling seized boats locally was bad, for there was no competition, and the smugglers could buy them for next to nothing. The pilots of Portsmouth and the Wight were noted smugglers, and if found ' towing ' goods they at once declared them to the officers as wrecked goods salved. The following extracts from reports made to the Board by confidential experts are strikingly illustrative :

' At present the sums expended in defence are very great, yet smuggling is carried on to such an extent that spirits of good quality are sold at 12s. and 14s. a gallon.' The writer goes on to state that there are three favoured methods of smuggling : first, by rafting tubs under water ; second, by running from hoverers ; third, by transhipping goods into coasters at sea. He knows that recently a hoverer manœuvred off Hastings with impunity, the blockade men ' having neither spy-glasses to see nor sails to pursue.' ' When such things take place as the run at St. Leonard's on Tuesday last at eight in the morning, it is a pretty good proof all is not right.' ' Smuggling has long been carried on, and it requires

SIR FRANCIS HASTINGS DOYLE.

('*Vanity Fair*' Cartoon.)

 *To face p.* 122.

people of the country, who know all its bearings—men, too, not overpaid, of the working class—to counteract it.'

The other expert states : ' At Portsmouth much is doing by the Isle of Wight people.   At Cowes the trade increases so much that spirits are sold at Newport from 10s. 6d. to 12s. a gallon.   There appear to be about thirty-six cutters and boats employed in smuggling to the Wight and Portsmouth.   Goods are often run in Southampton Water, and offered at 10s. 6d. a gallon.   Much must be doing on the Dorset coast.   Brandy is offered at Yeovil at 8s. a gallon. In Sussex the larger cargoes are run by French luggers, some by the Pagham and Brighton boats.   Tubs fell lately at Hastings to 7s.' (a gallon).   He proceeds that at Rye as much was run as the smugglers could find sale for, and that many people wished to sell their vessels and buy foreign-built craft, thinking the latter would not be liable to seizure unless found within a league of the coast.   Tubs were selling at 7s. a gallon at Dover, and at Rochester, though so far up river, the goods were even cheaper.

The Scottish Board announced a seizure at Greenock of twelve kegs Irish whisky concealed in barrels of salt meat (May 2, 1822).   The Irish Board announced information that tobacco, lace, and silk were extensively smuggled into Ireland, concealed in hollowed planks and pieces of lumber.

On August 30, 1822, the revenue cutter *Melville* seized in the roadstead at Burntisland the brig *Fortune*, with a cargo of wood and a ' false bottom.'   Access to the false bottom was obtained by way of the stern, the panels giving access being secured by screws made to appear like common bolts.   She was rigged with a false sternpost, which had to be cut away before the place of concealment could be entered.   Below is an account of the contraband goods found therein :

> 199 bales, containing 4,830 pounds roll tobacco.
> 3 bags and 2 parcels, containing 323 pounds roll tobacco.
> 1 keg, containing 10 pounds snuff.
> 303 kegs, containing 1,096 gallons Geneva.
> 33 boxes and 213 bags, containing 1,512 pounds tea.
> 1 box, containing 72 packs playing-cards.

A letter sent by the British Consul at Boulogne reached
the Scottish Board, stating that a fine lugger had left
Boulogne with a cargo of spirits. Her crew, principally
English, numbered about twenty. They had been sent
over to man the lugger by merchants interested in the
venture, and on the previous day had been seen about
Boulogne, *accompanied by Englishwomen.* The letter
stated that other luggers were being built, and that a
steady contraband trade was carried on by means of
galleys.

A letter from Governor Ainslie, Cape Breton, Newfoundland, reached the Board, complaining that large
quantities of coal were stolen from H.M. coal-mines in
that colony, smuggled into Halifax, and sold there at a
price ruinous to the fair trader. The governor stated
that the traffic was prejudicial even to the smugglers, as
they neglected their farms and fisheries to follow it, and
spent the proceeds of their trade in debauchery at Halifax.
He desired that a permit might be called for whenever
coals were discharged at Halifax. (Orders to the collector accordingly.)

Early in 1823 a tub of spirits was found on the beach
at Newhaven, made in the shape of a salmon-kit, and
' cemented over.' A boat was seized at Dover. Her keel,
made of tin painted to resemble wood, contained spirits ;
so did her ' hollow yards.'

Three casks were found floating in a sack off Sandwich.
A bag of shingle was attached as ' sinker,' and an inflated
bladder with a small tuft of feathers as a ' mark.' ' Such,'
states the report, ' was the exact nature of the experiment,
that the bladder kept the sack floating one foot under the
surface. Had an accident happened to the bladder, and
the sack sunk, the feathers were so fixed as to mark the
place. On the spring tides the rush of water over the
flats causes a quantity of froth. The bladder had the
appearance of a body of froth.'

Twelve tubs of spirits were found floating off Rye. A
circular piece of sheet-lead, weighing about 9 pounds, had

been affixed to each, and the tubs lashed together longitudinally. Thus weighted, ' they rolled unfettered in the tideway,' the lead sinking the casks to a depth of 2½ fathoms. Thus, if the officers were ' creeping,'* they would scarcely feel the casks.

The brigantine *John* was seized in Loch Mahon. She had a cargo of timber, and artfully concealed under the cargo and in a place between the cabin floor and sternpost were 773 bales of tobacco.

The following almost incredible information reached the authorities : ' A clinker-built boat of 26 tons, named the *St. Francois*, Jean Baptiste de la Motte master, from Gravelines, lately passed through the Forth and Clyde Canal to Glasgow. The crew brought over a quantity of lace, concealed in boxes made in the shape of apples, and painted so as not to be easily distinguished from real apples. She landed part of her cargo at Whitby, and, after discharging the remainder at Glasgow, cleared on the 27th May, 1823, for Gravelines.'

The Secretary to the Commissioners of Inquiry into the condition of the Customs and Excise departments called upon the Admiralty for a return of H.M. ships employed in the prevention of smuggling in Great Britain. The following is an extract from the official Minute upon this request : ' Acquaint him that all his Majesty's ships and vessels on the home stations are principally employed in the suppression of smuggling. It is, therefore, absolutely impossible to give any other list than a general list of all the ships in commission within the British seas.'

The English Customs reported to the Admiralty that certain members of the Board had surveyed the coasts of England. With this report went an informative return of the quantities of brandy, tea, and tobacco duty-paid during the past five years, from which it appeared that

* ' Creeping,' dragging or sounding for sunken goods, or prying into holes and gullies along the shore.

either the demand for tobacco had fallen off, or the illicit introduction of it had increased :

BRANDY (GALLONS).

1818.	1819.	1820.	1821.	1822.
731,277	964,814	1,021,576	1,140,304	1,221,140

TEA (POUNDS).

1818.	1819.	1820.	1821.	1822.
22,468,170	22,754,341	22,359,539	22,616,167	24,106,722

TOBACCO (POUNDS).

1818.	1819.	1820.	1821.	1822.
12,475,432	11,754,834	11,249,342	11,619,505	11,576,063

In the report made on the revenue of Scotland by the Parliamentary Committee of 1823, unfavourable comments had been made upon the Scottish system of prevention.   In answer to these reflections, Mr. Arrow, the inspecting commander of Coastguard in the Aberdeen district, furnished a long and interesting statement, in which the system as conducted by Mr. Arrow since the establishment of the Scottish Coastguard in 1819 was lauded to the skies.   While admitting that the Scottish fisherfolk and coast peasantry were inclined to assist smugglers, he pointed out that there were certain traits in their character which rendered the establishment of stronger coast patrols unnecessary.   ' If the Scotch fishers and coast peasantry had the daring, or, more properly speaking, the want of feeling, that the smugglers on most parts of the English coasts have, the weak patrols of the present force would not be effective.   So long as the above orders of society continue their present habits, and the wish to appear at kirk with a clean character, so long will the present force of the Coastguard be effective.'   He then furnished certain details as to the smuggling practised on the east coast of Scotland previous to 1819, details which to some extent contradicted his own argument, for, while they did not exactly disprove his statement that the Scottish ' runners ' were not violent folk, they proved that, at any rate before 1819, they had not been particularly anxious to preserve the purity of their characters, unless it were that smuggling, unaccompanied by violence, required but an occasional lustration.

He stated that before the establishment of the Coast-guard, the coast being left under the protection of the Customs and Excise cruisers and the riding-officers, there was a regular passage of smuggled spirits, tea, and tobacco from Flushing into Aberdeen. Two smuggling syndicates were established at Collieston. Each syndicate owned two vessels, which were kept constantly employed. One syndicate failed in 1802, but the other (directed by two notorious fellows named Mitchell and Christie) held on till 1817, and then 'broke.' But business began afresh in 1818 under the directorship of one James Dickie, who received from five to seven cargoes each ' season.' Arrow furnished a most interesting account of the doings of the old smuggling receivers, who, ' assisted by a Folkestone man named Dangerfield,'* supplied the coast from Aberdeen to Montrose most plentifully with contraband. He stated that in 1809 some fair traders of Aberdeen ' got up a movement ' against the Mitchell and Christie firm, and that Christie actually had the impudence to publish an advertisement of challenge in a local newspaper.†

Mr. Arrow insisted that he and his men had broken the back of the old contraband system in that locality. To prove the excellence of his methods, he stated that a person called at his house one night, and made the following statement :

* This desperado is named many times in the ' information lists ' as running goods in various parts of the United Kingdom. Many of the old smuggling skippers were Folkestone men, and quite a number of smuggling ventures, some into remote places, were financed by natives or inhabitants of Folkestone.

†This Mr. Arrow quoted as below :

' NOTICE.—Alexander Christie : Notwithstanding—has still on hand for his favourite customers a considerable quantity of anker gin, which cannot in point of quality and flavour be excelled, and a fresh supply daily expected : Also Highland whisky of best quality, and other spirits equal to his neighbours.

' In these pinched times, a discerning public will find this worth their attention.' (From the *Aberdeen Journal*, January 11, 1809.)

'I am employed by the smugglers. You know we
have had a vessel on the coast the last thirteen nights,
and that we want to land near Aberdeen. For the love
of God, let her come in, and give us fair play. You take
what you can ; let us get off with what we can, or she
will go away altogether, as she cannot keep on this coast
any longer.'

(This vessel, Mr. Arrow stated, had to run to sea in the
end, and was wrecked on one of the eastern islands.)

The testimonials to Mr. Arrow's vigilance and the
effectiveness of the force under his control were many
and influential. We furnish extracts from a few of
them :

Signatories.	Extracts (condensed).
A J.P. living near Rattray Head.	'Cargoes were landed in open day between Fraserburgh and Peterhead in 1818 and 1819.'
The Baron-Bailie of Peterhead.	'Many cargoes were run on various parts of the coast between Girdleness and Rattray Head, before the Coastguard was established.'
The Secretary to the Commissioners of General Assembly.	'For thirty years smuggling was carried on to a very considerable extent at Slains and Cruden.'
A Lieutenant-General and J.P.	'Until lately about two miles from Collieston was the emporium of smuggling. I have often seen one—nay, two— luggers at a time unloaded by twenty or thirty fishboats as regularly and systematically as the disembarkation of an army.'
The Minister of Slains.	'Collieston has been a well-known station for smuggling from time immemorial till within three or four years past. There never has been a year from 1794 to 1819 that there were not three or four cargoes of foreign spirits landed, and some years more than double that quantity.'

Signatories.	Extracts (condensed).
The Procurator-Fiscal.	(This gentleman stated that Mitchell at one time carried on a huge business, being financed by one James of Folkestone. When Mitchell failed, he owed James £5,000.* Before the establishment of the Coastguard, smuggled spirits were sold at every tavern between Peterhead and Aberdeen. 'Gin and brandy were presented to visitors in every farmhouse—nay, every cottar's house—in Buchan.')

(All these, and others, testified to a falling off in smuggling since the Coastguard 'arrived.' From a general study of statement and testimonials, it appears that prior to that period Scottish smuggling was carried on by vessels of from 100 to 200 tons, each bringing from 800 to 1,500 tubs spirits, and occasional cargoes of tobacco and tea. A run usually occupied about two hours. The fishermen and country folk, with their wives and daughters, assisted in getting the goods ashore, and stowing or distributing them.)

Early in 1824 the controller-general of Coastguard sent a statement to the London Board (whence it was transmitted to the Assistant Commissioners of Edinburgh) to the effect that he had received reliable information that a cutter called the *Eliza* had landed 700 bales tobacco at Luce Bay, Mull of Galloway ; that the tobacco had been stored in ' pits,' and was to be made up into small packages and smuggled into Ireland.

On February 19, 1824, the *Asp* was seized at Rye. She had a false bottom, extending aft as far as the ballast bulkhead, and in this space a quantity of silks and tobacco had been concealed.

Information reached the Assistant Commissioners at Dublin that a cutter of 160 tons, laden with brandy, hollands, and tea, would sail shortly from Flushing ; that

* See p. 127.

she carried forty men, was pierced for fourteen guns, was consigned to Ormsby of Sligo and Burke of Connemara, and might run at Clogher Head or on the coasts of Kerry and Cork. She had on board two 'spotsmen' (pilots). A smuggling lugger of 90 tons had left Flushing for Wexford.

On March 20, 1824, a piece of wood made to resemble an ordinary ship's 'fender'* was examined on board a vessel that arrived at Greenock, and found to have been neatly hollowed out and packed with 'crown glass' (eighty-eight panes). About the same time several pieces of timber which had been landed at an outport in Ireland were found to be hollow and to be stuffed with tobacco.

Information reached London that the *Aldborough* yacht had loaded with silks at Nieuport, run the goods in the Humber, and was back in Nieuport shipping another cargo.

On April 15, 1824, the *William and Mary* left London with a cargo of wooden hoops for Waterford. She arrived at Passage on May 7, and the suspicions of the customs men stationed there were aroused. A search was made, and soon it became evident that, after leaving London, she had made a trip to the Dutch or French coasts, taken in contraband, and stowed it beneath her original cargo. The officers found 291 bales of tobacco (weighing in all between 6 and 7 tons).

A clever fraud (repeatedly imitated in modern times) was discovered at one of the English outports. A number of copper cans had been imported, entered as containing orange-flower water. A tube led from the mouth to the bottom of each can. This tube was filled with the scented liquid, but the space between tube and sides was filled with essential oils, liable to a very high rate of duty.

---

* 'Fender,' a large cylindrical piece of timber with a rope rove through the end, suspended over the vessel's side when she approaches her moorings, to prevent injury to her timbers by contact with other ships or with the pier-head. (Sometimes a 'cork fender' is used—viz., a bag composed of closely interwoven cordage, and filled with pieces of cork.)

The Board advised the outports that information had been received of extensive smuggling by collier vessels, the goods being transhipped into them at sea.

Information was received of smuggling in Kent and Sussex by means of shrimping-nets fitted with hollow poles. In each pole was a tin tube containing about 2½ gallons spirits.

On June 10, 1824, Captain Brace, of H.M.S. *Ganges*, captured two smugglers and a quantity of contraband at Barbados. Under the Plantation laws he had no power to detain *the men* in custody, but, being unaware of this, he kept them in hand till apprised of his error by the collector. After the goods had been condemned the smugglers entered an action against him for illegal detention, which he was glad to compromise by paying them £35 each. The Treasury refunded the money paid by him, otherwise it would have been a disastrous business for Captain Brace, for, though the condemned goods realized £121, the expenses attending condemnation were over £90, made up as below :

	£	s.	d.
Collector's poundage	2	0	0 odd.
Controller's poundage	1	10	0 ,,
Advocate's and Proctor's fees	47	0	0 ,,
Judge's, Registrar's, and Marshal's fees	37	0	0 ,,
Watchman's pay	1	5	0
Advertising goods	0	16	5
Paid to drummers*	0	5	6

We cannot close this chapter more suitably than by reproducing two letters written by the Customs Secretary to informers. It will be seen that the informers were women. Many letters might be quoted from the revenue records which re-exemplify the old case of Samson and Delilah. (We suppress the names, but not the addresses.)

'*To Miss* ——, *Musical Museum, Spring Gardens.*

' MADAM,

'With reference to your letter of the 23rd ultimo, I have it in command to acquaint you that the coll^r. and

* Probably for tattoo at proclamation of sale.

cont^r. at Shoreham have remitted a bill for £8 12s. 7d.,
dated 11th instant, and payable at 20 days after date,
being your share of the fine recovered from John Boxall
for smuggling, and that upon your application at my
office you may receive the same on producing a proper
receipt.

' G. DELAVAUD.

' *September 13th*, 1822.'

' *To Miss* ——, *Lee Cottage, Lee, Kent.*

' MADAM,
        ' The Commiss^rs having considered your applica-
tion of the 9th ultimo, requesting to be allowed a maintenance on account of the evidence given by you on the
trial of the smugglers captured by the *Badger* revenue
cruiser, I have it in command to acquaint you that the
Board do not see fit to comply with your request.
        ' *March 15th*, 1824.'

The reports of seizures in the Plantations at this period
furnished ample evidence of immense colonial smuggling.
One seizure note from Jamaica, bearing date October 5,
1824, showed that the contrabandists not only went in
for ' running ' goods, but occasionally tried to smuggle
high-rated goods amongst low-rated.   Seventy barrels by
the American schooner *Resolution*, and reported as corn,
were found to contain amid the corn seventy kegs of
brandy.   Ten tierces, reported as rice, were found to
contain amid the rice twenty-two cases spermaceti candles
and three cases China crapes.
        The perils of a revenue officer's existence were not con-
fined to encounters with truculent smugglers.   Occasionally he came into collision with passengers or travellers
who were as truculent, mentally, as the most desperate
contrabandist, and if the revenue man happened to be
resentful he might be easily betrayed into expressions or
actions which would cost him dear.   An instance of the
kind occurred in 1825.   Lord Harborough arrived with

his yacht from foreign shores, and landed on the lower
coast of the Thames. His vessel was visited by the men
of the Coast Blockade, who afterwards admitted that the
noble lord's dress and general appearance led them to
believe that he was a smuggler. Perhaps Lord Harborough himself was conscious of this, for it appears that
he said to Lieutenant Graham, who was in charge of the
blockade men : ' Do you take me for a smuggler ?'
' Certainly not,' replied Graham, ' but you can't be
answerable for what your men might do.' Lord Harborough thereupon applied several racy epithets to
revenue men in general, and called Graham ' a highway-
man and a robber.' This, Graham afterwards stated,
occurred in the presence of many notorious smugglers,
who had strolled up to witness the dispute. Graham
replied : ' I don't care if this boat is Lord Harborough's
or a common man's. Here is my card. I must get the
satisfaction of a gentleman. If you don't give it to me,
I will kick you and post you.' For this display of manli-
ness the revenue officer was sentenced by the Court of
King's Bench, on May 13, 1825, to four months' imprisonment in the Marshalsea.

The chief characteristics of British Customs administration during the first twenty-five years of the nineteenth
century may be indicated with profit at the close of this
chapter. They took the shape of slow but effective
reform of departmental abuses, vigorous but unsuccessful
action against smuggling, occasional relaxations of the
navigation laws, and repeated consolidations of the Customs statutes. With respect to the first, it may be con-
ceded that the scope of patronage became considerably
narrowed, and the burden of Customs emolument was
gradually removed from the back of the mercantile community and placed upon that of the public. The second
feature has already been made conspicuously apparent to
readers. With respect to the third, only a few countries
had been favoured, notably the U.S.A. under the Con-

vention of 1819.   Wholesale repeal of hundreds of obsolete laws, and novel and effective consolidation of those
allowed to survive, were in contemplation, and will form
matter for the opening of our next chapter.

LIST OF AUTHORITIES.

Incidence of duties, etc. : The various Books of Rates.

Corn laws : Books of Rates ; Customs corn returns, reports, and
statistics.

Colonial revenue and smuggling : Jamaica, ' Treasury,' Antigua,
Nova Scotia, Montserrat, Trinidad, ' Treasury Warrant,' ' Council,'
Quebec, ' Reports,' Newfoundland and New Brunswick, and
' Promiscuous ' Files ; Plantation General Orders, 1814-1815.

British smuggling : ' Exchequer Trials ' (Solicitor's Depart-
ment, Customs) ; Letters to Outports ; Minutes of the English
Board, 1806, pp. 314, etc. ; Treasury Board Papers, 1806 ;
General Letters, 1780-1813, 1814-1823 ; General Letters, Scot-
land, 1821-1823 ; General Letters, 1824 ; General Letters, Dublin,
1824 ; General Letters, 1825 ; Treasury Customs and Excise
Book 52, Letter 6,207 ; Treasury Customs and Excise Book 54 ;
Assize and Promiscuous Trials (Solicitor's Department, Customs) ;
Customs Chairman's ' Private and Official Correspondence ';
Admiralty Papers (Coast Blockade), 1821 ; ' Illustrative Docu-
ments ' File (Customs Library) ; Thurso Letter Book, 1822 ;
Admiralty Papers, March 6, 1823, March 7, 1823.

Revenue legislation : The various statutes as quoted in text ;
Customs Chairman's ' Private and Official Correspondence.'

Statistics of revenue, etc. : 'Finance Accounts of United
Kingdom ' :   ' Income and Expenditure,' and various departmental reports and returns.

Reimbursement of Messrs. Frewen and Jickling : ' Gatley's
Memoranda ' (Customs Library).

CHAPTER II

THE PERIOD OF GRADUAL RELAXATIONS

1826—1844

On July 5, 1826, eleven voluminous Customs Acts, which had been passed during the previous year, came into operation. The first of these, Cap. 105, 6 Geo. IV., revoked all other enactments relating to the Customs. Its preamble echoed the opening clause of the Act which announced the consolidation of 1787. It stated that the laws of the Customs had become intricate, and that it was highly expedient for the interests of commerce and the ends of justice that all the statutes in force relating to the Customs should be repealed, and replaced by new enactments exhibiting more perspicuously and compendiously the various provisions contained therein. Three hundred and eighty-six Customs Acts relating to Great Britain, and fifty-six relating to Ireland, were repealed wholly or in part. Amongst the statutes affected were those historic productions, the Act of Frauds and the various Navigation Acts.

Cap. 106 provided for the management of the department, prescribing thirteen Commissioners for the United Kingdom and the British possessions abroad. One of these was to manage the Scottish Customs, and one the Irish, and each of these last mentioned had two ' Assistant Commissioners ' to aid him. The power of the Treasury to prescribe the official hours of attendance was reaffirmed, and the ' Customs holidays ' were specified as Christmas Day, Good Friday, and the King's birthday.

Cap. 107 contained the bulk of the departmental regulations of commerce. The law as to ' reporting ships ' and ' entering goods ' was clearly recited, and the usual meticulous ingenuity displayed in providing against evasion. All goods laden in British ships in foreign ports were to be certified officially at port of shipment, and the certificates produced when demanded officially in the United Kingdom. Goods shipped in the Plantations were to be attested, even as of old. Goods which, after paying customs, were liable to excise duties, were not to be delivered by the Customs except into the custody of an excise officer. The most important classes of foreign goods prohibited from importation were cattle, sheep, swine, and malt (in protection of the native agriculturist), tobacco-stalks (to protect the native tobacco manufacturer), and packages of tobacco and spirits which might be under the legal weight or size. Sworn declarations were required from exporters of drawback or bountied goods. Machines and parts of machinery, for use in manufactures in which the United Kingdom was eminent, were prohibited from exportation.

Cap. 108 dealt with the prevention of smuggling. The following offences entailed forfeiture of ship and cargo : (1) The bringing of prohibited goods by sea within four leagues of the coast between the North Foreland and Beachy Head, and within eight leagues of any other part of the coasts of the United Kingdom. (2) The navigating of square-rigged vessels within 100 leagues of the coast with illegal-sized packages of tobacco or spirits on board. (3) The throwing overboard of goods during chase. (4) The presence within the limits of a port of a vessel found to be ' unaccountably light,' said vessel having had previously cargo or part cargo on board. Gangs of smugglers, numbering three or more, carrying firearms, were made liable to the punishment for felony, persons who assaulted revenue officers to transportation for three years. The making of collusive seizures was rendered punishable by a fine of £500. Spirits found floating at sea were only to be taken up by revenue officers. One merciful provision reappeared, empowering the Commissioners of Customs to contribute, at a rate not exceeding 7½d. per day, towards the maintenance of poor persons imprisoned for smuggling.* (Most of the above were mere reaffirmations of old preventive measures.)

Cap. 109 was a new Navigation Act, on much the same lines as the older Acts. General trade *into* the Plantations was limited to ' British ships.' So was all inter-Plantation trade. Foreign ships might only carry to the Plantations goods which were the produce of, and direct from, the countries to which such ships belonged, but they might take in goods at the Plantations, and carry them to any *foreign* port. The usual ' enumerated ' *European* goods (wine, timber, corn, brandy, tobacco, oil, dried fruit, salt, timber, flax, hemp, etc.) might only come from Europe to the United Kingdom, for use therein, in British ships, or in ships of the country in which such goods were produced or from which they were imported. Most of the goods of Asia and Africa, and all goods of America, might only come to the United Kingdom, to be used therein, in British ships, except they were brought in the ships of the country in which the goods were produced, and direct from that country ; nor might such goods be brought at all if first landed in Europe. Trade between the United Kingdom and the Channel Islands was to be in British ships. So was all trade between the United Kingdom and the Plantations, and all coasting trade. (It will be noted that a few privileges were thus granted to foreign ships, notably that of trading to the Plantations direct from the ports of their own countries, and exporting foreign goods from the Plantations to any foreign country whatever.)

Cap. 110 reaffirmed most of the old provisions for registration of British ships. Registry was restricted to vessels built in the United Kingdom or the Plantations, and the register was forfeitable if more than 20s. per ton

* Originally enacted by Cap. 21, 53 Geo. III.

were spent at any one time on repairs in a foreign port. Foreigners might not hold property in British ships.

Cap. 111 provided a new tariff. The following extracts illustrate its tendency :

	£	s.	d.
Bacon, per cwt.	1	8	0
Beer, per 32 gallons	2	13	0
German sheet glass, per cwt.	10	0	0
Gloves, men's, per dozen pairs	0	5	0
Iron ore, per ton	0	5	0
Pig-lead, per ton	2	0	0
Linens (damask), per square yard..	0	3	0
Unrefined sugar, East India Possessions, per cwt.	1	17	0
Unrefined sugar, British Plantations, per cwt.	1	7	0
Unrefined sugar, foreign, per cwt...	3	3	0
Refined sugar, per cwt. ..	8	8	0

There were many *ad valorem* duties, the percentages ranging from 10 to 60. Whalebone of the British fisheries paid £1 a ton if of British taking, £95 if of foreign. Oil from the fisheries paid 1s. a tun if of British taking, £26 12s. if of foreign. ' Retaliation ' was provided for by a clause which empowered the King by Order in Council to levy an additional duty, not exceeding one-fifth of the original, on the goods of any country which surtaxed British goods, or imposed unfavourable tonnage duties on British shipping. He might also prohibit the importation of manufactured articles from any country if the said country prohibited exportation of the raw material to the British dominions. Only four articles of export were specifically taxed—coal, skins, wool, and woollen manufactures.

Cap. 112 provided for the warehousing of goods, or, rather, amended and extended the previous arrangements towards that end (see p. 21, etc.).

Cap. 113 granted export bounties on cordage, linens, sail-cloth, and Plantation sugar refined.

Cap. 114, which was passed ' to regulate the trade of the British Possessions abroad,' specified thirty-two ' free ports ' in the British American and West Indian colonies, of which no fewer than ten were in Jamaica. Foreign

trade into the Plantations was confined to these ports.
Foreign countries which had colonies might only enjoy
the privilege, granted generally to all foreign ships, of
trading into the British possessions goods the produce of
the countries to which the importing ships belonged, and
of carrying Plantation goods to any country whatever,
when British ships were treated under the ' most favoured '
method in the colony-owning countries in question.   Certain light duties were levied on British and Plantation
spirits imported into the North American possessions, and
all other goods (not British or colonial) into those colonies,
or into the West Indies or Mauritius, paid *ad valorem*
duties.   All duties collected in the Plantations (or colonies
as it will be best to call them in future), except certain
trifling duties still existing under Acts made in 1778 and
1791, were to be paid in by the collectors to the various
colonial treasuries, and applied to the use of the colonies.
The duties under the two Acts above mentioned remained
imperial, and it is possible they were preserved in order
to form a pretext for continuing the imperial staff of
collectors and officers, the Treasury's power of making
appointments, and the Treasury's and British Customs
Board's powers of control.   Thus still, and indeed for some
twenty-five years longer, the colonial Customs were staffed
and managed from Treasury Chambers and Thames
Street, and there is no more interesting phase of Customs history than that exemplifying the futility of this
continuation.

Cap. 115 regularized the previous Customs procedure
with regard to the Isle of Man, specifying the goods (wine,
brandy, geneva, from foreign countries ; and rum, tea,
tobacco, coffee, sugar, and playing-cards from or *via*
England) which might only be imported in stated quantities under licences granted by the Board of Customs.
The expenses of government and administration were to
be deducted from the Manx duties, and the balance paid
into the imperial Exchequer.

Cap. 116 embodied in its provisions the greater part of

the original Acts governing the carrying of passengers from the United Kingdom to foreign parts.

Before the new Acts came into operation, it was found necessary to pass another (Cap. 48, 7 Geo. IV.) to amend them by rectifying certain errors, supplying certain items previously deficient, and even altering some of the duties. A few Acts repealed were reinstated, and a number of other Acts repealed.

It will be seen that these eleven statutes consolidated the regulations neatly. A mass of puzzling matter was removed from the body of revenue law, yet it cannot be said that even in its new shape that fabric was quite free from complication. As regarded departmental work, a fruitful source of trouble had been retained by continuing the home control of the colonial Customs. The collectors in the colonies, smarting under the loss inflicted on them by the abolition of fees,* were inclined to throw every possible obstacle in the way of the colonial treasurers. The governors found it extremely difficult to obtain from their new subordinates, the collectors, such returns as were required for the information of the various colonial legislatures. Nor were the colonial legislatures or Houses of Assembly free from malicious intent. Cases occurred in which they refused to sanction payment, out of the colonial revenues, of the salaries which had been granted in lieu of fees to the Customs officers. Many disputes arose, but it is likely that in most instances the collectors were in fault.

On February 7, 1826, the collector of Montserrat reported to the Board that the revenue collected in that island was insufficient to furnish his salary. ' Not a shilling,' he wrote, ' has been taken since the commencement of the year.'

On April 2, 1826, the collector of Antigua wrote a passionate and erratically-punctuated letter to the Board, and sent with it a copy of an Antigua newspaper, containing an anonymous letter that cast reflections upon

* On January 1, 1826.

the collector's conduct.　It appears that he had made a
practice, when selling rum which he had collected under
the 4½ per cent. tax in kind, of making a charge for the
casks after the rum had been purchased, and that his
right to do this, and pocket the proceeds, had been challenged in the local press.　Part of the collector's report
ran thus :

'The Writer, whoever he may be, is too insignificant,
and dastardly, to be sought out by me as a gentleman ;
but when my Official Character is attacked and my Integrity challenged ; it becomes me to give to the Board
under which I have the honour to serve ; such an explanation of my conduct, in the discharge of my public
duty ; as to refute the calumny, of any one of the Inveterate Enemies, I have in this Island, who have been
raised up against me, from the Zealous and conscientious
discharge of my arduous duties, in it.'

The collector of Dominica had made himself obnoxious
to a certain section of the inhabitants of that island
by his persistent enforcement of the Acts relating to the
abolition of the slave trade.　This had produced an
extraordinary mass of correspondence, extending from
1819 to 1823, principally on the question as to whether
slaves who had escaped from the neighbouring French
colonies, and taken refuge in Dominica, should be ' condemned ' under the Acts (by which they became the
property of the British Crown, and virtually free), or
whether they should be restored to their masters if the
latter claimed them.　The Judge of the Vice-Admiralty
Court in Dominica decided against the collector's plea
for ' condemnation,' and this evoked a violent protest
to the Board, in which the collector declared that, having
been attacked in a Dominican newspaper, he had taken
proceedings for libel, and cast the paper in £639 damages,
and that the Judge, being editor of the paper in question, had given the recent unfavourable legal decision
as an act of retaliation.　Another huge mass of correspondence grew out of this charge.　In the end the

collector was censured by the Board, and the matter dropped.

Another skirmish occurred at Grenada. The governor directed the collector to prepare certain returns. After some delay the returns were sent, with a bill for £19 16s. (currency) for trouble attendant upon extracting the necessary information from the official records, the collector stating that there was a precedent for the charge, the Customs Board having allowed similar compensation in 1774. The governor replied that he had neither the means nor the inclination to pay the bill, and referred the collector to the Board. The Board declined to pay. Later another return was called for, and the collector suggested that the governor should send a clerk to compile it. The irritated governor wrote back demanding an answer—yes or no—as to whether the collector would prepare the report. The collector, in reply, stated that he was in a quandary, for if he drew up this report for the governor he would have to delay his periodical returns to the Custom House, London. The dispute was referred to the Treasury, and the collector was censured.

Much of the voluminous correspondence between the West Indian colonies and the London Board of Customs was due to colonial misconception of the complicated laws against the slave trade. During 1825 several slaves were detained by the Customs at St. Kitt's—one for being imported from the Dutch colony of Curaçao ; one woman and her child because they had been brought from Anguilla, and the woman had not been registered according to law ; and two others because they had been imported without being mentioned on the ship's report. The Board found that the slave from Curaçao did not come under the Act, he having been imported previous to the limit period therein stated, and they directed that he should be restored to his owner. But previous to this decision reaching St. Kitt's the governor had directed proceedings in the Vice-Admiralty Court of the island, and the slave had been ' condemned to the Crown,' thus gaining freedom. More reports, and then the Customs Lawyer in London opined that the Court's decision must stand, it having been arrived at by ' competent jurisdiction.' Many such cases occurred at various periods ; the colonial records teem with them.

More trouble occurred in Antigua, where the collector had taken it upon himself to cease paying the produce of the colonial duties into the island treasury, and in this case it is manifest that the sole reason was pique on account of loss of fees. (It should be stated that in most of the colonies local duties were collected long prior to 1826, under Acts passed by the various colonial legislatures. The Act Cap. 114, 6 Geo. IV., was in a way, though not professedly, a measure consolidating previous colonial revenue enactments.) Evidently the Commander-in-Chief of the Leeward Islands was in doubt as to the proper course of procedure, for, after issuing a peremptory injunction that the duties should be at once paid in, he weakened, and allowed the collector to retain them pending further orders. In the end the duties were paid over to the treasurer ; but it is amazing to observe the self-importance of these colonial collectors of old, and the lengths to which it carried them.

It seems as though there was a general conspiracy among the colonial customs men at this period to assert their independence of local legislative control. The collector of Jamaica complained to the Board that the provincial House of Assembly had issued *direct* orders to him to furnish certain returns, and he quoted a Board's Order of 1807, which enjoined that such directions should only be complied with when sent through the governor. He stated that he had been called before the Assembly to receive the command, and that he was liable to be arrested for contempt. The Board directed him to comply, and stated that if any further difficulty arose they would submit it to the proper legal authorities.

It was in Jamaica that the great battle between Customs and colonial control was most stubbornly contested.

Besides the duties levied under the new Act (Cap. 114, 6 Geo. IV., recently quoted), the House of Assembly levied other colonial duties, and insisted upon their collection by certain locally-appointed officials. The island treasurer and the collector disagreed on the point as to whether the salaries of the customs officers were to be provided, as directed by the imperial Act, out of a fixed proportion of the receipts under Cap. 114, 6 Geo. IV., or the same proportion of the receipts under that statute and under the ' permanent ' island Act as well, the collector insisting upon the latter course. The island treasurer refused to give the collector an account of the proceeds of the island duties, so the collector put into the king's chest the moneys received under the Act, locked the chest, and bided his time. The governor was drawn into the dispute. He failed to see why two sets of duties should be levied, and directed the collector to discontinue taking money under Cap. 114, 6 Geo. IV. The collector protested that this was illegal, and in his report to the Board stated : ' We earnestly entreat your Honours will prevent as far as possible the interference of the Colonial Assembly with your officers in this island, as their policy in commercial matters is opposite to that of Britain, and thus the carrying into full effect British enactments is not a popular duty.'

Downing Street, Whitehall, Thames Street, and the sun-scorched House at Kingston, were soon at it hammer and tongs. The island assembly forbade for a period the payment out of the colonial treasury for rations for the white troops quartered in Jamaica, and only rescinded this action after receiving an eloquent and serious letter from the Secretary of State for the Colonies. The difficulty was not adjusted till 1832. A Treasury Minute on the matter, issued on August 13, 1830, is worth quoting :

' My Lords do not wish to prolong any controversial discussion by entering into the several arguments which the Committee of the House of Assembly have thought it advisable to adduce, and of which my Lords can in no

degree admit the justice or utility.' The Minute proceeded to state that certain tonnage duties recently levied
by the Assembly to provide Customs salaries produced
more than was necessary for that purpose, and expressed
a hope that these new duties would be reduced, so that
what appeared to be a provision for salaries might not
become a source of island revenue. It also desired that
there should be no future lapse of the island grant for
victualling troops, and that, as the forthcoming arrangement for Customs salaries was to be retrospective, the
amount held back from the victualling grant should also
be made up promptly.

Cap. 56 of 7 and 8 Geo. IV. still further amended the
recently consolidated British Customs laws, and a few of
the duties. One rather interesting clause provided that
when goods were imported in packages, and the packages
had hollow sides or bottoms in which dutiable goods were
concealed, all the goods in the packages should be forfeited. Another stated that all trade with the British
possessions in America and the Cape of Good Hope should
be deemed to be trade within the limits of the East India
Company's Charter. The Navigation laws were slightly
eased.

During this year the collector of St. Mary's, River
Gambia, got into serious trouble, being suspended by the
governor of Sierra Leone (Sir Neil Campbell) on a charge
of misappropriation. The governor, in his report to the
Board, stated that the collector had furnished no account
of 'extra duty' paid on 1,781 gallons of wine, and had
allowed 2,385 gallons of spirits to pass duty-free. There
was a further charge against him of allowing several
consignments to pass, some duty-free, some free of the
'extra duty,' the quantities being as follow : 944 gallons,
' 3 puncheons,' 481 gallons, 694 gallons, 718 gallons, 710
gallons, 244 gallons, all ' spirits,' with 577 gallons whisky
and 93 gallons gin. He had issued ' auction licences ' to
three persons, and only returned the duty paid by one,
and had seized vessels and released them without attempt-

ing to secure condemnation.   The governor recommended
that another man be at once put in his place.   The Board
replied with considerable hauteur, stating they were not
in the habit of dealing with such cases summarily, but
always gave an accused official a fair chance of defence.
They suggested that Sir Neil Campbell should send them
a full account of any investigation which he might have
held, with the collector's answers to the charges.   The
final result does not appear in the records, but it is possible that ' spirits ' may have had much to do with the
whole matter, and have closed the case before Sir Neil
Campbell could reply.

Certain correspondence with the Mauritius at this period
throws light upon the complications of colonial revenue.
Several English merchants applied to Lord Bathurst,
asking that all moneys charged as duties upon their goods
at Port Louis under Acts passed in the colonies, such
moneys being paid since the issue of Cap. 114, 6 Geo. IV.,
might be refunded.   This being referred to Thames Street,
the Board reported against the application, and it appears
from the papers that the design of the Act was to establish
a *minimum* tariff, that the colonies still had the power of
taxing themselves, and that the Act did not abrogate any
duties previously levied under any colonial Act.   The
imperial laws were absolute as regarded trading privileges,
not as regarded revenue.   (A Treasury Minute confirming
this view was issued on April 10, 1827.)

Among the records of this period appears the journal
of John Fife, tide-surveyor, Quebec, a perfect example of
the art of ' cooking.'   Below are certain items :

' *May* 1st, 1827.—Employed boarding vessels arrived
from sea, making the necessary reports to the collector
and controller, boarding tide-waiters and visiting them,
cautioning them to be diligent and strict upon duty, and
injoining them at all times to be on the alert for the protection of His Majesty's revenue.   5 a.m. to 6 p.m.'

This record is repeated on most days, but the startling
item, ' mustering passengers from 5 a.m. till 7 p.m.,'

occurs once. (This would be in connection with the Passenger Acts, and indicates an immense influx of emigrants.) He is shown as on duty *every* day, Sunday included, never for less than twelve hours, usually for thirteen. Sometimes he appears as working from 6 a.m. till 7 p.m., then ' making a visit ' at two on the following morning, then going on duty at 7 a.m. and remaining till 9 p.m. ! There are no records of seizures. Men who ' fake up ' flamboyant journals have no time to keep a lookout.

A petition reached the Council of Trade from the lessees of the coalmines at Sydney, Cape Breton. It stated that in 1826 the king granted to the duke of York all the unreserved mines and mineral rights in Nova Scotia (Cape Breton was an appanage of Nova Scotia at this time), and that the duke leased them to the petitioners for sixty years. They had works at Sydney, at a place near Pictou, and in Lingan Bay, and they asked that ' free ports ' might be established at those three places. (Much correspondence occurred on this subject up to 1829. Sydney, Cape Breton, was made ' free ' about this period.)

On July 16, 1827, the American trading schooner *Potomac* arrived at St. John, New Brunswick. Two merchants of St. John paid duty on sixteen bales cotton-sheeting which formed part of the cargo. The master landed the goods, and was about to deliver them without waiting for their examination by the Customs. On being called to account for this, he gave vent to his feelings in the turbulent fashion common amongst American mariners of that day, by, as the report put it, ' damning the Customs and the laws.' This may have caused the officers to be dilatory in examination, for one of the importers, who was in attendance, forcibly took the goods away before the examination was completed, and when this was opposed he struck one of the officers a violent blow in the chest. He was proceeded against, and fined £200. An official squabble arose over the legal expenses of the trial, and endured till 1833.

Up to 1826 there had been no collection of customs duties at Labrador, though there were several large fishing establishments on that bleak and barren coast— at Esquimaux Bay, Dumpling Harbour, Sandwich Bay, Domino Harbour, Francis Harbour, Battle Harbour, Cape Charles, Red Bay, and Green Bay.   These, except the one at Red Bay, which was owned by a Canadian firm, belonged to various merchants of London, Poole, and the Channel Islands.   It should be explained that all stores sent from the United Kingdom to the fisheries in British North America were free of export duties, and duty-free on arrival, but the customs collectors in those colonies had to certify on the cockets that the stores were used by the fishermen only.   Therefore all such goods sent from the United Kingdom to Labrador had to be taken to Newfoundland, and inspected there by the Customs before being carried to their final destination.   Such respectable British captains as brought goods from foreign parts to Labrador also called at Newfoundland, and paid duty there on their cargoes.   Such as were not scrupulous took their foreign goods straight to Labrador, and landed them duty-free.   Many American vessels fished in the Labrador waters, and of course the shrewd Yankees did not call at Newfoundland on the way, but carried large quantities of tobacco, spirits, etc., straight to the fishing establishments.   Thus commercial honour was heavily penalized.

In 1826 the collector of St. John's, Newfoundland, observing that he received next to no duty on goods for Labrador, made an arrangement with William Langley, agent for one of the Labrador fishing firms, that Langley should survey the coast and collect such duties as were payable.   He was to receive no salary, but it was hinted that if results were favourable he might be appointed as collector of Labrador.   Langley made an elaborate and admirable report of his work.   He appears to have gone to considerable expense, and no doubt he sacrificed much personal popularity, for the fishermen were naturally averse to paying duties. In the sturdy old English way, they pointed out that the new system would harass British and favour American interests, for the turbulent Yankees despised all British revenue enactments. The fishers urged that if duties were collected a permanent customs official should be stationed on the coast, with power to protect the British fishermen from the arrogant and persistent encroachments upon the provisions of the Fishery Convention that were practised with impunity by the Yankees. Still, Langley managed to collect a few hundred pounds, and sent the money to Newfoundland. Whether he kept anything for his trouble does not appear. If he did not (the Newfoundland collector expressed full confidence in him), he had reason to repent him afterwards, as others may have done who have put faith in official generosity. He offered to provide a vessel, to visit the coast three times during each season, and collect as much duty as possible, at a salary of £400. No doubt he would have made an excellent officer, and have worked well in the suppression of smuggling and the prevention of encroachment. After doing his best for three years without pay, he had occasion to return to his native land of Devon, and from thence requested compensation for his services. After a deal of correspondence, in the course of which most ungenerous and unwarrantable suggestions were made as to his integrity, he was granted £150 ! He was a man of great intelligence, and well acquainted with the hard and dangerous life of the seafarer of that time, and it certainly appears that he was treated most scurvily. It is curious to note the departmental methods. In some instances men who did nothing wonderful were surfeited with grants of money and pelted with offers of promotion ; in others far superior men *voluntarily* performed the most difficult, distasteful, and dangerous services, and the very fact that they had performed them *voluntarily* was made an excuse for snubbing and starving them.

The Board in 1829 offered Langley the post of collector at Labrador, with an allowance of 25 per cent. on the takings.   Considering that at some comfortable ports collectors were maintained at salaries which exceeded their gross duty receipts, the offer was preposterous, and he refused it.   He would have had to give up his mercantile connections, to maintain an expensive vessel and crew, and in a way to collect the duties at the point of the cutlass, besides enduring the hardships of constant cruising on that terrible coast.   Indeed, the offer was an insult.   In no other part of the Empire was a customs man paid by results.   No doubt it was not a studied insult, and this puts the tenderers under still worse reflections.   It seems that they were unable to understand the extreme meanness of their own proceedings.   So, for some years longer, there was no duty collected at Labrador, the Fishery Convention regulations remained a dead letter, and the merchants of Jersey, Poole, and London craved in vain the protection that had been promised by strings of pompous legal clauses.   There are people who hold that laws *cannot* benefit commerce, that the trader must work out his own salvation.   Whether this be true or no is hard to tell, but it has been made painfully apparent in many a page of history that laws may *hamper and injure* trade, and that, as our plain-spoken fathers would put it, ' most damnably.'

The Corn Laws were amended by Cap. 60 of 9 Geo. IV. The duties under this Act stood thus :

WHEAT (AND IN PROPORTION FOR OTHER KINDS OF CORN).

Price per Quarter.			Duty per Quarter.		
			£	s.	d.
62s., and under 63s.	..	..	.. 1	4	8
63s., and under 64s.	..	..	.. 1	3	8
64s., and under 65s.	..	..	.. 1	2	8
65s., and under 66s.	..	..	.. 1	1	8
66s., and under 67s.	..	..	.. 1	0	8
67s., and under 68s.	..	..	.. 0	18	8
68s., and under 69s.	..	..	.. 0	16	8
69s., and under 70s.	..	..	.. 0	13	8
70s., and under 71s.	..	..	.. 0	10	8
71s., and under 72s.	..	..	.. 0	6	8
72s., and under 73s.	..	..	.. 0	2	8
73s., and above ..	..	..	.. 0	1	0

(If the price were *under* 62s., the duty was to be raised in the proportion of 1s. duty to 1s. price. If the price were 73s. or above, the duty was to be 1s. only. It is evident that the legislators considered 62s. a fair price— a duty exceeding £1 4s. 8d. would at the time be almost prohibitive—and 73s. unreasonably high.)

By Cap. 76 of 9 Geo. IV. several alterations were made in the Consolidated Acts, principally in the form of in- stalling certain provisions which had existed prior to the Consolidation of 1826, and had been overlooked by the compilers. There was a new proviso that manufacturers who claimed bounty on the exportation of double refined sugar should provide the Customs with samples of the goods they intended to export, which samples were to be retained as ' standards ' (of quality), and the bounty, previously granted only to sugars refined from goods of the British possessions, was extended to sugars refined from foreign goods. A few of the duties were altered.

In 1828, on account of abuse of the privilege granted to ecclesiastics of importing religious vestments duty- free, and of the same privilege granted occasionally to professional musicians and to surgeons or hospitals with regard to musical and surgical instruments, the Board announced that in future they would disallow all applica- tions to that end, except when ' a flute or a violin or a professional instrument in ordinary use ' was imported. (This reads as though an end were put to duty-free im- portations of ecclesiastical raiment, but the regulation was not enforced strictly, as later we shall take oppor- tunity of showing.)

In 1828 the first regular collector was appointed for Sydney, New South Wales, and the Board provided him with a roll of instructions. (Previous to this the governor had levied such duties as obtained in the colony,* under Cap. 114, 59 Geo. III. ; Cap. 8, 1 and 2 Geo. IV. ; and

* New South Wales and Tasmania were under one governor till 1825.

Cap. 96, 3 Geo. IV.) The collector was specially bidden to pay the money collected as duties (having first accounted for ' incidents ' and officers' salaries) into the hands of the colonial treasurer.

A complaint reached the Board from the governor of Nova Scotia that, although the Secretary of State had fixed the Customs expenditure of the colony at £6,422, the collector had kept back from the year's duties no less than £9,000. The Board inquired into this, and reported to the Treasury that of this amount £1,788 had been retained to meet the expenses of the first quarter of the following year. The Treasury stated their opinion that £1,788 was too much to keep in hand. Below is an extract from the Secretary of State's letter on the subject :

' Under the excitement which has for a considerable time prevailed, not only at the deduction of the salaries from the gross produce of the revenue, but at the large amount and extent of the Customs establishment, Mr. Huskisson considers the retention a proceeding which it would have been much better to avoid.' (The collector of Halifax had £2,000 a year as salary, the controller £1,000.)

The case of the *Adelaide* became very troublesome. She had been seized by Captain Jones, of H.M.S. *Orestes*, early in 1827, and taken to Bermuda. The Vice-Admiralty Court restored her, with costs and damages against Captain Jones. The reasons of seizure and restoration were as follow : Mr. M'Alister, a merchant living at Trinidad, went to Bermuda for his health, taking with him his family and a free coloured woman. At Bermuda he purchased a girl of twelve and a boy of ten to assist the woman, and, as the mother was loath to be separated from her children, he bought her and the rest of her family as well, making five in all. Before doing this he asked the collector of Bermuda if he would be acting legally in taking these people to Trinidad. The collector held that the laws did not define any particular number that might be reckoned as ' domestics,' and that M'Alister's position entitled him to at least the number bought. All that he required the planter to do was to see that the slaves were entered on the ship's clearance according to law, and to carry with him a certificate of the registry of the mother as an adult slave. This was done, but Captain Jones seized the vessel, alleging that M'Alister was *trading* in slaves.

When the Vice-Admiralty Court restored the *Adelaide*, Captain Jones gave notice of appeal. The collector surrendered the *Adelaide* to her owners, but took bond in a large sum to cover result of future proceedings. Then he referred to the Board for advice, and the Board expressed full acquiescence in the decision of the Vice-Admiralty Court. But Captain Jones prosecuted his appeal in the High Court of Admiralty, England, where the decision was reversed, and the penalty of forfeiture affirmed.

The Board, in their subsequent reports to the Treasury, tried to justify their action and that of the collector of Bermuda, maintaining their ground with a stubbornness almost heroic. Yet it is certain they were wrong. Three of M'Alister's slaves were mere children, one being only three years old. How could these be shown to be ' domestics '? By the letter of the law it was a clear case of trading in slaves, even although M'Alister bought most of the slaves from humane motives.

The costs and penalties, as in all such proceedings, were terrific. The owner of the vessel had to pay £748 (her appraised value under the bond) and a fine of £200. Mr. M'Alister lost his slaves (they being condemned to the Crown, and thus emancipated). He had also to pay a fine of £500. The captain of the *Adelaide* was fined £700. But the bill of costs ! So huge was it that the seizing officer actually suggested that the penalties might be waived provided the costs were paid (and £100 to the Treasurer of Bermuda, to be used in the education of negroes). We do not find that this was allowed, but the Treasury blamed both Board and collector most severely for giving unsound advice.

There was trouble in St. Kitts over the officers' salaries. In the quarter ending October, 1827, but £1,305 was collected, and only £565 of this went to the colonial treasury, the rest going as salaries and incidents. The island Legislature passed an Act authorizing the treasurer to proceed against the collector for the amount held back as ' salaries,' but the king disallowed the Act. A verdict had been obtained in the island prior to notice of disallowance, so a case went before the superior Court in England as to the costs incurred, the colony claiming that the costs up to date should be paid by the collector. We find no trace of the decision, but the Board, on February 25, 1828, instructed the collector to take credit for his own costs out of the moneys in his hands, so it seems the other costs went against the colony.

Cap. 43 of 10 Geo. IV. amended the Customs laws, and altered a few of the duties. The clauses most important were those limiting to six years the time during which goods which had been exported could be imported duty-free under ' Bill of Store,' and vesting the power of registering ships in the colonies (other than the East India possessions) solely in the collectors and controllers of customs. (Previously the colonial governors had part in the matter.) The Board directed their officers, when dealing with ether imported from the Channel Islands, to charge a countervailing duty of 17s. 6d. a gallon, as it had been found that to manufacture 1 gallon of ether in the United Kingdom $2\frac{1}{2}$ gallons of British proof spirits were required, which paid excise duty at the rate of 7s. per proof gallon. Another order directed the officers to scrutinize all passengers, and be vigilant in the examination of their baggage, as it was expected that a large quantity of jewellery stolen from the Princess of Orange was about to be brought to the United Kingdom. Another directed that an extract from one of the revenue Acts, fixing upon passengers the responsibility of declaring their dutiable goods, should be printed in French and English, and exhibited on board all passenger-ships arriving in the United Kingdom.

Disputes were still raging in the colonies. The collector of Savannah-la-Mar, Jamaica, complained to the Board that the House of Assembly called him up to Kingston on a frivolous pretext, that the journey cost him £30, and would have cost him £100 (currency) if he had not had horses of his own, and many friends who entertained him by the way. The Assembly refused to pay his expenses. It appears that the collector of Falmouth, in the same island, was also called up, and replied that he could not afford the expense, upon which the Assembly sent the sergeant-at-arms to bring him up to Kingston in a chaise. The chaise went over a precipice, and the collector was injured badly, yet the Assembly refused to compensate him, and even tried (unsuccessfully) to make him pay the expenses of their sergeant-at-arms. The Board declined to intervene.

On July 22, 1829, the Board reported upon an application from the Lieutenant-Governor of Malta as to proposed consolidation of Customs and Excise in that island. It appears that the cost of the Maltese Excise was £308, of the Customs £1,317. The Board drew up a scheme, and offered to propose a new tariff (the original duties had been low). They negatived a suggestion that the trifling manufactures of Malta should be allowed into the United Kingdom duty-free.

Some idea of the lucrative nature of a Resident Naval Officer's duties in the colonies may be gathered from the following. The office of Resident Naval Officer at Jamaica was held by patent up to November 22, 1827, the patentee being one King, of Marston House, Frome, England. Mr. King leased the office to one Atkinson, a Jamaican resident, who paid him £1,500 a year. When the patent was revoked, King received from the Treasury an annuity of £1,500 as compensation. Atkinson continued to collect the fees of the office up to 1829, and, when queried by the

Treasury, declared that the colonial Legislature had allowed him to do this up to the time when *they* abolished the office. This seems strange. Probably few in England knew till then whether the office had been abolished or not.

The first regular Australian Customs collector arrived at Sydney, New South Wales, early in 1829, and reported to the Board that on February 2, 1829, he, the controller, the landing-waiter, the collector's clerk, and the controller's clerk, waited on the governor and took the oaths of office. The late acting collector (an official employed by the governor—see p. 151) had rendered his account up to January 31, and paid the money into the provincial treasury. Later the collector reported that convicts were employed in minor public offices. The tide-surveyor's boat was manned by convicts, who received an allowance —the coxswain 10d. a day, the rest 5d. each. On August 17 another report was sent, stating that Newcastle was the only outport, that its import trade consisted of goods (principally British) previously duty-paid at Sydney, and carried to Newcastle by small craft. The exports were coals, and farm produce for the Sydney market. The landing-waiter had been appointed by the governor in 1828, and acted as pilot as well, the river Hunter being navigable forty miles above Newcastle. Along with this report the collector sent an account of the expenses of his survey of Newcastle, including his hotel bill. The items may be interesting. The packet-fare from Sydney was £3 return, the steward's fee 10s. Below is a copy of the hotel bill at Newcastle :

' Breakfast, 2s. 6d. ; lunch, 1s. ; wine, 1s. 6d. ; dinner, 4s. ; porter, 2s. 3d. ; tea, 1s. 6d. ; bed, 2s.

' Breakfast, 2s. 6d. ; bottle of porter, 3s. ; dinner for two, 8s. ; bottle of sherry, 6s. ; port, 3s. 6d. ; tea for two, 3s. ; bed, 2s.

' Settled, N. McCLYMONT, 12th August, 1829.'

(Thus it seems that prices were reasonable at Newcastle in 1829, except the price of bottled porter.)

Later the collector stated that application had been made to load coals at Newcastle, to be used in manufactures and steam navigation in India, and he asked whether such trade was sanctioned by the laws of Navi-

gation, Newcastle not being a free port.   The governor
had granted shipment provisionally.   The Board sanctioned the privilege, extending it to cattle as well.

On October 29, 1829, a person named Lucas wrote the
duke of Wellington, accusing the colonial customs officers
of conniving at fraud.   The duke referred him to the
Board, and he communicated with Thames Street.   After
repeating his previous accusations, he proceeded :

' If you give me encouragement it shall never go higher,
which is much to be wished, as if it is made more public
blame may be attached to your Honourable Board.   If
you will, therefore, give me a promise to employ me, you
shall know all before it goes to Earl Grey or into the
House of Commons.   I trust you will, therefore, have the
kindness to answer this free of expense, re-enclosing the
enclosed.   I need only add that the Custom-house officers
I mean are men that can hardly write their names, and
the lowest in the world, yet have most handsome salaries.'

Minute : ' *Read.*'   (Strange to tell, this person had been
a captain in the army.)

The Assembly of New Brunswick passed a resolution,
worded as follows, to the effect that the colony refused
to sanction payment of the Customs salaries out of the
colonial funds :

' On motion of Mr. Partelow : Resolved unanimously
that the House deeply lament that the proposal of H.M.
Government on the settlement of the Custom-house
question cannot be complied with.   The House, in unanimously coming to this determination, do it upon the
principle that the House of Assembly are the sole constitutional judges of the proper compensation to be
afforded public officers when their salaries are to arise
from taxation within the province, and although the
House are well satisfied of the necessity of making proper
provision for the officers of the Customs, . . . yet they feel
bound to say that the scale now proposed is far beyond
what the circumstances of the country will admit,' etc.

This resolution reached Sir George Murray, who sent it to the Board *via* the Treasury. Nothing appears as to the result, except an expression of opinion by the governor of New Brunswick that the Assembly were likely to reconsider matters.

During 1829 Mr. G. A. Thompson wrote the Board from ' Woodland Vale Cottage, Woolwich Common,' furnishing a list of subscribers to a supplement to his ' Alcedo ' (a dictionary of America and the West Indies, translated from the work of Colonel Don Antonio de Alcedo). The Board had subscribed to the original work, but they declined to patronize the supplement.

On January 21, 1830, Sir George Murray wrote the Board from Downing Street, asking whether the customs collector at Bathurst, River Gambia, was within his rights in levying fees on the following scale : For a ship's clearance, £1 1s. ; a manifest, 10s. ; a bill of health, £1 1s. ; ' *rol d'equipage*,' £1 5s. ; harbour fees, £1 10s. ; bond on appointment of a new captain, £1 10s. ; quarantine fees, £1 1s. The Board replied that he was, the place not being a Crown colony, and the fees being those leviable in Sierra Leone before that place became a Crown colony.

The Nova Scotian House of Assembly had for some time been behaving obstreperously, and it appears that matters had come to such a pass that communication between them and the officials of His Majesty's Council had been temporarily suspended, and the renewal by the Assembly of certain revenue Acts had not received royal sanction. The customs officers, who, of course, were pleased to get a chance of harassing the Assembly, continued to deliver goods from bond, but charged only the duties under Cap. 114, 6 Geo. IV., and let them go free of a certain impost previously charged under the colonial laws, the Act renewing that impost being unsanctioned. A less warrantable feature of their conduct lay in throwing obstacles in the way of furnishing returns which were required by the Assembly. For instance, when the customs warehousekeeper was called to the bar of the

House to give details as to the persons who had cleared goods without being charged impost, he declined to attend till ordered by his superior officers. In the end the collector furnished the returns required, and reported matters to the Board, commencing thus : ' As much temper has been exercised by the popular branch of the Legislature upon revenue matters, it was to be expected that this department would not fail to be visited with the usual share of narrow-minded jealousy from them.' The Attorney-General for the colony upheld the Assembly, and furnished what he considered to be statements of revenue law in support of their action. This brought him into grips with the Customs lawyer at London, who shattered his sophistries in masterly fashion. Below is a summary of the Nova Scotian lawyer's statements and the London lawyer's comments :

NOVA SCOTIAN ATTORNEY-GENERAL.

MR. WOODHOUSE, INSPECTOR AND EXAMINER OF PLANTATION ACCOUNTS, CUSTOM HOUSE, LONDON.

1. Warehoused goods are liable to the duties which were payable when they were first imported. Time of importation is time of entrance into port.

No. They are not held to be goods ' for duty ' till they are taken out of warehouse for home use.

2. The bond given as security on warehoused goods is treble the duty that was payable at time of importation. This proves proposition No. 1.

No. The bond is but a collateral security, and furnishes no evidence as to the rate of duty which will be charged at delivery.

3. It is the practice to base the *quantity* for duty at delivery upon the account taken at importation.

This is quite sophistical. The quantity has nothing to do with the rate of duty.

4. If the duties were increased between periods of importation and delivery, warehoused goods could not be charged with the extra duty unless a special clause were provided in the Act. Witness certain revenue Acts of the time.

Warehoused goods would be liable to the higher duty at any rate. The introduction of a clause is a mere explanatory device, not absolutely necessary.

(The Board agreed with their lawyer. The file ends April 25, 1832.)

The collector of Sydney, New South Wales, reported that Mr. Rame, of Sydney, had started a shipbuilding establishment at Hokianga, New Zealand, and desired a British register for a schooner which he had built there. The collector asked the Board's advice, as Sydney merchants were forming settlements at several places in New Zealand, intending to grow flax and export spars. A barter trade was already in evidence, muskets, gunpowder, coarse cottons, and spirits being exchanged for flax and spars. The natives, being under missionary influence, refrained from molesting the settlers. The Board replied that as New Zealand was not a British possession Rame's ship was not entitled to a register.

Later the collector announced the arrival of another ship, built at New Zealand by Rame. Her tonnage was 392, and she carried twenty-seven sailors, of whom fifteen were Maoris. Her cargo consisted of seven bales flax, value £15 ; 100 loads timber, value £700 ; and 130,000 feet plank, value £700.

It appears that Rame had memorialized without avail the Secretary of State for the Colonies, and then gone bankrupt. The trustees of his estate had brought the vessel to Sydney, and there, of course, she was detained— (1) for not being properly manned ; (2) for having no register. The trustees entered into bond with the Customs for £10,000, and the vessel and cargo were delivered up, the bond to await the Board's decision.

Soon a Sydney firm of merchants applied for a register for the *Olive Branch*. This vessel belonged to the Rev. William Williams, a missionary located at the Society Islands, and had been built there under his directions. The Naval Officer at the Bay of Islands granted her a pass, and she took a cargo to Sydney. The merchants urged that if she were not allowed to trade the natives, who at present were much attached to the British, and had helped to build the vessel, might admit the Americans. They stated also that a brig built by missionaries at Tahiti many years before had been allowed a register.

The matter was adjusted by the granting of *licences* to the three vessels in question—the *New Zealander*, the *Sir George Murray*, and the *Olive Branch*—to trade between Sydney and New Zealand, and the last-mentioned might also trade to the Society Islands.

Cap. 4 of 1 and 2 Wm. IV. abolished the system of oath-taking in connection with commercial declarations made to the Customs, and substituted written declaration. ' From the frequent occasions,' said the preamble, ' on which such oaths are required, the reverence and respect which should attach to such solemn obligations have been weakened.' A notable release was effected by Cap. 16, which abolished the coastwise duties on coal and slate, and the export duties on coal carried to the British Colonies. Cap. 30 substituted for the varying duties on wine a simple scale, Cape wine brought direct being allowed the easy rate of 2s. 9d. a gallon, and all other wines charged 5s. 6d. The few remaining Customs fees taken by certain clerks in the Long Room were abolished by Cap. 40.

During 1831 instructions were repeatedly issued as to the quarantining of vessels from the Elbe and Weser. Cholera was rampant in the northern parts of Europe. In October of the previous year the British ambassador at St. Petersburg had announced an outbreak of cholera morbus in the interior of Russia, and its resistless advance upon Moscow, and that at Astrachan the governor and nearly all the police had died of this terrible disease.

A Treasury letter of June 3, 1831, directed the admission of religious vestments duty-free, if proved to be *bona fide* effects, imported by a clerical functionary. Still, all such admissions were subject to the Board's permission, and we find it was sometimes withheld. Sacramental plate might only be admitted duty-free by special permission of the Treasury.

Another Treasury letter, dated June 21, 1831, announced that in future superannuation pay at the highest rate would only be granted to officers who had performed specially meritorious services. Another referred to the application made by a Mr. Hudson, of Hull, that leeches, imported in ships which were liable to quarantine, might be freed from the usual detention. ' Allowed, the bags containing the leeches being first immersed in water.'

In the Husband of the 4½ per cent. duties' account for the quarter ending January 5, 1831, appears a list of certain pensioners quartered on that branch of Customs who had not applied for their pensions. The sums thus outstanding were :

	£	s.	d.
Mrs. Batson ..	28	8	8
Lady Blackwood	56	11	10
Lady de Ameland	208	4	8
The five Misses Fitzclarence	686	16	3
Lord Farnborough	1,500	0	0
Duchess of Gloucester	250	0	0
Mrs. Gordon..	50	0	0
James Grange	62	10	0
Mrs. Hamilton	54	18	11
Miss Hamilton	27	9	5
The Princess Hesse-Hamburg ..	274	14	6
Messrs. Hosier and Bernard	150	0	0
Messrs. Hobart and Sullivan	400	0	0
Mrs. Huskisson	41	4	2
Sir Sidney Smith	500	0	0

(£5,200 had been paid into the Exchequer—it is to be presumed as the net quarterly proceeds.)

A gentleman prone to research apprised the Board that the Vice-Admiralty Court at New Brunswick was not legally constituted, as no patent or Admiralty warrant had ever been issued to that end. The Board at once communicated with the Admiralty through the Treasury.

Cases of illegal seizure of vessels, through misinterpretation of the Navigation laws, were frequent in colonial waters. The *Bristol*, a colonial ship registered at Kingston, Jamaica, was seized on March 26, 1831, it being discovered that, though registered as a British-colonial vessel, she was in reality owned by foreigners. Such seizure was, of course, perfectly legal. She was condemned in the Vice-Admiralty Court, and sold, the purchasers being her previous owners. She shipped a cargo for a foreign port, and the collector granted her a clearance, but when she reached Port Royal on her outward voyage Captain Gabriel, of H.M.S. *Magnificent*, seized her. When the report reached London, the Board stated that this second seizure was utterly illegal, as there was nothing to prevent foreign ships carrying goods from the colonies to any foreign country, although they might not *bring* foreign goods except direct from the country to which the ships belonged. The Attorney-General for Jamaica opined that the goods were liable to forfeiture, even if the ship were exempt, the captain being an Englishman, but the Board declared otherwise. Indeed, it is hard to discover on what the Jamaica lawyer rested this latter plea, for nothing appears in the Navigation Acts of the time to prohibit an Englishman from commanding a foreign ship owned by a friendly power. The Treasury decided that there was no legal reason for seizure of either ship or goods. Still the seizers carried the case into the higher Court, trying to secure a verdict of ' probable cause of seizure,' and thus escape the costs, even if the seizure were quashed. But the judge declined to certify to that effect, and the huge expenses fell upon the seizers.

Cap. 51, 2 Wm. IV., imposed a salutary check upon the extortion practised in the Vice-Admiralty Courts. It provided that the king might, by Order in Council, amend the practice and fees, and that tables of fees should be exposed in the various courts. Persons aggrieved might claim that the costs charged should be taxed in the High Court of Admiralty. Cap. 48, 2 and 3 Wm. IV., amended the Customs laws. It prescribed an allowance for waste on bonded spirits (much less liberal than the one at present existing). It remodelled the ' stores ' regulations. In the old days stores duty-free from bond had been allowed but to naval ships, and in course of time the privilege had been extended to merchantmen, but only as regarded the shipment of Plantation rum for use of crew. By the new Act, all vessels of not less than 70 tons proceeding on voyages likely to last forty days

were allowed stores duty-free.   The Prisage and Butlerage
of the County Palatine were commuted for an annuity of
£803, to be paid to the lessee, and after expiration of
lease to the Receiver-General of the Duchy, for the king's
use.   (The statute empowering purchase was passed in
1803 ; see p. 24.)   A few duties were altered and a few
drawbacks abolished, and certain treaties of reciprocity
existing between the United Kingdom and various foreign
powers were reaffirmed.

Cholera had for some time been prevalent on the Continent.   On January 27, 1832, the Customs were apprised
by the Privy Council that the disease had appeared at
Musselburgh, Fisherrow, Morrison's Haven, and Prestonpans.   Orders were issued that coasters from infected
British ports should be quarantined on arrival.   On
February 11, 1832, Stockton was scheduled as an infected
port, and London was added to the list three days later.
Generally speaking, the parts affected were Scotland, the
North of England, and London.   Canal-boats arriving
from infected towns were quarantined.   But it was soon
found that these drastic regulations were insupportable.

The Board issued a list of articles allowed to be shipped
duty-free from bond for use of crew and passengers, and
a comprehensive table of ' probable duration of voyages,'
by which the quantities issued were to be regulated.
Articles allowed : Tea, coffee, cocoa, spirits, raw sugar,
molasses, dried fruit, rice, vinegar, soap, and British-
manufactured tobacco, for all persons on board ; wine,
cigars, refined sugar, and beer, for officers and passengers.

Riots occurred in the Mauritius over the appointment
of an unpopular Procurator-General, and Mr. D'Epinay,
a member of the Council of Government, convened a
public meeting in the interests of tranquillity.   Colonel
Draper, the collector of customs, who was also a member
of the Council, seconded a motion that Mr. Jeremie, the
unpopular official in question, should be induced to quit
the island.   The motion was carried with acclamation,
and it appears that the Procurator-General was tem-

porarily removed by means which may almost be pronounced forcible. For initiating this action, Messrs. D'Epinay and Draper were ousted from their offices as members of the Council, and the latter was deprived of his collectorship. The despatch sent for this purpose by Viscount Goderich, Secretary of State, may with justice be described as extravagantly worded. Extracts are appended :

' Mr. Jeremie had been the object of the falsest and the basest calumnies. His life had been openly threatened. Sir Charles Colville appealed, with the utmost earnestness and solemnity, to all the better feelings of the community.' Mr. D'Epinay's action was described as ' proposing to calm ungovernable passions, and stifle the clamours of sedition, if not of treason, by defying the king's authority, and trampling upon his Majesty's rightful prerogatives.' Mr. Jeremie was described as replying ' with a degree of promptitude, courage, and ability which do him the highest honour.' ' It may reasonably be supposed that such a manifestation of spirit and talent in a man of unblemished character and spotless integrity, the victim of unjust prejudices and scandalous calumnies, would have had due effect upon his audience.' The despatch ended with a clang, thus : ' All confidence, therefore, between his Majesty's representative and Colonel Draper being thus destroyed, there is but one course to take : His Majesty can have no further occasion for Colonel Draper's services, and you will remove him at once from his office as collector of Customs, and from his seat in the Legislative Council.'

This thunderbolt reached Port Louis, and the governor launched it at Colonel Draper on February 1, 1833. The colonel wrote the Board at once, requesting their good offices. He stated that he had acted with a view to the salvation of the Mauritius and Mr. Jeremie, ' the colony being on the verge of interminable ruin.' ' In early life,' he continued, ' I was page-of-honour to George III., passed eighteen years in the Third Regiment of Guards, and was selected as aide-de-camp to his Majesty George IV. I can with a safe conscience lay my hand to my heart and say, " I have ever served his Majesty with fidelity, sincerity, and ever attached to his Royal Person, his Crown and Dignity." '

The Board referred this halting yet affecting memorial to the Treasury, and the Treasury merely apprised the colonel that the cause of dismissal was not anything he might have done as a member of the Legislative Council. Considerable ill-feeling was excited at Port Louis over Mr. Draper's case, and several members of the Mauritius Legislature temporarily refused to serve on that body, alleging that Lord Goderich's action was an infringement of colonial rights. This contention was undoubtedly just, but it failed to secure Mr. Draper's restoration.

Another case of Customs partisanship occurred in Jamaica. On January 3, 1832, the collector of Kingston had written thus to the Board : ' In consequence of the rebellion of the negro slaves in various parts of the island, and their firing many of the sugar estates, His Excellency the Governor, with the advice of his Council, has proclaimed the island under martial law, so that all business has been suspended during ten days past.' On January 13 the collector at Montego Bay, Mr. Roby, had sent the Board an account of the insurrection (*vide* Illustrative Document, No. 45). It appears that one Burchell, a Baptist missionary living at Montego Bay, had to some extent sympathized with the insurgents (probably but so far as to protest against the severities incidental to martial law). He was indicted on a charge of treason, but the grand jury threw out the bill. On March 13, 1832, a number of whites assembled at Montego Bay with the avowed intention of treating Burchell to a bucket of tar and a roll in feathers, but he succeeded in getting on board H.M.S. *Ariadne*. The authorities at once made arrangements for his removal from the island. This step was opposed by a number of his personal friends, who had assembled in his defence, well equipped to ' repel force by force.' Among these was Mr. Roby, who had armed himself with loaded pistols. Finding that the authorities were resolved upon Burchell's removal, and had actually allowed an American vessel, which had just arrived, to tranship her import cargo to the *Ariadne*, so as to be able to depart promptly to New York with Burchell on board, Mr. Roby seized the transhipped goods, which were technically liable to forfeiture, the vessel that brought them not having reported inwards. The governor freed the goods, and when Roby reported the matter the Board replied with what was practically a severe censure upon the officer, and threw all the expenses of detention upon him as well. But this did not daunt the heroic partisan. He persisted in attempting to justify his conduct, and came out of the trouble, not only much more easily, but to an immeasurable extent more creditably, than Colonel Draper, ex-page-of-honour, guardsman, and aide-de-camp to George III., had come out of his.

Yet another case occurred. On December 5, 1832, the Treasury ratified the suspension of Mr. Fawcett, controller at Savannah-la-Mar, for participation in ' the riots which led to the formation of the political association called the Colonial Church Union in Jamaica.' The Board sent a circular letter to all ' the slave colonies,'* warning their officers against partisanship.

Trouble occurred in Barbados, where the collector, previous to his retirement from the service on superannuation allowance, had kept back £6,037 10s. out of the last year and a half's collection of colonial duties, to pay the customs salaries. Disputes had been frequent in the island on the subject of salaries ever since January 1, 1826 (the date of abolition of the old system of small salaries and huge fees). The new collector had also kept back £1,006 5s. out of a quarter's duties, and the treasurer of Barbados had entered action against him and his pre-

* Antigua, Barbados, St. Kitt's, Nevis, Montserrat, Grenada, St. Vincent, Jamaica, Tortola, Dominica, Trinidad, Tobago, St. Lucia, Demerara, Nassau, Bermuda, and Mauritius.

decessor.   The situation was rendered still more interesting by the professed incapacity of the officers to produce the account of duties taken, they alleging that the
Customs documents had been destroyed by a recent
hurricane.   It certainly appears that colonial opinion was
rather unreasonable on the point in debate.   Under
the old system, in all the colonies, there had been con-
tinual protestation against the extortion of fees from
merchants.   So soon as the expense of maintaining the
officers was thrown upon the colonies at large, dissatisfaction of a more general kind obtained.   No doubt the
real reason for complaint was that the officers were not
appointed locally, and made responsible solely to the
various colonial Legislatures.

The Customs laws were reconsolidated in 1833, the new
system coming in force on September 1.   All previous
Customs and Navigation Acts were repealed by Cap. 50,
3 and 4 Wm. IV., except a few which related to trade
conventions existing between the United Kingdom and
foreign powers, registration of aliens, British and Irish
fisheries, importation of munitions of war, quarantine,
and the East India Company's privileges.   The management of the Customs department was reconstituted on
much the same lines as before, by Cap. 51.   The new Act
' for regulation of the Customs ' (Cap. 52) reaffirmed in
concise form most of the old enactments.   The usual
prohibitions of tobacco-stalks, tobacco-flour, counterfeit
coin, pirated books, certain agricultural products, etc.,
appeared, and a list of restricted articles.   The export
prohibitions showed that it was still held desirable to
protect British inventions, for they applied to many
engines and machines, production of which at the time
was almost exclusively British—viz., machines used in
woollen, cotton, linen, and silk manufactures, various
engines used in the iron trade and in the manufacture of
artillery, various presses and dies, all die-sinking tools,
machines used in the manufacture of paper and blowing
of glass, potters' and saddlers' wheels, and frames for

making clothing. The regulations applying to coasters were drastic, probably on account of the prevailing transhipment of contraband goods into coasters at sea.* The 'times of importation and exportation,' which had previously been on many occasions wrangled over in revenue and navigation cases, were clearly defined. ' Time of importation ' meant the time when goods were brought within the limits of the port at which they were afterwards discharged ; ' time of exportation ' meant the time when goods were shipped on the vessel in which they were afterwards carried abroad. These definitions were to apply in cases of dispute as to when duties were imposed, altered, repealed, or when made or repealed, etc. ' Times of arrival and departure' were also defined strictly. ' Time of arrival ' was the time at which report of ship was made or should be made ; ' time of departure ' was the time at which the proper officer of Customs granted final clearance. These latter definitions were for use when questions arose as to charges or allowances upon *ships*, irrespective of cargoes.

A new preventive Act (Cap. 53) appeared, with the usual comprehensive restrictions and appalling penalties as regarded running, signalling, assembling, aiding smugglers, obstructing and assaulting officers, etc., and the usual alluring hints to intending informers. The ancient and damnable proviso (see vol. i., p. 215) reappeared—a proviso that had instigated thousands of oppressive and illegal detentions—that when vessels or goods were seized, and on trial released, and the officers were able to induce the judge who tried the case to put a certificate on the record that there had been ' probable cause of seizure,' the person aggrieved should not be able, in any subsequent action taken by him for damages, to recover more than twopence, nor might the seizer be fined more than one shilling. The Act furnished specimens of the various forms of information, conviction, and commitment.

* Many of these regulations survive.

The new Navigation Act (Cap. 54) was much the same as that of 1826, except that it was more concisely worded. Cap. 55 reproduced most of the old laws of ship's registry under slightly different wording, and Cap. 56 instituted a new table of duties. Compared with the tariff as consolidated in 1826, it showed a few slight increases and a good many slight deductions. Below is a comparison of the two lists, as regards spirits, tea, and tobacco :

	Consolidated Tariff, 1826.	Consolidated Tariff, 1833.
	£ s. d.	£ s. d.
Spirits of British possessions in America, the proof gallon	0 8 6	0 9 0
Spirits of East India Company's possessions	1 0 0	0 15 0
Spirits of British possessions, sweetened	1 0 0	1 0 0
Other sweetened spirits	1 10 0	1 10 0
All plain spirits, except as above	1 2 6	1 2 6
Tea, per pound (excise duty only)	96 per cent. on gross sale price if 2s. a pound or less ; 100 per cent. if over 2s.	(Excise duty only, but later in the same year made a customs duty varying from 1s. 6d. a pound on common teas to 3s. a pound on the best.)
Tobacco of U.S.A., Russia, Turkey, or East India Company's possessions, leaf, per pound	0 4 0	(See all other tobacco, below.)
Tobacco of British American Plantations, leaf, per pound	0 3 9	0 2 9
All other tobacco, leaf, per pound	0 6 0	0 3 0
Cigars or manufactured tobacco, per pound	0 18 0	0 9 0

A new warehousing Act (Cap. 57) appeared in the Consolidation, and a new Act for bounties and allowances

(Cap. 58). British refined sugar was the only article
entitled to *Customs* bounty. Drawback was allowed on
silk goods manufactured in the United Kingdom, on
foreign barilla used in bleaching linen, on Norwegian
deals and timber used in the Irish, Devon, and Cornish
mines, on wrought gold and silver, on rice cleaned in the
United Kingdom, on tobacco manufactured in the
United Kingdom, and on foreign wine exported. The
excise drawbacks were on British beer, bottles, bricks,
glass, hops, paper, and soap. Many of these allowances
had existed prior to re-consolidation.

The new Act (Cap. 59) regulating the trade of the
colonies gave warehousing privileges to nineteen already
' free ' ports, and permitted private individuals, subject
to licence by the East India Company, to trade with
China. Another Act (Cap. 60) regulated Manx commerce, altering in some cases the quantities of tea and
sugar allowed to be imported there from Great Britain
under licence.

These repeated consolidations show that the aversion
of the mercantile community to dubiety and complication had its effect upon the legislative mind. This may
appear to prove that the legislative mind is not eminently
gifted with foresight. Most revenue legislation is opportunistic, for its evolution is really due to officials, and
there is no person less interested, as regards the future,
than your typical official.

Cap. 73, 3 and 4 Wm. IV., abolished slavery throughout
the British colonies. Cap. 85 limited the duration of
the East India Company's privileges of government till
April 30, 1854, and removed St. Helena from their list
of possessions upon April 22, 1834. From the latter
date, also, the Company's exclusive right of trading or
licensing others to trade in tea, or with China, was to
cease. The Company were to close their commercial
business as promptly as possible. Cap. 93 prescribed
regulations for the new ' open trade.' All British subjects might engage in commerce with the territories

' beyond the Cape of Good Hope as far as the Straits of Magellan.' Three officers were employed to supervise the trade with China, the expense of such establishment to be defrayed by slight tonnage duties levied in China on import vessels and on import goods. Cap. 101 regulated the tea trade. This Act was to come into force simultaneously with the cessation of the East India Company's trade privileges. The collection of the tea duties was to be transferred from the Excise to the Customs (see the new rate of duties quoted in parenthesis at p. 170). Under this Act tea might still only be imported into the United Kingdom from the territories between the Cape of Good Hope and the Straits of Magellan, and into the Channel Islands, the British American possessions, and the West Indies, from the said territories and from the United Kingdom.

Thus the mighty Company's trading privileges ceased, after continuing 233 years, but the directors retained the power (considerably cramped) of ' governing ' for a period the districts from which they had derived their revenues, except their victualling port of call, St. Helena. As a matter of course, the St. Helena Customs came under the London Board's control.

The waterguard, and some of the inferior landing officers, at Liverpool had for more than a year been in a state approaching mutiny. Southgate, a surveyor, and Ross, an inspector-general, were extremely unpopular with their subordinates. On October 28, 1834, the collector of Liverpool forwarded to the Board several anonymous threatening letters which had been sent to the two superior officers in question, and specimens of vilifying correspondence which had appeared in the local papers. He asked if any proceedings could be taken. The Customs lawyers stated that nothing could be done, *even if the writers of the letters were discovered.*

One of the letters to Southgate purported to be in the nature of a warning : ' I would have you to take care of yourself as there is a plot laid to take away your life and likewise the inspector-general's by a set of men that is prepared with Pistols and is determined to sell their lives dear. Take this as a warning for as God is my judge they are fixed upon your destruction,' etc. This was signed ' A Warehouseman.' One written to Ross commenced thus :

' MR. GENERAL,
        ' You are a great man to be sure and receive a great salary but could not your services be dispensed with and the salary you receive be bestowed on the poor men you think so little of. . . . What says the Author of your being if ye oppress the poor and they cry unto me I will hear and avenge them.'

Matters reached such a pitch that the Board resolved upon an investigation, but ere it commenced an officer named Walsh shot Southgate, who died soon afterwards. It appears that there was general exultation amongst the inferior officers over this event, and Mr. Ross received the following *billet-doux :*

' Hell yawns for another Tyrant. Justice calls aloud for a better sacrifice. The greatest wretch still survives. Heaven has decreed his fall and has numbered his days. Don't wrap yourself with the idea that all is over. Thy days are numbered.'

The investigation was held, and the minutes are rather interesting. Many Liverpool merchants gave evidence, and most of them suggested better pay and conditions for the lower outdoor Customs staff. During the year Mr. Walker, an ex-lieutenant of marines, was made inspector of the Liverpool waterguard. He retained that position till 1844, and it seems that the force during that period was but nominally under the control of the Board.

A curious illustration of the amenities of official life is

furnished by certain correspondence which passed between Quebec and Thames Street in 1834. A document signed ' Scrutator ' was sent to the editor of *The Settler*, a Montreal paper, accusing the collector of Quebec and the acting collector of Montreal of having obtained promotion by arranging for the undermanning of the Canadian Customs. The editor incautiously published this. About the same time the Board of Customs received an anonymous letter, accusing the collector of Quebec of soliciting influence in his own interest. Mr. Charles Secretan, who had been dismissed from the post of customs clerk at Quebec, was suspected of being the author of these communications. On being accused to that effect, he admitted writing to *The Settler*, but denied the authorship of the letter sent to the Board. For nearly two years longer this pestilent young fellow continued to bombard Board and Treasury with frothy charges against the Canadian Customs. (The volume of incidental correspondence is quite amazing, and productive of wonder that the Board postponed so long their final recommendation to the Treasury to take no further notice of Mr. Secretan or his charges.)

A striking instance of the villainies practised occasionally by colonial collectors occurred at the Mauritius. The American brig *Hindoo*, with a general cargo from Batavia to Amsterdam, put into Port Louis in distress. It was necessary to sell part of her damaged cargo, but this was opposed by the collector, as contrary to the letter of the Navigation laws. The matter was tried in the Vice-Admiralty Court. The Court allowed sale. The collector appealed. The Court upheld its decision, but declined to grant costs against the Crown. Thus the shipmaster, a distressed mariner, was saddled with his own costs, although the collector was merely insisting upon formalities. The collector, still craving power to seize the goods, submitted the case to the Board. The Customs Lawyer's report threw more light on the rascality of the proceedings than any comment of ours could do.

' A ship in distress is not strictly under the Navigation Acts.' It went on to state that, though not expressly exempted by the letter of the law, a distressed ship should be ' by that equity which is used in construing statutes.' But what of the poor shipmaster, who had been forced into enormous outlay ?

An extraordinary robbery was committed at the Custom House, London. There was an official there called the Accountant of Petty Receipts, and part of his duty lay in the receiving of moneys paid as fines and forfeitures, including, as a matter of course, the moneys realized at the Customs sales of seized goods. On the evening of November 27, 1834, he locked the ' King's Chest ' in his office as usual. It contained £4,000 in Bank of England notes, and £477 in gold. Another official locked it with a master key, then locked the cupboard containing the chest, delivered the key of the cupboard to the person appointed to receive it, and deposited his own key in the proper place in the office of the Accountant of Petty Receipts.

In the King's Warehouse, hard by, was employed one Mott, a customs officer, and he was very friendly with Mr. Huey and Mr. Seale, landing-waiters at the London Docks. These three gentlemen were, in unofficial hours, ' Corinthians ' of the deepest dye. Their little ventures with wine, lovely woman, the racecourse, and the prize-ring, had curtailed their resources, and they had laid a plan to rob the King's Chest on the eve following the next Customs sale. They had employed three eminent ' cracksmen,' May, Jordan, and Sullivan. Mott arranged that a friend of his should buy a cask of rum at the sale, and gave Jordan a £50 note with which to pay for it. Jordan went into the Accountant of Petty Receipts' office on the morning of November 27, tendered the note, observed the business of unlocking the chest, and noted also that there was a large sum of money in it. May managed to get himself locked into the Custom House that evening, found the keys, opened the safe, and carried off the contents, which the gang divided with scrupulous fairness the next morning. The consternation of the Accountant of Petty Receipts, when he opened the chest, must be left to the imagination of readers.

The criminals were not discovered till over a year had elapsed. Huey turned king's evidence. Mott, Seale, Jordan, and Sullivan were transported for life. It does not appear that May was captured. A curious circumstance was disclosed during Huey's statement of evidence —viz., that after the robbery he buried his portion of the plunder in Camberwell churchyard, and left it there for a considerable time.

The official papers connected with the robbery contain several documents illustrative of the morbid excitement generated by events of the kind. One is from a Jew, accusing another Jew, and implicating a young fellow who was a clerk in the office of Petty Receipts. (In consequence of this letter the young man was subjected to close surveillance and exceedingly unjust treatment.) Another letter is from ' Jane Wilson,' and conveys in execrable English the writer's suspicions of ' a person acquintit with the party as gout the notes.' A paper-hanger of South Lambeth also wrote of the suspicious conduct of his next-door neighbour, ' a young woman often visited by a round-faced young man.' And now and then came bewildering missives, addressed to the Custom House, from Miss Casey, an insane female who persisted in signing herself as ' Lady St. John.'

The Nottingham manufacturers had memorialized the Treasury in 1833, praying that stricter measures might be taken to prevent the exportation of bobbin-net machinery. The Board of Customs issued a minute inciting officers to vigilance, and instructing them to allow no machinery to be shipped until it had been inspected by the landing-surveyors. Meantime the Committee representing the manufacturers published a circular, dated from the Star Inn, Nottingham, offering rewards for information which might lead to seizure of the articles of machinery specified, or to the detection of foreigners engaged in pirating them, or in seducing artificers to go abroad. The Manchester Chamber of Commerce approached the Treasury in 1834. The petition commenced : ' Your memorialists have been informed and believe that machinery has of late been illegally exported to a great extent, and that doubts exist as to the powers of making seizures among the officers of Customs, some of whom have disputed the opinion of the law officers of the Crown.' It continued that there was a practice in vogue of obtaining licences for the shipment of ' unrestricted ' machinery, and under cover of the said licences exporting goods the shipment of which was prohibited. The memorialists asked that a bill making prohibition comprehensive and licence exceptional might be submitted to Parliament. ' The whole value of the machinery in our cotton mills, which we have been so many years in accumulating, falls greatly short of the value of one year's exportation of the produce of our cotton factories.' (From this they argued that the nation would lose comparatively little if the exportation of machinery were restricted more closely.)

By Treasury Minute of July 1, 1834, the following ports were approved for importation and warehousing of goods from China and the East Indies : London, Liverpool, Bristol, Hull, Leith, Glasgow, Greenock, Port Glasgow, Dublin, Cork, and Belfast. Newcastle was added later. This proceeding had been made necessary by the abolition of the East India Company's charter of trade, under which most articles imported from the Company's dominions had been landed at London, and warehoused under the Company's custody (see footnote, p. 23).

Cap. 15 of 4 and 5 Wm. IV. abolished the Exchequer offices of Auditor, Tellers, Clerk of Pells, and the ' offices subordinate thereto,' and established instead of these a Comptroller-General, with a salary of £2,000 only. This official and his subordinates were to execute their duties in person. The books, records, and standard weights, measures, coins, etc., were to be handed over to him on

October 11, 1834, and on that day the tellers were to pay into the Bank of England all the money in their hands that belonged to the Crown. All such public moneys as had, during at least 700 years, been payable into the ancient Court at Westminster, were in future to be paid into the Bank of England by the various collecting departments, to the credit of the national Exchequer, and were to form a special fund in the Bank's books. Issues were to be paid by the Bank under sign-manual or Treasury warrant. The Treasury might authorize payment without royal order, whenever money granted by Parliament was to be paid out of the Consolidated Fund, or any other fund specially appropriated to any particular service. In all payments fractions of a penny were to be disregarded. The Exchequer fees were abolished.

Cap. 34 abolished the system, enforced under Cap. 21 of 7 and 8 Wm. III., of deducting 6d. per month from the wages of seamen as a contribution towards the revenues of Greenwich Hospital. The average sum thus obtained had amounted to £22,000 per annum. Under the new Act an annual grant of £20,000 was made to the funds of the hospital.

Cap. 49* announced that, in spite of the provisions of Cap. 74, 5 Geo. IV. (see p. 46), many sets of weights and measures of the old types had been stamped and passed in the Exchequer as models of the standards prescribed by the said Act, although in some cases they were highly incorrect as regarded shape ; therefore so much of Cap. 74, 5 Geo. IV., as laid down that all weights and measures should be according to certain Exchequer standards was repealed, and the erratically-shaped articles were declared legal. But copies of the imperial standards were to be sent to the various counties and burghs, and the magistrates were to decide where these were to be located, and to appoint local inspectors of weights and measures. The ' stone ' was to be 14 pounds in all cases (previously the London ' stone ' had been 8). All weighed articles were

* Amended by Cap. 63, 5 and 6 Wm. IV.

to be sold by avoirdupois, except gold, silver, platina, precious stones, and retailed drugs. It is curious that most of the old Acts relating to weights and measures had to be amended owing to blunders made by the Exchequer officials.

Cap. 89 amended the Customs laws, providing that in future duty should be charged on salved goods sold to meet expenses in cases of wreck, that the provisions relating to spirits imported in casks should apply to goods of that kind when imported in vessels not strictly casks, but answering the same purpose, and altering the duties on a few articles. It provided that the East India Company, though their charter had expired, might still import and warehouse goods.

No Customs Acts of any importance appear on the statute-book during 5 and 6 Wm. IV.

Proclamations were made by the presidents of St. Kitt's, Nevis, and Montserrat, allowing temporary importation of articles, contrary to the laws of Navigation, and duty-free, on account of the great distress caused by the hurricane of August 12, 1835. The necessary bills were directed to be prepared, by which the imperial Parliament might indemnify the governors.

On February 23, 1835, the House of Assembly, Lower Canada, directed Mr. Jessopp, collector of Quebec, to furnish a return of passenger vessels entered at Quebec during 1834. He suggested that the order should come through the governor. On February 28 the Assembly passed a resolution, directing the sergeant-at-arms to arrest Mr. Jessopp for contempt. Mr. Jessopp apprised the governor, who supported his contention. But Mr. Papineau, Speaker of the Assembly (a representative of ' the extreme French party ' in the province), issued a warrant to the sergeant-at-arms, and on March 2 Mr. Jessopp wrote from Quebec gaol to the governor, stating that he was about to apprise the Board of Customs that he had been incarcerated. He wrote accordingly on March 6, informing the Board that the colony was in a state of great excitement. (Annexed to the file is a copy of *The Vindicator and Canadian Advertiser*, which bears out Mr. Jessopp's statement.) Many of the British-descended colonials formed themselves into a ' Constitutional Association,' and sent an address to the imperial Parliament, stating that their liberties were endangered by the preponderance of ' the French vote,' and lamenting the partial handing over of revenue administration to the House of Assembly. On March 19 the controller wrote the Board that the governor had prorogued the Assembly and released Mr. Jessopp. On June 13, 1835, Lord Glenelg sent a despatch to the governor, stating that the customs officers' duties were ministerial, and that there was no just reason for the officers objecting to answer questions put by the Assembly, or to furnish any documents required. The officers were to be directed to obey the Assembly's injunctions in future.

The encroachments made by American fishermen still formed ground of complaint by the British North American customs officers. The preventive officer at Gaspé informed the collector of Quebec that the Americans came close to the shore, and caught bait in defiance of the terms of Treaty and Convention, that they refused to obey his orders to quit, and that one of them—master of the *Bethel*—treated him ' with scurrilous contempt.' The collector apprised the Board, who referred the matter to the Treasury. The governor of Canada wrote to Washington, and the American Government directed the American collectors of customs to warn the fishermen against encroaching. Meanwhile the preventive man at Gaspé asked that an armed vessel might be sent to cruise between Anticosti and Point Miscou, and later the Quebec collector apprised the Board that H.M.S. *Champion* had been put to this employment.

The people of Carbonear, Newfoundland, sent a memorial, with 490 signatures, to the king, furnishing statistics of local shipping and trade, and praying that

Carbonear might be made a free port. The people of Harbour Grace, and the adjacent ports of Bay Roberts, Port de Grave, and Brigus, sent a similar memorial, with 1,074 signatures. (By Treasury Order of October 28, 1835, Harbour Grace was declared a free port.)

The newly-created Legislature of Newfoundland had framed certain laws of revenue, and directed the collector to gather the duties appertaining. It appears that he performed this with an ill grace, and during 1835 he complained to the governor, stating : ' I must observe that I consider this attempt to impose the collection of these duties on the officers of this department is illegal.' He asked the Board to secure him compensation for the additional work, but they directed him to comply with the Legislature's wishes as expressed through the governor, and to ask the governor to provide such assistance as was necessary. They also told him to bear in mind that his salary had been increased from £600 to £800, and that all the Customs expenses in Newfoundland were paid out of the proceeds of Newfoundland taxes.

On May 8, 1835, the Treasury apprised the Board that they had authorized the coinage of silver pieces of the value of $1\frac{1}{2}$d. and 3d. for circulation in the West Indies, and that the customs officers there might receive such coins at the nominal rate. (This was done at the request of the employers of apprenticed coloured labourers.)

The correspondence between the Antipodes and Thames Street during 1835 was rather interesting. First appeared a statement from the collector of Sydney that an establishment of British subjects, provisioned from Sydney, had been formed at Otago, New Zealand, for whaling purposes, by Mr. Joseph Weller, a Sydney merchant. The collector stated that this was but one of several establishments formed during the last ten years, and that the whalers had been in the habit of sending their oil to Sydney, where he had admitted it duty-free, as was the method with all New Zealand products, and then he had allowed it to be shipped to the United

Kingdom as of colonial taking.   Mr. Weller was desirous
of sending the oil *direct* from New Zealand to the United
Kingdom, and wished to know if it would be admitted
there at the low rate as colonial-taken.   The Customs
lawyers objected to this, stating that New Zealand was
not a British colony, and the goods would be liable to
the duty on foreign-taken oil (£26 12s. a tun, instead of
1s.).   The oil must first be shipped to Sydney, and its
method of taking certified there ; then it might be
admitted in the United Kingdom at the low rate as before.

An Order in Council of November 20 constituted
Sydney (New South Wales) and Hobart Town and
Launceston (Tasmania) free warehousing ports.

On account of repeated reports made since 1831, an
officer had been stationed at Botany Bay, to check the
extensive smuggling of spirits and tobacco that prevailed
in that district.   His quarters were in ' The Round
Tower.'   The collector of Sydney desired that an officer
should also be stationed at Broken Bay, ' one of the most
populous districts in the colony,' but it does not appear
that this was complied with.   It is hard to conceive that
a solitary officer could be any check upon smuggling in a
place like Botany Bay, the abode at that time of many
desperadoes.   The collector reported cheerily on the
matter in 1834 - 1835, stating that the contraband
trade had been subdued to a considerable extent, that
the population of Botany Bay was increasing, and that the
local Government had commenced to dispose of land in
small lots to private individuals ' of the humbler grade
of life.'

An application reached the Board from one Egan, a
bookseller living at Kingston, Jamaica.   In 1834 he had
purchased at the Jamaica Customs sales a number of
pirated books, seized on landing from New York, and condemned to be sold for exportation.   He shipped the
books for the United States of America, and then had them
re-landed, and the customs officers, being told of this,
re-seized them at his shop in Harbour Street, Kingston.

He was fined £100 and £98 costs, and petitioned the
Board for relief, but no relief was granted. We furnish a
list of the titles, which may supply a hint as to the
literature in demand at Jamaica :

Eugene Aram.	Moore's Melodies.
Devereux.	The Vicar of Wakefield.
Paul Clifford.	The Disowned.
The Water-Witch.	Love and Pride.
Lionel Lincoln.	Pelham.
The Bravo.	Mothers and Daughters.
Zohrab.	The Scottish Chiefs.
The Children of the Abbey.	Scott's Poetical Works.
The Arabian Nights.	Moore's Works.
The Pilot.	Byron's Works.
The Abduction.	History of England.
The Red Rover.	The Saracen.
Almack's Revisited.	

The collector of Port Louis, Mauritius, appealed to the
Board of Customs.   He had refused to pay the ' Caisse de
Bienfaisance,' a graduated communal tax, or poor-rate,
levied in the island on all persons ' not destitute of
means.' He pleaded that the commissariat officials in
the Mauritius were exempt, that the customs men had a
claim to similar immunity, and that a committee of
appeal which formerly officiated, and to which claims were
formerly submitted, was no longer in existence, so that
the tax was levied at the discretion of the Mauritius
officer of Inland Revenue (between whom and the
customs men it is likely no great love existed, if the
ancient histories of the rival departments, both in the
United Kingdom and the colonies, may be relied upon).
He also hinted that his salary was inadequate, but the
London Customs Lawyer, Mr. Thackeray, informed him
that he was liable as a resident.   (It may be interjected
here that there was still considerable tension of public
feeling in the colony, and that in 1833 a gentleman of
French extraction, named Malvery, had drubbed and
kicked the customs controller in the public street of
St. Louis, and escaped with a light sentence, to the unbounded and piteously-expressed disgust of Mr. Jeremie,
the unpopular Procurator - General.   And when the

matter was reported to the Customs Board the lawyers found fault with the collector's method of prosecuting Malvery, and the Board merely marked the paper ' Read.')

The practice of granting ' merchants' samples ' of spirits was regularized in 1836. One free sample was granted at importation. If the goods were bonded and required for sale a second free sample was granted. If they were afterwards exported a sample was allowed on delivery for shipment. Thus, if a merchant imported 100 casks, warehoused them for a few days, and then exported them, he could have 300 samples duty-free, though not a penny of duty would be paid except the 10s. per cent. on all exported goods.

During 1836 the Treasury directed the Irish Coastguard to cooperate with the ' revenue police,' a body under the control of the Board of Excise (with a view to the preventing of illicit distillation). The Excise Board issued over 100 excise commissions to officers of the Irish Coastguard.

The Treasury apprised the Board that the French ambassador in London had complained as to the seizure of certain goods at Berbice and Demerara in 1835. From an inspection of the files it appears that the collector of Berbice in 1835 was a thorough dipsomaniac, and that he was on terms of friendship with a notorious smuggler named Graimo, captain of the French schooner *L'Aurore*. Graimo had a smuggling connection in Demerara, and had managed to keep it going by the following ingenious method. He went to Surinam and loaded with Dutch gin. Of course he could not legally carry the goods into a British possession. They could only be taken thither in a Dutch ship, and direct from Holland. But Graimo carried them to Berbice, and the drunken collector allowed him to land them as though brought legally under the Navigation laws, and charged the duty (1s. a gallon). Then the goods were carried to Demerara by a colonial vessel, and landed there as from a British possession.

This breach of the Navigation laws endured until the governor of Berbice suspended the collector for being chronically intoxicated, and appointed an inquisitive deputy, who discovered the frauds. Only fifty cases of gin could be seized ; the rest had disappeared. The seized goods were forfeited, and Graimo was fined £100. In consequence of the interposition of the ambassador, the Treasury allowed the duty paid on the fifty cases of gin at Berbice to be returned, and waived the penalty of £100, apprising Lord Palmerston of their decision.

The collector of St. John's, Newfoundland, submitted a peculiar case for the Board's consideration. A British vessel from Lisbon had arrived at Newfoundland, and the captain in his report declared his crew as ' all British.' The collector found that three of the crew were foreigners, and took the Solicitor-General of Newfoundland's opinion on the matter, which was to the effect that the master was liable to a penalty of £10 for each foreigner reported as a Briton. The Customs Lawyers at London concurred, and stated that the master was also liable to a penalty of £100 for making a false report. But the Board declined to recommend proceedings.

The collector of Launceston, Tasmania, reported that part of the *Haines*, a hulk used as a place for convicts at that port, had been turned into a bonded warehouse, and that large quantities of the spirits stored there had been missed. On a search being made among the soldiers employed in guarding the hulk, many bottles of spirits were discovered, and others were found in the adjacent barracks.

The *Tres Milhas*, a Portuguese schooner with 282 slaves on board, was brought into Port Antonio, Jamaica, by H.M.S. *Racer* on June 14, 1837. Ten of the slaves had smallpox, and the whole consignment was quarantined at Navy Island. The Portuguese crew were released, and sent to Cuba. It appears from the report that the schooner was in a very leaky condition, and the slaves were packed so closely on board that they had barely room to stretch their limbs. ' The poor creatures,' wrote the collector, ' are in high spirits. It has been asserted that they were all inoculated for the smallpox previous to leaving Africa.' The Africans were released from quarantine and apprenticed on December 26, 1837, and the expense of their detention, being £1,837, was defrayed by the colony.

A meddlesome person wrote from Hobart Town to the Board, reminding them that some years back he had apprised them of extensive smuggling from Dieppe into Brighton, and stating that he had since discovered another fraud. He accused the Hobart Town merchants of buying American-taken oil, and shipping it to the United Kingdom as British-taken. He announced himself as an ex-shipowner, and forwarded the message through his son, a solicitor in Cheapside. It appeared on inquiry that the information was quite inaccurate.

On May 25, 1837, the collector of Grenada reported that H.M. brig *Harpy* had captured, off the coast of Martinique, the Portuguese schooner *Florida*, with 280 slaves. 112 of the slaves had volunteered for the 1st West India Regiment, and been sent to join that corps at Trinidad. The rest had been indentured to planters in Grenada. All the negroes had been vaccinated before landing, smallpox being rife at Grenada.

On May 24, 1837, the collector of Dominica reported the capture, by H.M.S. *Griffin*, of the Portuguese brig *Don Francisco*, with 433 slaves, all of whom were landed in good health and spirits, and apprenticed within seven days. The collector ignored the terms of the old indenture form enjoined by the Order in Council of March 16, 1808, which provided that in such cases the female slaves should not be put to field labour. That form, he pointed out, had been framed when slavery existed in the British colonies. (Why the fact that slavery had been abolished should warrant such disregard of an order which subscribed to the dignity of woman may not be evident to the reader, certainly it is not to the writers of these pages.) The *Don*

Francisco was condemned, sold to a Britisher, and granted a British register.

Cap. 92 of 1 and 2 Vict. repealed the 4½ per cent. duties. The Board communicated with the collectors of the Leeward Islands, asking what reductions might be made in the various colonial establishments on account of the discontinuance of the duties.

Cap. 113 of 1 and 2 Vict. abolished the Customs Receivers' privilege of appropriating the ' odd pence ' out of the final sixpence when duties were paid, and made droits of Admiralty liable to duty when sold. It contained a clause dealing with British marks on foreign goods, but applying only to cutlery and hardware. It freed officers of the Coastguard and Mounted Guard from turnpike tolls when on duty, and empowered the Board to render traffic between neighbouring colonies coastwise trade. The provisions of the Conventions of Commerce made in 1818 with the United States of America and Portugal were extended to all foreign countries with which treaties of commerce had been subsequently made, or might be made in times to come.

A firm of Liverpool bacon importers approached the Treasury, stating that the allowance for waste on foreign hams while warehoused under bond was insufficient. (The hams were weighed at importation, and on delivery from bond a certain deduction was made from the import weight for duty, to account for the ' waste ' that took place by drying.) The Treasury increased the allowance to 5 per cent. for the first twelve months, and 6 per cent. for any longer period.

A curious official dispute was reported to the Board from St. Kitt's. The controller charged his clerk, Mr. Charles Augustus Berkeley, with disobedience, disrespect, and an attempt to provoke a breach of the peace. Berkeley denied the charge ' totally and unequivocally.' (The customs men of the period were fond of ' fine writing.') He stated that the controller insulted him while he was ' anxiously and intently engaged in making

up the complicated quarterly accounts.' The statement
of exculpation continued : ' Casting upon me a look of
vengeance, he ' (the controller) ' said, " You are a d—d
impertinent fellow, and if you were not in a public office
I'd break your head." What reply did I make to this
abuse, this insult ? Not a word ! I felt, God knows I felt
keenly, but I governed my temper. I uttered not a reply,
but calmly continued to do the public business.' The
Board directed Berkeley to obey his superior officers, and
the controller to refrain from using intemperate language.

On November 6, 1838, four casks were landed at
St. John's, New Brunswick, the contents being entered
as ' copper spikes ' (duty-free). On being opened they
were found to contain copper tokens. (A specimen of the
tokens is annexed to the file. It is a fine copper coin,
almost the size of a penny. On one side is a head—
certainly not the queen's—and the wording, ' Pure
Copper, preferable to paper.' On the reverse side is an
allegorical figure, the date 1838, and the wording, ' Trade
and Navigation.') Inquiry elicited that the coins had
been made in Birmingham, to the order of a person living
at Strabane, Ireland, and this person had just been bailed
on a charge of uttering base coin.

The London Customs Surveyor-General and the Customs
Solicitor differed as to the legality of the importation, the
former holding that the goods were not liable to seizure, as
they did not purport to represent with any great similarity
coins then in use, but were merely intended to be used as
convenient articles of circulation. The Solicitor held that
the coins were base, though not counterfeit, and insisted
that the laws were intended to prohibit all but legal
tenders. The Bench officers in the Long Room were consulted, and they sided with the Surveyor General, holding
that the goods were ' not coins.' The Board directed
release, and when in the following year 25 hundredweight
of tokens were seized at St. John's, Newfoundland, they
made a similar order.

Lieutenant Robinson, of H.M.S. *Skipjack*, seized the

American schooner *Concord* for encroaching on the fishing limits.   The seizure note read as follows :

Cause of Forfeiture.	Goods.	Value.
At anchor off the S.W. Point of Grand Manan. For breach of treaty with H.B. Majesty and the U.S.A., having set nets to catch fish within the limits of the British territory—say, within three miles from the shore.	Quantity said to be about 30 quintals of cod, hake, and haddock (green),* caught by citizens of the U.S.A. in a vessel of that country called the *Concord*, of East Machias, burthen about 26 tons.	Fish, £25 (currency). Schooner, about £30 (currency).

(The master's name given as J. Adams ; the owners' names as J. Foster and Jabez Norton, all of Great Machias.)

After a month had elapsed from date of seizure (no word being received of appeal) the collector condemned and sold the vessel as though seized under the revenue laws (sect. 25, Cap. 89, 4 and 5 Wm. IV.).   He then submitted his proceedings for the Board's approval, stating : ' As this is the first case of the sort which has occurred at this port, we trust we have acted legally.'   The Customs Lawyers reported that the vessel was justly liable to forfeiture, and that the collector had dealt with her in the proper way.

Certain Liverpool shipping agents inquired of the Board whether a Sicilian or Neapolitan vessel, loaded or in ballast, might go from Liverpool to Newfoundland, take in a cargo of fish, and carry it to Italy or the Sicilies, also whether such a ship might go, loaded or in ballast, from England to Newfoundland, or whether she lay under any disability compared with British vessels.   The Customs Lawyer reported that she might not carry goods from England to Newfoundland, nor was he aware of any Order in Council permitting her to load there.   The Bench officers reported that no foreign ship might carry

* Uncured.

goods laden in the United Kingdom to Newfoundland, and that no Sicilian or Neapolitan ship might load there. (The prohibition of loading must have obtained because the King of the Sicilies did not grant reciprocal rights to British commerce. Otherwise the vessel might have gone from England in ballast, and loaded fish for any foreign port whatever.)

A British-American syndicate submitted a case to the collector of Jamaica, who referred it to the Board. They desired to establish a line of steamboats between New York and Kingston, and wished to know if they could obtain British registers for the ships. The collector opined that if the company were composed of Americans only the ships could only bring American produce. For instance, they could not bring goods from St. Thomas's. But part were Britishers. Could *these* have British registers for such of the ships as they owned ? No, because the profits were to be pooled with the Americans. But the Bench officers in London held that the pooling of profits would not affect the privileges of such of the ships as were *exclusively* owned by Britishers. The Board concurred.

Cap. 44 of 2 and 3 Vict. prohibited temporarily the carrying of cargo on deck by timber ships from British North America during the period from September 1 to May 1. This was on account of ' great loss of life and severe sufferings ' occasioned by reckless deck-loading. (The regulation was continued by subsequent enact-ments, and extended to ships from Honduras, and is still in existence.) Each captain on arrival in the United Kingdom was to produce a certificate from the British North American collectors of customs, to the effect that all the cargo was under hatches when the vessel left North America.

A Treasury letter of January 22, 1839, called for a report from all the collectors of the United Kingdom as to their method of enforcing the Emigration Acts. It appears that Dr. Poole, the ' inspecting physician of

emigrants' at Grosse Isle, Lower Canada, had reported
that the medical superintendence on emigrant vessels was
extremely defective. He stated that most of the persons
calling themselves surgeons of emigrant ships were un-
licensed students, or apothecaries' apprentices and shop-
men, with little professional knowledge, and that the lists
of passengers certified to by the British customs collectors
were seldom correct, which rendered it difficult to find out
the number of deaths during voyage. The passenger
accounts were falsified from two motives, the ages being
often understated so as to evade the colonial emigrant
tax, and the passenger space encroached upon by counting
adults as children.

A Liverpool merchant named Holt had entered at
various times large quantities of glass for exportation on
excise drawback, and the customs searchers of the port,
whose duty it was to examine the goods at shipment, and
ascertain whether they corresponded in quantity and
value with the statements on the specifications, had been
in the habit of passing them without examination, and in
some cases even allowing shipment before the specifications were produced. Holt had taken advantage of this
to ship ordinary rough goods not entitled to drawback,
and had thus defrauded the Excise to the extent of
£70,000. The fraud was discovered in 1839, and the
officers appear to have got off rather easily. The senior
searcher was dismissed, the others were reprimanded, and
the inspector-general and landing-surveyors of the port
were censured.

New instructions were issued as to dealing with packages
brought for foreign ministers. Any package produced by
a messenger, and declared to be a despatch-box, was to be
passed at once without search, unless the officers had suspicion, in which case they were to apprise the Board.
Packages declared to contain goods for foreign ministers
were to be put in the Queen's Warehouse, to await a
Treasury Order.

In paying to the island treasury the duties collected

under Cap. 59, 3 and 4 Wm. IV., the collector of Dominica tendered no less than £98 0s. 4d. worth of 2d. and 4d. silver pieces, which the treasurer refused to accept, but in the end the governor directed him to take the money.

The House of Assembly, Upper Canada, sent a petition to the queen, praying that the prohibition of the importation of tea from the United States of America to Canada might be removed, and that such tea might be allowed to come in on payment of a certain duty. The Customs Lawyers were accordingly directed to draft a bill to that end, the amount of duty leviable to be settled by colonial Statute. The file contains statistics of tea exported from the United Kingdom to British North America and the West Indies :

	To British North America.	To British West Indies.
	Lbs.	Lbs.
1837	1,193,987	64,330
1838	1,397,837	73,435
1839	1,722,622	59,795

The Board had directed inquiry to be made as to revenue matters at Broken Bay, New South Wales. The commander of the *Prince George* revenue cutter, stationed at Sydney, furnished a report, stating that about twenty vessels traded to the Hawkesbury, and that the population of Port Stephen was fast increasing. ' The Australian Agricultural Company hold all the land there.' He proceeded that Twofold Bay was used by vessels in the cattle trade, that Jervis Bay was used but as a place of shelter, and that there was a coasting trade between Port Macquarie and Wollongong. He had visited Western Port, but found no vessels there ; and he had not heard of any smuggling. In 1839 the collector of Sydney reported to the Board that Botany Bay had a revenue cutter to watch the large vessels that frequently put in in distress, and to check the smuggling. She had made no captures, but had been of service in recovering small vessels carried off by convicts, in saving wrecked mariners, and in communicating on Government business with various places along the coast.

A return of trade in Ceylon for the five years ending 1839 is annexed to the file, and reads as below :

	Imports (Value). £	Exports (Value). £
1835	352,076	199,267
1836	411,167	334,519
1837	541,239	326,860
1838	490,083	292,315
1839	510,664	375,608

(The principal article of export trade was cinnamon. From June 1, 1839, to May 31, 1840, 374,530 pounds cinnamon were exported.) A Customs survey of 1839 gives the following description of outports and commerce in Ceylon :

IMPORTS.	EXPORTS.
Jaffna: Paddy, rice, cloth, earthenware.	Madder, tobacco, ebony.
Manar : Paddy, rice, cloth.	Madder, dried fish, gingelly-seed.
Trincomalee : Paddy, rice, cloth.	Beeswax, gingelly-seed, ivory, ironwood.
Batticaloa : Paddy, rice, cloth, iron, brassware.	Beeswax, cocoanuts, ivory, timber.
Muletivu : Paddy, rice, cloth, earthenware.	Beeswax, cocoanuts, jaggery, bark, and timber.

Cap. 17 of 3 and 4 Vict. increased the Customs duties by 5 per cent. on all goods except spirits, corn, and flour, and the drawbacks, bounties, and allowances, in the same proportion. The duty on imported spirits was increased by 4d. a gallon. Cap. 19 removed this impost from timber, and replaced it by a string of additional specific duties. The Passenger Act was extended by Cap. 21 so as to apply to the passenger trade from the West Indies, Bahamas, and Bermuda. By Cap. 56 ships belonging to native princes or states having subsidiary treaties or being in alliance with the East India Company were admitted to the privilege of British ships within the limits of the East India Company's charter.

II.   13

The Treasury apprised the Board of a despatch from Lord Palmerston, stating that information had been received that the Carlist commander, Cabrera, had sent money to England for the purchase of 20,000 muskets. An order was therefore issued that all shipments of arms should be notified to the Treasury.

The first consignment of fish-oil from the Malabar coast arrived. The quantity was 15 butts only. It was admitted by Treasury order at the low duty (1s. a tun), and directions were issued that all subsequent consignments should be passed at the same rate if caught by his Majesty's subjects.

The first case of removal of coffee from bond for husking purposes occurred at Greenock. (This is a common practice at the present day. The goods are frequently imported in husk, and removed under bond to places where the husk is removed. They are then returned to bond, reweighed, and taken to account for duty at the new weight.)

An order was issued in November, 1840, to the effect that, the Baltic traders and whalers having returned, the Coastguard officers and collectors were to use their best endeavours to obtain able volunteers for the navy.

The Governor-General of Canada informed Lord Russell that the provisions of the Passenger Acts were still in many cases disregarded (see p. 191). He instanced two vessels which had brought emigrants from Westport. They had been seven weeks on the voyage. Provisions ran short, and for a long period the steerage passengers were in a state of semi-starvation. In another case the captain had charged extortionate prices—37s. 4d. a hundredweight for bread which cost 17s. 6d., 3d. a pound for barley which cost 1½d., ' and other things in proportion.' (These matters illustrate the spirit in which the collectors and Emigration officers approached their work, and prove that the average shipmaster is by no means the jovial, open-handed, open-hearted person that song and story have combined to make him.)

The collector of Dominica reported that on April 26, 1840 (Sunday), he went on board three vessels belonging to St. Kitts, St. Lucia, and Dominica, seized their pendants, which they were flying in contravention of Sect. 11, Cap. 13, 4 Wm. IV., and then informed the captains they were liable to a penalty of £50 each. This produced petitions from the terrified shipmasters, which the collector forwarded, with a statement that he had taken bond for the penalties, pending the Board's decision. The Board directed him to cancel the bonds, and to refer to the governor for instructions in future, before seizing pendants or flags. It is evident the penalty was one of a kind frequent in the British Statute-books—a ' bogey ' penalty—and the law on the matter one of those peculiarly British laws which shrewd men never dream of enforcing.

It appears that the colonial governors still shared in the proceeds of seizures under the revenue and Navigation laws. On June 5, 1840, the earl of Gosford applied to the Board from Park Place, St. James's, London, for his share of the Montreal seizure proceeds, due to him as governor of Lower Canada. The amount (£85 3s. 1d.) was paid to him.

During 1840 a committee of the Nova Scotian House of Assembly made certain statements to the governor. They recommended that the Nova Scotian Customs and Excise should be amalgamated, and stated that under the existing system, when goods were cleared at landing, three customs and two excise entries were required, and that when goods were warehoused four customs and three excise entries were called for, and that at some of the outports the customs and excise offices were miles apart. They urged that the collectors should be placed under local control, and the London Board's powers abolished. (It appears that in Canada and Newfoundland the customs and excise duties were collected by one staff.) The committee also stated that some of the officers appointed by the home authorities were unsatisfactory, and when the governor asked for proof the following reply was given : ' The House has considered that the statement did not require any evidence in support thereof, the same being well known to many of the members and to the public, and accordingly no evidence was taken by the committee thereon.' The papers were referred to the London Board, who merely marked them ' Read.'

The Roman Catholic vicar of Newfoundland memorialized the Board, stating that he ordered three church organs for the use of various Catholic churches in the colony, that the goods were sent out in a colonial-built ship via Hamburg, and that in consequence of the vessel's having called at Hamburg the Newfoundland customs officers charged him the duty payable upon foreign manufactured organs (£71 0s. 8d.). On inquiry in London, it was found that the master had not cleared his ship for Hamburg, also that the organs had not been entered outwards, nor had the British export duty been paid on them. Still, the Treasury authorized the Board to refund the extra amount paid in Newfoundland. The shipmaster was fined.

Fifteen years had elapsed since the Privy Council for Trade and the Customs Board had been made aware of the startling fact that, although Labrador had been included in many revenue Acts, there was not a single established customs officer on its extensive coast, yet no regular appointment was made there till 1840. True, Mr. Langley (see p. 148) had, much to his own disappointment and detriment, acted as collector for a year or two, and the sheriff who accompanied the judge on his annual visits to Labrador had occasionally attempted to act under instructions from the collector of St. John's, Newfoundland, but the results had been as vague as the systems of appointment. In 1840 the Newfoundland Legislature appointed Mr. Elias Rendall as collector of provincial customs at Labrador, and the collector of St. John's instructed him to levy the imperial duties as well. He was not particularly successful, the British

fishermen stationed there declining to pay duty, the
reason assigned being that they were not protected in
their fisheries.   Said one of the fishing agents : ' The
Americans who swarm on the coast visit most of these
harbours and creeks with goods for sale.   Were it possible
to enforce a general payment, the British resident would
not seek any immunity.'

To show how cautiously the warehousing privileges
were extended to ports, we give a summary of the proceedings on the memorial of William Burge, of Falmouth,
Jamaica.   He informed the Board that the trade of the
port in 1838 had been as below :

Tonnage of vessels inward	..	.. 11,457
Tonnage of vessels outward	..	.. 11,688
Customs collected	..	.. £1,764 11s. 2d.

He stated that the Jamaica Assembly had passed a
resolution declaring it expedient to establish a bonded
warehouse at the port of Falmouth, and that he was prepared to provide such a warehouse, if an Order in Council
could be obtained sanctioning the proceeding.   The
requisite order was issued on March 1, 1840, and the
warehouse was opened on October 1.

The amount of customs duties collected in Jamaica for
the quarter ending April 5, 1840, shows that trade was
increasing fast.

	£	s.	d.	
Kingston and Old Harbour ..	.. 18,182	13	8	(sterling).
Port Morant	.. 856	15	11	,,
Port Antonio	.. 146	8	2	,,
Port Maria and Annatto Bay	.. 663	14	9	,,
Montego Bay and Lucea	.. 4,004	14	11	,,
Savannah-la-Mar and Black River	.. 1,645	6	4	,,
Falmouth, Rio Bueno, and St. Anne's Bay	.. 3,626	17	10	,,
	29,126	11	7	,,

It appears that Newcastle, N.S.W., had experienced
peculiar vicissitudes.   In 1834 a petition, signed by sixty-
nine merchants, had been sent to the governor of N.S.W.,
asking that the customs officer at Newcastle might be

allowed to enter and clear vessels. The petition stated that three ships had been laden with wool at Newcastle recently, and that there was a considerable export trade in maize, tobacco, coal, butter, and cheese to Tasmania. The governor allowed the privilege requested. (Previously vessels discharging and loading at Newcastle had been entered and cleared at the head port, Sydney, and all duties had been paid there as well.) The Sydney collector apprised the Board of the governor's action, stating that Hunter's River was the most productive part of the colony, especially with regard to wool, and that the trade of Newcastle was increasing with great rapidity. In 1838 he reported that during the last quarter of 1837 seventy-one vessels, tonnage varying from 14 to 344, had cleared out from Newcastle, the cargoes being maize, coal, sheep, hides, tallow, and wool, but the imports were trifling, as follows :

Spirits : 3 cases, 17 casks.	Sugar : 1 ton, 16 mats.
Tea : 28 packages.	Porter : 1 barrel.
Beef : 40 barrels.	Timber : 38 loads.
Wine : 1 cask.	Flour : 72 bags.

The value of the wool shipped from Newcastle to the United Kingdom in 1837 was £20,000. Soon afterwards the port began to go down. In 1840 the landing-waiter was removed to Sydney, the exportation of wool to the United Kingdom having ceased, and a tide waiter only remained at the port, to look after the coasting trade.

The collector of Colombo reported to the Board that an article had appeared in the *Bombay Courier*, commenting upon a growing practice of ' sailing vessels under more than one flag.' The collector supported this by quoting the case of the *General Wood*, a ship which had been sailing under various flags and names ever since she was built in 1816. He also stated that the provisions of the Navigation Acts were rarely observed in the East India ports. But it appeared upon investigation that there was no law prohibiting a *British* ship from trading under false colours, or with false papers.

The inspector of Waterguard at Liverpool informed the
Board that several of his officers had become Socialists,
and proceeded to comment upon the matter in the high-
flown language so often used by the higher officials whenever they dealt with matters outside the scope of ordinary
routine. ' I have read,' he stated, ' several Socialist
publications. The doctrines they contain are as blas-
phemous as they are inimical to the constitution of
this country. They tend to equalize all classes of society,
and to deny all authority from superiors. These dangerous
principles partake of neither religion nor morality. They
have substituted a new and specious system of their
own, a system contrary in spirit to the queen's
proclamation against vice and immorality, contrary in
spirit to the Treasury Minute of March 18, 1836, which
goes to inculcate good order in Society. This delusion is
daily increasing in these parts, and I have felt it my duty
to bring it forward. I cannot but look upon this as a
most serious matter, for I must doubt the trustworthiness
of that officer who denies in principle any control but
his own will. Can his oath be depended upon ?' The
collector, controller, and inspector-general of Liverpool
furnished supplementary statements, couched in language
equally turgid and ambiguous. They agreed with
Mr. Walker that Socialism was ' likely to be attended
with the most baneful and pernicious consequences to the
community at large, and to man in his social state.'

Now, the Minute quoted by Mr. Walker as inculcating
' good order in Society ' had been issued in consequence
of an address to the king by the Commons in 1836, praying
the discouragement of all *political* associations that held
communication by means of secret signs and symbols, or
excluded people of a different religion, and had been
levelled particularly against Orange Lodges. Yet the
Board thought it applicable to the Socialists, and in their
covering report to the Treasury they expressed a deadly
determination to carry it out. But the Treasury held
that the Minute was inapplicable. Yet they desired the

Board to communicate the following message to the Liverpool iconoclasts : ' My Lords learn with the sincerest regret that any officers in H.M. Service have connected themselves with a Society so subversive of morality and religion.'

The first consignment of guano from the Pacific arrived in 1841. The Treasury waived the duty of 5 per cent. *ad valorem* to which the guano would ordinarily have been liable as ' unenumerated goods,' and rated it at 5s. per ton only. Later they allowed preserved turtle to enter duty-free—a privilege which live turtle had always enjoyed. A later Minute announced that the queen, by letters patent under the Great Seal, had been pleased to ' erect ' the islands of New Zealand into a separate and distinct colony. Another directed that Mr. Gray, customs controller at Aberdeen, should be censured for inducing the provost and chief magistrate of that substantial town to apply to the Treasury, praying that Mr. Gray might be appointed to the vacant collectorship.

Although in 1841 the Customs establishment at Port Adelaide was not under the control of the Board, but appointed solely by the governor, the collector managed to gain what may with fairness be called unenviable distinction. On June 29 the French-built vessel *Ville de Bordeaux* anchored in Glenelg Roads. The captain reported her as from St. George's Sound to Tasmania, he being commissioned to buy stock at the latter colony for transport to West Australia, and stated that he had put into Port Adelaide because he had reason to think stock could be procured there more readily. He ordered a number of sheep, and entered his vessel for Bourbon. The officious customs clerk who took his entry thought fit to tell the collector that he had observed that the captain was uneasy while making it, so the collector examined the ship's register and log, made certain inquiries, took it upon himself to detain the vessel under suspicion of contemplated infringement of the Navigation laws, and then apprised the governor, explaining the causes of detention. He stated that the vessel had previously been taken to Sydney in a leaky condition, and that her owners, a French firm located at Bordeaux, made a pretended sale of her at Sydney to one Joubert, a Frenchman, who had been naturalized there as a Britisher. The transfer had not been properly endorsed on the register. She was manned at Sydney by a mixed crew of Englishmen and Frenchmen, and provided with an English captain, and the new captain's name had not been put on the document. And there was an entry in the log which showed that she had previously made an illegal voyage from Lombock (a French settlement) to West Australia. (It is apparent, however, that she had been furnished at Sydney with a register *de novo*, although the document had not been properly completed.)

When the sheep were brought to the quay the man in charge refused to disclose their destination. The collector became still more suspicious, and declared the ship seized. He sent the tide-surveyor to put a tidesman on board, and the captain threatened to pistol the tide-surveyor, but that official got on board with his tidesman, and then the captain put to sea. It appears that the English portion of the crew had not been well treated, and they at once volunteered to overpower the Frenchmen and seize the ship, if the tide-surveyor would order them to do so. That gentleman, however, was not prepared to take the risk just then. According to his subsequent report, the captain went below, destroyed the incriminating entry in the ship's log, and substituted a fresh statement. Then he navigated the vessel off and on, threatening to shoot the officers if they did not consent to leave her. In the end the English sailors rushed aft, overpowered the captain, and took the ship back to the roads. There she remained, and the intending exporter of the sheep sold his flock by auction, getting a poor price, but the collector insisted that this was but a dodge to incense the public against the Customs. If it were, it succeeded, for the public took sides with the captain, and the local press assailed the collector with much vituperation. Mr. Joubert claimed the vessel, and the judge of the Supreme Court allowed his claim, on condition that he gave security for the expenses incurred. The governor of South Australia transmitted an account of the proceedings to the Secretary of State for the colonies, who referred it to the Treasury. It was sent to the Board, and their report on it was singularly perspicuous. Below is a summary :

'The matter should not have been thus referred. South Australia at present a chartered, not a Crown, colony, and the Board have no supervision. Still—

'1. The collector for South Australia not legally empowered to carry out either the Navigation or the Ships' Registry laws.

2. 'Even if thus empowered, has done wrong. *Ville de Bordeaux* arrived *in ballast,* so, even if French, had right to enter port. She cleared out for Bourbon, a French settlement. Collector's statement that she is really for West Australia merely the result of hearsay.

'3. Collector's statement that she has made a previous voyage from a French settlement to West Australia cannot be proved. No Customs in West Australia to prove it.

'4. Collector claims power to condemn vessel and cargo, they not having been claimed by the appellant Joubert within prescribed period. But Joubert's neglect does not enable collector to do an unjust thing, and does not deprive Joubert of power to claim indemnity on an equitable plea.'

The Treasury Minute on this report must have startled the collector. It directed the governor to restore the vessel at once. If sold, her proceeds were to be given to the owners, without any deduction for expenses. If sold, and governor not satisfied as to *bona fides* of claimant, the proceeds were to be sent to the Treasury, and that department would deal with the matter of claim. The collector was censured, and admonished not to deal on his own responsibility with such matters in future, and that the law providing for summary sale of unclaimed seized vessels was intended to prevent unnecessary legal expenses, not to shield unauthorized seizers. The Minute proceeded thus : ' The collector has incurred great personal responsibility by the course which he has pursued, and his want of caution in the transaction may prove the source of much embarrassment to himself and to the colony.'

Undoubtedly the collector had strained matters. (It should be mentioned that when he saw the vessel leave the roads with the customs officers on board he actually seized the bleating innocents that were waiting shipment on the quay, and did not restore them till the vessel was brought back, also, that the value of the *Ville de Bordeaux* was estimated at between £8,000 and £10,000, and that, had he secured her forfeiture, he would have pocketed a very pretty sum.)*

The account of the customs survey of the port of Launceston, Tasmania, in 1841, is rather informative. The customs duties collected during 1840 were £33,727. The tonnage inwards was as follows : ships from the United

* The marginal comments pencilled on the reports by Mr. Dean, the Customs Chairman, are amusing. One of them is worded thus : ' The affair seems to partake of a little robbery, a little piracy, and a little buccaneering ' (the difference between buccaneering and piracy he did not explain). ' With the exception of carrying goods from Lombock to West Australia, I can discover no grounds for seizure under the Customs laws. Even on this point you have only the log to help you, and the log would appear to be altogether a fiction. The French Government may demand restitution of the British Government.'

The bad phrasing may be overlooked. Mr. Dean was a remarkable man, extremely clever and industrious, yet eccentric—witness his habit of jotting down little explosive comments on the papers he dealt with. Some of the comments are intensely amusing. For instance, when, in conducting an inquiry, he listened to the statements of an incoherent and unwilling witness, he remarked in pencil : ' What a —— fool this fellow is !'

On another occasion, when reading a verbose statement penned by a Scottish officer who was desirous of initiating a scheme of ' official reform,' and obtaining thereby an increase of his own salary, the observant Dean ornamented the margin of each paragraph with a pencilled ' Hum-m !' till he reached the one that suggested profit to the applicant ; then Dean wrote, ' Aha, I thought we should come to this !' and straightway damned the whole scheme.

Kingdom, 4,379 tons ; colonial ships, 29,839 ; foreign, 547. Outward ships for the United Kingdom, 3,521 tons ; colonial, 33,275 ; foreign, 1,136. Value of imports, £303,140 ; exports, £452,870. In the bonded warehouse were 91,152 gallons spirits ; 208,398 pounds tobacco ; 4,589 pounds cigars, and 66 casks wine. The staple articles of export were bark, flour, hay, potatoes, whale-oil, bones, cattle, horses, wool (6,161 bales), and sheep (78,028). The surveying collector thought the smuggling was decreasing, the settlers being afraid of the convicts, who gave information whenever they witnessed a run, ' that being the surest way to obtain a ticket of leave.'

Sir William Colebrooke approached the Treasury with a scheme for altering the bonding system in the Leeward Islands. He suggested that importers should be given six months' credit for duties on their goods, to date from the period of entering the goods for home use. Sir William opined that this method would assist traders, and lower the price of commodities. The scheme was referred to the Customs Board, and they reported on it with considerable freedom, pointing out that there were many free warehousing ports in the West Indies at which importers might bond their goods duty-free till required for home use—or bond them for exportation. They hinted that Sir William's propositions were not so clearly worded as they might be. ' Nevertheless, we gather from his communication that he proposes to deliver goods at once into the hands of the importer, without payment of duty, merely taking security for the payment of the same within a stated period.' They proceeded to pooh-pooh the whole suggestion.*

A dispute arose in New Brunswick on the matter of goods for the fisheries. Articles such as biscuit, meat,

* It is evident that Sir William desired to save importers the expense of warehouse rent. Before the system of bonding in warehouse was introduced into Great Britain, the method suggested by Sir William had been in general use, and most of the duties were thus bonded. If an importer paid at importation, he was granted discount.

cordage, hooks, lines, nets, anchors, for use by the fishers, were allowed to be imported duty-free, or warehoused if necessary, and afterwards cleared duty-free. Certain merchants of New Brunswick complained to the Board that in some instances the collector had refused to deliver, duty-free, molasses and sugar warehoused for the fisheries. They had accordingly paid the duty under protest. The collector justified himself by stating that he had charged duty in the cases mentioned because the merchants had failed to furnish satisfactory proof that the goods would be used by the fishermen. He had reason to believe that in the past large quantities of goods had been cleared duty-free for fishery use, and afterwards consumed by the general public. The Board endorsed his action.

Cap. 3, 5 and 6 Vict., Sect. 2, settled a curious point. The lieutenant-governor of Tasmania had by proclamation of February 4, 1829, imposed certain rates of customs in the colony, and an excise on distilled spirits. He derived the authority to do this from Cap. 114, 59 Geo. III., and Cap. 96, 3 Geo. IV. Cap. 83, 9 Geo. IV., made the last-quoted Act perpetual, but provided that, as New South Wales and Tasmania had become separate colonies, the *two* governors should henceforth administer affairs *with the advice of their respective Legislative Councils*. On January 2, 1834, the Tasmanian Council had confirmed the governor's proclamation of 1829. Soon there arose doubts as to whether the duties taken between 1829 and 1834 had been legally collected. In 1842 the matter was adjusted by the Act quoted at the beginning of this paragraph, announcing that the proclamation was legally binding, and indemnifying all concerned in the collection of the disputed duties.

The Anti-Corn-Law League, formed in Manchester in 1838, had become extremely powerful. There had grown up at the same time a disturbing factor of a far different type—Chartism. It does not appear that there was ever any great sympathy between the leaders of the two movements. Such men as Cobden and Bright could scarcely be expected to run in harness with Ernest Jones and Feargus O'Connor. The men of the Manchester school were essentially opportunistic and 'utilitarian.' They had noted the effect of many years of past legislation —legislation directed principally towards the benefit of 'the landed interest.' Legislation performed in the interests of rent had starved the weavers and spinners. They believed that they could bring about a new Britain— a Britain of cotton lords and wizened operatives, cheap bread and dear exports. Britain was to become one gigantic workshop, and to distribute for ever her bales of prints and her cases of machinery to an admiring and un-emulative world. (The universal contempt of agriculture displayed in the legislation and literature of the sixties, seventies, and eighties of the nineteenth century was entirely due to the teaching of the Manchester school.)

Yet it must be admitted that something had to be done. The people could be starved no longer. It must be admitted, also, that the thing could not have been *safely* done by any but the Manchester politicians. The temper of the modern British is extremely peculiar ; there must be some element of what is called 'practicality' in a movement ere they can be brought to bestow abiding sympathy upon it. Widespread Industrialism—the de-votion of masses of people to the production of mean things for everyday use—is responsible for this new phase of the national temper, under which no risks must be taken, but every revolution must have its register and ledger, its dreary diary and misleading statistics. 'We will make work plentiful and bread cheap,' said the Manchester men ; and the tame cry captured the lower classes, who were not aware that under rigid Protection their ancestors had cheap bread (and something with it) for centuries and centuries.

The Chartists were altogether different. Such men as Shelley and Byron, men whose names will be honoured when those of Cobden and Bright have been relegated to the list of doctrinaires, would have thrown themselves heart and soul into the Chartist movement—a movement which conveyed promise to the souls of all who refused to have their mouths stopped with cheap bread, and their aspirations limited by a twelve-hour day and the white-washed walls of a factory.   One must study the poets of the two systems to achieve suitable comparison.   Most of Ebenezer Elliot's verse reminds one of the yelping of a hungry dog, but there is true vehemence, there is a touch of the old elemental fire of revolt, in, ' We're low, we're low, we're very, very low.'

After this little outburst, which may refresh if it fails to convince readers, we proceed to state that though Chartism and Cobdenism marched toward widely diver-gent goals, their potentialities in disturbance combined to influence the thoughts of the great Conservative statesman of the day, and the result was Cap. 14, 5 and 6 Vict., under which the corn duties were lowered consider-ably.   Below is a comparison :

WHEAT FROM FOREIGN COUNTRIES.

	Previous Duties.			New Duties.		
	£	s.	d.	£	s.	d.
When price of British wheat under 51s. a quarter	A sliding scale of duties, rising from £1 16s. 8d. when the price was 50s. and less than 51s., to £2 8s. 8d. if the price went under 39s.			1	0	0
Do., 51s. and under 52s.	1	15	8	0	19	0
Do., 52s. and under 53s.	1	14	8			
Do., 53s. and under 54s.	1	13	8	0	18	0
Do., 54s. and under 55s.	1	12	8			
Do., 55s. and under 56s.	1	11	8	0	17	0
Do., 56s. and under 57s.	1	10	8	0	16	0
Do., 57s. and under 58s.	1	9	8	0	15	0
Do., 58s. and under 59s.	1	8	8	0	14	0
Do., 59s. and under 60s.	1	7	8	0	13	0
Do., 60s. and under 61s.	1	6	8	0	12	0
Do., 61s. and under 62s.	1	5	8	0	11	0
Do., 62s. and under 63s.	1	4	8	0	10	0
Do., 63s. and under 64s.	1	3	8	0	9	0
Do., 64s. and under 65s.	1	2	8	0	8	0
Do., 65s. and under 66s.	1	1	8	0	7	0

WHEAT FROM FOREIGN COUNTRIES (*continued*).

	Previous Duties.			New Duties.		
	£	s.	d.	£	s.	d.
When price of British wheat 66s. and under 67s.	1	0	8 ⎤			
Do., 67s. and under 68s.	0	18	8 ⎬	0	6	0
Do., 68s. and under 69s.	0	16	8 ⎦			
Do., 69s. and under 70s.	0	13	8	0	5	0
Do., 70s. and under 71s.	0	10	8	0	4	0
Do., 71s. and under 72s.	0	6	8	0	3	0
Do., 72s. and under 73s.	0	2	8	0	2	0
Do., 73s. and upwards	0	1	0	0	1	0

WHEAT FROM BRITISH POSSESSIONS OUT OF EUROPE.

Previous Duties.			New Duties.		
	s.	d.		s.	d.
When price of British wheat under 67s. a quarter	5	0	Under 55s. ..	5	0
			55s. and under 56s. ..	4	0
			56s. and under 57s. ..	3	0
When price 67s. or more	0	6	57s. and under 58s. ..	2	0
			58s. and upwards ..	1	0

(Proportional rates for other kinds of corn.)

The prohibitions of colonial and foreign malt, and of all foreign and colonial ground corn except wheat meal, wheat flour, and oatmeal, survived.

This important measure was followed by a new copyright Act (Cap. 45, 5 and 6 Vict.). It repealed the copyright Act, Cap. 19, 8 Anne, and the Acts amending it (Cap. 107, 41 Geo. III., and Cap. 156, 54 Geo. III.). The new Act provided as below :

1. The word 'book' to signify every volume or part, pamphlet, sheet of letterpress or music, chart, or plan, separately produced ; the words 'dramatic piece' every play or scenic, musical, or dramatic entertainment ; the word 'copyright' exclusive right of printing and multiplying copies of the above ; the words 'personal representative' every person entitled to rights of administration ; the word 'assigns' every person in whom the author's copyright interest might be vested ; the words 'British Dominions' the United Kingdom, Channel Islands, and all other possessions of the Crown.

2. Copyright to endure for author's life and seven years

longer, or till forty-two years after first publication (if last term the longer). If published posthumously, to endure for forty-two years.

3. If after author's death his assign refused to republish, the Privy Council might license any complainant to publish.

4. The usual free copies to be delivered to certain institutions.

5. Copyright might be registered at Stationers' Hall.

6. Actions for piracy to be in the Court of Record, in that part of the dominions in which the offence was committed.

7. Importation of pirated works to be punishable by forfeiture, and fine of £10 and double value of goods. Pirated books might be seized by Customs or Excise.

8. The Act to apply to musical compositions.

9. Seized pirated books to become property of holder of copyright.

10. Registration of copyright necessary before action taken, but copyright to exist even if unregistered.

Such were the main provisions of the new Act. Whether it or any Statute moulded on similar lines could be held just to authors may be worth a few moments thought. The Copyright Acts were the first British Socialistic laws, for they decreed that literary work should not be assignable beyond a certain period. Then it was to become public property. It is curious that literature—the poorest-paid work performed by man—should be treated thus.

Cap. 47, 5 and 6 Vict., amended the Customs laws. It repealed the long-existing prohibition of importation of foreign cattle, sheep, swine, beef, pork, mutton, and lamb, of fish imported in foreign vessels, and of fish of foreign taking. (But in the last case the fish—with certain exceptions—had to be brought from a foreign port ; it might not come direct from the fishing-ground.) It repealed the stipulation for a separate manifest for imported tobacco, and declared bonds entered into by merchants with the Treasury or Customs valid in law.   It re-amended the Copyright laws, by enacting *complete* prohibition of books produced in the United Kingdom and reproduced abroad (but the copyright-holder was to apprise the Customs of his rights before such prohibition could be enforced).   It abolished the exemption of coastguardsmen and revenue patrolmen from tolls, and gave the Treasury power of amending duties towards reciprocity.   It provided for the assaying of gold and silver plate imported for sale.   It repealed the previous duties and drawbacks, and granted a new scale, by which the dutiable goods, which had previously been arranged alphabetically, were assorted under nineteen headings for imports and one for exports.   The duties were still in many cases preferential with regard to British possessions.   The duties on tea, tobacco, silks, and spirits, were still tremendously high.   The only export duties were on coal, clay, china stone, cement stone, flint, wool, and skins.

The Act was scarcely passed when it was amended by Cap. 56.   Certain new duties on timber were postponed for a year ; the meaning of ' parts,' applicable to regulating the duties on copper ore, was explained to be ' parts of a hundred ' ; the statement that goods of the Channel Islands were to be deemed foreign was qualified so as to read ' goods produced in the Channel Islands from foreign materials '; a misleading parenthesis was corrected ; specimens illustrative of natural history were included in the list of ' exemptions from duty '; the law as to assaying foreign plate was relaxed so as to admit antique plate free of assay ; the export duty on cement stone was repealed, and certain new regulations as to delivery of bonded goods were deferred.   These might be called a tolerably large bunch of alterations, and there can be no doubt that they were the result of protests from merchants, which proves that the mind of the high revenue official is not always clear.

The time-honoured Excise survey of tobacco manufacture had been discontinued under an Act of 3 and 4 Vict. The result had been wholesale adulteration, sometimes to the extent of 70 per cent. The Excise control was renewed by Cap. 93, 5 and 6 Vict., and many stringent regulations were reimposed.

Considerable misapprehension had arisen in some of the colonies as to duties leviable under the Act 59, 3 and 4 Wm. IV. There had been in that Act a clause stating that whenever any goods chargeable with duty under its provisions were also chargeable under colonial laws, the duties mentioned in the Act were not to apply except they *exceeded* the duties leviable under the colonial laws, and then only to the amount of such excess. In some of the colonies the local duties had exceeded those under the Act 59, 3 and 4 Wm. IV., yet the colonial legislators had insisted on full collection. Cap 49, 5 and 6 Vict., accordingly, made all such proceedings in the past legal, and imposed a new scale of duties. (The complications in the colonies over the collection of revenue were indeed extraordinary. To them, and to the greed and arrogance of some of the imperial collectors, was due the approach of the abolition of the home control.)

During 1842 the Roman Catholic Bishop of Montreal applied for remission of duty on vestments, etc., imported for religious purposes, and the collector of Montreal, in reporting to the Board on the matter, stated that he did not think the privilege should be granted, as he had reason to believe that if it were similar applications would at once be made by the priests of the seminary of St. Sulpice, Montreal. The Board reported to the Treasury that indulgences of the kind were occasionally extended to indigent priests, but that in this case the applicant was surrounded by an opulent clergy.*

* An application had been made in 1839 by the Catholic clergy of Trinidad, who alleged that similar privileges had been granted to the Catholics of that island ever since 1797. The Board recommended the remission, although the collector's valuation of the articles differed materially from that furnished by the clergy on their entry. For instance, they had valued ten fine Italian

On August 3, 1842, the officers at Halifax, Nova Scotia, seized a number of copies of the *New World*, a New York publication. A copy is appended to the file. It is a curio, being merely a complete reproduction of a novel by Lady Blessington, entitled ' The Lottery of Life.' The motto of the paper is, ' No pent-up Utica contracts our powers, for the whole boundless universe is ours '—a motto distinctively American, and highly expressive of the American publishing methods of that day. The collector stated : ' The importation of this and similar reprints is considerable, and occasions much dissatisfaction to the booksellers of this port, as it greatly interferes with the sale of the English books which are imported from the United Kingdom.'

No doubt the New York publisher had gauged the literary tastes of the Nova Scotians. Their character may be best displayed by a reproduction of the opening and conclusion of Lady Blessington's novel, which contains all of ' The Lottery of Life ' that we have found ourselves able to read.

Opening : ' Born of humble but honest parents, I was so fortunate as to attract the notice of Abraham Mortimer, a retired banker.'

Conclusion : ' A letter despatched a few days after to her dear friend, Lady Frances Lorimer, in answer to one from that young lady announcing her approaching nuptials, contained such excellent advice on the danger of young wives exacting attentions only paid during the days of courtship, that it had the best effect on that lady.

---

devotional paintings at £8 the lot. Still, the collector let them pass duty-free on receipt of the Treasury order to that effect, remarking that he preferred doing that to arguing with the Bishop. Soon the clergy imported other articles, and claimed them duty-free, and the governor sanctioned delivery, relying upon the previous Treasury Order. When the Board heard of this, they surcharged the unfortunate collector with the amount payable. In 1844 the priests imported various church ornaments and two casks of wine, but, needless to state, had to pay duty. (The Catholic clergy of the Mauritius claimed remission in 1845, but were refused.)

This judicious counsel considerably lowered the exaggerated and romantic expectations she had previously indulged of the unbroken felicity of wedded lovers, and saved the husband of Lady Frances from the scenes of domestic chagrin that had clouded the conjugal happiness of Lord Henry and Lady Emily Fitzhardinge, during their first entrance as a wedded pair into fashionable life in London.'

It appears from the advertisement list of the *New World* that the other books most in demand, and therefore diligently pirated, were ' Morley Ernstein,' ' Zanoni,' ' The Jacquerie,' ' Summer and Winter in the Pyrenees,' and ' The United Irishmen.'

The traders of St. Kitts and Nevis had petitioned at various periods between 1828 and 1842 that the Customs establishments of those islands should be consolidated, and all traffic between them deemed ' coastwise ' trade. The Board had replied that though they were empowered to regulate coastwise traffic in the colonies, their powers did not extend to making intercolonial into coastwise trade, and had pointed out that the customs duties in the respective islands were paid in to separate colonial treasuries. But in 1842 they departed from this decision, and allowed the privilege requested, so far as regarded vessels owned in the two islands.

The sub-collector of Wellington, New Zealand, reported as to the lack of protection of British and colonial trade in his district. He stated that American fishing vessels frequently came close to the shores of Stewart's Island, and traded in contraband with the settlers and natives ; also that a colonial schooner brought a cargo of tobacco (duty-paid), and it was found impossible to sell the goods, the Americans having supplied all requirements. He was of opinion that a revenue cruiser should be stationed at Cloudy Bay. The Board merely inscribed the damning word ' Read ' on this important epistle.

On July 4, 1842, the governor of Ceylon, in his address to the Council, stated the total revenue for 1841 as £344,463, and announced a deficit of £16,870, which had to be paid out of the balance previously remaining in the public chest.

Cap. 29, 6 and 7 Vict., referred to an Act passed in 1842 by the Legislature of Canada, imposing a duty of 3s. a quarter on all wheat imported into Canada, except from the United Kingdom. It appears this Act had been passed with the view that the United Kingdom should act reciprocally by lowering the duties on Canadian wheat. They were accordingly, by Cap. 29, reduced to 1s. a quarter. Cap. 79 affirmed certain provisions, made by a Convention, regulating the fisheries between Great Britain and France. It enjoined that the French might not fish in the waters between France and the British Islands, except at a distance exceeding three miles from low-water mark. The Board of Trade might draw up by-laws applicable to the fisheries. The British revenue officers were authorized to examine the registry certificates and tackle of British fishing vessels, and to execute warrants granted by justices of the peace on account of infringements. Proceedings against French fishers for offences committed whilst encroaching were to be dealt with by the magistrates of the adjoining counties. Offences committed by the French outside the limits were to be deposed to before the magistrates, and the depositions sent to the British consul at the offender's place of residence. Cap. 84 amended the Customs laws. There had been much fraud, especially in the Port of London, by entering high-duty goods ' on sight,' carrying them away unexamined, and producing for examination low-duty goods made up in similar packages. It was provided under this Act that all ' sight entries ' were to be accompanied by a declaration from the importer as to the amount of duty reasonably likely to be due, and that amount was to be deposited before the goods were examined. If on examination it was found that more duty was due, the balance was to be paid before any of the packages were delivered. It was also provided that colonial vessels might deliver in the United Kingdom oil, blubber, etc., of British or colonial taking, at the low rates of duty, as was allowed with British vessels, and that the queen, by Order in Council, might from time to time define the reciprocal export privileges granted to certain foreign States, and specify the colonial ports at which goods might be warehoused for exportation. The Act concluded by repealing the prohibition of exportation of many kinds of machinery. (This last proviso was no doubt incited by two circumstances : 1, The rapid spread of Free Trade principles ; 2, a recent astounding revelation of Customs connivance at evasion of the prohibiting laws. See pp, 261-269.)

On March 21, 1843, lists of copyright works were for the first time sent to the various ports. Only books advised to the Customs by the copyright-holders were included in the lists.

A Treasury Minute of July 25, 1843, stated that certain revenue officers in Ireland had joined Repeal Associations, and warned them to abjure membership at once, on pain of dismissal.

By an Act of 6 Vict. the Legislature of New South Wales had allowed goods of Tasmania and New Zealand to enter New South Wales free of duty. (All Acts passed by this Legislature had to be submitted to one of the imperial Secretaries of State, it being provided by a Statute of 9 Geo. IV. that the king should thus have an opportunity of signifying his approbation or disapproval.) On August 31, 1843, Lord Stanley apprised the governor of New South Wales that the recent Act was disallowed. ' The principle,' he stated, ' of establishing differential duties in favour of particular colonies is so objectionable that Her Majesty's Government cannot consent to any further extension or recognition of such a system. If allowed, it would inevitably give rise to retaliating measures on the part of other colonies, and a system of protection and preferences would gradually be established among the several colonial dependencies of the Empire, by which the operation of commerce would be embarrassed.'

On becoming aware of the nature of this despatch, the Sydney collector took it upon himself to impose the *ad valorem* duty of 5 per cent. on Tasmanian grain imported into Melbourne. (It had been duty-free under *previous* colonial Acts. The Acts had not been clearly worded, and the collector took advantage of their ambiguity.) Both governor and Board supported his action, the latter recommending that the levy should be continued, and the importers be left to take legal action for recovery of the duties if they felt disposed.

An extraordinary squabble amongst customs officers was reported from Kingston, Jamaica. It appears that the trouble started in the Custom-house, several of the participants (Messrs. Elliott, Evans, Davis, and Morphy) coming to blows. The collector admonished the parties concerned, but did not apprise the Board. On June 12, 1843, Davis and Morphy were at a club in Kingston, when Elliott and Evans entered. Elliott observed in staccato tones to his friend, ' Who introduced these blackguards here ? Who brought the —— snobs into this place ?' Morphy at once struck him with a cane, and a mêlée ensued, all four using their sticks freely, Elliott shouting, as he belaboured Morphy, ' You —— scoundrel ! I'll knock out your brains !' and then, as he bestowed similar favours on Davis, who was a mulatto, ' You brute beast, you woolly-headed scoundrel, I can find no brains to knock out in you !' Davis replied, whilst defending himself, to the effect that Elliott's mother had been a camp-follower, and that Elliott's position in the Service was the result of Elliott's sister's good looks and extreme complaisance. Several members of the club intervened, and parted the enraged officials.

Later in the evening Elliott and Evans, armed with stout canes, placed themselves in ambush on the Parade. Perhaps the wine of the island had obscured their faculties, for they fell upon an inoffensive stranger, and gave him an unmerciful drubbing. On discovering their mistake,

they begged a thousand pardons, and explained that the
drubbing was intended for Morphy.

This quarrel, at first exemplified in wood, was soon
transferred to paper, Elliott reporting Davis to the Board
for casting aspersions upon the female branch of the
Elliott family. The Board directed the collector to
censure all concerned.*

During 1843 a person signing himself ' William Large,
gentleman, Warren's Place, Cork,' wrote the Board,
asking for compensation for certain services which he
claimed to have performed as waiter and searcher in
Surinam in 1801-02, during the time the place was a
British possession. The Customs Solicitor dismissed the
claim, stating that all papers connected with Surinam
had been lost in the fire that destroyed the London
Custom-house in 1814. The Roman Catholic Bishop of
Cape Town memorialized the Board, praying that certain
materials for church-building, etc., might be admitted to
the colony duty-free. The list specified the following
goods :

7,312 feet timber.	2,000 feet window-glass.	100,000 bricks.
1,200 slates.		Certain altar-pieces.
6½ tons sheet-lead.	170 gallons oil and turpentine.	Certain pictures.
1,860 pounds nails.		Certain statues.
8,000 pounds iron bolts, etc.	1,250 pounds paint.	Certain bells.
	3,000 pounds cement.	An organ.

All the above were for a church at Cape Town, and there
was another list for a church at Grahamstown. The
memorial stated that indulgences had been extended to
certain Protestant churches, both Dutch and British-
colonial. The collector admitted that the governor had
remitted certain duties in the past, but reminded the
Board that they had pronounced against any subsequent
indulgence of the kind. The application was rejected.

The International Copyright Act of 1 and 2 Vict.
(amended by Cap. 45, 5 and 6 Vict., see p. 208) was re-

* Undoubtedly the Board made allowance for temperature,
and the potency of the cooling drinks used so freely in the West
Indies at that time.

pealed, and Cap. 12 of 7 and 8 Vict. provided that works
first published abroad might enjoy the privilege of copyright, provided that an Order in Council specified that
the copyright privilege should be extended, and on condition that the works were produced in the particular
foreign country specified. If published in one foreign
country and produced in another, they were to be prohibited from importation into the British dominions,
unless the proprietors of the copyright sanctioned such
importation. All such privileges were to be reciprocal.
Cap. 66 removed many of the restrictions upon aliens. It
provided that any person born of a British mother should
be capable of holding real or personal estate, that subjects
of a friendly State might hold lands, etc., in residence for
a term not exceeding twenty-one years, that aliens might
become naturalized, and that naturalization should
attach to any woman who married a British subject.

Cap. 43, 7 and 8 Vict., amended the Customs laws relating to the Isle of Man. Trade from the United Kingdom to that island, and *vice versa*, was no longer to be
deemed foreign. All ships thus employed were to be held
coasting ships, yet specific Manx duties were payable on
certain goods. Some of these goods might still only be
imported from Great Britain, and these were liable to the
restrictions applying to foreign goods.

The Board issued instructions to collectors as to carrying out the provisions of Cap. 79, 6 and 7 Vict. (see p. 214).
All British fishing-boats were to be numbered in series
according to the customs districts to which they belonged,
and were to be marked with the initial letters of their
respective districts. All derelict fishing-gear, etc., was
to be delivered to the Customs, and the collectors were
empowered to restore such goods to their owners, and to
award the finders salvage.

Incredible though it may seem, up to 1844 the method
of taking bottled spirits to account for duty at the outports had been different to that used at London. In the
former case the goods had been estimated at 6 reputed

quarts to the gallon—an extremely slipshod method.
The outport officers were directed by a ' General Letter '
of August 27, 1844, to conform to the London practice,
under which the quantity per case was estimated by actual
measurement of certain bottles.

On June 10, 1844, the collector of Dominica reported
that the island was in a state of rebellion, and had been
placed under martial law. The coloured people had
committed many outrages. The militia had been called
out, and had fired on the mob, killing two and wounding
several others. Two hundred persons had been taken,
and were to be tried by court-martial. The trouble had
arisen through a provincial Act enjoining the taking of
the census, the coloured people believing that this was
a device towards re-enslaving them.

A letter from the Postmaster-General reached the Board,
stating that the postmasters at the frontier offices between
Canada and the United States had not been supplied
with the usual list of British copyright works, and were
therefore unable to cope with the introduction of pirated
books into Canada. Later he wrote asking that the
customs officers in New Brunswick might be instructed
to cooperate with the postal authorities there in preventing the smuggling of letters (to evade postage expense)
from the United States.*

Major Smith, ' a shipowner and merchant of Port Elizabeth, Algoa Bay,' applied to the Board, representing himself as a trader with Bengal, Mauritius, and the Cape
coasts. He stated that he had established a depot on
the coast of Kaffraria, and imported goods at Algoa Bay
for exportation thither. The collector of Cape Town had
called on him for the duties on these goods, although other
goods imported at Table Bay for a similar purpose had
been delivered duty-free. The major pointed out that
the British Government had by treaty disclaimed all

* The incessant complaints as to smuggling, literary piracy,
and unfair trading, on the part of Americans, tend to show that
commercial morality was even scarcer in the United States than
in the United Kingdom.

control of Kaffraria, and that it was preposterous to levy duty on goods imported at Algoa Bay for exportation to an independent State.

Later he found it was necessary to get a licence for the trade, and applied to the governor at Cape Town. The collector recommended that the licence should be granted, on condition that no arms, wines, or spirits were to be landed, and that the duties on the goods were paid. Smith got his licence, and then renewed protest against paying the duty. But the governor enforced payment.

The collector's report on Smith's application was interesting. It described Port Elizabeth as a free warehousing port in the eastern part of the colony—the colony being bounded east and west by the mouths of the Great Fish River and the Unizimkulu. The territory ceded to the Kaffirs lay within the eastern boundary, and the dominance of the British Government had been asserted in the treaty. Till recently there had been only a land trade from Cape Town and Natal to the Kaffir territory. All goods taken thither had been first duty-paid, and the traffic was tolerably extensive, larger quantities of Kaffir produce returning by the same route. Smith's trade by sea to the coast of the territory was a recent venture, and the collector insisted that if goods were allowed to go there duty-free they would be smuggled into Cape Colony. In the end it was decided that no goods should be thus shipped till duty-paid (unless they were products of the colony). The object seems to have been to discourage the traffic, it being thought that an open sea trade would favour the introduction of arms. The Board refused Smith's application. (It appears he was not a merchant and shipowner, after all, but agent for Messrs. Hawkins, of Great Tower Street, London.)

Mr. Furlonge, landing-waiter at Montserrat, caused some little trouble during 1844. He commenced by sending word to the Board that the Hon. I. P. M. Trott, senior assistant judge of the Court of Queen's Bench in Montserrat, had been concerned in extensive smuggling transactions.   Later he wrote again, complaining that he had been persecuted by Trott.   ' I am now,' he wrote, ' confined in the common jail with a heavy fine, for a trifling assault upon a gentleman who had grossly insulted me.   The collector was one of the judges who assented to this cruel persecution.'   He proceeded to insinuate that the collector was Trott's intimate friend, and had connived at the latter's frauds.   But the Board, no doubt realizing that this was another case of over-indulgence in ' sugar-cane wine,' treated the reports with contempt.

During the same year the President of Montserrat queried the collector for failing to carry out an Act passed by the Montserrat Legislature in 1748.   The collector stated that he could not undertake to enforce colonial Acts which were repugnant to the imperial laws.   The matter dropped.   Below is an extract from the Montserrat Act of 1748 :

' Whereas frequent and great losses happen by the clandestine carrying off of the inhabitants and other people, their negroes and substance, from this island, etc.'   It proceeded that no vessel might depart till the master had entered into bond of £1,500 that he would carry off no one till authorized by a ticket from the island Secretary's office.   The collector was to withhold clearance till the bond had been entered into.

During several years there had been a deal of correspondence on the question of establishing a Customs station at Labrador (see p. 196), an arrangement much desired by some of the settlers in that territory, while others opposed the idea.   In 1836 Lord Glenelg had described the situation in a despatch to Captain Prescott, governor of Labrador, stating that the Planters believed they were separate from Newfoundland, and still under the authority of the king in Council, but that this view was not correct, Cap. 27, 49 Geo. III., and 59, 6 Geo. IV., being against it.   He also quoted the decision arrived at by a recent Commission, which had stated that the coast of Labrador, east of a line drawn north and south from the harbour of Blanc Gablon, was annexed to the colony of Newfoundland.   Lord Glenelg was of opinion that the Labrador settlers could claim to be represented in the Newfoundland Legislature.

In 1843 the Attorney-General for Newfoundland delivered an opinion upon the matter.   He recommended the appointment of two customs officers, to remain on the Labrador coast from June to September.   He pooh-poohed the idea that the expense would exceed the collection, pointing out that the colonial customs officers were not appointed simply to raise revenue ; they were the enforcers of the Navigation laws and of commercial treaties. He referred to illicit trade on the coast of Labrador, conducted by ' vessels of the United States fitted out for fishing and trading.   Against such proceedings,' he observed, ' the customs officers would be some check, and their appointment is, I think, essential for the reasonable and consistent maintenance of the system.   At the conclusion of the late war, when peace restored to France, as well as the United States, their privileges of fishery in these parts, the coast of Labrador was resorted to by numerous planters from the settlements of Newfoundland, who during the war had enjoyed the exclusive benefit of fishing between Cape St. John and the straits of Belle-isle.'   He proceeded to state that these settlers were supplied with stores from Newfoundland, and returned each year the produce of their fishery.   English and Jersey merchants also erected establishments at Labrador, importing their supplies direct from Europe, and carrying their fish and oils direct to European markets.   Of late these industries had become depressed, British-taken fish being subjected to heavy duties in foreign countries, and the French and American fisheries being supported by liberal bounties.   Thus most of the colonial settlers and English merchants had abandoned their Labrador establishments.

In 1844 the Customs Lawyers in London made a vague and half-hearted report upon the case.   They suggested that it was a matter that the governor should deal with, and they thought the appointment of ' transient officers ' would be inexpedient. It appears that in the end the governor of Newfoundland decided to appoint officers, and to place a suitable vessel at their disposal. Thus it is clear that at Labrador up to 1845 there was no regular collection of duty, and that the fishing treaties and conventions, and the laws of Navigation, were as nothing.

On May 14, 1844, an American brig was discovered derelict and ashore at Stewart Castle, near Falmouth, Jamaica. Her name was the *Gleaner*, and she had a full cargo of pipes of gin and wine. The lord of the manor impounded her, and soon afterwards the American consul put in a claim. On May 22 a claim was made by the Receiver of Admiralty Droits. Then began a paper war among the claimants three—manorial, national, and departmental. The consul became importunate, and quoted instructions from the American Secretary of State. The collector who held the vessel in custody apprised the Board, and was instructed to keep ship and cargo till the case was decided in the Vice-Admiralty Court of the island. Unfortunately we are unable to discover which claim succeeded.

The matter of trade marks appears to have possessed the minds of the Jamaica customs men at this period. Several detentions took place under the Acts relating thereto. One was of two gold Swiss watches marked ' Tobias, Liverpool,' and another of six gold Swiss watches, with English words on them denoting quality, movement, etc. (Sec. 11, Cap. 47, 5 and 6 Vict.). The Board in this case directed forfeiture of the goods marked ' Tobias, Liverpool,' and release of the other consignment. Another detention was of cheese from New York, marked ' English Dairy.' The importer furnished proof that the cheese was made at an American farm called ' The English Dairy,' so the goods were released.

The Legislature of New Zealand, by Ordinance of

June 20, 1844, had abolished all the old tariff exemptions
and preferences, and imposed duties as below :

	£	s.	d.
Spirits, per proof gallon	0	5	0
Leaf tobacco, per pound	0	0	9
Manufactured tobacco, per pound	0	1	0
Cigars and snuff, per pound	0	2	0
Wine .. .. .. 20 per cent. *ad valorem.*			
Malt liquors .. .. 15 ,, ,,			
Arms and ammunition .. 30 ,, ,,			
All other goods .. .. 5 ,, ,,			

Three firms of merchants protested against paying
these duties upon their imports from the United Kingdom.
They urged that the ordinance was repugnant to the
imperial laws, but the Board sanctioned collection. On
September 28, 1844, the Legislature changed round, and
produced one of the most striking fiscal ordinances on
record, repealing all customs duties, and directing that
revenue should be raised solely by a tax on property.
The preamble ran : ' Whereas the commerce, agriculture,
and general prosperity of New Zealand would be greatly
promoted by removing all restrictions on the free intercourse of shipping with its numerous ports and harbours,'
etc.

A copy of this Ordinance was forwarded to the Board
by the collector of Hobart Town, Tasmania. He had
been instructed to send an officer to Auckland, New
Zealand, and to pay the officer's salary till he arrived and
took up his employment. The bewildered collector asked
what he was to do, as there was no employment for the
officer to take up. He also bewailed the new measure,
stating that it would have an evil tendency upon the
revenues of the adjacent colonies. For instance, when
goods were cleared duty-free from bond at Hobart Town
for shipment to New Zealand, their arrival could no
longer be certified, there being no Customs to do the certifying, and thus such goods might be brought back, and
run almost with impunity on the coast of Tasmania.

The Ordinance earned the approval of the governor of
New Zealand. He stated in his speech at the opening of

the Session that the Maoris were anxious for free trade, that their friendship should be secured at any price, that it would be impossible to check smuggling on 3,000 miles of coast, and that the amount of customs previously collected was but £18,000 a year, while the expense of collection was nearly £5,000.

The Board referred the Ordinance to the Treasury, and directed that the officers sent to New Zealand should remain there. It is not exactly apparent how long the Ordinance endured, but the Customs were soon in operation again. Soon, too, there was a new governor, and a flaming, destructive war with the Maoris.

The imports into Port Adelaide during 1843 had been :

			Value.
From the United Kingdom..	...	..	£50,053
From other British colonies	..	..	1,680
From foreign countries	..	..	25,842

The collector of Hobart Town, Tasmania, in his account to the Board of his survey of Launceston, reported that trade was declining (imports rapidly, exports slowly).

	1843.	Value.		1844.	Value.
Imports	..	.. £705,260	Imports	..	.. £442,988
Exports	..	.. 439,890	Exports	..	.. 408,799

The collector of Colombo, in an account of his survey of Galle, stated the value of the trade there at £68,425 (imports) and £25,794 (exports). Most of the goods imported were from the British colonies ; most of those exported went to England. There was much smuggling of spirits and tea from passing vessels, and he suggested that three fast-sailing canoes should be manned and appointed in prevention. He stated that the tide waiters, who were natives, were overworked and badly paid. They had only three nights a week in bed, and their pay was but 18s. a month.

The canoes were procured, and the governor issued an injunction ' To the District Modliars and Fisher Head

II.   15

Men along the coast ' to do their duty in preventing smuggling. During the following year the collector reported that the smuggling had been checked so far as the port of Galle was concerned, but the smugglers had taken to landing their goods ' farther down,' storing them on the coast, and smuggling them from thence ' into the bazaar.' Two of their hiding-places had been discovered, and one contained over 1,000 flasks of spirits.

In closing the portion of this chapter that deals with tariffs and departmental practice, a few remarks should be made on the general aspect of affairs. We furnish an account of the Customs revenue for 1844. (We have had choice of three sets of returns, and find that they all differ slightly ; therefore we can only give the amount as *approximately* correct.)   Shillings and pence omitted.

GROSS CUSTOMS REVENUE, 1844.

				£
England	..	..	..	.. 19,993,273
Scotland	..	..	..	.. 1,918,887
Ireland	..	..	..	.. 2,362,826
Total	..	..	..	24,274,986

The cost of collection was about 5·2 per cent. on the gross takings (4·75 in Great Britain, and 9·12 in Ireland). The repayments, drawbacks, etc., amounted to £170,129. Besides the cost of collection and the drawbacks, other charges were made on the revenue—viz., the expenses of quarantine and warehousing establishments, certain amounts in adjustment of light dues, compensation to certain Irish civil servants and to naval officers of the coastguard, payments in support of the civil government of Scotland, etc., besides which about half a million was retained as an outstanding balance. The amount actually paid into the Exchequer was £22,504,821. London's gross return was £11,778,516 ; Liverpool returned £4,487,664 ; Bristol, £1,007,832 ; Hull, £607,963 ; Leith,

£631,926 ; Glasgow, £551,851 ; Greenock, £367,465 ; Dublin, £1,043,466 ; Belfast, £366,414 ; Cork, £302,207. *Chester* actually returned £75,985, while the once famous Chichester only accounted for £834. The most ' barren ' ports were Aberystwith, with £82, and Campbeltown, with £4 17s. 4d. (*gross*, be it remembered). Manchester, which had been granted bonding privileges, figured in the returns for the first time, with £1,991. Twenty-eight ports in England and Wales, eight in Scotland, and three in Ireland, yielded no ' net '; indeed, on most of them there were deficits.   Below is the list of undesirables :

Aberystwith.	Padstow.
Aldborough.	Poole.
Arundel.	Ramsgate.
Blackney and Clay (of old a stirring port).	Rye.
	St. Ives.
Bridlington.	Scilly.
Bridport.	Southwold.
Cardigan.	Wells (once important).
Chichester (another famous port of old).	Weymouth (once important).
Cowes.	Ayr.
Dartmouth.	Banff.
Deal.	Campbeltown.
Faversham.	Kirkwall.
Fowey.	Lerwick.
Gweek.	Stornoway.
Harwich.	Stranraer.
Llanelly.	Wick.
Lyme.	Baltimore.
Maldon.	Coleraine.
Milford.	Tralee.

Public opinion was veering towards Free Trade. The Navigation laws, praised by most historians of the eighteenth century as the noblest productions of patriotic foresight, were rapidly falling into disrepute. Much was urged against continuance of even the *disjecta membra* of those assertions of British dominance. They were decried in many quarters as utterly incompatible with the spirit of modern commercial progress, but close scrutiny of many cases arising from them leads to the conviction that much of this outcry was due to a brace of causes—causes likely to escape the notice of the ordinary historian.   One was the inherent villainy of many of the administering officials.   The other was the greed of certain shipowners, who, improving upon the growing desire for cheaper commodities, wished to cheapen manhood, and to substitute for the sturdy breed by Nature and training fitted to hand, reef, and steer, and to wield boarding-pike and rammer, bandy-legged Lascars, frowsy niggers, and squinting Mongols.

The reports made by Committees of Inquiry into Revenue during the early forties testify to a growing dislike of protective duties.   Undoubtedly the chief cause of this was the bad influence of the later Corn laws, an element of evil which, as has been shown, sprang into existence during the last ten years of the eighteenth century.   These pages form no suitable lists within which to wage the bitter controversy as to whether Free Trade is or is not completely suitable to the needs of a nation. But, as they have here and there exhibited the dents and rents in the Protectionist panoply, room may be reasonably found for the assertion that many of the arguments by which the country was being converted to Free Trade were utterly specious.

To prove this, quotations must be made from the evidence of two ' experts,' both officials of the Board of Trade.   One insisted that certain protective duties then imposed, notably the tax on imported woollens, were useless from a revenue point of view, and unnecessary as instruments of protection.   The tax on woollens, said he, brought in little revenue, and was never intended to be anything but protective.   But the woollen trade did not need protecting, for the exports of woollens had become vast.   Now, any straight-thinking reader will perceive that it is difficult to prove such a statement, especially when the intending prover goes on to argue from it that protective duties do not protect.   For the history of the restrictions on the importation of woollens—and, in fact, the whole history of the English woollen manufacturing trade—prove that that trade was for ages systematically fostered at the expense of the foreign purchaser of wool and of the English agriculturist, and the very figures quoted proved that the shutting-out of the foreigner did not prevent the foreigner from buying extensively from the shutters-out.   But to sneer at a tax as ' merely protective,' and then repeat the sneer because the tax is unproductive, is highly characteristic of your ' expert.' For it is abundantly clear that a tax on imports, to be genuinely protective, *must* be unproductive.

The other Board of Trade witness made a profound impression upon the Committee that examined him—at least, the report stated thus ; but it is likely that a deal of the praise bestowed on him was due to the fact that, though the initials differed slightly, his and the Chairman's names were similar.

It is easy to perceive that Mr. James Deacon Hume, of the Board of Trade (formerly of the Customs), was a dull disciple of the old Adam and the young Richard. He enunciated the childish maxim that the way to make foreign countries open their markets is to import large quantities of foreign goods.   Then the people in the protected foreign countries will find it difficult to ' get their returns,' and will agitate for the removal of their own protective duties, so that their customers oversea may be able to ' pay with goods.'   Of course, no merchant in the possession of his wits would ever dream of acting as pioneer in such a venture, unless he intended roguery, but that signifies nothing to an ambitious official who is suffering from too much Adam Smith and too little knowledge of the ways of men.   Many such chirping absurdities did Mr. Hume tender to the Committee.   But the item most curious was his excursion into the realms of prophecy.   ' I feel the strongest confidence,' said he, ' that if we were to give up our protective system altogether it would be impossible for other countries to retain theirs

much longer.' Students of the course of events from
1840 to 1910 will be able to judge of Mr. Hume's reliability
in the prophetic line. The framers of the final report
stated, ' Mr. Hume's words are remarkable.' (Barring
their occasionally ungrammatical arrangement, it is hard
to detect anything remarkable in them, or in the utter-
ances of his brother official.)

The Committee made many palpable slips in their
report. France, for instance, was quoted as an example
of a country committed thoroughly to Protection, and
unable to obtain importance as a manufacturing centre.
Yet the evidence had revealed that the thing most
dreaded by British manufacturers of silk, lace, and other
fancy goods was French competition. History was at hand
to prove that for ages France had supplied us with wines,
brandies, and delicacies innumerable, and had dictated
the fashion of attire ; and her supremacy in many important lines of manufacture had been proved by the
circumstance that when all intercourse with her was prohibited thousands of English coast-dwellers had risked
the press, the hulks, and the gallows, to flood England
with contraband French manufactures ! Switzerland was
quoted as a country unprotected by tariffs, yet excelling
in manufactures. But the secret of Switzerland's success
was sedulously concealed : the fact that men, women, and
little children drudged in the châlets from dawn to dark
at monotonous and soul-paralyzing occupations, for wages
that would not have been tolerated in England, even in
the blackest days of the old factory system.

We introduce these excerpts and comments mainly to
illustrate the absurdity of taking too much notice of
interested ' experts,' and of making long doctrinal reports.
No doubt the members of this and other Committees
meant well. They knew that the country was in a parlous
state, that the Customs department was badly officered
and, now and then, corruptly administered, that bread was
dear, and their occasional excursions into the manufacturing towns had made them familiar with a type of

juvenile physiognomy far different from that which
elicited the historic ' *Non Angli, sed Angeli.*' It was convenient to ascribe all the effects of the manifold villainies
of Greed and Unreason to Protection. Children were
wailing in the streets ; the wolf of Starvation was at many
a door. Any truncheon was good enough to slay Lupus
with. And the result ? Good was done—harm here and
there, which future legislation may attempt to rectify—
but good in the main.

We now furnish an account of the various preventive
measures, and some of the remarkable seizures and
smuggling episodes, during the period extending from 1826
to 1845.

Early in 1826 the smacks *Fox* and *Lovely Lass* were
seized at Portsmouth with tubs of spirits concealed in the
spaces between waterline and keel, the concealment being
contrived so that access to the goods could not be gained
till the vessels were laid ashore.

On the night of February 24, 1827, Lieutenant Digby,
of the Coastguard, found about eighty smugglers on the
beach at the Devil's Gap, Rottingdean, engaged in signalling to a vessel that was hovering on the coast. They
advanced upon him, and he drew his pistol, which flashed
in the pan. One of the smugglers knocked him down
with a bludgeon, and another disarmed him. Then he
was beaten till he became insensible. Two men named
May and Palmer were convicted at the Horsham assizes
for this offence.

At the same assizes Abraham Cox, a labourer, was
charged with attempting to bribe Timothy Harrington, a
naval sailor employed on the Coast blockade. Harrington
stated that the prisoner approached him on the night of
April 1, 1826, while he was on patrol at Newhaven, and
offered him a bribe to allow a ' crop ' of tubs to be landed
on the following night. Cross-examination elicited that

when a seaman made a statement of this kind he was at once relieved from the irksome and dangerous duty of patrolling, so that he should be kept out of the way of the smugglers, and that the patrolmen would do almost anything to obtain this relief. The defence set up was that Harrington was unworthy of credence. Cox was acquitted.

No doubt there was a deal of false testimony and straining of evidence in some of the revenue cases. A poor rustic lad named Hazelgrove was charged with making a fire on the coast at Middleton on January 4, 1827, to signal to smugglers, but it was proved that the fire was lit for other purposes entirely, and the boy was acquitted.

A coral smuggling case was tried in the Exchequer on May 29, 1827. Two Italians, Guecco and Mazzinchi, bought a large quantity of coral, which had been warehoused at the London Docks for exportation, sent it to Rotterdam, and then re-imported the goods, concealed in kegs of butter. They imported five consignments between July, 1824, and July, 1825—in all, nearly 8,000 ounces of coral. One day, while the customs officers were weighing the butter at importation (butter being, of course, liable to a low duty), one of the casks fell and burst, and out rolled a tin containing coral. Mazzinchi promptly turned king's evidence. Guecco was fined £400.

On February 13, 1827, the officers at Roseau, Dominica, seized two sloops and their cargoes because the goods were being landed prior to report of ship. There being no direct evidence of fraud, the seizure was a mere arbitrary enforcement of the strict letter of the law. When the seizure note reached London, the Customs Lawyer reported that the officers had no right to seize the goods, the ship only being liable to forfeiture. On inquiry, it appeared that this could not be rectified, for the Dominican officers had promptly secured condemnation and sale of both ship and goods. All the Board could do was to direct that the net proceeds of the sale of the goods should be paid to the owners. Why, because the officers were either ignorant or greedy, the costs of condemnation and sale should be deducted out of the proceeds of goods illegally seized and perhaps corruptly sold, will be past the comprehension of any plain-thinking person. Yet such was the invariable practice ; this is but one case among hundreds. Of course, the aggrieved parties might go to law for damages, and then the whole of the Crown's legal phalanx would be pitted against them, *at no extra expense to any official concerned.*

Fraud was extensive in connection with the shipment of bountied linen, the manufacturers enclosing ' Unions,' a mixture of linen and cotton, in bales of genuine linen, and claiming bounty on the whole. The fraudulent goods were made by means of a ' devil.' Several cases of the kind were discovered during 1827.

The Board altered the regulations with regard to ' head-money ' (awards made to officers for capturing smugglers). The £15 previously given for capture and committal, and the £20 for capture and transfer of the offender to the navy, were not to be granted in future, except when *armed* smugglers were captured on the coast.

Early in 1828 the boat *Mary* of Dover was found to have a double bottom and double sides, containing thirty tin cases filled with spirits. In May information was received that the sloop *Farmer's Delight* of Hastings had been sold to a Boulogne merchant for use in smuggling. The barge *Alfred* of London, bound coastwise from Arundel to London with wood hoops, was seized off Birchington by the revenue cruiser *Vigilant*. She had taken on board at sea no less than 1,045 tubs of spirits, which were found beneath the wood hoops.

By Cap. 23 of 10 Geo. IV. the scale of rewards for seizing smuggled silks was substantially increased. The seizing officer was to receive the full value of the goods seized, and half of all penalties recovered. (The duties on silks were increased by the same Act.) The usual strings of information reached the Board, one item containing a description of four vessels which had recently gone into the smuggling trade, and another announcing that foreign silks were extensively imported in bales of rags.   The seizures were many ; we quote two or three of the more illustrative cases.

Early in the year the *Lucy* of Fowey was seized at Chichester, with 100 tubs of spirits in her false bottom and sides.   In March the barge *Independence* of Kinsale was seized at Galway, with kegs of brandy concealed in her storeroom, and tobacco and cigars in the cabin ceiling. In April a number of cases containing eggs from Jersey were found at Southampton to have hollow sides, with silks packed in the spaces.   The trawler *Two Brothers* of Falmouth was advertised as ' wanted ' for having sunk 152 tubs of spirits at Coverack.   A large quantity of tobacco and tea was found in casks of resin, landed in the Port of London by an American ship during August.

(The following are quoted from the general list of merely ' huge ' seizures.)

A boat seized by the Shoreham Coast blockade, with 1,245 gallons spirits and 1,950 pounds tobacco ; and two boats seized at one time by the Arundel Coast blockade with 1,117 gallons spirits, 54 pounds tea, and 2,083 pounds tobacco.

To prove that many consignments went clear, it will be necessary to quote one or two specimens of reliable information.   A huge run took place on March 20, 1829, ' between Jew's Gut and the Ness Point.'   The goods passed through Lydd at 8 a.m. in twelve carts, escorted by about eighty armed smugglers.   (The Lydd people came to the doors and cheered as the cavalcade went clanking by.)   A run took place between Winchelsea Watchhouse and Cliff End early on June 5, 1829.   Seventy or eighty men, each carrying two tubs, went through Winchelsea about 4 a.m.   Another consignment of tubs, numbering ninety, was floated up the Brede Channel the same night, and run at Winchelsea Sluice.   On July 23, 1829, a large run of half-ankers took place near East-bourne, and the goods were loaded in carts *at noon*, and

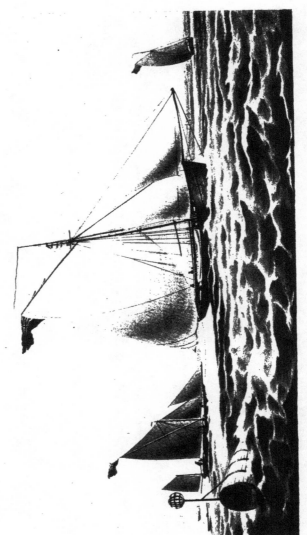

Revenue Cruiser 'Vigilant', with Barge 'Alfred' in Tow.

To face p. 234.

carried inland. 'Midway between Eastbourne and Willingdon,' wrote the informer, 'one cart overturned, and caused some delay.'

On October 1, 1829, a cargo of tubs was run on Romney Sands, and a gang of men carried the tubs inland, and loaded them up on carts. Early on October 2, 1829, a galley, 44 feet long, 4 feet 5 inches broad, and 2 feet 6 inches deep, was rowed through mountains of surf and beached near the 'Ivy Cottage,' on the Shorncliffe station. Her cargo was landed and carried inland, but the boat's back was broken. The Coast blockade found her on the beach at daylight. (A similar run took place near Dungeness, and again the long galley used was swamped and disabled. The carriers were not at hand, and the blockade men found and seized boat and goods, but the crew escaped.) On October 29, twenty large bales, supposed to be tea or silks, were run on Dover Beach, 'near the bathing-machines.' Twelve men were in waiting, who put the bales into a coal-cart, and conveyed them into the town. (A few days prior to this daring run the Dover customs officers had found sixty-five half-ankers sunk near Shakspeare's Cliff.) A *chasse-marée* was sighted hovering off the coast in the Arundel district on October 29. H.M.S. *Cameleon* chased and boarded her, but found nothing. She had no boat, so officers scoured the coast, and found a boat lying derelict. It transpired afterwards that she had landed 200 tubs, and the Frenchmen had assisted to carry them inland.

Desperate resistance was not so frequent as of old, yet it occurred occasionally. One hundred and fifty tubs were run at Cliff End, in the Rye district, on the morning of December 3, 1829. The blockade men arrived just as the tubs had been loaded up. The smugglers, armed with 'bats,'* at once engaged them. Four of the blockade men were badly injured. The run was effected successfully, though several of the 'batmen' were wounded and one killed.

* 'Bat,' a long stick used with both hands.

News reached Thames Street that the collector of Dominica, while searching a house for contraband, was assaulted by a crowd of coloured people, and badly injured. Annexed to the report was a copy of the *Dominican Colonist*, containing the following letter : ' As it is more than probable that the coloured gentry of this island who are in the habit of smuggling are unacquainted with Sec. 54 of the Act 114, 6 Geo. IV., do me the favour of inserting it in your next number. Mr. Evans, some time ago, was thrown overboard by a coloured man while in the execution of his duty, Mr. Constable was beaten and maltreated by another, and within the last few days Mr. Redman suffered similar treatment.'

The officers asked for permission to offer a reward for the discovery of the parties. The Board's minute of reply was rather discouraging : ' We see no grounds to comply with this request.'

Cap. 10 of 11 Geo. IV. and 1 Wm. IV. provided that smugglers who were allowed to escape sentence by joining the navy should receive but half the pay at which they were rated ; and if their wives or families became paupers the other part should go to the parish supporting them.

On February 10, 1830, the landing-waiter at Sandy Point, St. Kitts, informed the collector that he had tried to seize a boat that was engaged in smuggling, that a mob collected and stoned him almost to death, and that two of his assailants had been convicted, fined £50 each, and imprisoned for three months.

Certain smuggling cases at the port of Kingston, Jamaica, produced in the end a remarkable decision by the Board—a decision which appears to go beyond the law entirely. Seizures were as plentiful as usual ; on June 14, 1830, the officers seized five cases of gin in a house in White Street, Kingston ; on July 1, in a house occupied by a Spaniard, they seized forty ' jugs ' gin and 400 pounds brown sugar, which had been landed from a schooner from Cuba ; and two chests of tea on board the same schooner. In August, 1830, other seizures of gin

and wine were made ashore, and in the house of one
Hyman Levy the officers found forty-nine barrels of salt,
in which were concealed carboys of gin. On the premises
owned by one Cohen they found many other barrels of
salt, but these had been opened, and the precious carboys
disposed of. And one Solomon Lazarus was concerned
with Cohen and Levy in importation of said salt and gin.
Each Jew protested his innocence and accused his confederates, and the Board directed that proceedings might
be waived against Levy if he would pay £100, and *consent
to give evidence against the other parties!* He promptly
decamped to the United States. Proceedings were waived
against Lazarus on his paying £459 penalty and £105 15s.
costs. (Levy returned to the island in 1836, and paid a
heavy fine.) There was not sufficient evidence to carry
proceedings against Cohen.

The United Kingdom smuggling records (second-hand)
for 1830 are voluminous. Of course, we can only quote
a few cases, which we select as fairly illustrative of the
various phases of the trade.

A seizure of a large quantity of eau-de-Cologne was
made at one of the outports. The goods had been put
into long-necked bottles, the corks covered with gilt foil,
and the consignment labelled and entered as champagne.

Books which had been printed prior to 1801 were
allowed importation at a much lower rate of duty than
was payable upon books printed subsequently (£1 per
hundredweight against £5). A large consignment, entered
at Dublin as printed prior to 1801, turned out on inspection to be fitted with false title-pages.

A quantity of silks had been smuggled ashore at
Rochester, and the receivers were chary of conveying
them by road to London, fearing they might be discovered
by the mounted patrol; so they had a number of egg-
boxes constructed with hollow sides, in which they packed
the silks. They imported a cargo of eggs, landed and
cleared them, packed them in the silk-lined egg-boxes,
and sent them to London by waggon. Someone con-

nected with the business gave information to the Customs, and eggs and silks were seized on arrival.

Repeated information arrived as to the doings of the *Grace* of Gweek. She was stated to have been often at Roscoff, engaged in loading contraband, and to have frequently met French vessels at sea, taken in contraband goods, and landed them near Land's End. Her crew were described as ' the three brothers Carlyon of Coverack, reputed smugglers.'

We quote from the Dover list (April 5, 1829, to June 5, 1830) the seizures made by the officers employed in examining imports and clearing passengers' baggage.

April 6, 1829.—2 pairs silk stockings, 2 lace veils, 1 lace scarf, 132 yards lace.

April 9.—24 pieces of chip (for hats).

April 14.—44 yards silk, 1 silk handkerchief, 1 pair silk braces, 1 silk waistcoat, 1 silk cravat, 3 yards merino, 3 pairs leathern gaiters, 14 pairs leathern gloves, 1 book containing 50 prints, 2 pairs earrings, 6 buttons, 6 metal forks, 1 inkstand, 1 piece porcelain, 5 yards thread lace.

Another seizure of 2 yards velvet, 31 yards silk, 4 silk handkerchiefs, 1 reticule, 12 reels and 21 skeins floss silk, 1 silk band, 1 cushion, 2 worked muslin caps, 5 necklaces, 66 buttons, 1 pair bracelets, 6 snuff-boxes, 3 pairs leathern gloves, 1 book containing 50 prints, 1 piece glass, 3 ounces beads, 2 salt glasses, 4 decanter-stands, 2 pairs earrings, 1 pair eardrops, 1 cream-jug.

Another of 12 yards silk, 3 yards merino, 4 wineglasses, 3 fans, 1 necklace, 4 pairs earrings, 2 glass balls, 5 papers pins, and sundry beads.

April 23.—224 yards silk riband.

April 30.—446 yards blond lace.

May 2.—13 pairs leather gloves.

May 8.—22 yards silk, 2 flasks eau-de-Cologne, $2\frac{1}{2}$ pounds tea.

May 10.—1 clock.

May 13.—16 flasks eau-de-Cologne, 136 yards silk riband.

May 14.—47 yards cotton fringe, 24 flasks eau-de-Cologne, 2¾ pounds tea, 1 trunk.

May 17.—8 pairs silk stockings.

May 19.—1 merino shawl.

May 23.—9½ pounds tea, 6 pairs gloves.

June 10.—3 cambric petticoats.

June 11.—6 cartons manufactured hair.

June 16.—36 packs playing-cards.

June 19.—22 pieces lace.

July 8.—3 musical boxes, 26 musical snuff-boxes, 18 gold watches.

July 11.—14 ounces plain silk, 10 ounces figured gauze, 1 ounce silk gauze, 2 ounces figured silk.

July 13.—7 pounds tea, 7 flasks eau-de-Cologne.

July 15.—46 bottles and 50 flasks perfumery, 4 silk umbrellas.

The list proceeds in much the same fashion up to June, 1830. Now and then larger seizures occur, of which a few appear below.

A seizure of 55 pounds vultures' feathers. Another of 44 yards silk riband, 2,170 ' porcelain teeth,' 300 human teeth, and 1 bracelet. Another of 2 silk bonnets, 8 silk dresses, 2 silk aprons, and 2 silk waistcoats. Another of 16 silk dresses, 24 pieces trimming, 4 silk tippets, 26 embroidered caps, 37 embroidered tippets, 42 pieces embroidery, 1 embroidered dress, and 8 bonnets. The list shows seizures of musical instruments, percussion caps, stained paper, ostrich feathers, and many other curios.

The rummaging staff at Dover are credited with three tolerable seizures during the same period—one of a sloop and 27 casks brandy ; one of a boat with 789 yards silk and 544 yards riband ; and one of a ' raft ' of spirits, containing 65 tubs. The Coast blockade at Dover seized during the same period a boat with 14 tubs spirits, a boat with 9 tubs, a four-oared boat with 167 tubs, 4 boats with 32 tubs, 2 boats with 229 tubs, a boat with 47 tubs, a boat with 23 tubs, a boat with 37 tubs, and a boat with 35 tubs, amounting in all to about 1,914 gallons spirits, besides an immense number of ' sunken tubs crept up,' in parcels of from 1 to 10.

Below is a list of large seizures made during 1830-31 :

March 22, 1830.—By the Hastings Coast blockade. The boat *Mary*, with 1,706 pounds tobacco and 487 pounds snuff.

March 31.—By the Hastings Coast blockade. The smack *Neptune*, with 2,971 pounds tobacco and 1,389 pounds snuff.

May 29.— By the Margate Coast blockade. 2,439 yards figured silk, 1,265 yards black silk, 3,667 yards coloured silk, 35,825 yards silk gauze, and 4,607 yards Petersham gauze.

June 23.—By the Rochester Coast blockade. The coasting brig *Industry*, with coals, and concealed beneath the coals 1,850 gallons spirits, 2,688 pounds tea, and 41,110 yards silk gauze, which had been taken on board at sea.

September 22.—By the Rochester Coast blockade. The coasting sloop *William*, laden with oats, and 1,974 gallons spirits and 1,203 pounds tea as above.

January 16, 1831.—By the Ramsgate Coast blockade. 3,940 pieces silk gauze, 1,515 ells crape, 5 silk dresses, a velvet skirt, 1,591 pounds tea, and a half-anker of brandy.

An ingenious fraud was discovered at Southampton early in 1831. A consignment of casks of cider from Jersey was examined closely, and the officers found that sections of the upper part of each cask were diagonally ' blocked off,' and that tobacco had been packed in the spaces thus created.

The Coast blockade was abolished in 1831, as previously stated. This force had been established in 1817, for special protection of the coast of Kent and Sussex. The blockade men had made many important seizures, yet the authorities had never imposed implicit confidence in them. The force was practically independent of the Board's control, yet disagreements often occurred between the Board and the Admiralty on account of its proceedings. A committee inquired into the protection of the Revenue in 1821, commented unfavourably upon the constitution and discipline of the force, and urged that it should be governed by the Customs Board. Much correspondence ensued, the Board losing no opportunity of belittling the blockade men, a task in which they were ably supported by several of the collectors at the outports—notably by the collector of Shoreham, whose confidential reports on the matter contained most remarkable statements. He declared that the force was composed principally of ' raw Irishmen,' who had never been on board ship previous to their taking passage for England, and of old and worn-out seamen ; that the discipline enforced was barbarous, there being many cases of brutal flogging ; and that when seamen were required for the expedition to Navarino in 1829 not one-third of the men were found fit for naval service. (After the Coast blockade was abolished, the Revenue Coastguard took over the duties, and the Board thus regained control of the whole of the preventive service.)

A report made by a revenue spy in May, 1831, seems to show that there had been good reason for suspecting the integrity of the blockade men. It stated that smuggling was suspended in Kent and Sussex since the abolition of the Coast blockade, as the various contraband syndicates were busily studying the methods of the new force, but that at one of the ports the smugglers had actually stolen an eight-oared galley belonging to the Coastguard, and taken her to Calais. A fleet of galleys lay at that port, waiting orders from England. Later came a report from Rye that in consequence of the suspension of smuggling the price of spirits had risen from about 50s. to £4 a tub.

The preventive regulations were strengthened during 1832 by the clauses in Cap. 84 enacting forfeiture of goods fraudulently concealed in packages entered on bill of sight, and liability of unauthorized enterers of goods and of hirers of smuggling parties, and giving power to customs

II.   16

officers to stop and examine vehicles without being liable to action at law if such examination were fruitless. It was also directed that fishing and pilot vessels should be painted black (that they might be readily distinguished from hoverers).

It had become a common practice with smugglers to furnish false information, and to make demonstrations of runs at certain places, in order to lure the preventive men into watching and visiting the places in question. While the guards were thus occupied, genuine runs were made at other places.

There can be no doubt that some of the preventive men were inclined to use weapons with remarkable promptitude. Early in the morning of December 23, 1832, two coastguardsmen named Carter and Lovell, stationed at Weymouth, saw a fore-and-aft vessel hovering off ' the old Sluice.' Then a boat with five men appeared, ploughing through the surf, and beached safely. The coastguardsmen fired a rocket as a signal for assistance, and ran towards her ; the smugglers leaped out and escaped. Attached to the boat by a warp were many tubs of spirits. The coastguardsmen loaded their pistols, expecting an attempt at rescue ; nor were they deceived, for up came a number of men armed with sticks, who began to cut the tubs loose. One of the men knocked Lovell's cutlass from his hand, and another attacked Carter, who at once opened fire. The smugglers then dispersed, carrying off many of the tubs. Assistance arrived, and the officers collected 65 tubs of spirits, and found two of the smugglers, named Webber and Burt, lying dead on the beach. Mr. Thackeray, the Customs Lawyer who was sent from London to attend the inquest, reported thus on the result : ' The jury came to the best conclusion I have ever known a Dorsetshire jury to do where smugglers were concerned.' The verdict ran thus : ' The deceased, James Webber and George Burt, came by their deaths by being shot with pistol balls by some officers in the service of the Coastguard in the execution of their duty, for the

preservation of themselves and to prevent the rescuing
of contraband goods which they had seized in the king's
name.'

Another and much more desperate mêlée occurred in the
Folkestone district. Information having been received
by Lieutenant Parry of the Coastguard that a 'forced
landing' would be attempted at 'No. 5 Guard,' that
officer placed himself in ambush with a party of his
men, and soon after nightfall a boat laden with kegs of
spirits ran in through the surf.   On the officers attempting
seizure, about 200 people, armed with clubs and guns,
appeared on the beach, and a battle-royal ensued.   The
smugglers were beaten off, and one of them was killed.
Two of the coastguardsmen were badly injured, and Lieutenant Parry received seven severe wounds, all in front.
The officers captured the boat and kegs, and took them
into Rye, bearing their wounded and the dead smuggler
with them.   The Admiralty Minute on the papers read
thus : 'Inform the Board of Customs and Lieutenant
Parry that in approbation of the gallant conduct of the
lieutenant their Lordships have promoted him to the
rank of commander.'

Another battle-royal took place at St. Leonards.   The
coastguard, under the command of Lieutenant Palmer,
came upon a party engaged in a run, and were at once
attacked by a squad of 'batmen,' who beat them most
severely ; but Palmer and his men killed several of the
smugglers, and captured a boat and 46 ankers of brandy.
(Palmer was promoted for this and similar services in 1839.)

It must not be thought that all revenue officers were
like Messrs. Parry and Palmer. The inspecting commander of Coastguard at Carne, Ireland, was by no means
inclined to take risks.   On January 26, 1832, he apprised
the controller-general of Coastguard that the Carne district was in rebellion. 'The tricoloured flag,' he stated,
'is displayed in open day. . . .   The Rev. Mr. Staples,
the magistrate, was in conference with me this day,
intimating that he was fearful of an attack, and that he

should be obliged to call out the revenue police and the Coastguard. At Clonmelly they pulled their priest on Sunday from the altar, set fire to several stacks, houghed cattle, etc. May I request to know, as there is no provision made for naval officers in this service in case of loss of life, whether I am to order a civilian to take charge of the party when called on by a magistrate ?'

The controller-general drew his pen under the concluding lines, and reported to the Board thus : ' An officer who under such circumstances is capable of offering such a suggestion for the purpose of avoiding personal risk is utterly unfit for and unworthy of the office he holds.' The Board referred the papers to the Admiralty. Admiralty Minute : ' Direct his immediate removal. Acquaint the Customs. Nominate Commander Henry Parker.' The most amazing part of the business was that the superseded officer actually wrote the Admiralty, trying to justify his previous letter. He asked : ' When naval officers are called upon to act offensive instead of defensive, are they to be considered as acting afloat, and remunerated in case of wounds ?' He ended with this peculiar statement : ' These are times when it renders it necessary to act with the greatest caution.' He received no reply.

The Admiralty had adopted a method of promoting specially each year from among the coastguard officers one captain, one commander, and one midshipman, for distinguished services, the appointments being made on the recommendation of the Customs Board. We furnish a summary of one of the reports of recommendation.

Report on Commander Langharne : ' Employed for the last eight years in Ireland. Was instrumental in bringing about the capture of the *Elizabeth and Grace* by H.M.S. *Semiramis* on the Irish coast, and the capture of the *Marie Theresa* by H.M.S. *Pike*. In March, 1827, prevented the landing of a large cargo, and captured several persons who were signalling. In October, 1827, again frustrated the plans of the smugglers, earning Board's special approval.   In March, 1829, was on leave.   A run took place during his absence.   Returned, captured the run goods (492 bales tobacco), dispersed a crowd several hundred strong, that attempted rescue.   Secured conviction of instigator of run (penalty £10,876 10s. 9d.).'

Report on Lieutenant Neame : ' Fourteen years in coastguard, first at Mersea, Essex.   Detected and convicted principal smugglers there.   Went to Ireland in 1820 ; was very successful.   Large run in Bray district, February, 1820.   Neame and party attacked by several hundreds of the country people.   Beat off the rioters, killing and wounding forty or fifty of them, and captured forty bales tobacco, fourteen horses and carts, and nine men, seven of whom were convicted and transported. Afterwards went to Antrim, and reorganized the Coast-guard there successfully.'

Report on Midshipman Hay : ' Instrumental in capture of several vessels, and about 2,000 kegs spirits.   Saved many shipwrecked people, notably when the *Mary Ann*, East Indiaman, went ashore on the Devon coast in 1827, and when H.M.S. *Echo* was wrecked on same coast in 1831.

' Langharne to captain, Neame to commander, Hay to lieutenant.'

About the middle of 1832 the Treasury approved an arrangement for filling vacancies in a new ' Mounted Guard ' appointed for Kent and Sussex, by volunteers from dragoon regiments, at the following rates of pay : Sergeants, 5s. a day ; corporals, 4s. 6d. ; troopers, 4s., and allowances for the horses.   Forage, saddlery, weapons, and veterinary attendance to be paid for by the Crown. (In the following year this force was increased so as to guard the whole of the English coast.)

Another ingenious fraud was discovered by the Southampton officers.   A number of coops containing poultry arrived from Guernsey.   It was found that the coops had false bottoms, filled with tobacco.

The various Government postal packets were deeply

suspected at this period, and on January 26, 1832, a special rummage was instituted on board the *Messenger* packet, which had arrived at Falmouth from Gibraltar. Below is a list of the contraband goods found :

414 pounds leaf tobacco and 44 pounds cigars under the planking of the coal-hole ; 60 pounds cigars under the plates of the engine-room ; 15 pounds cigars under the cinders in the smith's forge on deck ; $2\frac{1}{2}$ pounds cigars in the starboard paddlebox ; $2\frac{1}{4}$ pounds cigars under the sails in the sail-room ; 16 pounds leaf tobacco under firewood in the forehold ; 12 glass tumblers under a false sill in the engine-room.

Said the rummagers in their report : ' The officers gave us every assistance, with the exception of the boatswain, who, with the engineers, stokers, and coal-trimmers, acted in a very insubordinate manner, and threw every impediment in our way.'

An important seizure was made on June 13, 1832, by the Newhaven Coastguard. The victim was a vessel named the *New Speedwell*, with 23 pounds cigars, 990 pounds leaf tobacco, 1,095 pounds tobacco-stalk flour, and 12,986 pounds tobacco-stalks (in all nearly 7 tons).

To display the course of smuggling in the West Indian colonies, we quote the following curious list of seizures, made in Dominica in November, 1832 :

1. In a negro hut (for being illegally landed), 2 barrels flour, 1 barrel bread, 1 barrel tar.

2. In the house of François Brown (for being illegally landed), 1 barrel fish. (The above were American goods.)

3. In the house of Frederick Smith (illegally landed), 1 basket anisette, 3 baskets onions, 1 basket oil, 1 pair shoes, 21 snuff-boxes.

4. In the house of Joseph Rolle (illegally landed), 2 baskets anisette, 2 baskets onions, 1 box candles, 18 earthen pots, a firkin of butter, a box of raisins, 6 boxes oil.

5. In the house of Jeanne Rose (illegally landed), 18 drinking-glasses, 1 box eau-de-Cologne, 1 box candles.

6. In the house of Julienne Marceau (illegally landed), 1 box soap, 30 earthen pots. (The above were French goods.)

7. In the house of Charles Melangam (illegally landed), 2 barrels flour, 36 earthen pots.

8. In the houses of Martial Roger, Mordesin de Blanc, and Mariette Bellot (illegally landed), 1 barrel pork, 4 barrels flour, 2 boxes oil, 2 firkins butter.

In the Bay of Colihaut, 13 dozen ' goglets,' 22 firkins butter, 12 boxes oil, 1 bag corn (two canoes used in conveyance).

At Souffriere, 5 barrels flour, 2 barrels pork, 12 dozen claret. (The above were partly French and partly American goods.)

The Board directed forfeiture of goods in all the cases, but declined to authorize prosecution of the smugglers, they being indigent coloured people.

Early in 1833 a number of bales of cotton, which had been delivered into a lighter at Belfast from an American ship, accidentally took fire, and it was discovered during salvage that a large bale of leaf tobacco was concealed within each package of cotton.*

A new system of rafting tubs was discovered at Langstone Harbour. Sixty-three tubs had been lashed together ' in the form of a pile of shot.' Each tub had a sling attached to it, and to each sling was fastened an iron plate weighing about 8 pounds. The upper tiers of tubs were painted white. This raft had grounded in 7 feet of water, yet but three of the tubs were visible, and they from a short distance only. Two grapnels were attached to the raft, so as to be caught by dredging with a ' sweep line.'

On September 13, 1833, the coasting barge *Rebecca*, with a cargo of limestone, arrived at St. Germain's Lake, Plymouth. The coastguardsmen overhauled her, and

* In 1835 a number of barrels of pitch were landed from the same vessel, and it was found that a block of tobacco, weighing 100 pounds, was secreted within each barrel of pitch.

found 211 tubs spirits beneath the limestone. The tubs had been taken on board at sea from a ' hoverer.'

Below are illustrative extracts from the seizure lists of Port Louis and Montreal.

PORT LOUIS, MAURITIUS.

Quarter ending January 5, 1833.—This includes cigars and straw hats seized on a vessel from Calcutta ; coffee on a vessel from Bourbon ; smoked salmon on a vessel from Salem ; and coffee thrown overboard from a French schooner, and recovered by divers.

Quarter ending April 5, 1833.—Muskets and bayonets found on premises occupied by one Pyton ; loaf sugar and the boat conveying it ; cigars and the boat conveying ; coffee on a ship from Bourbon ; gunpowder and spermaceti on an American ship from Salem.

Quarter ending July 5, 1833.—Arms and gunpowder run ; sundry goods from Calcutta ; sundry goods from Singapore ; cigars and preserved ginger on a ship from Batavia ; arms on a vessel from Bourbon.

(The inhabitants were in a state of excitement over the reinstallation of the unpopular Procurator-General, Mr. Jeremie. This may account for the smuggling of arms and gunpowder.)

MONTREAL.

December 2, 1833.—Seized on the highway from a non-resident foreigner, 1 horse, 1 sled, 132 gallons of American whisky, and 156 pounds of coffee of the French West Indies.

December 30.—On the premises of I. Mack, innkeeper, 1 bale American bristles.

December 30.—On bank of St. Lawrence (owner unknown), 6 cases of clock movements, 156 dozen boxes of combs, 9 gross of buckles, 1 bridle, 1 horse-collar, 1 saddle, 1 umbrella (all American).

January 16, 1834.—In the street, ' from a non-resident,' 12 pounds of tea.

February 3.—In a cellar under a stable, owner unknown, 1,530 pounds of American tobacco.

February 4.—On premises occupied by N. C. Kurcyan, 1,200 pounds of American tobacco.

February 10.—On premises occupied by P. Darragh, 4 chests of tea, 2 packages of tobacco.

February 15.—On premises occupied by C. Wilkinson, 78 gallons of American whisky.

February 18.—On premises occupied by J. Craig, 1 chest of tea, 4 packages of tobacco.

February 26.—On premises occupied by J. Brown, 1 bag of coffee.

February 27.—On premises occupied by Louis Gareau, 2 chests of tea and 23 pairs of American gloves.

February 27.—On premises occupied by Stephen Franchiri, 2 boxes of tea, 194 pounds of tobacco.

February 28.—On premises occupied by Stephen Dier, 10 kegs of tobacco, 1 bag of coffee.

March 7.—On premises occupied by W. Megill, 2 boxes of tea, 232 pounds of tobacco, and 360 pounds of American butter.

March 26.—' In the cellar of a Frenchman ' (name unknown), 2,160 pounds of American tobacco.

March 26.—In a barn owned by one Morrison, 840 pounds of American butter.

During 1833 the collector of St. Kitts forwarded to the Board a deposition made by the master of a colonial sloop, to the effect that in the previous year he had conveyed the Honourable R. W. Pickwoad, judge of the Vice-Admiralty Court, and Lieutenant Hutchinson of the 86th Regiment, ' to the French islands,' that they bought there a considerable quantity of wine and perfumery, that he brought the sloop back to St. Kitts, and landed the goods without the knowledge of the Customs, and that the said goods were surreptitiously conveyed to the Honourable R. W. Pickwoad's residence. Both Pickwoad and Hutchinson denied the charge, and the former wrote the Board, stating that he had previously found it necessary to complain to the Secretary of State as to the conduct of Lieutenant-Colonel Nickle, the officer who administered civil government at St. Kitts, and also that of the Attorney-General for the island, and that those officials had induced the informer to make the statements in question. (Considerable correspondence ensued, ended by a statement from St. Kitts, on February 27, 1835, that Mr. Pickwoad was dead.)

During 1834, by Cap. 13 of 4 and 5 Wm. IV., the practice of sending convicted smugglers to serve for five years in the navy was abolished. The pecuniary penalties prescribed for certain smuggling offences were also abolished, and justices were granted power to imprison offenders instead.

During 1835 the Board received information of a subtle fraud. A quantity of brandy had been cleared duty-free from bond for exportation, carried to sea, transhipped to a coaster ; the casks had been placed inside puncheons containing sugar, the consignment landed as British refined sugar removed coastwise, and the brandy thus taken into home consumption free of duty.

Many ingenious ' concealments on the person ' were discovered. One man was found to be wearing a corset with eighteen quilted spaces, and a pair of drawers secured at the ankles, carrying in all 24 pounds of tea. Six men were captured wearing waistcoats, ' thigh pieces,' and ' shin pieces.' Two of them had in these receptacles nine parcels of lace each. The remaining four had eight parcels each. Several Deal boatmen were found to be fitted with ' shin pieces,' ' bustles,' ' stays,' ' thigh pieces,' and ' cotton bags to fit the crown of the hat.' Each boatman carried 30 pounds of tea.

A French sloop, laden with a full cargo of tobacco, intended for the coast of Ireland, and carrying an Irish pilot and an Irish supercargo, was driven by storm into Douglas, Isle of Man, and captured.

A petty squabble between merchants and customs

officers in Ceylon led to revelations of much illegal trading in that colony.   On September 20, 1835, Messrs. Ackland and Boyd, merchants, landed at Colombo from the barque *Anne*.   They had six turkeys with them, and it appears that they went on shore with these birds at a place not approved by the Customs for the landing of baggage and effects.   A customs officer saw them land, and insisted upon detaining the turkeys, although turkeys were duty-free, basing his action upon the circumstance that landing had occurred at an unapproved place. Ackland refused to allow him to seize the birds, and sent them back to the ship.   The officers then instituted proceedings in the island Courts for obstruction.   Ackland was acquitted, and when the report reached London the Board expressed an opinion that the officers had acted unwarrantably.   Ackland and Boyd then complained to the Board that entry had since been refused to certain wines, imported by them from Tutticorin. Inquiry elicited that the merchants had been evading the Navigation laws by importing wine from France to Colombo ' for exportation,' transhipping it to Tutticorin, and then importing it thence as goods from a British possession. (Subterfuges of this kind were common during the times of restricted trade.)   They pleaded that other merchants were allowed to do this, and indeed it seems, to one who reads between the lines, that Ackland and Boyd's goods would never have been restricted but for that unfortunate affair of turkeys.   The Board intimated that a new controller was on his way to Ceylon, and that no doubt he would try to prevent squabbles between merchants and officers, and evasions of the laws of Navigation.

Cap. 60 of 6 and 7 Wm. IV. relaxed to a certain extent the preventive regulations as to size of package and tonnage of importing vessel, allowing spirits to be imported in casks containing not less than 20 gallons, and tobacco or snuff in packages not less than 300 pounds in weight, and reducing the legal tonnage for import ships to 60 tons. It extended the powers of the Board with regard to the granting of general transires for coasting vessels. At the same time it empowered magistrates to deal with *petty* cases of smuggling without an order from the Board. This provision extended merely to cases in which the goods seized, being spirits, did not exceed a gallon, and, being tobacco, did not exceed 6 pounds. The magistrates under such circumstances might inflict fines not exceeding £5, or imprisonment for not more than one month.

In 1836 a steamer trading to London was found to have her paddle-boxes lined so as to contain a considerable quantity of contraband goods. The smack *Tam o' Shanter* was seized by the Coastguard at Padstow, 72 tubs of spirits being found concealed in spaces between the cabin and the outer timbers. She was a coaster, carrying coals.

During March, 1837, a curiously-built boat was found on the beach at Bognor. She had no thwarts, and was flat-bottomed. Her bottom was pierced so that when loaded she would sink just below the surface of the water. A net was found on board, and it was evident that she had been used for running tubs. When loaded, the net had been laced from gunwale to gunwale to keep the tubs in position, and she had then been set adrift. The smugglers had unloaded her, and left her on the beach.

On March 14, 1837, the *Sylvia* revenue cruiser seized the *Good Intent* schooner at Mount's Bay, on account of the following concealments : 26 tubs in false lining near sail-locker ; 138 tubs in a space formed by double bulkheads between hold and cabin ; 26 tubs in the coal-locker, under the coals ; 148 tubs in a space formed by double bulkheads between forepeak and hold ; 21 tubs under flooring of forepeak. The bulkheads and flooring had been newly tarred, so that the odour of the spirits should not be apparent.

On July 1, 1837, the same revenue cruiser took the *Spartan* schooner off Land's End. She had a hollow beam under the cabin floor, and a double bulkhead between the hold and the coal-hole. These spaces were filled with compressed tobacco.

There was considerable smuggling at Sydney ; witness the following seizures :

December 5, 1837.—On the brig *Gazelle*, from Boston, U.S.A., 1,211 pounds of tobacco.

June 9, 1838.—On the *Mary Ann*, of London, 503 pounds of tobacco, 115 gallons of whisky, 45 gallons of geneva.

September 14.—On the ship *Earl Durham*, 478 pounds of tobacco.

November 24.—Found in possession of a dealer at George Street, Sydney (had been shipped from bond for exportation to New Zealand, and afterwards run), 356 pounds of tobacco.

Many seizures were made in the United Kingdom on board Her Majesty's ships. We quote three specimens only :

Portsmouth.—Seventy pounds of tobacco, found concealed between bulkheads on board H.M. cutter *Seaflower*, from Jersey.

Dover.—Sixty pounds of tobacco, 10 packages of cigars, and 2 casks of spirits, found in the engine-room of H.M. Post-Office packet *Widgeon*.

Jersey.—Two hundred and fifty-two pounds of tobacco, part found ashore alongside H.M. Post-Office packet *Dasher*, part in the engine-room (illegal shipment for England).

The collector of Colombo informed the Board that the governor had prohibited the traffic hitherto carried on with passing vessels by the boatmen of Galle. The Board concurred, while hinting that care had better be taken as to the forfeiture of boats engaged in the trade, the law not being fully applicable to such cases.

In 1839 the collector of St. Kitts reported that the customs officer at Sandy Point pursued a smuggling boat, overtook her, and stepped on board to seize certain ankers

of gin. The smugglers, named respectively Lammond
and Parsons, took the officer by the neck and heels, gave
him a couple of swings, and, Lammond calling out
' Now is the time,' threw him into the sea. Then they
rowed off with the gin. They were afterwards arrested,
and Lammond was sentenced to twelve months imprisonment. Parsons was acquitted—why is hard to
discover.

The *Lady de Saumarez* arrived at Southampton from
Jersey. Part of her cargo consisted of bundles of laths,
and in the middle of each bundle was found a roll of
tobacco, weighing about 4 pounds.

A peculiar fraud was discovered at the London Docks.
It was the practice to gauge quarter-casks of brandy for
duty by the ' diagonal,' a graduated rod being inserted
in the bunghole diagonally, so that its end touched the
bottom chimb of the cask, and the gallons being read as
marked on the rod. A shrewd merchant turned this to
account by importing casks the diagonal of which was
shortened artificially, the bung stave being depressed,
and the heads put in obliquely. By this means he had
succeeded in getting his casks through each at 3 gallons
less than the actual content (the usual content of a
brandy quarter-cask being 29 to 30 gallons).

On November 19, 1839, the tobacco manufacturers of
Edinburgh memorialized the Treasury, complaining of
the injury done to their business by smuggling, and
stating that they had reliable information of a recent
transaction at Leith, where over 2 tons of cavendish were
landed ; also that they were of opinion that the customs
staff at Leith, which had been recently reduced, required
strengthening. The Board reported on the petition,
stating that they believed smuggling had increased of
late. They had recently sent officers to search certain
suspected houses in Leith and Edinburgh, and five
seizures had been made (356 pounds of cavendish in all).
In connection with this paper there is a quotation from
the London tobacco brokers' circular, calling attention

to the fact that the quantity of tobacco duty-paid during the year ending October 5, 1839, was at least a million pounds less than in the preceding year.

On November 20, 1839, four large cases were landed at one of the London legal quays, from a vessel from Hamburg, and entered on ' sight.'   The Customs received information that an attempt would be made to run these goods, and produce four substituted cases for examination.   The cases were opened at once, and found to contain about a ton of tobacco and cigars.   The goods were not seizable in a strictly revenue sense, being entered on ' sight,' a method of declaring that the contents of the packages are unknown to the importer, but they were seized as infringing the laws of Navigation, being the produce of Asia, imported from Hamburg in a foreign ship.

The following statement appeared in the *Hampshire Telegraph :* ' The Adelaide revenue cutter has recently been twenty-three weeks in this harbour (Portsmouth) refitting, in which time she was recoppered, and supplied from London with a new set of rigging.   A continuance of such gross robbery on the Government ought immediately to be remedied, and these craft should be sent to the dockyard for stores and repairs in future.   Had this been the case in the present instance the vessel in question would not have been delayed more than ten days or a fortnight.'

A seizure was made at one of the Irish ports of a quantity of English-manufactured arms, packed in large cases, the arms being concealed beneath parcels of snuff-boxes and corkscrews.

The Deal punt *Canning* was seized at Deal.   She had been ostensibly engaged in catching shellfish, but was found to have sixteen large tin cases of spirits concealed beneath her bottom boards.

A number of tin cases, each containing 63 pounds tobacco, were found in the water-tank on board an American trader.

An Ordinance of the island of Mauritius, issued on March 2, 1840, had prohibited the importation, culture, or sale of a substance called ' gandia,' formerly much used by the labouring population of that colony. The Ordinance described it as a most pernicious drug, causing furious excitement. Forty-two bales, weighing in all 1,907 pounds, were seized by the collector of Port Louis, but, it being proved that the goods had been shipped at Bengal prior to the issue of the Ordinance, the Board allowed them to be exported.

In 1841 new regulations were issued with respect to British 'open boats,' as below :

	Between Beachy Head and North Foreland.	On any other part of coast.	Along coast.
Fast rowing-boats might not go more than	4 leagues from coast	6 leagues from coast	} 20 leagues
Open boats for sailing and rowing, under 15 tons	4 leagues from coast	8 leagues from coast	} 50 leagues
Open boats for sailing and rowing, 15 tons and above	4 leagues from coast	8 leagues from coast	} 70 leagues
Decked vessels, under 15 tons	4 leagues from coast	12 leagues from coast	Around coast

(Extra privileges might be granted to fishing-boats if the masters were of good character.)

A vessel which had brought herrings from the Orkneys was seized in the Dunfanaghy district (Donegal), it being found that she had 187 bales of tobacco on board (about 10,000 pounds).

A large seizure of pirated books was made at Kingston, Jamaica, including parcels of volumes under the following titles : ' Nicholas Nickleby,' ' Oliver Twist,' ' Pickwick Papers,' ' Sketches by Boz,' ' Miss Austen's Novels,' ' History of Rome,' ' Smollett's Works,' ' Chitty's Medical

Jurisprudence,' 'The Pathfinder,' 'Moore's Life of Byron,' 'Fielding's Works,' 'Mrs. Hemans' Poetical Works,' etc., etc. This seems to have been a bad case, for the goods were entered 'on sight,' and it was afterwards found that the importer had a complete invoice. But the Board allowed the goods to be returned to the United States.

Below is a copy of the seizure list of Sydney, N.S.W., in 1841 :

May 12, 1841.—22 gallons brandy in the Commercial Inn, smuggled thither by the waiter.

102 pounds tobacco near the Queen's Wharf (seized by police).

May 26.—70 barrels beef and pork on the *Lapwing* from New Zealand, entered as 'British.' Had been originally sent from London to New Zealand, but had lost their ' British ' privileges through being landed there, New Zealand not being at the time a Crown colony.

June 4.—42 gallons brandy, seized by a civilian in Rushcutter's Bay. (The goods had been landed from a boat belonging to a passing Calcutta trader. The boat escaped with a number of other casks, but was afterwards captured and seized—the casks not found.)

September 4.—13 gallons brandy in a house in Erskine Street, Sydney.

49 cases spirits in a public-house in King Street, Sydney.

September 6.—74 gallons spirits and 60 pounds tobacco in a house in Erskine Street, Sydney.   174 gallons spirits in a public-house in Erskine Street.

September 16.—154 pounds tobacco at Kissing Point, Parramatta River.

November 23.—84 pounds snuff and 6 pounds cigars on the *Lady Raffles*, from New Zealand.

Most of the goods thus seized formed part of a huge run previously made by a notorious smuggler. It appears that a cargo of spirits and tobacco had been shipped duty-free from bond in Sydney for New Zealand, and the smuggler in question had effected the re-landing and

II.   17

distribution of the whole consignment. ' Robert Henderson,' said the report, ' has been long suspected, but living until lately in a wild and extensive harbour twenty-one miles north of Sydney by sea and seventy by land, so many obstacles have presented themselves in the way of detection that nothing before has been brought against him.'

Below is a copy of the seizure list for the Jaffna district, Ceylon, for the first four months of 1841 :

January 25, 1841.—2 shawls, on board a ' dhoney ' at Manar.

January 28.—13 skeins silk thread, concealed among rice on a dhoney.

February 1.—32 bags rice, landed without report.

February 7.—14 silk handkerchiefs and 1 silk shawl, for being landed on a Sunday.

February 8.—22 hundredweight of coriander seed and 1 hundredweight of garlic, imported in a vessel of less than the legal tonnage.

March 12.—34 pieces cloth, transhipped without entry.

March 24.—3 chelas and 1 somen (manufactures of India).

April 1.—15 bags rice and a quantity of paddy (transhipped without entry).

April 7.—6 whips, 5 pairs slippers, 17 pieces soap, 32 chowries, 4 shawls, 16 pieces cloth, 40 handkerchiefs, 2 wrappers, 2 looking-glasses, imported in a vessel of less than the legal tonnage.

April 8.—30 pounds coffee (prohibited goods), 7 yards cloth, at Point Pedro (not reported).

April 22.—4 shawls, for being unstamped.

In 1842 the revenue cruiser *Vulcan* seized the French smack *Le Courier* off Weymouth. She had arrived in ballast, and on rummaging her the revenue men found that she was provided with most ingenious ' concealments.' Between the ballast and the keelson was a false keelson, fitted with ten tanks containing spirits, each tank having an aperture leading into the next tank.

The vessel's pump was aft, and within the lining of the pump was a tube that extended from the end tank to the deck. Forward an 'air tube' extended from the deck to the false keelson, and along the tops of the tanks. Filling and emptying might be performed through the pipe that passed up the pump-lining aft (see diagram).

A few weeks later the Weymouth tide-surveyor seized the schooner *Sea Flower* for being fitted up with various elaborate concealments.

There were many seizures of British-made soap at

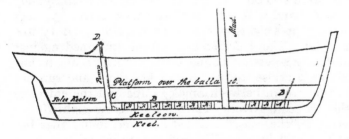

Irish ports in 1842. There was an excise duty on soap manufactured in Great Britain, and when such soap was shipped for Ireland a drawback equal to the duty was paid to the shipper. When this drawback was paid the Excise granted a 'sufferance,' which went with the goods. If the sufferance were not produced in Ireland, the goods were seizable, it being presumed they had been manufactured in Great Britain, and shipped without paying the excise duty.

On the night of December 5, 1842, the officers at St. John, N.B., seized fifteen casks of rum on the highway outside the town. Soon after they were attacked by a crowd of armed people, who tried to rescue the goods. The officers fought their way successfully, and captured four of their assailants.

As population increased in the Australian colonies, smuggling became rife. On May 30, 1842, the commander of the revenue cutter stationed at Sydney reported to the Board his recent cruise to Trial Bay to intercept the *Velocipede*, a schooner which had cleared out from Sydney to New Zealand with a cargo of 100 casks spirits, 59 kegs tobacco, 7 cases cigars, and 1 case snuff, shipped duty-free from bond. The *Velocipede* had been informed against after clearance, as not bound to New Zealand at all, but merely on a cruise, to return in a few days, and run her cargo somewhere between Smoky Cape and the entrance to the McLean River. The cutter's crew sighted her hovering off the coast, boarded her, and found that her cargo was still intact. The master stated he had been to New Zealand, and, finding that there was no sale for his goods, had decided to go to Singapore. (If he had really been to New Zealand and back, he had made a remarkably fast voyage. And why he should have called at Smoky Cape on his way to Singapore was past mortal understanding.)

Nothing could be done. There was no absolute proof that he intended to smuggle, yet there were many grounds of suspicion. For instance, the cutter found a large schooner, belonging to the owners of the *Velocipede*, lying at anchor in Trial Bay. The master stated he had come for a cargo of cedar, but it did not appear that any such cargo was in waiting. Later, too, it was found that the *Velocipede* had hovered on the coast of Broken Bay, and been warned off by fires, lit ashore by confederates who had observed that the revenue men were on the alert. Nothing could be done, but the cutter followed the *Velocipede* along the coast till she lost sight of her in

the darkness, and then a gale sprang up, and the cutter
returned to Sydney. There is nought to show what
became of the *Velocipede,* but it is likely she ran back to
Trial Bay, and transhipped her goods into the coasting
schooner, or landed them in some secret place where they
would be safe till the receivers arrived.

It is evident that the colonial revenue men made many
gross blunders. On November 6, 1842, Captain Nagle,
of H.M. colonial brig *Victoria,* while lying at Kapiti,
Cook's Straits, New Zealand, was informed by certain
Maoris that they had witnessed a run of contraband, and
that the goods had been taken to a store kept by one
Mayhew, a merchant who acted also as American vice-
consul. Nagle accordingly went to Mayhew's store, and
seized a great roll of tobacco and 200 gallons of rum.
He left the goods with the sub-collector of Wellington for
condemnation, and then it was found that Mayhew had
cleared the rum from bond, and paid the duty on it, and
that the tobacco had been imported prior to January 1,
1842, when it was exempt from duty. So the goods had
to be restored.

The year 1842 is memorable from a Customs point of
view as that in which an immense system of fraud, connived at, and partly suggested, by certain officers of the
Port of London, was laid bare. It is necessary to go back
a year or two to describe fully the circumstances of the
case. It appears that for a considerable time there had
been much confidential intercourse between many of the
London landing-waiters and certain wealthy city men
who were importers of French silks, gloves, and lace.
The waiters had the entrée of the merchants' parlours,
their wives were frequent purchasers on credit at the
merchants' wholesale stores, and able to procure expensive
dresses and all kinds of costly frippery for themselves and
friends, the goods being charged to them at wholesale
prices, and payment rarely pressed for. Some of the
waiters kept up most expensive establishments, and were
heavily in debt, their bills being backed by their merchant

friends.   The result was wholesale fraud and unblushing connivance.   Of course we can but quote from evidence, but it should be stated that undoubtedly only a few of the frauds committed came to light, and there is every reason to believe that though only a few landing-waiters were exposed and punished, the landing department was, and had for many years been, utterly corrupt, that the superior officials had winked at their subordinates' mis-doings and indirectly shared in the proceeds, and that one or two members of the Board were not above suspicion.

The arch-villain of the piece was a landing-waiter named Burnby.   The general course of his conduct may be best displayed by a few quotations from his own and his accomplice's confessions.   In 1837 he induced a landing-waiter named Homersham to join him in a profitable scheme of connivance, which consisted in allowing prohibited machinery to be exported.   As our readers will have gathered, the exportation of many kinds of machinery was forbidden by law, and consequently attempts were frequently made to export such goods surreptitiously, very high prices being obtainable in foreign countries.   Burnby and Homersham established an understanding with certain manufacturers and foreign buyers, and no doubt made a deal of money.   Soon they gained another connection, the merchants exporting dummy packages, and the officers certifying that the packages contained goods entitled to drawback.   In 1839 they connived at the introduction at St. Katherine's Dock of a large quantity of cigars in cases entered as containing marble.   In 1840 their proclivities had become so well known that a clerk employed by one of the houses in the City approached Homersham with an inquiry as to whether they ' could do business,' and a fresh arrange-ment was at once made.   The firm imported a large con-signment of gloves.   Homersham took an exact account of them in his ' rough book,' entering the particulars in pencil.   It was quite usual at the time for the landing-waiters to ' give credit,' by examining and delivering

goods before the duty was paid.   Homersham acted thus
with the gloves.   As soon as they had reached the warehouse and been dispersed among the other stock, Homersham was apprised.   Then he erased the correct account
in his rough book, and made a fresh entry of the goods,
which showed them at about half the proper quantity.
The firm entered them, and paid duty according to the
new account, and then divided the amount saved between
themselves and the officers concerned.   Thus things went
merrily on.   Soon the waiters came in touch with a large
firm of silk importers (afterwards exchequered for
£35,000), and then with another firm, so that they seemed
to be on the highway to fortune.   (Yet it appears that
Burnby had lent Homersham much money, probably to
make him secure.)   They forged entries in the official
books, taking the books to the merchant's house for that
purpose.   In short, they were extremely busy, yet they
were merely the worst of a very bad gang.   The other
waiters were engaged in frauds not quite so extensive and
daring—good old time-honoured Customs villainies, such
as deliberate undervaluing of *ad valorem* goods, and the
' faking ' of Customs tares.   Much roguery was practised
with goods imported ' on sight,' cases of high-duty
goods being entered thus, landed, and swiftly delivered,
similar cases of low-duty goods previously landed and
duty-paid, but not delivered, being brought into the
examination-room.   This last trick was done with the
connivance of both Customs and dock employés.   The
Customs and dock officials were on extremely friendly
terms ; indeed, one of Homersham's sureties was a dock
official.   This surety was convicted of extensive
smuggling, and imprisoned, yet the clerk at the Custom-
house, who was supposed to examine into the security of
officers' sureties, knew nought of the matter till years
later, when the great exposure occurred.

   Towards the end of 1841 Burnby, for some reason or
other, decided to ' peach,' and made a communication to
his brother-in-law, Captain Morgan, late of the Coast-

guard. Morgan communicated with Sir George Cockburn, and a private meeting took place on November 9, 1841, at the Admiralty : present, Burnby, Morgan, the Chancellor of the Exchequer, and the Chairman of the Customs Board. Burnby made a confession, and inculpated twenty-one landing-waiters and many London merchants. The sneaking villain then proposed, as a means of proving his statements, that packages should be imported, and the inculpated officers allowed to deal with them. This proposal was rejected, but he was put upon duty with several of the officers, with instructions to watch them and report their proceedings. Things went on without any public exposure till 1842, when Burnby induced Homersham to peach. Then a number of landing-waiters were suspended from duty, and it is evident that Burnby was blamed for informing, for things became so uncomfortable between him and his brother officers that he fled to France, but was induced to return and continue his disclosures. A Committee was formed to inquire into the matter ; members, Lord Granville Somerset, Mr. Gladstone, Mr. Baring, Mr. Milnes-Gaskill, and Mr. Pringle. Several curious episodes marked the proceedings. For instance, a return was asked for of the quantities of silks and brandies imported from France during the years 1827-1841. The Board of Trade furnished one, showing the quantities shipped in France, according to the French Customs returns, and the quantities landed in the United Kingdom, according to the British Customs returns. The French return of silk showed that during the fifteen years in question 5,344,416 pounds silk manufactures had been exported to the United Kingdom. The British return showed that 2,652,550 pounds only had been received. It would appear, therefore, that more than half the goods had either been smuggled directly, or not taken to account by men of the type of Burnby and Homersham. Yet conclusions must not be formed too rapidly. For, turning to the brandy account, we are confronted by the following

statement : From 1827 to 1833 inclusive the account of
brandy exported from France to the United Kingdom
was much larger than the import account thereof into
the United Kingdom. Then—amazing to note—*the
proportions varied the other way.* In 1834, 1,747,827
gallons were exported from France, and 2,999,012 gallons
(French brandy) imported into the United Kingdom.
And thus the imports continued to exceed the exports
down to 1841. The Committee made no comment upon
this staggering return, except a hint that the *French*
account might be wrong. Then why did they publish
it in the report ?*

Another curious episode. The Committee asked the
Chief Jerquer of the Customs to produce his book, in
order that they might ascertain the method of checking
the landing accounts of goods. The Chief Jerquer was
sorry ; his book had just been destroyed (it is to be
presumed by accident).

The Commissioners of Inquiry found many things to
complain of, but the methods of Customs management
displeased them most of all. They discovered that
though there were nine gentlemen on the Board only
two, the Chairman and Deputy-Chairman, had done any
work worthy the name. Few personal visits had been
made, and seven of the Board had next to no knowledge
of the officers they were put to control.† The seven

---

* Perhaps it is good for the believer in statistics that he has
little opportunity of intelligent comparison. Otherwise people
would have less faith in Blue-books, and many a long financial
oration which has become historical might appear a wind-borne
bag of unreliability.

† Next to no knowledge of their official qualities, but the
social excellences of certain men were well known to certain
Commissioners. The following is from a letter written by a
member of the Board to a colleague, with reference to the contemplated special promotion of Mr. ——, of the Coastguard :

' ——, you perhaps know, was introduced to ——' (one of the
Board) ' by ——, whose brother, the collector of Wells, thought
highly of him, and ——, as I think, a little irregularly, induced
—— to move him to the Isle of Wight. It was there he became
acquainted with ——' (another member of the Board), ' who, I
believe, saw a good deal of him, and thought very well of him,

' walking gentlemen ' came at eleven (eight months out
of the twelve ; they were on leave the other four), and
left at three. Even the parenthetical sentence ' eight
months out of twelve ' needs qualification. During that
eight months' spell the seven ' lay figures ' stayed away
on every Monday, and but four of them came during the
rest of the week. Thus life was one bright holiday.
Yet during the whole of the proceedings the industrious
and eccentric Chairman, Mr. Dean, continued to write
letters of indignant protest to the Commissioners of
Inquiry—letters in which, although he had every chance
of obtaining credit by comparison, he almost demanded
that scrutiny of the habits and official methods of his
colleagues should cease. ' They are gentlemen—men of
education,' was his chivalrous contention ; ' they should
not be subjected to such indignity.' One of his letters
to Mr. Gladstone was especially characteristic. It expressed the opinion that the Board's attendance should
not be regulated as though they were artisans or school-
boys, yet admitted that men were not made Commissioners of Customs because they possessed any special
aptitude. Mr. Dean then proceeded to exhibit his
incompetency as a reasoner. He stated that Government
should rely more upon men than measures. (Yet it was
evident that seven of his colleagues were incompetent,
and what self-respecting Government would rely upon
incompetent men ? And why, in the name of reason, if
the character of men was so much more important than
the issue of regulations, had the Board in the past relied
solely upon regulations—regulations which were admitted
to be utterly beyond practice—and never taken the trouble

---

and when ——'s ' (another member of the Board) ' son was about
to join Sir R. Stopford's ship at Portsmouth, —— took great
notice of him—I believe took him ' (the boy) ' into his own house,
and was very kind to him—and I am advancing nothing but what
I believe to be true by saying that —— has lost no opportunity
of ingratiating himself with any members of the Board with
whom he may have communicated, and I wish much you could
privately hear what Gowland says and thinks of him, who would
speak his mind honestly, and is no bad observer of human nature.'

to make themselves acquainted with the officers' methods of work ?)   What Mr. Gladstone, then in the full tide of his intellectual powers, thought of Mr. Dean's letters is not manifest, but it is possible they may have inspired him with that contempt and dislike of the Customs which he displayed through his subsequent career.

During September, 1843, Mr. Dean's indignation was excited still more by the appearance in the *Times* of two articles headed '.Customs Frauds,' articles which reflected upon the character of certain members of the Board.*

* The articles in question were extremely bitter.   The Board were accused of partiality and vindictiveness in their proceedings, both against certain firms which had been concerned in the frauds and the conniving officers.   It was stated that the Customs, before entering action, seized the property of the merchants who had offended, and then complicated the proceedings in a remarkable manner.   For instance, they arrested the principals of the firm of Candy and Co. several times within an hour, obliging them to secure bail on each occasion, the total sum covered by the several securities amounting to nearly £22,000.   They were not satisfied with dismissing the officials implicated ; they inquired into the pecuniary circumstances of others, some of whom had given bills upon their property.   ' Yet,' stated the article, ' the paper of some of the Commissioners themselves has been about in the market under circumstances not particularly creditable to those parties.'   The Board were also accused of resorting to discreditable proceedings and compromises in order to gain information.   ' What can we say of a surveyor-general who takes down to his private residence a parcel of dismissed officers, and who, over his own bread and cheese and ale, seeks to worm out of them their secrets ? . . . What can be gained by employing Burnby to pump a fellow now in a spunging-house for frauds on the revenue, which he ' (Burnby) ' has done by working on his victim's hopes and fears in the daytime, so that he might be primed at night to make the necessary disclosures implicating others ?'
The writer insisted that, revengeful and underhanded as their proceedings had been, the Board had taken no judicious steps to remedy the abuses existing in the department.   ' Has anything,' he asked, ' been done effectually in the corn trade, where the fraud committed in drawback upon damaged corn is as notorious as the sun at noonday ?   What has been effected in the tobacco trade, where more cheroots have been smoked in one night than have paid duty in a year ?   Have the frauds in the export of cloths been probed to the bottom ?   With the exception of the Chairman and Vice-Chairman, the Commissioners know as much of the affairs passing through their own department as their own washerwomen.'

The Board applied to the editor, demanding the name of the writer ; the editor replied that it was known to the Committee of Inquiry. The gallant old official Dean then sent Lord Granville Somerset a letter, declaring that the articles were libellous, and the Board despatched a protest to the Commissioners of Inquiry, stigmatizing the writer of the article as a ' hireling caterer to an able and unprincipled public journal.' (Later they offered to expunge these expressions.)

The inquiry proceeded, and in the end even Mr. Dean

He accused one of the surveyors-general, who had been entrusted with the task of investigating some of the frauds, of direct connivance, especially in the way of screening the informer Burnby, stating that this official had upon one occasion apprised Burnby that a special search of the station under his survey was about to be made, and adjured Burnby to conceal or remove certain incriminating packages ; also that the surveyor-general had written to an implicated officer, stating that the officer might send him on as much wine as he could get, ' at the same price.'

He blamed the Board (and not without reason) for conducting their investigations *in camera*, stating that it was only in the Customs that such unfair proceedings were carried on. The defendants, he insisted, did not hear the evidence ; the only thing communicated to them was the charge. In Customs investigations the defendant was presumed to be guilty till he proved himself innocent (a diabolical inversion of legal practice common with the higher officials of that day). In some of the cases in question the defendants were impeached *in camera* by the informer Burnby, and tried by an official who was a personal friend of that informer, and the said official made a *secret* report of the proceedings to the Commissioners.

Then he treated his readers to a few paragraphs of lurid scandal. He referred to two high officials who had taken a prominent part in the investigation, and declared that years back, when they were landing-surveyors, they were in the habit of deciding contentions as to the *ad valorem* rates chargeable on certain high-duty goods by spinning a coin on the counter of the ' Ship ' tavern, Water Lane. He stated that the Commissioners, with two exceptions, were of no use as business men ; that they were entirely in the hands of the surveyors-general (a most damning statement, if his charges against the surveyors-general were even partially correct). He then furnished a comparative statement of the official doings of several members of the Board, and of their private transactions, of which statement we supply a summary, arranged for the convenience of readers :

felt himself compelled to descend from the pedestal of
indignant challenge, and to own that there was much
need of reformation in the Board Room as well as on the
quays. The old hero admitted that he was overcome
with mortification at the turn affairs had taken. ' I had
a better opinion of the department,' he wrote, and it is
likely that his pad was blotted here and there with
scalding tears. It is certain that if any man in the
department had earned his salary Mr. Dean had. The
quantity of work got through by him was simply pro-

Official Procedure.	Semi-Official and Private Transactions.
Dismissal of a certain officer for giving a bill on effects.	Drawing bills on each other, and getting them discounted by merchants and wharfingers.
Prosecution of an ordinary smuggler for 50s. worth of contraband.	Release, without inquiry, of an opera-singer's baggage, containing hundreds of pounds' worth of contraband.

(The above, it was stated, were seizures made simultaneously
and by the same officers.)

Issue of a report condemning and forbidding the making of purchases by officers at wholesale houses.	Collusion with an inferior officer to purchase goods in the manner reprobated.

(The writer announced that he held the incriminating letters.
He even quoted them.)

The articles wound up with a statement that the Board, as
constituted, were utterly incompetent. ' The department must
have at the helm something more than mere men of family and
fashion. We want men of character and talent, who, knowing
their duty, have nerve enough to act up to it.'
Thus the *Times*, and though there can be no doubt that the
journalist responsible stuck at nothing to make attractive copy,
and that he had as suppliers of information one or two of the
subtle rascals who had been dismissed, and certain vindictive
persons in the department who had considered themselves overlooked by the Board, it is likely most of the statements were
true, and that the action of the ' Thunderer ' was to a certain
extent warrantable. (Sorrow must be expressed for Mr. Dean,
that he should have been included, even by the mere circumstance of proximity, in so public and sweeping a censure.)

digious, and may have induced the Commissioners of Inquiry to make the suggestion they did—viz., that a ' Director ' and ' Vice-Director,' with a few intelligent subordinates in close touch, would form a better staff of control than (to quote Dean) ' nine gentlemen of birth and education.'

A tremendous outburst of vigilance took place in 1843. The seizures increased in number to an amazing extent, and some of them were exceedingly creditable to the officers concerned. It had become quite evident that smuggling, especially the smuggling of tobacco, had been on the increase for several years. The manufacturers clamoured that the duties might be reduced to 1s. a pound, in order to remove the incentive to smuggling. They protested that they had been placed in the embarrassing position of either throwing themselves into the arms of the smugglers or drifting into bankruptcy. There can be no doubt that they did their very best to ' make a case ' for reduction of duty ; still, after every allowance has been made for exaggeration on their part, and also on the part of some of the notorious smugglers who about this time furnished much information to the authorities, we come to the conclusion that smuggling had never been so extensive, or carried out with such ingenuity, as between 1835 and 1843.

Early in 1843 a quantity of tobacco, cut in pieces exactly resembling shoe-soles, was seized at Portsmouth. Soon after it was found that alcohol had been extensively imported as turpentine, and passed at the turpentine rate (5s. a hundredweight). The goods were in reality only slightly flavoured with turpentine. After landing, the flavouring matter was removed by distillation, and a pure spirit obtained (strength, 60 O.P.). Information was received of an extensive fraud effected by making up tobacco in rolls resembling ' junk,' and introducing it amid coils of old rope.

The following are a few of the large seizures of tobacco made in 1842-1843 :

At London :   1,389,   11,280,
    5,242,   1,906,   3,377,   6,030
    pounds.
At Holyhead : 7,047 pounds.
At Boston : 2,172 pounds.
At Dover : 2,652 pounds.
At Goole : 11,482 pounds.
At Harwich :   3,340,   7,222,
    6,153 pounds.
At Hull : 4,560 pounds.
At Lyme : 2,705 pounds.
At Stockton (Yarm) :   5,918
    pounds.
At Arundel : 6,174 pounds.
At Exeter : 9,471 pounds.
At Grimsby : 4,161 pounds.
At Plymouth : 3,457 pounds.

At Southampton : 5,922 pounds.
At Kirkaldy : 2,063 pounds.
At Downpatrick : 1,122 pounds.
At Waterford : 28,620 pounds.
At Belfast : 3,042, 3,386 pounds.
Off the Lincolnshire coast, by
    revenue cruiser *Lapwing* :
    9,271 pounds.
In a tugboat at Tynemouth :
    8,788 pounds.
Same   locality   (seized   by
    revenue   cruiser   *Scout*) :
    6,153 pounds.
In Holyhead harbour, by the
    tide-surveyor : Two smacks
    and 7,047 pounds.

But it must not be thought that the quantities seized
bore any appreciable proportion to the quantities run.
Indeed, it was stated boldly by many experts that not
above a third of the tobacco used in the United Kingdom
paid duty.   The tobacco goods most frequently smuggled
were leaf, negro-head, and cheroots.   The smuggling was
principally from Holland, Belgium, and Prussia.   Information was tendered of one enterprising contrabandist
who made a trip every two months from Holland to
Belfast, conveying each time 40,000 pounds of tobacco.

Much of the information given came from tobacco
manufacturers, who had been compelled by contraband
competition to dabble extensively in smuggling and
adulteration.   Some of the statements made were simply
astounding.   One eminent firm of London tobacco
brokers declared their belief that from 20,000,000 to
25,000,000 pounds of tobacco were smuggled into the
United Kingdom every year.   A well-known manufacturer stated that he had been approached by a notorious
smuggler, who offered to run cargoes at £100 a time, taking
all risks.   The manufacturer thereupon cleared 49 hundredweight of tobacco duty-free from bond for exportation,
and shipped it to Holland.   The smuggler followed, took
the tobacco on board his lugger, sailed across the North
Sea, ran the goods in Deptford Creek, and brought them

by cart to the City.   This traffic was continued.   On one
occasion the smuggler had very bad weather, and lost a
man overboard.   He managed to reach the Thames, but
in a distressed condition, and he put into Leigh, Essex.
The fishermen of Leigh* helped him to land his cargo
(3 tons of tobacco), and carried it on their backs to Roch-
ford, where it was repacked into casks, and then brought
by carrier's cart to London.

A certain smuggling syndicate owned several ' hatch-
boats,' which were supposed to be engaged in fishing off
the North Foreland.   The syndicate had a regular ' buyer
and packer,' who lived at Rotterdam.   He made a practice of buying 20 tons of tobacco at a time, and repacking
the goods into small bales.   The hatch-boats sailed
across, took in cargoes of about 3 tons, covered the goods
with fish, and ran them over into Barking Creek.   During
1843 about 15,000 pounds were seized from them.   Still,
they did very well, for they succeeded in running 85,000
pounds safely.

Another syndicate imported herrings from Holland, and
landed them in casks at Billingsgate.   Along with the
herrings they brought an equal number of casks of
tobacco.   ' A few barrels,' stated the informant, ' are
opened in the salesman's presence ' (it is to be presumed
they had been previously passed by the Customs).   ' The
smugglers' agent buys the whole consignment.'   It was
stated that this syndicate had been known to land 15 tons
of tobacco during one Saturday afternoon.

At this time there were but few steamers in the coasting
trade.   That trade, including the huge coal traffic between
the North of England and London, was principally carried

---

* The fishermen of Leigh were incorrigible smugglers, and it
is only during recent years that their enterprise in this direction
has lapsed.   There may still be people in Leigh who remember
the doings of ' old ———,' a well-known smuggler, who, if information be correct, right up into the recent eighties, was in the habit
of running over to the Continent in his ' bawley,' and bringing
back cargoes of contraband goods.   It is stated that he was
caterer for the light-ships, for many of the river bargemen, and
for most of the good people of Leigh.

on by means of small sailing vessels.   Between 20,000 and
30,000 coasters and collier brigs came up London river
each year.   Many of these vessels were engaged in
smuggling.   Sometimes a coaster would ' break her
voyage,' while on her way to London, by running across
to the Continent, taking a cargo of tobacco, overstowing
the goods with coasting cargo, and then recrossing and
proceeding to her destination.   But oftener the practice
was to run the goods over in a cutter, pick up the coaster
at a place agreed upon, and tranship them into her.
Much tobacco was smuggled in this way from the Channel
Islands into the United Kingdom, Jersey in particular
being a notorious place of output of contraband.   Information was given of one inhabitant of that island who
made fifteen trips in a year, carrying 15 tons of tobacco
each time.   The goods were transhipped off the Nore
into coasting ' billy-boys.'   The importing syndicate
hired a wharf below Blackwall, at which all the goods
were landed safely.   Another venture from Jersey consisted of over 20,000 pounds of tobacco, packed in iron-
hooped bales, so as to resemble ordinary merchandise,
transhipped into a coaster in the Channel, and landed
openly in London as coastwise cargo.

A curious statement was made as to a smuggling ex-
ploit at Stockton.   A vessel loaded oak-bark at Newcastle, left for Stockton, ran over to Rotterdam, took in
a great quantity of tobacco, overstowed the goods with
bark, and then sailed to Stockton.   Vague information
as to her proceedings had reached the Stockton Customs,
and three officers were put on board on the night of her
arrival, to watch her until daybreak.   The captain got
into the confidence of one of the officers, and bribed
him.   The other two were made helplessly drunk, and
the whole of the tobacco delivered into a lighter before
morning.   The lighter was taken up the river to Yarm,
and the tobacco run into the churchyard.   A carrier
was engaged, and the whole of the goods were conveyed safely to Sheffield.   In the morning the vessel

was searched by the Customs, and nought found but oak-bark.

A great deal of tobacco was run ashore from the Pool, London, by the sailors on board the packets and cargo-boats that plied between London and the Continent. The most daring and skilful dealers in this line were the sailors of the General Steam Navigation Company. Most of these men came from the neighbourhood of Folkestone, and were the descendants of incorrigible smugglers. A great part of the goods brought by them was conveyed ashore on the persons of professional ' carriers,' and taken to the dwellings of professional receivers. The most famous receiver of all was ' Mother Gregson.' She had a tobacco-dealer's licence, and kept a chandler's shop in Barking Churchyard, a shop which was practically a ' clearing-house ' for smuggled goods. She employed a number of lads (all under sixteen years of age, and there-fore immune from prosecution), who did nothing for a livelihood except carry tobacco ashore on their persons from the vessels lying in the Pool and at the London wharves, and tramp with it down to her shop. This juvenile smuggling force was known among the waterside folk as ' Mother Gregson's gang.'* Some idea of the extent to which the conveying of tobacco ' on the person ' was carried on may be gleaned from the evidence of a waterside police expert of the time, who stated that, though 210 persons were convicted of this practice in 1842-43, it was his firm conviction that not more than one offender out of a hundred was detected. It should be borne in mind that a practised ' carrier ' could convey with ease from 8 to 20 pounds of tobacco on his person (one man was caught carrying no less than 47 pounds). Information was given, after the event, as to an extra-ordinary venture in this line. The crew of a Dutch vessel

---

* Mother Gregson was in touch with many City tobacco merchants and shopkeepers. On one occasion a large quantity of tobacco was found at her shop. The goods were undoubtedly contraband, but she escaped by producing false invoices, which, said the information, ' she procured at a few hours' notice from some of the most respectable people in the tobacco trade.'

(ten in number) brought 2 tons of tobacco to London, concealed among the cargo on board. They carried this huge quantity ashore upon their persons within a week, making several trips each day. It was stated that the customs officer who was employed to watch the vessel winked at their proceedings, receiving as reward the paltry sum of £3.

There was much smuggling of tobacco-stalks, the goods being used in the illicit manufacture of snuff. Many large manufacturers of snuff dabbled in this business. In 1844 a huge seizure of stalks was made in the Minories by several of the London police. The goods had been landed ' down the river,' and thence conveyed to the premises of an eminent London firm, a firm whose name is a household word with snuff-takers.

Flushing, Rotterdam, Antwerp, Hamburg, Bremen— all these were places where much pains were devoted to the packing and manufacture of tobacco for smuggling into the United Kingdom, principally into the great centre of absorption, London. The quiet and winding creeks and rivers of East Anglia had become favoured running-places, the goods being afterwards taken to London in market-carts and carriers' vans. But London was not the only great smuggling port. Hull ran her very close ; indeed, the records of information dealing with the ancient port on the Humber are most picturesque of all. We quote two or three :

1. A billy-boy left the Humber, ostensibly to procure ballast at Spurn Point. She ' ran over,' took in 140 bales of tobacco and stalks, and landed them on the Humber shore without a hitch. ' Part,' said the informant, ' went to ——, part to ——, the rest came to me.'

2. A smack, belonging to Faversham, went foreign, took in 3 tons of tobacco (cut, leaf, and stalks), and landed the goods on the Humber bank close to Hull. ' The shag,' said the informant, ' was brought to me by a truckman, packed in hampers.'

3. The same smack made a second trip, and arrived in

the Humber in a blinding snow-storm, after a terrible passage. She lay off Grimsby a whole day, *close alongside the revenue cutter*. Next morning she got under weigh early, and landed her cargo at Stone Creek. ' I kept the cut tobacco,' said the informant, ' and sent the stalks to Sheffield.'

4. Another vessel landed between 10 and 11 tons in one run on the Holderness coast. ' Any quantity of tobacco,' said the informant, ' may be landed at Hull.'

5. An American smuggling agent approached a Hull manufacturer, and offered to supply him with any desired quantity of smuggled tobacco. ' Leave your warehouse door open,' said the persuasive Yankee, ' and we will take care the tobacco is placed there. If it is seized, we will not ask you for any money; if it goes through safe, we shall ask you 2s. a pound in a banker's bill for two months.'

The Americans were not in ' the trade ' as much as formerly, so far as Great Britain was concerned. Their greatest feats of smuggling were performed in Ireland, but even there not to the same extent as during the 1810-1819 period. (It should be remembered that prior to 1819 there had been next to no purely preventive force in Ireland. Then the Irish Coastguard was formed, the first station manned being on the coast of Cork, where great smuggling had been transacted by Americans. It was the opinion of experts that prior to 1819 about 6,000,000 pounds of tobacco had been smuggled annually on the south-western coast of Ireland, and that the ordinary customs staff there had connived at the trade.) Still, great runs took place occasionally on the Irish coast. It was not uncommon, when a run was made, for a thousand or more of the country people to muster, armed with sticks, scythes, and pitchforks, and assist the smugglers. ' Not one of these,' ran the information, ' will incriminate the purchaser.' On p. 277 is an accredited statement of the expenses and proceeds of a run made in Ireland by Americans for an Irish purchaser, and connived at by the Coastguard.

GOODS SHIPPED (60,000 POUNDS TOBACCO).

To	£	s.	d.	By	£	s.	d.
Original cost at 4d. a pound ..	1,000	0	0	56,000 pounds tobacco sold at 2s. a pound ..	5,600	0	0
Freight cost at 1½d. a pound—	375	0	0				
Wages of ship's company ..	59	0	0				
Douceurs to ship's company ..	180	0	0				
Interest on ship's cost, depreciation	102	0	0				
Loss on weight of goods	66	0	0				
Loss by 'decoy' (so many bales to be left for the officers to seize)	150	0	0				
Bribe to Coastguard	200	0	0				
Expense of conveyance inland	250	0	0				
Extra expenses (roughly) ..	118	0	0				
	2,500	0	0				
Profit ..	3,100	0	0				
	5,600	0	0		5,600	0	0

(The transaction occupied two months.)

It was stated that many people in the Channel Islands had made large fortunes by smuggling. The supervision of cargo-boats that left Jersey and Guernsey for England was extremely slack, the Jersey and Guernsey officers merely making perfunctory surveys, ostensibly to see that no contraband goods had been shipped. So lax were the searches that in 1842 one Guernsey vessel laden with stone actually brought 12 tons of tobacco, and landed it safely in the Regent's Canal Dock, London. There was much smuggling of tobacco in casks of apples, the Customs scrutiny of the apples on shipment at Jersey being practically nothing more than a journey to obtain a declaration for the Jurat that the apples were the produce of the island. The examination of the goods on their arrival in England was equally slipshod. There was also much smuggling from the Channel Islands into France —information said more than into England.*

It is apparent that the Coastguard in the United Kingdom had for some years been miserably inefficient. The force numbered about 11,000 men, nearly two-thirds of whom were employed afloat. During the five years 1839 to 1843 inclusive this large force seized only 89,691 pounds of tobacco and 4,908 pounds of cigars. Of this the greater part was seized in 1843, through the sudden vigilance inspired by the current inquiries into revenue and revenue fraud.† It should be noted that against this the regular Customs staff had seized, in 1843 alone, 93,000 pounds of cigars and tobacco, while the excise officers had seized over 15,000 pounds as smuggled, and about an equal quantity as adulterated.

Although (thanks to contraband) tobacco must in many places have been tolerably cheap, there was much adulteration—probably resorted to in self-defence by such of the manufacturers as did not deal with smugglers. It should be observed, too, that Mr. Baring's Act, which tacitly permitted the adulteration of tobacco, had been in operation several years. The adulterants used were rhubarb-leaves, foxglove-leaves, brown paper saturated with sarsaparilla, syrup of sugar, powdered chicory-root, glutenized Irish moss, carbonate of potash, sulphate of potash, carbonate of magnesia, carbonate of lime, terra japonica, alum, sand, salt, crude nitrate of ammonia, muriate of potash, and *bread* (this last being cut up with the tobacco).

Other circumstances combined to favour fraud. The

* The manufacture of tobacco in France was granted as a licence by the Crown to various companies, who regulated prices as they chose. The smuggling into France was even worse than that into the United Kingdom. Most of it was across the Belgian frontier, and was performed by dogs specially trained to carry the goods to the various receivers. It appears from a return made in 1830 that in ten years the French revenue officers had killed no less than 40,278 of these dogs.

† Late in 1843 they made three large hauls (on the Lincolnshire coast and off Tynemouth).

regulations, circumlocutory as they were, were terribly imperfect. Leaf tobacco, stripped of the stalk, and imported in a high-dried condition, paid no more than leaf imported with the stalk in, and containing a normal amount of moisture. Thus it became a practice to ship tobacco from bond, duty-free, for exportation to the Channel Islands, dry it till it had lost a third of its weight, and then reimport it promptly for duty. A few weeks after duty had been paid the bales regained their ordinary moisture, and then they were sold to dealers at the normal weights.

The exposures of Customs connivance and rampant smuggling narrated in the last few pages did not fail to discredit certain members of the Board, and several ' retirements ' took place. It is possible that the Chairman, Mr. Dean, despite his well-known zeal and efficiency, did not escape blame, for his connection with the department ceased soon afterwards.

Large seizures were still reported from the Colonies. Early in 1843 the *Jane* arrived at Launceston, Tasmania, from Manilla, and landed, amongst other goods, seventeen butts of molasses. Ten of these were transhipped on board the *Westbrook* for Sydney ; the other seven were duty-paid as molasses. Several days afterwards a cooper observed a heap of remains of dismantled casks lying in a corner of a wharf at Launceston, and noticed that wooden cleats were nailed to the inside of some of the staves. He told one of the customs officers, who inspected the staves, and came to the conclusion that they were the remains of the casks which had been cleared as containing molasses. He went on board the *Westbrook*, examined the ten casks which had been transhipped, and found a large jar inside each cask, fastened to the inside of the staves by cleats. The ten jars contained 110 gallons of spirits.

On March 25, 1843, a large seizure was made at Sydney, N.S.W. A customs officer observed a dray, loaded with casks and escorted by Lascars, passing along Clarence Street. It stopped near ' the Albion Mills,' and unloading commenced. The officer examined the casks, and found that they contained sugar, with kegs of tobacco inside. He seized horse, dray, and goods, and sent for his surveyor. That official brought a writ of assistance, searched the mills, and found several other casks of sugar containing tobacco. Forty casks were also found in a store hard by. The total amount of tobacco seized was 17,343 pounds. The goods had been landed from the *Duchess of Kent*, a vessel recently arrived from Calcutta, and they had been cleared by the Customs as sugar.

A dispute at once arose between the Solicitor-General for the colony and the customs collector as to whether the vessel was liable to seizure, the Solicitor-General opining that she was exempt, the goods being seized after landing ; the collector that she had been liable to seizure from the moment she reached harbour, the goods having been reported under a false denomination. The case was referred to the Board, who agreed with the Solicitor-General.

It appears that another vessel belonging to the same owners was on her way from Calcutta with a similar consignment. As soon as she arrived she was searched from stem to stern, but the only goods seized were 3,000 cigars, belonging to the captain and not reported, and 80 pounds tobacco, which had been concealed by the Lascar crew. Then one of the passengers came forward, and stated that a sailing-boat had intercepted the ship off Jarvis Bay, and had put a letter on board, upon reading which the captain had directed the Lascars to take off the hatches and throw a number of large casks into the sea. Then the Lascar serang turned informer, and corroborated the passenger's statement, mentioning incidentally that the captain had given the Lascars the 80 pounds of tobacco recently seized as compensation for their trouble in jettisoning the rest. The captain was convicted, but the ship was held exempt from forfeiture, she being outside the limits when the offence took place. No proceedings were entered against the owners ; they became bankrupt.

On October 27, 1843, a Chinaman imported and entered 180,000 cigars at Port Louis, Mauritius. When the officers came to weigh the goods, they found 96 pounds of opium concealed among the cigars. The whole of the goods were forfeited.

In June, 1843, the searcher at Woodbridge Bay, Dominica, received information that goods were to be run in the neighbourhood by a sloop from Martinique. He placed himself in ambush, and soon a boat came ashore laden with contraband goods. He seized her. Then another boat put off from the sloop, making for a distant part of the bay. The searcher pursued and captured her, and found that she was also loaded with contraband. Later he attempted to seize the sloop, but was violently assaulted and repulsed. Proceedings were taken against his assailant in the Court of Grand Session, Dominica, but the grand jury returned ' no true bill,' although the defendant had admitted the offence. The collector reported that this was ' mainly to be attributed to the feeling that exists in the community against revenue officers.' But the Board did not advise any further proceedings.

On May 27, 1843, an officer at Montreal seized a trunk, landed as baggage by ' a non-resident foreigner.' It contained the following works : ' A Guide to Family History,' by the Rev. Fletcher, Finsbury Chapel (399 copies) ; ' Gallery of British Arts,' by Finden (6 copies) ; ' Scenery and Antiquities of Ireland,' by N. P. Willis (36 copies) ; ' Canadian Scenery,' by N. P. Willis (50 copies) ; ' The Parent's Gift,' by Susan Jowett (5 copies).

It appears that they were seized as landed without payment of duty, not as piracies (Willis and Jowett, we presume, would be American authors). The seizing officer's report stated : ' I found the case had been landed as baggage, with instructions that it should be sent to a tavern in this city. The individual stated that the package had been forwarded here in mistake. As he is known to be engaged in the contraband trade, I did not place any faith in his statement.' The books were forfeited, but the smuggler was not prosecuted. It is evident that books were smuggled extensively from the

United States into the British North American possessions, merely to escape the duty.

Cap. 16 of 7 Vict. declared tobacco-stalks to be tobacco within the meaning of the revenue Acts (this was not to repeal the existing prohibition of their importation), and extended the liability of detention, attaching to persons found on ships that had contraband goods on board, to persons on foreign mail-packets. It also provided that the penalty for an offence against the revenue in which several persons were concerned should attach to each offender, and that smugglers convicted more than once should become liable to imprisonment with hard labour.

The Lieutenant-Governor of St. Vincent wrote to the Treasury, suggesting certain measures for the repression of smuggling in that island. It appears that much gin was run, the coloured people preferring it to the rum manufactured in St. Vincent, and that the Legislative Assembly of the island objected to the appointment of an extra customs officer, they being doubtful whether the finances of the colony would bear the strain, but they recommended that the police should be stimulated by a grant of the whole of the ' officers' share ' of reward for seizure. In this recommendation both Board and Treasury concurred.

Dr. Bartlett, editor of the *Albion*, a periodical published at New York, complained to the Treasury through the governor of Jamaica that the Kingston customs officers had seized as piracies several hundred copies of his paper. He forwarded eight specimen copies, and the Customs lawyers thought they did not warrant seizure. But when the Board's notice to release the goods reached Jamaica the collector replied to the effect that some of the copies contained matter entitled ' Life and Adventures of Martin Chuzzlewit,' and other extracts from works which were on his copyright list. Then Dr. Bartlett stated that he had authority to publish ' Martin Chuzzlewit.' All the Customs lawyers continued in the opinion that the papers were not seizable. Things looked rosy for the American editor, till the Customs secretary thought of applying to

Mr. John Murray for an opinion. Mr. Murray's reply was so emphatic that we reproduce it :

'*June 27*, 1844.

'DEAR SIR,
    'I now return the numbers of the *Albion*, and enclose for your perusal letters from Mr. Colburn, the publisher, and from Mr. Turner, who is well versed in the law of copyright.
    'Were such a paper as the *Albion* published in Great Britain, I should feel myself called upon to bring an action against the publisher of so gross a piracy. I have no doubt I should obtain an injunction. It is little more than a selection of the best articles from our best periodicals, which are copyright as much as any separate volume. I see our paper from *The Quarterly* among others, for which £80 was paid, printed here *in extenso*.'

(Letters were enclosed from Colburn and from Mr. Turner, solicitor to the Society for the Protection of British Literature, stating the papers contained glaring piracies.)
    This correspondence was referred to the lawyers, and they at once qualified their original opinion. A Treasury Minute of July 20, 1844, confirmed the seizure.
    The sub-collector at Black River, Jamaica, seized fifty-five smuggled Panama hats, and the horse carrying them, on the highway between Black River and Savanna-la-Mar, on December 5, 1844. The goods were escorted by a Spaniard named Juan Ernandez. The sub-collector took Ernandez and the seized goods into the yard of a settlement close by, and asked one George Adams to act as interpreter, Ernandez being unable to speak English. Adams entered into conversation with the Spaniard, but declined to interpret the meaning thereof. Suddenly he and the Spaniard set upon the officer, dragged him across the yard, and threw him with great violence against a gate, injuring him seriously. For this they received twelve months' imprisonment.

It will be seen from a perusal of the foregoing that there had been little or no improvement in commercial morality. Some of the old methods of smuggling had become unfashionable, but they had been replaced by new ones. Concealments on board, transhipment into coasting craft, the running of goods which had been cleared duty-free for export, and the rafting and sinking of tubs of spirits, had become the favourite manœuvres. The old fighting methods had been abandoned. The practice of mustering ' batmen ' to protect a run had practically ceased since 1832, when the whole of the preventive men were supplied with firearms, for the smugglers found that the long hard ' bat,' which in the hands of an athletic longshoreman had often overcome dirk and cutlass, was of little use against a loaded musket. Another new phase of the contraband trade was the extensive smuggling of tobacco in preference to spirits.

LIST OF AUTHORITIES.

Revenue legislation : The various Acts quoted in text.

Incidence of duties, etc. : The various books of rates and Service handbooks.

Colonial revenue and smuggling : Antigua, St. Kitt's, ' Reports,' ' Treasury,' Dominica, Jamaica, ' Promiscuous,' Quebec, Newfoundland and New Brunswick, Australia, Tasmania and New Zealand, Nova Scotia, Mauritius, Ceylon, Montserrat, and Montreal files.

British smuggling : London *Times*, March 30 and 31, and May 30, 1827 ; General Letters, 1827, 1828, 1829, 1830, 1831, 1832, 1834, 1835, 1836, 1837, 1839 ; Admiralty Papers, 1832, 1833, 1839 ; Treasury Papers, 1834, 1835, 1839, 1840, 1841, 1842, 1843 ; ' Remarkable Seizures ' (Customs Library), 1842.

Departmental regulations : General Letters, 1828, 1829, 1830, 1832, 1833, 1836, 1839 ; Treasury Papers, 1834 ; General Letters, 1840, 1841, 1842, 1843, 1844.

Liverpool : ' Inquiry into Condition and Discipline of Liverpool Customs ' (Customs Library) ; General Letters, 1839, 1840.

Theft of public money : ' Robbery of the King's Chest ' (Customs Library).

Botany Bay and Broken Bay : ' Curious Board's Papers' (Customs Library).

Carlist purchase of arms, Malabar fish-oil, coffee-husking, and guano : Treasury Letters, January 3, January 16, and May 6, 1840, and September 21, 1841.

Infringement of Passenger Acts : General Letters, 1840.

Seizure of flags : Dominica file.

CHAPTER III

PERUSAL of that portion of the preceding chapter which deals with tariffs and departmental history will have revealed to readers that the duties imposed by the Consolidating Acts of 1833 were in many instances altered during the eleven years following. Other important alterations had been made in the revenue laws, notably the substitution of hard labour for impressment into the navy as a punishment for smuggling, and the removal of the prohibition of exportation of machinery. In 1845 it was considered necessary to issue ten new statutes, re-consolidating the Customs.

The first of the new Acts, Cap. 84 of 8 and 9 Vict., repealed the ten Consolidating Acts of 3 and 4 Wm. IV., as well as fourteen Customs Acts passed subsequently. Cap. 85 regulated the management of the Customs. Cap. 86 recited the usual provisions as to report, entry, times of work, Customs right of search, method of securing *ad valorem* duties, returned goods, ships' stores, certificates for goods entitled to special import privileges, and derelict goods. It also contained the usual list of restricted and prohibited articles. The restricted articles were fish of foreign taking, which might only come in vessels regularly cleared out from foreign ports as traders ; goods from places within the East India Company's charter, which might only come into certain approved ports ; infected hides, etc., which might be prohibited from time to time by Order in Council ; parts of articles, which might only come in packages containing the other component parts ;

285

tea, which still might only come from the Cape of Good
Hope and places eastward towards the Straits of Magellan ;
gloves, silks, spirits, and tobacco, which were subjected
to the restrictions as to tonnage of importing ship, size
of package, etc.   The goods prohibited without qualification were articles of foreign manufacture marked as the
produce of the United Kingdom, pirated books, paper
printed on in English, clocks and watches improperly
marked, counterfeit money, malt, snuff-work, spirits
from the Isle of Man, tobacco-stalks, and tobacco-stalk
flour.   Arms and ammunition might only be brought
under royal licence, and no goods might come from the
Isle of Man except foreign corn and flour, and such articles
as were produced in the island.   (It should be understood
that all the above articles, except arms, ammunition,
pirated books, infected articles—and silks, gloves, tobacco,
etc., in illegal packages—might be *imported and warehoused for exportation*.)   With regard to export goods,
arms, ammunition, pearl ashes, military and naval stores,
and provisions, *might* be prohibited by Proclamation or
Order in Council.   Exportation of clocks and watches
' without the movements,' and of metal-work inferior to
silver and set upon lace, was utterly prohibited.   The
coasting regulations were also recited.   Cap. 87 consolidated the preventive regulations, introducing little
that was new, except that it extended to customs officers
the powers held by excise officers of search in connection
with illicit distillation or brewing, and that it defined the
Customs power of search of the person, and granted
power to customs officers to execute revenue warrants
within the metropolitan police district.   The Navigation
laws were reaffirmed by Cap. 88, and the laws governing
registration of ships by Cap. 89.
    Cap. 90 recited the duties.   The following articles,
previously dutiable, were made free : Agates not set,
alkali, alkanet root, bitter almonds, aloes, alum, rough
amber, ambergris, amboyna wood, angelica, annatto,
antimony, argol, aristolochia, arsenic, asphaltum, un-

BOARD-ROOM, CUSTOM HOUSE, LONDON.

(*Present day.*)

To face p. 286.

enumerated balsams, barilla, bark, barwood, basket-rods, beef-wood, unenumerated berries, singing birds, bitumen, judaicum, bladders, bones, boracic acid, borax, certain kinds of bottles, box-wood, brazil-wood, brimstone, bronze works of art, camomile flowers, unrefined camphor, cam-wood, candlewick, canes not mounted, caoutchouc, carda-moms, cassia, castor, unmanufactured chalk, cedar-wood, china-root, chip, cinnabaris nativa, citrate of lime, citric acid, civet, coal, cobalt, cochineal, colocynth, columba-root, copperas, coral, cotton yarn, cream of tartar, rough crystal, cubebs, cutch, divi divi, down, unenumerated drugs, ebony, undressed feathers, flax and tow, flocks, flower-roots, fustic, galls, gamboge, gentian, ginseng, glue waste, grease, greaves, guano, unenumerated gums, gunstocks, gypsum, unmanufactured hair, heath, helle-bore, hemp, undressed and unenumerated hides, hides only tanned, hones, hoofs, hoops, horns, indigo, unwrought inkle, unwrought iron—the irons known as cast, bloom, chromate, rod, and hoop—jalap, jet, unset jewels, lemon and orange juice, kingwood, sticklac, lapis calaminaris, lard, shaven latten, lavender flowers—all lead except pig, sheet, and manufactured—leaves of roses, leeches, lentils, litharge, logwood, madder, mahogany, manganese ore, manna, unenumerated manures, bell-metal, moss, mother-of-pearl, musk, myrrh, certain nuts, oakum, ochre, many kinds of oil (including train-oil, etc., of British taking), oilcake, olibanum, olive-wood, orange-peel, orchal, un-enumerated ores, orpiment, orris root, unmanufactured painters' colours, palmetto thatch, pink root, pitch, plaster of Paris, platina, chip plait, pomegranate peel, quicksilver, quills, radix, rags, redwood, rhubarb, rose-wood, rosin, safflower, saffron, sal, saltpetre, sanguis draconis, Santa Maria wood, sapan wood, sarsaparilla, sassafras, satin wood, saunders, scammony, certain kinds of seeds, senna, shumac—raw, waste, and undyed thrown silk—skins, sponge, stavesacre, unwrought and scrap steel, straw for plaiting, sweet wood, talc, tar, tarras, tartaric acid, teasels, terra japonica, terra sienna, terra umbra,

terra verde, tin ore, tincal, tornsal, unmanufactured
tortoiseshell, tulip wood, turmeric, the rougher kinds of
turpentine, valonia, ancient vases, vermilion, walnut
wood, mineral water, beeswax, myrtle-wax, weld,
British-taken whale-fins, certain kinds of staves, teak,
New Zealand wood, wool, camel yarn, and raw linen yarn.
It was also provided that any unmanufactured goods
which might be imported subsequently, and which were
not specified, either as free or dutiable, in the new tariff,
should be free.

The only export duty that survived was on coal exported
in foreign ships (4s. a ton).

This tedious list of exemptions is quoted to show the
extent to which the tariff was simplified. Most of the
articles made free had been previously subjected to
nominal duties only, and collection had in many instances
been complicated by provisions favouring British shipping.
It will be observed that the articles were principally
' raw ' products. The momentous duties on lace, manufactured silks, tea, tobacco, wine, and spirits remained
unaltered. The rates were still in many instances
preferential as regarded goods from British possessions.

Cap. 91 dealt with the warehousing of goods. The
Commissioners of Customs might still appoint the tobacco
warehouses, providing for them out of the Customs
receipts, and levying rent on packages for reimbursement.
Warehoused goods on delivery were to be duty-paid at
the original landing quantity, except sugar, tobacco,
wine, coffee, cocoa, pepper, and corn, on which goods
allowance was to be made for natural waste.*

Cap. 92 dealt with bounties on exported goods. The
only goods thus favoured were the various kinds of
refined sugar.

Cap. 93 regulated the colonial trade on much the same
lines as previously. The Board of Customs had power to

---

* The allowances on wine, coffee, cocoa, and pepper were only
granted when the goods were delivered from warehouse for
exportation.

transform intercolonial into coasting trade, and the governors to appoint custom-houses. The queen by Order in Council might establish 'limited' as well as free ports. The old provisions as to permission to foreign nations to trade direct with the colonies, bringing only their own products, but carrying goods for export from the colonies to any place, were reaffirmed, with the usual conditions as to reciprocity.

Cap. 94 regulated the trade of the Isle of Man, the duties being as before. The quantities of spirits, tobacco, and cigars which might be imported into the island remained unchanged, and so did the management and application of the duties, except that a repealed grant of harbour duties to the Harbour Commissioners was made good by a grant out of the island Customs.

Among the confidential letters of 1845 we find a curious communication signed 'Strathallan.' It was originally sent to the Treasury, and desired that 'young Burnett' (a customs landing-waiter in Tasmania) might be favoured. It quoted certain statements made to the writer in a letter from Burnett, which represented the colony as a sink of iniquity, a receptacle for rogues and vagabonds from all parts of the world, etc., and attributed this unsatisfactory state of affairs to the measures taken by Lord Stanley for the settlement of the colony.*

For several years the Board had been vexed with complaints from shipowners that British trade to the Mauritius suffered through a practice by French vessels of bringing wine from France, touching at Port Louis, and apprising the wine-merchants there, then going to the adjacent French settlement of Bourbon, and waiting the arrival of craft from Port Louis, into which the wine was transhipped, and then conveyed to Port Louis, where the Customs allowed it to be landed at the low rate as brought in British ships. 'The General Shipowners' Society'

* It is likely the letter had effect. Burnett was made collector of Launceston, Tasmania, by Treasury Warrant of August 22, 1848. (His father was sheriff of Tasmania, and related to a certain noble Scottish family.)

stated that out of 9,332 casks of French wine imported into Mauritius in 1831 nearly two-thirds arrived by this crooked line of traffic.   There can be no doubt that this practice was adopted to evade a special Order in Council of 1827, and that it was just a cumbrous way of breaking the regulations ; yet, though the correspondence on the matter was voluminous and amazingly intricate, it appears that the Customs lawyers shirked giving a decision.   Hair-splittings most microscopic, opinions most contradictory, pervade the papers, yet nothing definite was delivered till 1846, when the Board announced that such traffic was legal.

A list of emigrants, forwarded by the collector of Quebec to the Board in connection with an unfounded charge of infringement of the Passenger Acts, furnishes instructive information as to the usual type of settler in Canada. The vessel concerned left London in 1842, but the investigation did not terminate till 1845.   She carried 134 passengers, the greater part being women and children. Of the adults one was a tanner, one a dentist, one a teacher, one a doctor, one a carpenter, four were drapers, four servants, three dealers, and no fewer than twenty-five were farmers.   Only three of the farmers were over thirty-five, and all bore distinctive Midland-English names. It is worth a little mental debate as to whether the reduction of the corn duties had anything to do with this preponderance of agriculturists.

Cap. 22 of 9 and 10 Vict. amended the corn laws, providing that the following duties should be paid on foreign wheat till February 1, 1849 :

AVERAGE MARKET PRICE OF BRITISH WHEAT.

				Duty Payable.		
				£	s.	d.
Under 48s.	..	..	..	..	0	10	0
48s., and under 49s.	..	..	..	0	9	0
49s., and under 50s.	..	..	..	0	8	0
50s., and under 51s.	..	..	..	0	7	0
51s., and under 52s.	..	..	..	0	6	0
52s., and under 53s.	..	..	..	0	5	0
53s., and upwards	..	..	..	0	4	0

(Proportionate rates for other corn and for flour and meal.)

On February 1, 1849, these duties were to be abolished, and a tax of 1s. per quarter to be imposed on *all* foreign *corn*, and of 4½d. on every cwt. of foreign flour and meal.

Cap. 23 amended many of the duties leviable under the Consolidating Act of 1845, abolishing those upon animals, bacon, beef, bottles, casts of figures, caviare, cherry-wood, cranberries, cotton manufactures not made up, enamel, gelatine, glue, hay, certain hides, printers' ink, wrought inkle, lamp-black, unenumerated linens not made up, magna grecia ware, manuscripts, maps and charts, mattresses, meat, medals, parchment, partridge-wood, pens, plantains, potatoes, pork, purple-wood, dyed thrown silk, telescopes, unenumerated thread, unenumerated woollens not made up, vegetables, and vellum. It also lowered the duties on many kinds of wood and seeds. Cap. 94 gave power to the Legislatures of the colonies in America and the Mauritius to reduce or repeal the colonial Customs duties. Customs officers were made competent to conduct proceedings in Customs cases, under the direction of the Commissioners. Cap. 102 slightly reduced the duties on colonial spirits.

An anonymous letter reached the Board from Manchester, England, complaining of the customs men at Montreal. It stated that the collector and controller were interested in pushing forward the supposed pending transference to the Colonial authorities of the power of appointing officers, as they were desirous of recommending their own nominees, who were brother ' Odd Fellows.' It went on that when ' the navigation ' opened in spring there was always a rush of business at the Custom-house, and that the merchants were much obstructed by the dilatoriness and circumlocution practised by the officers. The complaint was sent to Montreal, and evoked an indignant denial, the officers furnishing an account of the duties taken from May 5 to 31 (the ' busy time ') in 1845 and 1846. (Amount in 1845, £79,329 currency ; in 1846, £67,580.) The officers stated that nearly all the respectable people of Montreal were ' Odd Fellows '—' the late

Lord Metcalfe was one.' And they sent on a testimonial to their own capacity and alertness, signed by many merchants of Montreal.

The Governor-General of Canada complained to the Treasury that Mr. Jessopp, collector of Quebec, had refused to furnish him with a list of seizures. The Treasury directed Jessopp to comply, but the undaunted collector merely stated that there were no seizures to return, and hinted that the governor should first have applied to the Board. (Jessopp was an old offender in this way. See p. 179.)

The gradual narrowing of the London Customs Board's influence in colonial matters is exemplified by a letter from the Treasury to the Board, dated August 4, 1846. Their Lordships referred to a recent complaint made by the governor of New Brunswick as to appointment of customs officers, and directed the Board to forward all future communications, intended to reach colonial governors, through the Treasury.

The sale of bait to foreign fishermen by certain inhabitants of Newfoundland had become a burning question in the North American colonies, and with the various British firms that continued to send vessels to fish on the Banks. The administration of most of the regulations affecting the Newfoundland fisheries had been for many years vested in the North American customs officers. They supervised the delivery of stores duty-free for the British and colonial fishers' use ; they took charge of foreign vessels seized for encroaching, etc., and either condemned them if no appeal was made, or, if the seizure were disputed, entered the necessary action in the Vice-Admiralty Court of the colony concerned. The sub-collectors along the coast were expected to apprise the proper authorities of any foreign encroachments that came to their knowledge. It appears that the customs men tried their best to enforce the Fishery laws, but were foiled by the apathy and timorousness of the British controlling departments. The treaties between Great Britain and France and the

United States had been drafted vaguely, and without due consideration of the importance of the issues involved. Thus report after report was transmitted of insolent trespass by American fishermen, and of the uninterrupted smuggling of bait, yet little notice was taken. The Board either evaded the issue, being, it appears, dubious as to their powers, or referred the reports to the Treasury or Foreign Office, and those departments were equally cautious. It is evident, too, that colonial feeling on the matter varied considerably. The better class of people in the North American colonies were anxious that British and colonial priority in the fisheries should be preserved. The ' scallawag ' class, especially in Newfoundland, revelled in evasion, in the open sale of bait to foreigners, and in welcoming their encroachments, which gave abundant chances of exchanging fish for contraband. There can be little doubt that the annihilation of the ancient British fishing industry on the prolific Banks was due to the milk-and-water policy of the imperial administrators. Evidence on the point may be gleaned in plenty from the Customs files.

In 1844 the governor of Newfoundland asked the Secretary of State whether the provisions of Cap. 26, 26 Geo. III., prohibiting the sale of bait, etc., to foreigners, were still in force, or whether they had been repealed by Cap. 59 of 3 and 4 Wm. IV. and subsequent Acts. The law officers of the Crown had given quite a non-committal opinion, implying that the Act was in force, but that the practice had changed, and hinting that the new principles of Free Trade were against rigid enforcement of such statutes. The Customs lawyers also thought the Act applied, but that its provisions should be enforced by the colonial governors, not by the Customs.

The Newfoundland Assembly forwarded an address to the queen, extolling the Fisheries as a time-honoured nursery of naval seamen, and alluding to the many natural advantages possessed by the colony. They described the population as 100,000, all of British extraction. They

valued the annual imports at £800,000, and the exports
at £1,000,000. But they bewailed the existing illicit
traffic in bait with St. Pierre and Miquelon, stating that
it would destroy the local fishery, as the cod were desert-
ing their old haunts, and congregating on the shores of
the French islands. The French fishery had increased to
nearly 300 square-rigged vessels of from 100 to 400 tons,
and a multitude of open boats. The French import of
bait from Newfoundland reached 70,000 barrels caplin
and 28,000 barrels herring per year. Twenty thousand
men were employed in the French fishery, and in 1843
they had caught 1,400,000 quintals of cod, against
1,000,000 quintals caught by British and colonials.*

What was the reply? A tame letter from Lord Stanley
to the governor, asking if it would be practicable to carry
into effect Cap. 26, 26 Geo. III., and hinting that the Act
might be deemed obsolete. The governor, no doubt
accepting the hint towards temporizing, replied that it
would be inexpedient to enforce the Act, as the (illegal)
exportation of bait was *the poor man's trade!* Thus it
came about that the Newfoundland legislators were induced to compromise by levying a small duty on exported
bait. The whole of the official proceedings seem contemptible.

In 1845 the customs sub-collector at Little Bay reported
that little duty could be collected on bait unless cruisers
were kept on the coast to enforce compliance with the
Act. The Customs lawyers replied that the responsibility
lay with the colonial authorities.

In 1846 a cruiser was appointed to supervise the trade
in bait, and to check encroachments by the French. To
form an opinion of the extent of successful protection of
an important industry likely to accrue, one has but to
read the instructions given to Commander Oke. He was
told that under the existing treaties the French might not

* The British and colonial fishermen complained much of the
French system of fishing on the Banks with the 'bultow,' an
immense tangle of wires and lines covering a huge space of water.

fish or take bait nearer than three miles from the south-west coast of Newfoundland or east of Cape Ray, and nearer than mid-channel directly between Newfoundland and the French islands.   Penalty, forfeiture of ship and tackle.   But, to avoid international complications, he was not to seize encroaching vessels.   He was to identify them, and then wait on the Commandant of St. Pierre, and desire him to punish the offenders under the French laws. Oke was to carry a pendant and colours, and not to use arms except in self-defence.   Thus it will be seen that, if an offending vessel tried to escape identification, he might not even fire an unshotted gun ; that if he desired to board her to see the master's papers, and the crew resisted, he might not sustain his search, for he could not then be said to be acting in self-defence ; and that, whilst assuming the power of enforcing the conditions of a treaty, the legality of any action he might take was to be determined in the end by laws other than those embodied in the treaty.   An officer thus hampered would, it may be conceived, read between even the non-committal lines of his instructions, and take care not to bestir himself much.

By Cap. 1 of 10 and 11 Vict. it was prescribed that the reduced duties on corn, meal, and flour imposed by Cap. 22 of the preceding year should be suspended from January to September, 1847.   Cap. 2 allowed the importation during the same period of corn, rice, flour, meal, and potatoes in any ships from any country, the Navigation laws notwithstanding ; and Cap. 3 extended the suspension of import duties to buckwheat, maize, and rice. These temporary Acts of relief were passed on account of the partial failure of the home and colonial corn crops. Cap. 23 complicated revenue matters considerably by differentiating the duties on colonial spirits according to country of importation.*   This queer statute disarranged collection as below :

* To meet the wishes of West Indian traders.   (The Excise duty on home-made spirits varied proportionately.)   Differentiation continued, with slight variations, till 1858.

Rum of British possessions within the East India Company's charter, spirits and strong waters of the American colonies, and rum-shrub of the British possessions within the East India Company's charter or in America.	Previous duty : the proof gallon in the United Kingdom, 8s. 10d. Duty under this Act : In England, 8s. 7d. ; in Scotland, 4s. 5d. ; in Ireland, 3s. 5d.

Under the new arrangement no foreign spirits might be removed from one part of the United Kingdom to another except first warehoused in bond, and when they arrived in the other country they were to be duty-paid at the rate obtaining there. Spirits duty-paid in Ireland were not to be taken to Scotland or England, and no warehoused foreign spirits were to be taken to England from Scotland except by sea.

Cap 64 of 10 and 11 Vict., passed on July 9, 1847, under prospect of another bad harvest, extended the suspension of duty on foreign corn, etc., till March 1, 1848, and Cap. 86 extended the privilege of importation of those articles in any ship from any country till the same date.

The Chairman of the Board (Sir Thomas Fremantle) issued a circular, stating that since his recent appointment he had received many letters from noblemen and gentlemen, soliciting the promotion of certain officials, and that he was convinced these applications had been instigated by the officers concerned.

It appears that up to 1847 the bottles allowed to be used by merchants in taking their duty-free samples of wines and spirits had been smaller at the outports than in London. This is but one instance of the many discrepancies that prevailed in ancient Customs practice.

During 1845 the Board had refused to grant a British register to the British-built ship *Ecuador* (belonging to the Pacific Steam Navigation Company), because certain foreigners held shares in the concern. The Company took proceedings in the Court of Queen's Bench, and the Court directed that a peremptory mandamus should issue, requiring registration of the vessel. This decision was based on the ground that the Company applied in its corporate capacity, on which account the Court could not take notice as to whether the constituent members were foreigners or not.   (This seems an extraordinary verdict.) The Board referred the matter to the Privy Council for Trade, asking if it would be necessary to alter the Navigation laws on account of the decision.   The Council replied that they did not think any alteration necessary, and directed the Board to notify all the customs collectors, which was accordingly done in 1847.

As this treatise is approaching the period at which the severance of the British and colonial Customs was initiated, we supply a list of the colonies for the year 1847 :

Antigua.	New South Wales.
Bahamas.	New Zealand.
Barbadoes.	Nevis.
British Guiana.	Nova Scotia.
Bermuda.	St. Helena.
Canada.	St. Kitts.
Cape of Good Hope.	St. Lucia.
Ceylon.	St. Vincent.
Dominica.	Sierra Leone.
Gambia.	South Australia.
Grenada.	Tasmania.
Jamaica.	Tobago.
Mauritius.	Tortola.
Montserrat.	Trinidad.
New Brunswick.	Victoria.
Newfoundland.	

The establishments of many colonies which are now important were at this time imperfect, large stretches of coast being left unprovided with custom-houses and collectors.   Below is an account :

Canada.—A collector at Quebec, a collector at Montreal, sub-collectors at Gaspe and New Carlisle (two ports and two ' outbays ').

New South Wales.—A collector at Sydney (one port only).

South Australia.—A collector at Port Adelaide (one port only).

Victoria.—A collector at Melbourne, a sub-collector at Portland Bay (one port and one outbay).

Tasmania.—A collector at Hobart Town, a sub-collector at Launceston (one head port and one minor port).

New Zealand.—A collector at Auckland, sub-collectors at Wellington, Russell, Akaroa, Nelson, and New Plymouth (one head port and five minor ports).

Cape of Good Hope.—A collector at Cape Town, sub-collectors at Simon's Town, Port Elizabeth, Mossel Bay, and Port Beaufort (one head port and four minor ports).

Ceylon.—A collector at Colombo, sub-collectors at Jaffna, Galle, Trincomalee, and Pantura (one head port and four minor ports).

During 1847, the few imperial duties remaining having been abolished in Nova Scotia, a new official, called the ' Controller of Navigation laws,' was stationed there. This appears to have effected abolition of the Board's control of *revenue* in that colony, and in the following year several other colonies were dealt with similarly. In most instances the imperial staff remained, and took office in the provincial Customs. The new ' Controller's ' duties were defined as below :

1. To enforce the surviving Navigation laws.

2. To issue certificates of registry to British and colonial-built ships.

3. To enforce the laws governing colonial commerce— viz., to preserve the exclusive privileges of the numerous ' free ports,' to see that the various Orders in Council that dictated occasional relaxations were not abused, and to grant the certificates for colonial produce exported to other colonies and to the United Kingdom.

4. To assist in the compilation of statistics by furnishing the returns required by the home statists.

5. To compile annual returns for the imperial Parliament.

6. To enforce the Passengers Act, the Merchant Seamens Act, and the consolidated Acts for the suppression of the slave-trade.

Some of the new controllers soon caused trouble : see

the following brief account of the situation at Halifax and Nevis :

Pending arrival of the controller at the former port, the governor appointed an acting controller, who at once began to air his self-importance, insisting that the provincial collectors of customs should send their letters to the colonial Secretary through him (the controller). The Board soon disabused his mind on this point. The real controller arrived (he had been imperial collector at Antigua), and it appears that he made himself more agreeable than his predecessor had done, for the governor gave him the job of collecting the colonial customs at Halifax, but only paid him £300 a year in currency. The Board objected to his taking over the job, hinting that, as his pay from the imperial funds was £600 sterling, the governor was trying to economize at the expense of the United Kingdom. The Treasury were inclined to allow him to officiate, but the Board made a telling and spirited statement, urging that the Navigation laws, under which he acted, were almost amended out of existence, and would soon be repealed, and that he was therefore overpaid already as controller. They reiterated their former hint that the colony proposed to profit at the expense of the United Kingdom, and pointed out that, as provincial collector of Halifax, he would deal with about £60,000 a year, principally collected from distilleries. In the end the Treasury forbade him to accept the additional employment.

The controller at Nevis obtained the job of collecting certain colonial duties, his compensation to be a percentage on receipts, and the Legislature of the island embodied his appointment in an Act, but this did not prevent the Board from insisting that the governor should obtain the sanction of the Treasury. The additional appointment was not sanctioned till 1851, and then it was directed that the sum received by the officer as percentage should be deducted from his pay as controller. He soon resigned the extra employment,

stating that his remuneration from it was insignificant.
' Although I have advanced a step in rank, I have lost
in pocket.'

Considerable trouble was given during 1847 by Lord
Howard de Walden. That nobleman, who had recently
assisted in arranging at Lisbon a Treaty of Commerce
between Great Britain and Portugal, sent his effects,
consisting principally of British goods and the wines of
Oporto, direct to Montego Bay, Jamaica, where he had
an estate. He went to London and thence to Jamaica,
and was much annoyed to find that the articles had been
charged with duty as foreign goods. He declined to
pay, urging that his effects, being originally British,
should be duty-free, and that he should pay no higher
duty on his wine than if he had imported it from the
United Kingdom. He referred to the share he had taken
in the Treaty as a proof that he might claim to understand matters of trade between Portugal and the British
possessions. Undoubtedly he was in error, but the
Board remitted the duty on his effects, while insisting
that he should pay the foreign duty on his wine.

A curious question arose at Kingston, Jamaica. One
Watson arrived at that port on July 20, 1847, in command of a cutter called the *Sun*, registered at London.
He carried cargo from the Spanish Main, and claimed
exemption from tonnage duties because he held a commission from the king of the Mosquito Islands, and his
vessel was thus a foreign man-of-war. He stated that
he had refrained from cancelling his British register
because the Mosquito Government was not recognized
by the adjacent states, and he therefore wished to retain
the protection of the British flag. The Board decided
that he was only entitled to the privileges of an ordinary
British trader.

The coast-waiters' boats at Broken Bay and Botany
Bay, New South Wales, had up to this time been manned
by selected convicts. In 1847 the waiter at Broken
Bay apprised the Sydney collector that his boatmen had

been apprehended for robbery, and soon afterwards the
waiter at Botany Bay sent word that his crew had
received their tickets-of-leave and abandoned their
occupation. In August the Superintendent of Convicts
informed the collector that no more convicts would be
supplied. It was accordingly arranged to employ ' free
men ' at £4 a month (it would seem that wages were low
prior to the discovery of gold).

On June 15, 1847, the Treasury transmitted to the
Board a revenue Ordinance, recently passed by the
Legislature of South Australia, and asked in the usual
way whether it contained anything objectionable. The
Board pointed out the following imperfections :

1. The Ordinance had prescribed a method of dealing
with undervalued *ad valorem* goods similar to that
obtaining in the United Kingdom. The Board (perhaps
bearing in mind how badly the British system worked)
thought the appointment of an expert appraiser would
be preferable.

2. The governor and the naval and military officers
were allowed drawback of the import duty upon such
spirits as they consumed. The Board thought this
unusual.

3. The Ordinance tampered with the Navigation laws
in a way only allowed to the king in Council.

4. The tariff was extremely complicated, and there
were many differential duties.

The Treasury communicated with the governor, up-
holding the Board's opinions. All the objectionable
clauses were removed except the first, which was retained
on the strength of a report from the collector of Port
Adelaide to the effect that there had been much undervaluing prior to the issue of the Ordinance, but only one
case since.

On July 30, 1847, the collector of Hobart Town
informed the Board that the Tasmanian revenue sustained loss through the issue of duty-free rum to the
troops. He stated that there were 1,500 soldiers, and

that each received $\frac{1}{7}$ quart per day (say a total annual
issue of 19,500 gallons). Much of the rum was transferred to tavern-keepers, who paid the soldiers for it at
the rate of 2½d. a daily ration. The collector mentioned incidentally that an attempt was once made at
Sydney to commute the issue of rum at the rate of
1d. a day per man, but that the regiment concerned
mutinied. Later he reported to the colonial Secretary
that he had news of illicit distillation, and that the spirit
thus obtained was mixed with the rum which the troops
sold. It is evident he was suspected of a vivid imagination, for nothing was done.

By Cap. 97, 11 and 12 Vict. the sugar duties, which
had been arranged so as to decrease annually till a certain
rate was reached, were altered so as to reach a still lower
rate. Cap. 127 effected a substantial reduction in the
duties on unmanufactured copper and on pig and sheet
lead.

The various collectors in the United Kingdom were
directed to make known to masters of whaling-ships the
rewards offered for information as to the *Erebus* and
Terror, employed under Sir John Franklin.

Precautions had been taken in 1847 to prevent the
importation of sheep affected with the ' variola ovis.'
In 1848 the collectors were exhorted to special vigilance, as the disease was spreading fast in Norfolk and
Suffolk.

During 1832 Anguilla had been made a ' free port,' at
the request of the St. Kitts Council of Assembly. In 1848
the council asked the Treasury to abolish the Customs
establishment at Anguilla, as it was a drain upon the
colony, the expenses greatly exceeding the receipts.
Many unreasonable appeals had been made by the colonial
Legislatures, but none so unreasonable as this. The
establishment had been made against the Board's wish,
and it could not have oppressed the colony, for the
officers' salaries, the rent of the custom-house, and the
expense of the customs boat, were paid out of the United

Kingdom Customs. It is worth noting, too, that the Customs takings *in the Island of St. Kitts* failed to cover the expenses, and the deficit had to be made up annually by the London Receiver-General.

On October 18, 1848, the English brig *Croxdale* arrived at Rio de Janeiro. She had left Liverpool on July 12 with twelve seamen and over 120 passengers. The British consul at Rio inspected her, and found that she carried no medical man ; that her medicine-chest was imperfectly supplied ; that the master, his son, the mate, and four passengers were down with typhus ; that there had been much sickness during the voyage, also two cases of child-birth, in which both mothers and children had died ; that the vessel was but 290 tons, and altogether unfitted for her employment ; and that the unfortunate passengers (all Irish emigrants) were unclean and dejected. They had been half starved during the voyage, and deprived of lime-juice, though it had been served out to the crew. The Admiralty transmitted this depressing report to the Board (the Customs being considered the department empowered to prosecute). Thereupon arose the usual quibbles, the Customs lawyers urging that it was not a Customs matter, and much correspondence with the Emigration Department took place, till in the end it was arranged that the Customs should prosecute. It seems that the only person responsible was the shipowner, and he but for failing to provide a surgeon. He was prosecuted before the Liverpool justices under sections 18 and 62 of Cap. 112, 7 and 8 Vict., and cast in the mitigated penalty of £33 6s. 8d. Then arose another discussion as to which department should bear the expense of prosecution. This endured till the Treasury directed that the cost should be paid out of the Customs revenue.

On September 11, 1848, three forged £1 notes were foisted upon the Customs at Sydney. The fraud was discovered when they were paid by the Customs into the Bank. It appears that there were many of these in

circulation—indeed, two were presented by innocent
people at the duty-counter on the following day, but the
clerks detected them in time. The governor relieved the
clerks from surcharge. (A £1 note converted into a £5
note had been passed in payment of duty at the same
Custom-house in 1841.)

The collector of Hobart Town applied to the Board for
advice. Under two colonial Acts recently passed the
ad valorem duty on foreign goods had been raised from
5 to 15 per cent., and all preferential duties had been
abolished. Thus the produce of New South Wales,
hitherto admitted into Tasmania duty-free, had been
made liable to the duty on foreign goods. Nearly all the
payments of duty since the passing of the Acts had been
made under protest, the merchants insisting that the
Acts were not drafted in accordance with the provisions
of the imperial Act empowering the governor in Council
to make laws for the colony. The defect alleged was
absence of statement as to how the duties were to be
appropriated. It appears the Council had previously
enacted a similarly defective dog tax, and the Judge of
the island had decided that it was illegal. (The Board
declined to interfere.)

The pertinacity in economizing, characteristic of many
officials, was illustrated during 1848 by one of the
customs officers of Jamaica. Being on leave in Scotland,
he wrote the Secretary of Customs, calling attention to
a clause in the agreement between the Admiralty and the
Royal Mail Steam Packet Company with regard to the
mails, under which clause the Company undertook to
carry certain officials (when proceeding on duty) to the
West Indies, free of all except mess expenses. ' I would
go by an early steamer, as it will make a material difference in expenses, which is an object of moment to me.'
He received a curt intimation that he was not entitled
to profit by the clause. (The wonder is that so frugal a
man had taken leave.)

The Navigation laws were further ' amended ' by

Cap. 29 of 12 and 13 Vict.* It is apparent that many people in high administrative positions had become tired of the ancient regulations that had done so much for the achievement and maintenance of British mercantile supremacy, and that had produced and fostered that wonderful exemplar of hardihood, endurance, and nautical dexterity, the ancient British seaman. Readers will have perceived, by inspection of such extracts as have been furnished from the records, that in many instances lawyers and high officials interpreted these statutes in opportunist fashion, and that the customs men who were appointed to enforce them, especially in the colonies, often used the laws in the way that a footpad uses a loaded bludgeon. The public mind was inclined towards general relaxation. ' Free trade and open ports ' was the cry. The public eye, in its scrutiny of measures, beholds but two colours : every measure is either black as the pit or white as driven snow, and it is certain that the ' amendments ' mentioned captured public approval.

A number of Navigation Acts and parts of Acts were accordingly repealed, and the poor remnant put together in a statute that contained the following provisions :

1. Coastwise trade in the United Kingdom, the Isle of Man, the Channel Islands, and the colonies was still to be conducted in British ships ; but if two or more colonies agreed to desire that their mutual trade should be made coastwise, or if any colonial Legislature prayed the queen that its coasting trade should be thrown open to foreign ships, the privileges might be granted by Order in Council.

2. The coastwise trade of India might be thrown open to foreign ships if the Governor-General chose to direct the same by his Order in Council, the document to be laid before the imperial Parliament.

3. To constitute a ship ' British,' she was to be registered. If she was in the coastwise or fishing trade of the United Kingdom, Channel Islands, or Isle of Man, all

* The new Act was to operate from January 1, 1850.

20

her crew had to be British ; if in any other trade, the master and three-fourths of the crew ; but there were several insidious exceptions attached to the last proviso.

4. Any natural-born subject of the queen, any holder of papers of naturalization or denization, any person who had served three years on a British ship of war, and *any Lascar from a place within the East India Company's charter*, might be deemed a British seaman. No imaginative person can read certain clauses in this Act without calling to mind the immortal line—

> ' Here, a sheer hulk, lies poor Tom Bowling.'

The Customs laws were amended afresh by Cap. 90 of 12 and 13 Vict. thus :

A package of imported tobacco legal as to weight might not be made up of illegal internal packages. (This was to combat a recent smuggling practice.)

If any dispute arose between importer and officer as to duty payable, the importer was to deposit the duty demanded, pending action if desired.

Goods discharged from vessels lying afloat, to be taken to a quay for examination, were to be landed promptly.

Persons concerned in importing prohibited or restricted goods were to be liable, even though such goods had not been unshipped.

All corn, meal, etc., was to be duty-paid on importation. (Previously the duties had been allowed to be bonded.)

(Most of the ' amendments ' were either legal devices to check recently-discovered methods of fraud, or time-honoured provisions forgotten at the time of re-con-solidation.)

During 1849 great public excitement was caused by the murder of Patrick O'Connor, a customs gauger employed at the London Docks. Perusal of O'Connor's official records reveals that he was a usurer, an exploiter of the poor, a man without either morals or scruples—in short, a precious scoundrel. It appears that he engaged with a dock foreman and an adventurer named Fitzgerald in a pretty enterprise. When young Irish labourers came to London for work, they were approached by Fitzgerald, who told them that he had a friend in the Customs who would secure them permanent employment in the docks, purely out of Christian charity, but it was necessary that plump fees should be paid to Fitzgerald. When the money was down the unfortunate fellows were taken on, but in every case the foreman soon found occasion to dismiss them. Meantime O'Connor, Fitzgerald, and the dock bully divided the spoil. One turbulent Irishman attempted to blackmail O'Connor, but the crafty gauger stationed a detective in ambush, and had him arrested. The fellow got twelve months' imprisonment, but the revelations during the trial were of so lurid a nature that the Board declined to promote O'Connor when his turn came.

Meantime he had formed an illicit connection with Mrs. Manning, an attractive and buxom creature, who was married to a railway guard, and whose husband appears to have winked at his wife's flirtations on the condition that O'Connor, who was quite a wealthy person, contributed most of the housekeeping money. Perhaps O'Connor was penurious, for in the end the Mannings laid a deadly trap for him. He was going on leave to Ireland, and they induced him to deposit his trunk, containing valuable securities, etc., at their house in Rotherhithe, and to come and dine with them on the Sunday preceding his departure. On the Saturday they procured a fat goose and other delicacies, and dug a hole under the hearthstone in the kitchen. On the Sunday morning, while Manning basted the goose at the kitchen fire, his wife went upstairs and shot O'Connor through the head. The body was stowed beneath the hearthstone, and the two wretches sat down above it, and dined off the goose and trimmings.

Afterwards they gave up the house, and travelled here and there, disposing of O'Connor's ' paper.' Some little clumsiness caused them to be arrested. O'Connor's absence was noted, and a search was made at the empty house in Rotherhithe. During the search a stray dog entered the kitchen, and began to sniff and whine above the hearthstone. The stone was taken up, and the corpse discovered. Both the Mannings were hanged.

Below is quoted O'Connor's last official letter—an application for promotion :

'HONOURABLE SIRS,

'As there is now a vacancy in the department I belong to, by the superannuation of Mr. Robinson, inspector of gaugers, I beg most respectfully to express my hope that your Honours will not on this as on a former occasion think it right to pass me by in the expected promotion, for whatever offence I may have given your Honours by my having on former occasions long ago brought trouble on myself for repeating a few words told me by a tide-waiter, and not being able then to prove it to your Honours' satisfaction, as I had no writing, and he denied it, and also by lending money to different officers, now most of them out of the Service, and in doing which I had lost the most part of what I had got together after about twenty years of economy and frugal habits.

'I do then respectfully and most humbly intreat your Honours will give every consideration to my case, as I have at all times attended strictly and honestly to my official duties, and never had my honesty questioned. I beg again to repeat my strongest hope that I may be allowed to go forward to the next class of gaugers, and to resume my former position.

'Respectfully submitted by your Honours' most obedient and very humble servant,

'P. O'CONNOR.'

Beneath appears this note in the inspector's handwriting, dated August 20, 1849 :

'Mr. P. O'Connor was found dead on the 17th inst., under circumstances that leave but little doubt he has been murdered.'

On July 28, 1849, the governor of the Gold Coast, who was on leave, wrote from Clifford's Inn to the Secretary of State for the Colonies, recommending the establishment of a tariff and of Customs at various ports under his control. (It would seem there was no Customs staff except at Sierra Leone and Gambia. About £20,000 a year was collected at these two ports.) The articles proposed to be taxed at the new ports were spirits, tobacco, gunpowder, and firearms, ' the goods most extensively used.' The proposed duty on firearms was 6d. each, on gunpowder 5s. per 100 pounds, on spirits 3d. a gallon (the governor did not state whether liquid or proof), on tobacco 2d. *a gallon* (evidently the governor meant ' a pound ').

The Act dated Cap. 1, 12 Vict., passed by the Legislature of Jamaica, had imposed duties for the period from February 15, 1849, to October 1, 1849. On September 30 (Sunday) a vessel arrived at Kingston from Halifax, N.S., with a cargo of fish, oil, shingles, etc., and reported on the following day. The captain then applied to the collector for a pass, to proceed to sea again ; the collector granted it, and the vessel was taken outside the limits of the port. She returned on October 3, and her cargo was entered with the Customs. No new revenue Act had been passed, but the collector made the importers pay duty on the cargo under the old Act, insisting that it had been in force till midnight of October 1, 1849. It seems that the importers, Messrs. Darrell and Barclay, had expected this, and, to enable themselves to raise an objection, had taken the vessel to sea during the 1st, and brought her back when the Act could not be held to operate. They paid the duty—£233 odd—under protest.

The London Customs lawyers held that this trickery did not affect the issue. The vessel came first within the port on September 30, and that circumstance rendered her cargo liable under the Act. The Act did *not* cease, as the collector had maintained, at midnight on the 1st, but at midnight on the 30th. Such was the con-

struction to be placed upon the words 'till October 1.'
Still, they were doubtful whether, if the duties had not
been paid, they could have been recovered in the colonial
Courts. The Board ordered that the duties should be
retained, they being due when the vessel first entered
port.*

It appears that the merchants of Jamaica were spirited
litigants. On December 15 one of them asked the collector to grant him an allowance out of duties paid on
certain goods—the goods turning out damaged. The
collector declined, stating that the merchant should have
claimed the allowance before delivery, so that the
Customs might have surveyed the goods and formed an
estimate as to their depreciation. The merchant applied
to the Board, furnishing a certificate of survey, and insisting that the collector was merely using routine to
render the law as to abatement inoperative. The Board,
against the advice of their own lawyers, directed the
collector to grant the allowance, unless he had good
reasons for suspecting the accuracy of the claim.

Other Jamaica merchants asked the Board to inform
them as to the precise limits of the port of Kingston
(perhaps on account of Darrell and Barclay's case).
The collector was directed to inquire, and replied that he
had failed to find any specifying document except an
island Act (Cap. 39, 8 Vict., reaffirming a provision of the
repealed statute, Cap. 39, 41 Geo. III.), which stated
that the harbour included the waters ' between the shores
in the parishes of Kingston and Port Royal, and the
shores in the parishes of Kingston, St. Andrew, and
St. Catherine, and the shores in the parishes of Port Royal
and St. Catherine, and extending from the head of the
harbour to a right line from Gallows Point, in the parish
of Port Royal, to the southernmost point of the Twelve
Apostles' Battery.'

Cap. 95, 13 and 14 Vict., amended the Customs laws,
providing that the rules, orders, and regulations issued

* See p. 313 for another case.

by the Board should be valid until rescinded by the Board, even though the statutes that influenced their issue might no longer be in operation ; also that no superannuation allowance granted to a Customs official should be legally assignable. It allowed the importation duty-free of goods from the Channel Islands, provided they were goods of Channel Island growth, or manufactured from materials produced in the Channel Islands, said materials being of a kind not dutiable in the United Kingdom. The importation into the United Kingdom of extracts of coffee, chicory, tea, and tobacco, was prohibited. The only remaining export duty—that of 4s. a ton on coals exported to foreign countries in foreign ships—was repealed.

The Board regularized the system of dealing with small quantities of tobacco and cigars brought by passengers. If the quantity were under half a pound, and the passenger not a frequent traveller, the goods might pass duty-free.

The ways of petty legal practitioners were illustrated by the case of a Liverpool tide-waiter named Thomas. He had been arrested for debt, and the collector advised the Board. It appeared that a London solicitor had apprised Thomas that his wife had been left £154. The various legal expenses swallowed all of the legacy except £23 10s. This remnant Thomas expended. Then the lawyer sent in a bill for ' proctor's charges,' amounting to £20 7s. 2d., sold him up, and threw him into gaol.

The Plymouth tide-waiters petitioned the Board, stating that they were sometimes kept on small foreign craft for preiods ranging from forty to eighty days. (This must have been an utterly barbarous and useless formality.) Thus they suffered in health, and had few opportunities of seeing their families. The Board did not lighten their lot to any great extent. It was merely directed that when a tide-waiter had been on duty *seven successive days and nights* he should be allowed a night's rest before being boarded again !

The inspecting commander of Coastguard at Seafield,

Miltown Milbay, Ireland, reported an extraordinary riot in that locality. The brig *Andrew White*, laden with timber, went ashore on the coast, and the rabble of Miltown Milbay (described by the officer as ' the most unruly population in the kingdom ') mustered, on plunder bent, armed with reaping-hooks, hammers, axes, crow-bars, sticks, and stones. The officer asserted that some of the wealthier inhabitants, who desired to profit by the plunder, supplied the mob with whisky. The police and Coastguard did their best, but it seems that the rabble carried off most of the cargo, and that certain responsible citizens purchased it from them.

Part of the correspondence connected with this case is ludicrous. One of the rioters fell and broke his thigh, and then put in a claim for ' salvage ' ! One of the ' receivers ' sent the following modest though garbled petition to the Board :

' The police seized a cross-cut saw of mine which was in care of one of my laborers, and in his absence it was taken by some men who the police found on the shore and also found the saw. I sent to the Sergeant, who said it could not be given without your authority. I will feel obliged your ordering him to return it to me.
                    ' And you will oblige,
                              ' faithfully,
                                 ' THOS. H. MORONY.'

On February 19, 1850, the U.S.A. Consul at St. John, New Brunswick, applied to the controller of Navigation laws for enlightenment as to the state of affairs under the recently-amended Navigation Acts. Below are the questions and replies, the latter sanctioned by the Board :

1. ' May American vessels trade coastwise in the provinces ?' Reply : ' No ; but they may trade between province and province, to and from ports provided with custom-houses.'

2. ' May an American vessel from a foreign port trade to a colonial place other than a " free port," or load at

such place for foreign ?' Reply : ' She may trade to or from such place if the place be provided with a custom-house.'

3. ' May an American vessel be made British ?' Reply : ' Yes ; the full conditions of registry, etc., being complied with.'

When the Newfoundland Customs were handed over to the colony, the gauging and testing instruments, stationery, etc., went as well, under stipulation that the colony should pay for them. In 1850 the controller of Navigation laws wrote to the Board thus : ' It will surprise your Honours to learn that, although these articles were actually necessary to the colonial officers, the House of Assembly twice rejected the proposed vote, and it was not until after a third application had been made by the Executive that the amount was granted.'

The Jamaica revenue Act alluded to at p. 309 had been replaced by another statute—a statute drafted rather more carefully, for it provided that the tariff should expire on *December 31*, 1850. It was not passed until several days after the previous Act had determined, but it was made retrospective. Messrs. Scott and Leaycraft, Kingston merchants, refused to pay duty on certain goods imported by them during the interval. Thereupon an American resident, rejoicing in the illus-trious name ' Benjamin Franklin,' followed suit. A decree was obtained against Scott and Leaycraft, with costs, in the Vice-Admiralty Court of the island. They gave notice of appeal, but did not persevere. A decree was also obtained, with costs, against Franklin, and he deposited the duty and costs in the Customs chest, stating that he intended to lay his case before the queen. A deal of trouble was gone to in the United Kingdom to provide defence against Franklin's expected appeal, and there was much discussion as to whether the imperial or the island Customs should bear the expense if he carried it into the higher Court. All this, it seems, might have been spared, for there is no record of any further steps taken by him.

Questions from foreign shipowners, as to the purport of the amended Navigation Act, continued to trouble the Board. One, transmitted by the Jamaica collector, was from the British consul at St. Jago de Cuba, asking whether a Spanish vessel might trade as a mail-packet between Cuba and Jamaica. The consul was doubtful on the point, as the Spanish regulations were not reciprocal. The Board told him the vessel might trade, and hinted that the collector might have dealt personally with so simple a matter.*

An account of the finance of the colony of South Australia appears in one of the returns. The total revenue for 1850 was £147,455. Of this, £80,000 was raised by Customs, the duty taken on spirits and tobacco alone realizing £42,000. There was a 'bonded debt' of £15,000. The Customs expenses were extremely moderate. The collector had but £500 a year. The total charges on the Customs establishment were £3,719 for salaries, and £455 for incidents. Another return states the nature of New Zealand products exported from Auckland during 1848-1850 : 1848, £15,525 ; 1849, £27,092 ; 1850, £45,765. The chief articles exported were cordage, flax, grain, ' houses in frame,' black oil, sperm oil, spars, timber, copper ore, and potatoes. The exports of copper ore had increased in value from £500 in 1848 to £14,887 in 1850 ; of potatoes, from £121 to £5,780. Another return states the trade and revenue of the port of Geelong in 1850 : Imports, £40,883 ; exports, £359,687 ; Customs revenue, £11,348. (In 1851 the Geelong return was : Imports, £113,672 ; exports, £392,950 ; Customs revenue, £16,037.)

The only revenue Act of 1851 was Cap. 62, 14 and 15

* The best definition of the new state of affairs that we have been able to find is that furnished by the London ' Bench Officers ' (Customs) in 1850. They stated that all limitations were removed, save that foreign ships might not trade with or in the Channel Islands, or coast in the United Kingdom and the colonies.

Vict., which reduced the duty on foreign coffee and several kinds of foreign timber. The goods in question, when imported from British possessions, had been previously admitted at low preferential duties. The Act abolished such preference, and made the duties equal.

During 1851 the mayor and burgesses of Cork memorialized the Treasury, stating that the copper coinage in the south-west of Ireland was defective, much bad coin being in circulation, and a number of ' tokens ' issued by irresponsible persons. It was suggested that the collector of customs at Cork should be allowed to sell £1,500 worth new copper coin. Copper coin to the value of £500 was sent to the collector at Belfast. The officers were directed to remit in all £2,000 to the Bank of England, to the credit of the Master of the Mint.

The Customs return to the Census officers in 1851 was as below :

	Established Officers.	Temporary Officers.	Superannuated Officers.
London	1,736	367	408
English outports	2,236	533	645
Scotland	528	59	131
Ireland	476	193	177
	4,976	1,152	1,361

Late in 1850 one of the Southampton officers reported to the Board that a sealed bag had been shipped by a vessel for Lisbon ' by a Spanish gentleman.' The bag, he thought, contained letters, but he had not presumed to detain it, although he intimated suspicion that the postal regulations with respect to foreign letters might have been evaded. The Board communicated with the Postmaster-General, who referred to the Spanish minister in London, who in turn applied to the Spanish consul, who denied knowledge of the transaction, and sent an indignant demand for explanation, which the minister transmitted, along with a few severe remarks on his own account, to the departments interested. Early in 1851 it was found that the bag had been sent from the *Portu-*

guese Legation, under the Portuguese Consulate seal, and quite in accordance with official routine.

A Bideford ship cleared out from Westport for the North American colonies with sixty-seven emigrants. She displayed her proper complement of boats when the collector made his inspection, but when she arrived in the colonies the Customs found she was one short. Inquiry was made, and the Westport collector ascertained that the captain borrowed a boat prior to inspection, and returned it ' from sea ' after leaving port. The matter was allowed to drop, the vessel having gone into the foreign trade.

On January 17, 1851, the *Emerald Isle*, with emigrants from Sydney to San Francisco, left the former port without Customs sanction. Clearance had been withheld, and a tide-waiter put on board to insure detention, because the Emigration agent had declared the vessel unseaworthy. She took the officer to sea with her. The governor reported the affair to the Privy Council for Trade, and intimated that the colonial law officers opined that no proceedings could be taken, the law being defective on the point at issue. The matter was referred to the London Customs lawyers, who opined differently, pointing out that prosecution might be effectively sustained under the following Acts : Cap. 33, 12 and 13 Vict., against the master, for sailing without the Emigration agent's certificate ; Cap. 13, 9 Vict. (New South Wales Act), for sailing without Customs clearance, and also for carrying the officer away. These proceedings should be taken in New South Wales, but if the master came to the United Kingdom, he might be prosecuted under Cap. 87, 8 and 9 Vict. (The vessel was not liable to seizure.)

Meantime the *Emerald Isle* put in to Honolulu, and landed the officer, who in course of time found his way back to Sydney. She proceeded to San Francisco, and her company promptly deserted her, except the chief mate, who after a time succeeded in obtaining fresh hands. She was in England in 1852, and the new captain furnished a statement to the Board, from which it appeared that the previous skipper had not been much to blame, for it was shown that he had an independent survey made at Sydney, under which the ship was declared ' tight, staunch, and strong, and fit to proceed to any part of the world '; that he offered to put the officer ashore along with the pilot, but the officer would not budge ; that when he landed the officer at Honolulu he gave him £20 to pay his expenses back ; and that the consul at Honolulu surveyed the vessel, and testified to her seaworthiness. The matter was dropped.

The first section of the imperial Act 59, 13 and 14 Vict., had decreed the separation of Victoria and New South Wales. This exercised the minds of the New South Wales Crown lawyers and the collector of Sydney. The lawyers thought that only goods which were *shipped* from Victoria after date of separation should be charged with duty. Otherwise, they held, duty-paid goods shipped— say, in Melbourne—prior to separation, might arrive at Sydney on the day after separation and have to be duty-paid again. (The mere layman might think that it would be an equal hardship if the merchant shipped such goods after separation. In either case he would pay twice.)

On November 1, 1851, the collector of Melbourne informed the Board that the governor had made substantial increases in the pay of all the inferior officials, ' under the present unprecedented circumstances, consequent upon the discovery of gold in this colony.' Many officials of other departments had deserted and made off for the diggings, but the Customs men had pledged themselves to stick to their posts.

During this year the Board of Customs furnished Government with various accounts of large shipments of arms and ammunition to the Cape. The foreign office directed that inquiries should be made as to the ultimate destination of these goods, and the Cape Town collector furnished in reply a statement tending to show that the

smuggling of arms and ammunition across the boundary
of the colony to the Boers, Kaffirs, ' bastard Hottentots,'
and Portuguese, had ceased years ago.   Yet he failed to
explain satisfactorily the deliveries of gunpowder from the
two colonial storehouses, Craig's Tower and Amsterdam
Battery, which during three months of 1851 had reached
41,200 pounds.   Later he seemed to think that most of
this went to the Boers, and was used in protecting their
stock and in killing game.   ' The Boer and his gun,' he
stated, ' are constant companions, and to deprive him of
the use of it would undoubtedly be deemed a great
grievance.'   He also procured statements from vagrant
traders, which went to show that if the sale of weapons
and powder to natives had ceased it must have ceased
rather suddenly.   Said one : ' I have seen black people
(bastard Hottentots) bartering for gunpowder, giving in
exchange corn, skins, ostrich eggs, ostrich feathers, etc.
I have seen a trek-ox bought for half a pound of gunpowder, and three oxen for a gun ' (worth about five
dollars).   Another expert stated that twenty Boers
bought 1,000 pounds of powder from him in one lot ; and
another stated that the Boers frequently paid their Kaffir
labourers in arms and ammunition.   (This man had seen
a large quantity of gunpowder run on the coast from a
Liverpool vessel.)

Later Earl Grey wrote complaining bitterly of the
running of guns, powder, and bar lead to the hostile
Kaffirs.   Soon came a report from the commander of
H.M.S. *Rhadamanthus*, who had been sent to Espiègle
Bay and the mouth of the Orange River to investigate.
He had found no unauthorized supply on hand, except
five barrels of powder intended for blasting purposes,
but he had collected much information from Field-Cornet
Cornelissen and a trader named Dickson.   These concurred in stating that the smuggling of arms, etc., was
nearly ended ; but Dickson's admissions as to his dealings
in the past cause us to think he might still be active, as
soon as H.M.S. *Rhadamanthus* departed.   Not only did

he give details of his own doings, but of certain traffic by missionaries, and of direct landing of guns and powder by European vessels at Angra Pequena and Walwick Bay. There can be no doubt that ' gun-running ' was a profitable business, and that many unworthy British merchants made a good thing of supplying weapons to the enemies of their country.

The New Zealand collectors were empowered by the governor to allow tobacco to be mixed in bond with spirits of tar or turpentine, and then delivered duty-free for manufacture into sheepwash.

Provision had been made by treaty in 1819, and ratified by Cap. 54, 59 Geo. III., for reciprocity in commercial arrangements between the United Kingdom and the United States of America, and the United Kingdom and Portugal. Cap. 90, 8 and 9 Vict., had extended reciprocity so as to apply between the United Kingdom and all foreign powers that had entered into similar treaties. Cap. 47, 15 and 16 Vict., conferred still greater elasticity, for it provided that the queen by Order in Council might at any time establish reciprocity as regarded commerce and navigation between the United Kingdom and any foreign power that gave to British goods and shipping the same privileges as to its own, such reciprocity to endure as long as the foreign power continued to grant the privileges, even though no treaty had been entered into. The places that enjoyed Treaty privileges were : Austria, Belgium, Bolivia, Costa Rica, Denmark, the Dominican Republic, ' the Republic of the Equator,' France, the city of Frankfort, Greece, Guatemala, Hanover, the Hanse cities (of Bremen, Hamburg, and Lubeck), Liberia—the Duchies of Mecklenburg-Schwerin, Mecklenburg-Strelitz, Oldenburg, and Tuscany—Mexico, Holland, New Grenada, Turkey, Peru, Portugal—Prussia, and the various states forming the German Commercial Union—Rio de la Plata, Russia, Sardinia, Sicily, Sweden and Norway, the United States of America, Uruguay, and Venezuela.

In 1852 the Board issued directions as to dealing with

a new article of import 'known as Semolina.' It was to be admitted as wheat-meal, at 4½d. a hundredweight duty.

The once famous port of Chichester was made a creek (head port, Arundel) on December 5, 1852.

A Treasury Order of November 29, 1852, directed that all tobacco, except cigars, in the Queen's Warehouse as 'seized,' and all such tobacco seized thenceforward, should be destroyed, instead of being disposed of by auction at the Customs sales. The order stated that it was apparent that the sale of seized tobacco 'led to fraud,' and injured the honest trader, 'by displacing in the market a corresponding quantity of tobacco which would otherwise be entered for home consumption.' (This order, slightly modified, is still in force. Why it should apply only to tobacco is difficult to discover.)

By a Board's Minute of 1852 certain privileges had been granted to merchants of unshipping duty-free goods in the Port of London before and after legal hours without any expense for Customs attendance. Later the merchants of Liverpool asked that the privilege might be extended to that port. The Board replied that the measure was but experimental. The Liverpool merchants applied afresh, declining to consider it 'experimental,' it having been extended to Leith, Kirkcaldy, and Dundee. The Board referred the petitioners to the collector at Liverpool, but they refused to accept the recommendation, and soon the Liverpool Chamber of Commerce moved the Board upon the matter. Then a full report was called for, and the Customs surveyor-general tried his best to make out a case for the preferential treatment of London, stating that the London dock and wharf hours were similar to the Customs hours ; that few goods were un-shipped in London before and after the usual hours, except into craft, to be cleared by Customs during the legal period ; but that at Liverpool nearly all the goods were landed, and required to be cleared at once, and that if the Crown had to pay the officers for the extra attend-dance, great public expense would be incurred. He thought that ' the American portion ' of the Chamber of Commerce had inspired the memorial. The request was afterwards granted, and later still one from the Bristol merchants.

During 1850 and 1851 the Customs Board had been considerably embroiled with the directors of the London and St. Katherine's Docks. The trouble arose in 1849,* when information of fraud in connection with ' sweepings ' in the St. Katherine's Docks was given privately to the Solicitor. To make things quite clear, it may be necessary to explain the position of a dock company with respect to the Customs. In the first place the dock company was under a heavy bond to the revenue department—a bond liable to be put in suit if any fraud were discovered for which the company might legally be held blamable. The directors were bound to provide all reasonable facilities for the customs men to take account of goods, and might deliver no goods, either dutiable or free, without Customs sanction. In connection with the unpacking, repacking, weighing, etc., of certain kinds of dutiable goods, especially such goods as raw coffee and cocoa, there was frequently an accumulation of ' sweepings '—viz., litter from the various packages—and when the floors were cleared at the end of each day the ' sweepings ' were put away by the dock company's servants. In course of time they grew into a large quantity, and it was the practice of the dock company to assume possession, clean them, lot them, and either pay duty on them and sell them, or export them duty-free. In short, they became the company's perquisites, it being held that they could not be justly allotted to the various merchants' goods. It will be evident to readers that if the dock company's officials happened to be astute and unscrupulous people, they had here a chance of committing fraud. In the first

* A case much similar had occurred in 1816, when, acting upon information received, the Customs seized goods to the value of about £12,000 for being found in various places in the London Dock, and not accounted for in the Company's books.

21

place there could be no exact check on the quantity of
'sweepings' till the period arrived when the bulk was
weighed and lotted.   During the interval much might be
done.   'Sweepings' of dutiable goods might be slyly
conveyed from the dock, or used in making up deficiencies
in goods which had been taken to account (deficiencies
caused by neglect or abstraction).   There can be no
doubt that something of the kind had been practised
pretty freely at the St. Katherine's Dock.   A sudden
search was made by the Customs on December 4, 1849,
and several packages, some containing 'sweepings,' and
other goods which had not been entered with the Customs,
were seized.   Other searches were made during the early
part of 1850, and many packages detained.   The total
value of the goods seized (mostly coffee, indigo, and
pepper) was £8,392.

On March 2, 1850, information was tendered as to
similar irregularities in the London Dock.   Several
searches were made, and goods to the value of £10,467
were seized.

The directors of both dock companies displayed great
hostility, and combated the proceedings of the Customs
in every possible way.   It is likely that the searches were
conducted in an arbitrary manner, that many of the
packages were seized on mere suspicion, and that the
Customs Solicitor was a little too masterful and dexterous
in his efforts towards securing the conviction of offenders
and the inculpation of the dock companies.   But the
dock directors behaved in obstinate fashion, refusing to
accept the slightest blame for what must at all events
have constituted gross neglect, championing certain
employés of theirs who certainly did not deserve protection, and levelling accusations wholesale against the
customs men.   They even insisted that large losses
discovered upon wines housed in the vaults were due to
the bibulous habits of the officers.   The Customs Solicitor
entered actions in the Exchequer against both companies.
The St. Katherine's Dock Company compromised the

matter by paying £100, and admitting that great irregularities had prevailed. The London Dock Company fought their case, and, after a verdict had been given which satisfied neither Customs nor company, the latter did the same as the St. Katherine's Dock company had done. Yet, though both companies thus admitted that they were wrong and the Customs right, the latter were not to come off with flying colours.

Fiery articles, denouncing the Customs Board, began to appear in certain journals, and indignation meetings were held at several influential ports. A petition, signed by numerous merchants, was presented to the House of Commons, and a Parliamentary Committee, of which Mr. Gladstone was a member, sat to inquire into Customs matters generally. While this Committee was at work a separate Committee of merchants, elected by the trade, also sat in Charlotte Row, heard much evidence, and forwarded many recommendations to the Parliamentary Committee. Afterwards the proceedings of this self-appointed body were published in a volume, together with many remarkable reflections upon the British Customs, and especially upon the Customs Board.

The number of witnesses called up and examined by the Parliamentary Committee was remarkable. Extremely remarkable, too, was some of the evidence given by the witnesses, especially those who were hostile to the Board. Ship-owners, smack-owners, merchants, lightermen, and wharfingers, joined in complaining bitterly of Customs incompetence, circumlocution, and greed. Some of the complaints appeared justifiable ; others were manifestly made by men who had been trying to break the regulations, and who, having failed and suffered, had evolved burning grievances.

The Parliamentary Committee's report was decidedly unfavourable to the Board as constituted. It stated that the Commissioners' holidays were excessive, and recommended that at least one person from the mercantile class and one practical customs officer should be admitted as Commissioners. It proceeded that the inferior officers were shut out unfairly from promotion. There were six classes of these officers, and, although they all entered under educational tests that differed but little, promotion from one grade to another was rare, and none could rise from the five lower classes into the highest. The Committee found fault with the *ad valorem* duties, stating that they produced little and were extremely troublesome, and that the system adopted by the Crown of buying undervalued goods and selling them by auction caused a loss to the public. It was urged that greater powers in the disposal of questions raised should be granted to the higher outdoor officials, as under the method in use vexatious delay was often inflicted on the mercantile community. It was also suggested that in Customs trials, when the duty involved did not exceed £100, a much cheaper tribunal could be found than the Court of Exchequer ; also that the owners of vessels should not be fined for acts of smuggling committed by their employés, except when the fraud was extensive, or the captain or chief officer was implicated. Another reform suggested was the transference of liability for duties on bonded goods from the original importer to the warehouse-keeper, the Customs to give the latter a voucher in all cases of delivery of goods, and the Crown to take stock periodically, so that the then owner of the goods might be made to re-enter them. Simplification of the method of entering free goods was also recommended. Under the system in vogue each entry passed through the hands of nineteen customs officers. The Committee thought all entry of free goods by the separate consignees might be dispensed with, and the ship's report be accepted.*

The Committee commented severely upon certain tactics pursued by the Customs Solicitor in conducting the case against the dock companies. It appears that

* This would have been impracticable, as there would be nothing to make the consignee liable if his goods contained contraband.

during the proceedings six labourers were charged by the Customs as assistants in the assumed frauds. Five of these men were bailed, the other remained in prison three weeks, and was then bailed. Finally the dock company took steps to have them defended. The informations against them were filed by the Customs in December, 1850. Early in 1851 the defending solicitors asked four times for particulars of the informations. These were never furnished, nor were the informations tried, and at the time of the Committee's report in 1852 the defendants were still under bail, the charges against them being for penalties amounting to £10,800 !

Two prominent members of the Board resigned, and it was not deemed necessary to fill up the vacancies. Undoubtedly the Consolidation Act of the following year resulted from the strong agitation against many Customs restrictions that was kept up by the mercantile community. Yet, while this agitation was going on, a huge memorial was presented to the Commons by the shipowners, bewailing the repeal of the bulk of the Navigation laws ! To suit all classes of the commercial community is as hopeless a task as that essayed by Æsop's old wittol, who, in trying to please everybody, pleased nobody, and lost his ass into the bargain.*

The Tasmanian Act 5 of 15 Vict., passed February 19, 1852, for regulating the Customs in that island, stated that the discovery of gold in the neighbouring colonies had raised the price of goods in Tasmania, and made it necessary to increase official salaries. It repealed certain previous revenue Acts, and imposed a tariff upon imported spirits, wine, tobacco, tea, sugar, coffee, dried fruit, hops, and malt liquors.

Up to 1852, the maritime revenue in Victoria had arisen from harbour, entrance, lighthouse, and tonnage dues, and a comprehensive tariff with many *ad valorem* items. In 1851 the dues had produced but £6,501, and the tariff £106,260, of which £91,688 came from spirits,

* See pp. 150, 151, vol. i., ' The King's Customs.'

wine, tobacco, tea, sugar, and coffee. A Victorian Act
of 1852 abolished the vexatious dues, and all import
duties except upon the six prolific articles.

(These colonial revisions are mentioned to show that
the progress of opinion in some of the colonies was similar
to that in the United Kingdom.)

Among the Customs ' Plantation ' documents for 1852
appear many cancelled commissions from Australia and
Tasmania, illustrating the complete severance of colonial
Customs control and the home supervision. (The controllers of Navigation laws, etc., still continued to report
to the Board upon matters such as trade and copyright.)
The Customs in New Zealand completed severance in
1853.

On April 21, 1853, a remarkable debate on Customs
reform took place in the House of Commons. The
Secretary for the Treasury opened the proceedings by a
recapitulation of the circumstances attending the dispute between the Board and the dock companies, and
referred to a deputation of City men that had waited on
the Chancellor of the Exchequer early in 1853, when it
had been promised that matters should be improved and
a Customs Consolidation Act passed. He stated that the
weighers and tide-waiters might with fairness be admitted
to higher appointments, and that certain arrangements
had been made in that direction. He described the
system previously obtaining as one which seemed ' to
savour more of the spirit of Eastern caste than of English
freedom.'* On account of the many under-valuations
of *ad valorem* goods, it was intended that there should be
as few *ad valorem* duties in the forthcoming tariff as
possible. Every person who considered himself aggrieved
by a Customs seizure, detention, etc., might be allowed
to have his case dealt with in open court by one of the

---

* It cannot be truly said, even at the present day, that any
branch of the Civil Service is free from the influence of ' the
spirit of caste.' There is a strong prejudice against ' outdoor
men.' Talent and energy count for little, unless the exponent
be a ' clerk ' or a ' University man.'

Commissioners if in London, and at an outport by the collector. The Treasury stated that arrangements would be made allowing the inland carriage of transhipment goods from one port to another, so as to foster British shipping, and predicted that this would work wonders in the way of making the United Kingdom a place of transhipment. He declared that British shipping had increased considerably since the repeal of the Navigation laws in 1850. The Government were also prepared to rescind the prohibition of importing arms in transit, and to allow the transfer of goods in bond. They would abolish the varying warehouse privileges, and make all bonded warehouses subject to the same restrictions (the warehouse-keeper to be responsible for losses). But the Government declined the Committee's suggestion that there should be no entry for duty-free goods except the ship's report, and here the Secretary enlivened his audience by a few anecdotes of smuggling—viz., of the ' oil-cake case ' (see p. 347), of tobacco found in casks of potatoes, tubs of butter, tierces of provisions, and barrels of resin ; of the ' rape-oil case ' (see p. 364) ; and of a recent capture of the mate of a steamer from Boulogne, who was preparing to walk ashore wearing a corset containing forty watches. (The Secretary produced the corset to his audience. This was probably the first time that a smuggler's panoply had been exhibited in Parliament.) He then told an amusing tale, illustrative of the impudent and false charges occasionally brought against the Customs. A merchant doing business in Holborn employed as receiver a woman who lived near Bedford Row. Eleven cases of smuggled watches were found in her house. After the receiver had suffered and the watches had been sold, the merchant came forward and claimed restoration of the goods, and made abominable and unfounded charges against the seizing officers. For instance, he accused them of wrongfully detaining his personal correspondence, although it had been restored to him long before, and although it furnished evidence that he was not only the importer of the watches seized at Bedford Row, but a patron of the corset-wearing mate of the Boulogne steamer.

The Secretary then proceeded to lay an extra coat of flattery upon the already overlarded James Deacon Hume, consolidator of Customs laws, describing the work done by him as ' one of the greatest mental wonders ever achieved by man !' Then he made cheerful comparison between shipping in 1817 and in 1850 ; but we will refrain from quoting his statistics, whilst expressing hope that they were correct. Then came a list of exports, which showed that the export trade of Liverpool was more than double that of London, while that of Hull nearly equalled London, and that the shipping of London was less than that of Liverpool. Yet the Customs revenue of London was more than three times that of Liverpool, which, even when we take into account that all exports were free, leaves room for scepticism. But the most remarkable comparison was that between London and Hull.

London's tonnage was 3,289,000 ; Hull's was 836,000. (It should be remembered that this was a statement on foreign trade, so we may presume coasting ships were not included.) London's exports were of the value of £14,137,000 ; Hull's, £10,366,000. London's Customs revenue (all from imports) was £11,285,000 ; Hull's £353,000. Therefore, if the imported goods were at all similar at each port, London's imports would be about thirty-two times the bulk of the Hull imports. London's exports slightly exceeded those of Hull, so we may leave the relative bulk of goods, export and import combined, as 32 to 1. Yet the relative tonnage of shipping was exactly 4 to 1. The Financial Secretary seems to have perceived that there was a discrepancy, but he kept on quoting statistics. It is to be wondered if he had ever given a few moments' thought to the question whether this statistical porridge with which, since the days of Adam Smith, the British voter and member of Parliament had been so liberally dosed, was made of corn or of powdered chaff.

After the Financial Secretary had ended, the member for Bridport criticized his speech, and was severe on the Chairman of the Customs Board, stating that his administration was responsible for the late vengeful proceedings. He said that ninety-four informations were framed against the dock companies, that the case against the London Dock cost the defendants £12,000, and that the only verdict obtained in the Exchequer was one condemning two boxes of sugar. Then he had a slap at the Customs Solicitor. 'A few years before,' said he, 'this solicitor, Mr. Hamel, was an obscure attorney at the inland town of Tamworth. . . . Here was an ignorant and vain man, who said to himself, "I will distinguish myself; I will show by my conduct that I have the talents to justify my appointment," ' etc.

The member for Sunderland took up the cudgels on behalf of Mr. Hamel, stating that gentleman had been Sir Robert Peel's solicitor, and Sir Robert Peel had put him in his present position. Mr. Hamel had been spoken of as an obscure country attorney. Why should a man's original obscurity be a bar to his filling an important office? etc. (Other members defended the Customs Chairman.)

Cap. 95 of 16 and 17 Vict. prolonged indefinitely the provisions of the Act of 1833 (see p. 172) as to government by the East India Company of the territories within their charter. But the Governor-General's previous powers of control were amplified, and it was provided that the imperial Commander-in-Chief should be Commander-in-Chief of the Company's forces in India. (The Company were allowed to increase the number of their European soldiers from 12,200 to 20,000.)

Cap. 106 announced the promised Consolidation and the new tariff. The following goods were still subject to *ad valorem* duties : Agates, boxes, *unenumerated* cotton manufactures, unenumerated embroidery, essence of spruce, extracts (of cardamoms, coculus indicus, grains of paradise, liquorice, nux vomica, opium, Guinea pepper, Peruvian bark, quassia, radix rhataniæ, and vitriol), unenumerated extracts, unenumerated manufactures of hair, iodine, japanned ware, jewels set, hand-made lace, unenumerated leather manufactures, unenumerated linen manufactures, unenumerated musical instruments, foreign ships for breaking up, unenumerated manufactured silks,* gauzes, velvets, and mixtures of silk with other materials, unenumerated wood, unenumerated woollens, and all goods partly or wholly manufactured and not prohibited which had not been mentioned in the tariff list.

The goods liable to specific duties were certain kinds of almonds, almond-paste, apples, arrowroot, pearl barley, baskets, beads except of glass, beer, biscuit and bread, books of editions printed since 1800, certain brass manufactures, gold and silver brocade, bronze manufactures, butter, candles, certain sticks, caoutchouc manufactures, capers, playing-cards, cassia lignea, cassava powder, cheese, cherries, chicory, chinaware, cinnamon, clocks (varying according to value), cloves, cocoa, coculus indicus, coffee, comfits, confectionery, unenumerated copper manufactures, coral négligées and beads, corks (except fishermen's corks), corn, flour, and meal, cotton fringe, gloves, and stockings, currants, daguerrotype plates, dates, dice, unenumerated earthenware, eggs, certain kinds of feathers, figs, fig-cake, artificial flowers, unenumerated raw fruit, ginger, certain kinds of glass, grains of paradise, grapes, gutta-percha manufactures, hats and bonnets, hops, iron and steel manufactures, lace, lead manufactures, enumerated leather manufactures, certain kinds of linen manufactures, liquorice, matches, macaroni, mace, mandioca flour, manna croup, marmalade, medlars, millboards, morphia, enumerated musical instruments, mustard, nutmegs, certain kinds of nuts, nux vomica, certain oils, oilcloth, onions, opium, oranges

* Some manufactured silks, etc., might be charged with either specific or *ad valorem* duties at customs option.

and lemons, paper, pasteboard, pears, pepper, percussion caps, perfumery, pewter manufactures, pickles in vinegar, pimento, gold and silver plate, platting, preserved and French plums, pomatum, potato flour, hair powder and starch, prints and drawings, prunes, quassia, quinces, sulphate of quinine, raisins, rice, sago, salicine, unenumerated sauces, scaleboards, caraway-seeds, semolina, enumerated manufactures of silk, gauze, and velvet, and of silk mixed with other stuffs, soap, soy, spa ware, unenumerated spelter manufactures, spirits, stearine, succades, sugar and molasses, tallow, tapioca, tea, tinfoil and unenumerated tin manufactures, tobacco and snuff, toys, turnery, varnish containing spirit, veneers, vermicelli and macaroni, vinegar, washing-balls, watches (varying according to value), Cologne-water, wine, enumerated wood (except small staves, hoops, teak, waste wood, stringy bark, red and blue gum, green-heart, certain kinds of tree-nails, shovel-hilts, wood for herring barrels, and colonial firewood), woollen carpets, rugs, shawls, scarves, handkerchiefs, and gloves, and worsted yarn for embroidery. On most of these the rates were much reduced. The tea duty was to diminish annually till it reached 1s. a pound in 1856, and several other articles were also subject to diminishing duties—in some cases until they became free. The only preferential rates on colonial goods allowed to remain were those on apples, books, butter, cheese, eggs, unenumerated embroidery, ginger, liquorice paste and powder, caraway-seed, unenumerated silk manufactures, spirits, sugar and molasses, tallow, wine, and wood.

There were no export duties. Drawback was payable at export upon rice cleaned in the United Kingdom, sugar refined in the United Kingdom, tobacco manufactured in the United Kingdom, and wine ; and there was an export allowance upon British manufactured plate.

Such articles as had previously been liable to duty in the Isle of Man, and had been made duty-free into the

United Kingdom, became duty-free into the dependency. The duties on two or three of the other articles into the island were increased, but the vexatious licence and quantity regulations were abolished.

The other alterations effected by the Act have been foretold in our account of the Parliamentary debate at pp. 326, 327.

The above scale of duties will appear formidable to readers, yet it is diminutive compared with the previous list.

Below is an account of the ports and creeks of the United Kingdom, as shown in the Customs records of 1853 :

PORTS.	SUBPORTS AND CREEKS.
First Class.	
Bristol.	Uphill.
Dublin.	{ Balbriggan, Howth, Wicklow, Arklow, Kingstown.
Glasgow.	Renfrew, Bowling Bay.
Greenock.	{ Holyloch, Lochgilphead, Oban, Tobermory, Rothesay.
Hull.	Bridlington.
Leith.	{ Newhaven, Cockenzie, Fisherow, Dunbar, North Berwick, Eyemouth.
Liverpool.	Runcorn.
London.	Gravesend.
Second Class.	
Belfast.	Donaghadee, Larne.
Cork.	{ Kinsale, Clonakilty, Youghal, Robert's Cove, West Passage.
Newcastle.	Amble.
Plymouth.	Devonport, St. Germains, Calstock.
Southampton.	Lymington, Christchurch.
Waterford.	Passage, Dungarvan, Dunmore.
Third Class.	
Aberdeen.	Peterhead, Stonehaven, Newburgh.
Dundee.	Ferryport-on-Craig.
Exeter.	{ Topsham, Exmouth, Teignmouth, Seaton.
Gloucester.	Lydney, Beachley.
Limerick.	Tarbert, Kilrush, Clare, Dingle.
Londonderry.	Greencastle.
Portsmouth.	Fareham, Emsworth.

PORTS.	SUBPORTS AND CREEKS.

Third Class.

Sunderland.	Seaham.
Stockton.	Cleveland Point, Middlesbrough.
Whitehaven.	Ravenglass, Millom.
Yarmouth.	Lowestoft, Beccles, Southwold.

Fourth Class.

Douglas.	Derbyhaven, Peel, Ramsay.
Dover.	Hythe, Sandgate.
Lancaster.	Glasson Dock, Arnside, Ulverston, Ireleth, Angerton, Barrow, Walney, Poulton.
Lynn.	Heacham.
Newry.	Warrenpoint, Newcastle, Ardglass, Killyleagh.
Rochester.	Sheerness, Maidstone.
Shoreham.	Brighton.
Sligo.	Killala, Donegal, Ballyshannon.

Fifth Class.

Berwick.	Budle Bay, Holy Island, Alnmouth,
Boston.	Wainfleet, Saltfleet, Spalding.
Bridgwater.	Combwich, Minehead, Watchet.
Cardiff.	Aberthaw, Barry, Sully.
Carlisle.	Allonby.
Chester.	Flint, Wepra, Mostyn, Rhuddlan.
Cowes.	Newport, Yarmouth, Ryde.
Dartmouth.	Brixham, Torquay, Salcombe.
Drogheda.	
Dumfries.	Annan, Carsethorn, Barlocco, Kirkcudbright.
Dundalk.	
Falmouth.	St. Mawes, Penryn, Gweek.
Fowey.	Pentewan, Mevagissy, Charlestown, Par, Polkerris, Looe.
Galway.	Clifden.
Goole.	Selby.
Grangemouth.	
Inverness.	Cromarty, Burghead, Findhorn, Lossiemouth, Portmahomack, Fortrose, Fort George, Fort William.
Ipswich.	
Kirkcaldy.	Leven, Largo, Dysart, Burntisland, Anstruther, Pittenweem, St. Andrews, Crail.
Milford.	Little Haven, Nolton, Pembroke, Saundersfoot, Haverfordwest.
Newhaven.	Eastbourne.
Newport.	
Penzance.	

PORTS.	SUBPORTS AND CREEKS.

Fifth Class.

Poole.	Swanage.
Port Glasgow.	
Preston.	{Hesketh Bank, Skippool, Freckleton, Lytham.
Ramsgate.	Margate, Sandwich.
Rye.	Hastings.
Shields.	Blyth.
Swansea.	{Newton, Oxwich, Penarth, Aberavon, Neath.
Truro.	
Weymouth.	

Sixth Class.

Arbroath.	
Arundel.	Littlehampton, Chichester.
Ayr.	Girvan.
Baltimore.	{Castletownsend, Bear Haven, Bantry, Skibbereen.
Banff.	Fraserburgh, Garmouth, Buckie.
Barnstaple.	Ilfracombe.
Beaumaris.	{Holyhead, Amlwch, Conway, Aberffraw.
Bideford.	Appledore.
Borrowstoness.	{Brucehaven, Limekilns, Charlestown, Inverkeithing, St. David's.
Bridport.	
Carnarvon.	Pwllheli, Barmouth, Portmadoc.
Chepstow.	
Clay.	Cromer, Mundesley, Wells.
Colchester.	Brightlingsea.
Coleraine.	Portrush, Ballycastle.
Faversham.	Whitstable, Herne Bay, Milton.
Folkestone.	
Gainsborough.	Stockwith.
Grimsby.	
Guernsey.	
Hartlepool.	
Harwich.	Mistley, Walton, Thorpe, Holland.
Irvine.	Troon, Saltcoats, Largs, Ardrossan.
Jersey.	
Llanelly.	Pembrey, St. Clair, Carmarthen.
Maldon.	{Burnham, Bradwell, Leigh, Rochford.
Montrose.	Johnshaven.
Padstow.	Port Isaac, Bude, Boscastle.
Perth.	Newburgh, Errol.
Ross.	
Scarborough.	
Scilly.	
St. Ives.	Hayle, Portreath.

PORTS.	SUBPORTS AND CREEKS.
Sixth Class.	
Stornoway.	
Stranraer.	{ Drummore, Portnessock, Port-patrick.
Westport.	
Wexford.	
Whitby.	Sandsend, Robin Hood's Town.
Wick.	Helmsdale, Thurso.
Wisbech.	Sutton Wash.
Woodbridge.	Aldborough, Orford.
Supernumerary Ports.	
Aberystwith.	{ Aberdovey, Llansantffraid, Aberayron, New Quay.
Alloa.	{ Stirling, Kincardine, Kennetpans, Clackmannan, Cambus.
Ballina.	
Campbeltown.	Islay, Tarbert.
Cardigan.	Fishguard, Newport.
Deal.	
Fleetwood.	
Kirkwall.	Stromness, Sanday.
Lerwick.	
Lyme.	
Maryport.	
Strangford.	Killough, Quoile.
Tralee.	
Wigton.	Gatehouse of Fleet, Creetown Garliestown, Port William, Whithorn.
Workington.	Harrington.

Up to 1853 it had been the practice to mark each package of imported goods taken into bond with the initials of the ship and her captain. This had been found inconvenient, and on February 21 the Board instituted the present system of marking the packages with the year and a number denoting the ship, the number being taken from a series corresponding with the arrival of the ships in each year. Thus packages from the first ship in 1854 would be marked $\frac{1854}{1}$, and those from subsequent ships in sequence, and the accounts were to be kept accordingly.

The system of granting 'satisfactions' to detaining

officers after release of goods detained for mere informalities (the ' satisfactions ' taking the form of payments by owners of goods) was discontinued.

The Board announced that, in accordance with the recommendations of the late select Committee on Customs, and the provisions of the recent Consolidation Act, a room had been set apart in the London Custom-house for investigating disputes between officers and the public, and that a Commissioner would attend for that purpose on Tuesdays and Fridays.

Among the 1853 Customs records is a return sent by the controller of Navigation laws in Victoria, which bears striking testimony to the sudden increase of trade consequent upon the discovery of gold in the Australian colonies. Five ports are shown—Melbourne, Geelong, Portland, Port Fairy, and Port Albert. The Customs revenue from imported spirits, tea, wine, tobacco, and coffee was £765,728.   Trade as follows :

IMPORTS.

			£
From Great Britain	..	..	8,288,226
From British possessions		..	5,064,844
From the United States ..		..	1,668,606
From other foreign States	..	..	820,961
			15,842,637

EXPORTS.

			£
To Great Britain	..	..	9,875,624
To British possessions	..	..	942,741
To the United States of America ..		..	19,646
To other foreign States	..	..	223,532
			11,061,543

£8,644,529 of the ' exports ' stood under the heading ' gold.'   The greater part of the rest was under ' wool.'

Repeal of the Navigation laws, so far as the United Kingdom was concerned, was completed by Cap. 5 of 17 Vict., which opened the coasting trade of the United Kingdom and Channel Islands to foreign ships.

Cap. 28 and Cap. 29, 17 and 18 Vict., placed certain temporary imposts upon sugar and molasses, increased the duties on spirits of the British possessions in Scotland, and fixed the sugar duties at a higher rate than had been provided for under the Consolidation Act. It abolished the refining of sugar in bond.

Cap. 77, 17 and 18 Vict., provided that the Governor-General of India might from time to time, with the consent of the East India Company's directors, take under his authority by proclamation any part or parts of the Company's territory.

Cap. 94, 17 and 18 Vict., altered the dates of the financial quarter-days, April 5, July 5, October 10, and January 5, to March 31, June 30, September 30, and December 31, and made the end of the financial year March 31 instead of January 5.

Cap. 122, 17 and 18 Vict., imposed a duty on imported arms and ammunition. (These articles had been previously on the ' prohibited ' list, except when imported in transit.) It altered the duties on a few articles, abolishing one or two, and in other instances either reducing them or changing them from *ad valorem* to specific.

Under the provisions of Cap. 73, 16 and 17 Vict., the Board directed the comptroller-general to select 1,500 men from the Coastguard, to serve in the navy.

Great Britain being at war with Russia, the various collectors of customs were authorized to carry out the Order in Council of March 29, 1854, that all Russian vessels in ports of the United Kingdom should be allowed a period within which to load and depart, or if on the way to any port in the United Kingdom should be allowed to enter such port and discharge. Later this was extended to the colonies, and the period warranting entry and discharge was also extended so that all Russian vessels that had left Russian ports prior to May 15, 1854, should be allowed to complete their voyages to the United Kingdom, discharge, and depart.

22

Messrs. Longmans and Co., publishers, addressed a letter to the Chairman of the Board. They enclosed a communication from an agent in Sydney, urging them to have their books at once put on the Customs list of copyright works. The agent stated that large importations had recently been made of American piracies of Macaulay's works, Ure's ' Dictionary,' and McCulloch's ' Dictionary,' and that these books had not been entered on the list, yet he had succeeded by threats of legal proceedings in inducing the importers to send them back. On investigation, the Board found that the books named *were* on the Customs list.

Later, Longmans transmitted another letter from the agent, stating that a leading article had appeared in the Sydney *Argus*, advocating evasion of the copyright laws, and that a flood of piracies had recently been put on the market ; also that things were worse at Melbourne, where the booksellers' shops were full of piratical reprints. The controller of Navigation laws at Sydney (who was also collector of customs) was communicated with, and stated that all books which could be identified from the Customs list as piracies were detained and destroyed. He forwarded an account, from which it appeared that many such books had been seized, and a deal of indecent literature as well.

The conclusion of the Board's correspondence with the colonies is marked by a quaint series of papers dealing with applications made by the controller of Navigation laws, Halifax, Nova Scotia. On July 20, 1854, he asked the Board to recommend him for an additional office— that of Government Accountant in the colony. (Evidently he anticipated the speedy lapse of his own office.) The Board declined. Early in 1855 he wrote again, referring to his approaching retirement, and asking to be made collector of customs at Kirkwall, Scotland, at a salary equal to the pension due him on retirement, ' thereby effecting a saving to Her Majesty's Government, and relieving me from the great depression I feel on being totally unemployed.' 'The late M.P. for the Orkneys,' he continued, 'was a relation of my wife's, and her family connections still reside and have much influence there.' In spite of the delicate hint thus conveyed, the Board refused his request. He wrote again, evidently determined to acquire something beyond his mere pension, and asked the Board to give him the office table. Even this request was refused, and he retired, no doubt with a string of burning grievances.

The account of smuggling from 1845 to 1847 inclusive has had to be collected from various sources. As hinted in our ' Introduction,' there is but little first-hand material prior to 1848. From 1848 onward the hand of the foolish destroyer has been to some extent fettered, and thus we are enabled to furnish extracts from original memoranda—the *actual* reports of seizures and proceedings. As usual, we can only find space for a few, and these must be reported as briefly as possible.

Early in 1845 the Plymouth officers seized forty-two tins containing tobacco—the tins being soldered and painted so as to resemble ordinary red bricks—in casks of pitch imported from that hotbed of smuggling, Jersey.

During May in the same year the Liverpool officers seized a large quantity of tobacco, concealed in hollowed deal ends on board an American ship.

A vessel arrived at London from Jersey with a number of empty casks as deck cargo. The casks were found to have two sets of staves, the spaces between the staves being packed with cigars.

The collector of St. Andrews, New Brunswick, reported that he had information that goods were often smuggled into the town at night, concealed under hay and straw in carts, and he desired instructions as to whether the British revenue law, which empowered customs officers to stop carts on suspicion, and exempted them from liability if such suspicion proved groundless, applied to the colonies. The Board replied that it did not, and advised him not to stop any carts unless he was certain that they contained smuggled goods.

On October 19, 1845, the tide-surveyor at St. John's, Newfoundland, attempted to seize a lighter containing a large quantity of tobacco. The owner of the lighter instructed his men to resist seizure, with the result that the tide-surveyor and his subordinates were violently assaulted. It afterwards turned out that the tobacco was duty-paid. The Board refused to sanction prosecution of the tide-surveyor's assailants.

On January 6, 1846, the customs tide-waiter stationed at St. George's, Charlotte County, New Brunswick, visited certain mills in the neighbourhood, to search for smuggled goods. He made several seizures, and then one of the owners menaced him with a loaded gun, and forced him to abandon search. The Board declined to sanction proceedings against the offender, but recommended the officer to apply to the provincial authorities.

On December 9, 1846, Madame Soulìè, an actress, landed at Port Louis, Mauritius, and, on her baggage being examined, seizure was made of the following ' French goods ': 29 pairs stays, 31 pieces ribbon, 28 pieces silk trimmings, and 2 pieces lace. The lady petitioned the governor as follows :

' EXCELLENCE,
    ' La soussignée " Veuve Soulìè," artiste dramatique, a l'honneur d'exposer bien humblement. Que dans un voyage qu'elle a fait a Bourbon, elle a reçu en paiement quelques objets de mode de mince valeur, pour son usage personnel comme artiste. Que ces objets sont indispensables a l'exposante comme artiste, que n'ayant jamais en l'intention de les vendre, etc.
                                    ' ROSALIE SOULÌÈ.'

But the officers insisted that the goods had been concealed in false bottoms in Rosalie's trunks, and the

REVENUE CRUISER CHASING SMUGGLER BY NIGHT ON THE KENTISH COAST.

To face p. 361.

governor declined to interfere. On which the lady petitioned afresh : ' Ces objets sont des articles de mode indispensables à une actrice qui obligée d'avoir un grand nombre de costumes pour ses rôles.' She protested that she put them in ' les derniers compartiments de ma malle de voyage,' to prevent their being damaged.

The collector's report to the Board seemed to show that Madame Rosalie might have been devoid of fraudulent intention, for it appeared that the so-called ' false bottoms ' occupied the greater portions of the trunks, and the goods were examined on ' baggage sufferance ' (a form of entry generally held to be non-committal). Yet the collector sold the goods before making his report. The Board directed that the net proceeds of the sale should be given to the lady (which was tantamount to acknowledging that they did not hold her to blame). But the collector was unable to secure the lady's receipt for the moneys till 1848, ' in consequence of the illness of the party alluded to.' He stated that he had not deducted the duties from the gross proceeds, as he thought the party had been ' injured and greatly inconvenienced ' by the seizure. The London lawyers hinted that the duties were due, and that the collector should be surcharged ; but the Board remitted the duties. (It appears that the seizure was a scandalously harsh proceeding, that may have utterly ruined the unfortunate actress.)

The Mauritius officers were extremely zealous in the detection of opium-smuggling. Below is an account of several cases, extending over a period of three years. On December 9, 1844, a landing-waiter at Port Louis apprised the collector that he had seized a large quantity of opium in a store kept by two Chinamen, and that the Chinamen had offered him £80 as a bribe to ignore the concealment. The Chinamen were prosecuted in the V.A. Court, fined £200 and costs, and the £80 offered as a bribe was declared forfeited. The opium was sold for exportation, to be shipped either to Indian ports, where its importation was not prohibited, or to Great Britain, for manufacturing into morphine. The Chinamen prayed the governor to relieve them from two-thirds of the penalty, but he declined, so they paid the fine and the enormous costs. Then the collector made a subtle suggestion to the Board that the £80 offered as bribe should be given to the seizer, and that a third of the £200 fine should be given to the collector, to compensate him for his trouble in prosecuting. The Board considered this modest request, awarded the seizer his proper share of the fine, ordered the £80 to be paid in to the Crown's account, and gave the collector nothing. The Chinaman who landed the goods was captured soon afterwards, and fined £100 and costs. He went to prison in default, and the Queen's Proctor, who had prosecuted (the collector declining to officiate in this case), sent in a bill of costs to the Customs for £165 18s. 11d., £61 of which was under the heading of ' Registrar's fees.' The prisoner memorialized the governor, stating that he employed a lawyer to defend him, and that the lawyer charged him £140, which he had paid. It appears the poor fellow's health had broken down in prison. He produced the lawyer's receipt for the costs, and the governor released him. (The papers connected with this seizure convey ghastly impressions to the reader. It is manifest that the case was ' loaded ' by the seizing officer. No proceedings could be taken against a mere *importer* of opium ; the goods had to be landed and deposited for use ere action could be taken, so the seizer, who had been informed of the arrival of the opium from Calcutta, had allowed it to be unshipped, and watched it to its destination. When this is considered, along with the brazen extortions of the Mauritius lawyers, one is inclined to think that the officers and lawyers should have been imprisoned instead of the Chinamen.)

In 1847 a vessel arrived at Port Louis from Calcutta. She had two screwed and hooped bales of cotton on deck, and when the officers opened these they found in each a large tin case containing opium. As the goods were seized prior to landing, no proceedings could be taken, but the opium was sold for exportation. Soon after a Chinaman was caught on a vessel from Pondicherry with twenty boxes and three bladders of opium.

A squabble arose over the proceeds of sale, the officers insisting that the goods should be assessed for the purpose of award at 40s. a pound, although they fetched but 16s. a pound. The Board dealt summarily with the matter, giving the greedy fellows one-third of the *actual sale price*.

Later, one of the officers made a report which fills the reader with irksome suspicions. He stated that he was informed that a quantity of opium had been deposited on his premises. He made for home, and on his way observed his own servant in the company of a Chinaman. The men were carrying a trunk, and he found in the trunk forty-four boxes of opium. The colonial law officers held that there was not enough evidence to convict either servant or Chinaman, but the opium was condemned. (A reasonable opinion is that the officer found it on board ship, and sent it home by his servant, intending to sell it privately, and, becoming fearful that he might have been observed, charged the servant with the offence, and inculpated the first unlucky Chinaman he could get hold of. Things quite as villainous were done in the colonies in those golden days.)

The seizing officer fought tooth and nail for assessment at 40s. a pound, but the Board were firm. Then he applied to the governor for a further award, but was told no grant for that purpose could be made out of the colonial funds. After studying the practice of the Mauritius lawyers and officials, one is inclined to doubt which could be the worse, removal of all restrictions upon the importation of the drug, or the employment of such a set of sharks to detect it.

The collector of St. John, New Brunswick, reported detention of a number of pirated copies of ' The Emigrants,' consigned to Messrs. McMillan, booksellers, at

St. John. He suggested leniency, the importers having searched the 'prohibited' list prior to importing the books from Boston, U.S.A. (The list containing the entry did not arrive till after the order was sent.)   The copyright was held by Mr. John Murray. McMillan petitioned the Treasury, but without avail, the Customs lawyers insisting upon the forfeiture of the books, and stating that the Treasury had no control in the matter of prohibition under copyright.

The Board, by their General Letter of October 2, 1848, sent to all ports of the United Kingdom, announced that several flagrant cases of collusion between informers and seizing officers had been brought to light. In future, whenever an officer received information, he was to communicate the informer's name confidentially to the collector if at an outport, to the Solicitor if at London. All rewards to informers were to be paid through collectors or the Solicitor, and they were to satisfy themselves that the persons claiming such rewards were the actual informers.

During 1848 the Jersey officers began to entertain profound suspicion with regard to the *Eliza*, a cutter belonging to that island. On November 30, 1848, Richard Butt, master of the *Eliza*, was induced to make a statement as to his recent misdoings.   It appeared that on June 8, 1848, he cleared from Jersey for France, but instead of proceeding thither went to Bonne Nuit Bay, Jersey, and took in a quantity of spirits in kegs, and about $2\frac{1}{2}$ tons of tobacco-stalks, cigars, and snuff.   He then proceeded to Fishguard Bay, but was signalled to keep off for a time. About eleven at night he crept in and ran his cargo, then went over to France, took in sheep, and conveyed them to Jersey.   On September 22 he left St. Heliers without clearance, proceeded to Greve de Lecq, took on board 5 tons of leaf tobacco, snuff, and cigars, and a number of bags of tea and cases of spirits, sailed to Fishguard Bay, ran the goods, then took in stone ballast, and made for Jersey.   On the way home he was met by a revenue cruiser, and the captain boarded him, and found he had no papers. Butt explained this by stating that he had piloted a vessel down Channel. He reached Jersey, and claimed his pay from the syndicate that had employed him. Instead of paying him, according to agreement, at the rate of £50 a ton, they gave him but £10. His deposition concluded thus : ' In consequence thereof, as well as for other misunderstandings between deponent and the above parties, he has considered it a duty which he owes himself to make the present declaration.'

The persons composing the syndicate absconded, but in 1849 one of them wrote from France, offering to become an approver. His offer was accepted, but it does not appear that any of the other principals were captured. (The cutter was condemned in the Exchequer.) Several of the receivers suffered. The excise officers of Haverfordwest heard of the transactions, and instituted a search in the neighbourhood. They seized two horses and a waggon, conveying two large casks addressed to a person living in Farringdon Market, London, to be forwarded by rail from Bristol. The casks contained tobacco stowed beneath layers of bones, the goods having been repacked thus after landing. On the following day they found a quantity of tobacco in a hay-loft, but the total quantity seized (1,408 pounds tobacco and 32 pounds snuff) was a mere fragment of that originally run.

Many other remarkable cases appear in the 1848 record ; see below :

March 8.—Two horses, a waggon, and 912 pounds tobacco, seized by excise officers at York Railway Station (goods landed at Goole).

In May.—The *Jane and Nancy*, seized off Stonehouse, after she had thrown her cargo overboard (sixty bales tobacco—say 3,000 pounds).

July 16.—Information received of a run of 1,008 gallons spirits at Penryn.

October 30.—968 pounds tobacco and 180 pounds stalks seized in a storehouse at Plymouth.

November 30.—224 pounds tobacco seized on board the *Good Intent* at Fowey. (All the ship's company implicated.)

December 2.—195 pounds tobacco and cigars found on board a ship at Liverpool, concealed in tins of biscuit.

On September 4, 1848, the coastguard at Salcombe observed a boat entering the harbour at nightfall. They went off to board her, and she at once headed for the shore, and her occupants, two men and a woman, jumped out and took to their heels. One escaped, the other two were captured. The boat contained thirty bales of tobacco-stalks, weighing 1,598 pounds. The man taken was Richard Pepperell, probably the most daring and notorious smuggler in the West of England. He escaped after capture, by jumping from a window three stories high, but was retaken, convicted, and imprisoned in default of paying a fine of £100. The woman was acquitted on the plea of her being a passenger. (We shall have occasion to describe other transactions in which Pepperell was concerned.)

A seizure reported on March 24, 1848, from Auckland, New Zealand, throws light upon the methods of bartering for contraband in the colony. One Henry Atkins was captured with 138 pounds tobacco, which he had obtained from an American vessel lying at the Great Barrier, in exchange for nine hogs. On December 9 in the same year a smack was seized with 86 pounds tobacco on board, which the master had bought from an American whaler. On January 9, 1849, the Auckland officers seized ninety-one casks wines and spirits, landed without entry from the American ship *Robert Pulsford*. This last seizure appears to have been unjust, for the goods were shown on the ship's manifest ; but the magistrates, perhaps influenced by Uncle Sam's general record as a smuggler, condemned the goods, and the Board refused to intervene, though appealed to by the shipowners. The authorities were not always so severe. In November, 1848, the collector at Russell, New Zealand, had seized a large quantity of tobacco at a whaling settlement near Wanganui. The goods were removed to the Custom-house at Russell, and the owners were prosecuted and fined £100. For some reason or other the governor remitted the penalty, and soon afterwards unknown adventurers broke into the Custom-house at night and carried off the goods. It was found that they had been originally run from an American whaler, and when this vessel came into port the collector detained her, and placed a tide-waiter on board. As soon as darkness fell the Yankee skipper began to get his vessel under weigh, so the tide-waiter went ashore and apprised the collector, who at once went off in a boat and asked the captain what he was doing. The captain answered, ' Guess I'm goin',' and shot off into the night. Even then there was not an end of the trouble. In June, 1849, a Maori found a large case of tobacco concealed in the scrub near the whaling settlement. He mustered his tribe, who divided the tobacco and made off. Then the finder reported the matter to the collector, doubtless expecting a reward. (The papers close with a pathetic statement from the collector that he has lost his original action, lost the reward he expected, lost the goods, lost all chance of making the American skipper pay, lost the whole of a second seizure except the package, been put to expense which he cannot charge to the Customs account, and is now derided and persecuted by the whalers and settlers.)

During 1849 a French smack was seized at Plymouth with tanks of spirits concealed between double bulkheads, and a huge seizure of compressed snuff was made by the London officers, the goods being made up as ' oilseed cake,' and packed with the genuine article. Thieves broke into the Custom - house at Newry, and stole 607 pounds tobacco. On April 21, 1849, about 2½ tons of tobacco were found floating off the Essex coast.

The following illustrative cases of seizures are quoted from the 1849 papers :

March 3.—Horse, cart, and 993 pounds tobacco, seized by excise officers and police near Shield Row, Durham.

May 3.—122 pounds tobacco, seized on a ship in Leith Roads.

May 16.—150 tubs spirits, seized in Portsmouth Harbour, while being towed by the steam tug *Royal Charter*.

May 24.—96 tubs spirits, found sunk off Challaboro', Devon.

May 25.—128 pounds tobacco, seized on a ship at Liverpool (concealed in casks of biscuit).

July 30.—74 tubs, 31 flagons, and 8 half-flagons spirits, seized on a vessel in the Itchen River (concealed under concrete along the keelson).

October 15.—799 pounds of tobacco-stalks, seized on a vessel off Challaboro', Devon. (The incorrigible Pepperell was concerned in this case. He had just been released from prison ; see p. 346.)

October 29.—Cutter *Lion* and 335 gallons spirits, seized at Jersey.

October.—1,038 pounds tobacco, seized at the Eastern Counties railway station, London. (The goods had been landed at Woodbridge, Suffolk, and forwarded by rail, packed in hampers and advised as fish.)

November 18.—The *Deux Amis* and 1,189 pounds tobacco and cigars, seized at Jersey. (The goods were intended for illegal exportation to France.)

November 27.—168 pounds tobacco, seized in a cab outside the Liverpool docks.

November.—1,096 pounds tobacco, seized at Newry on a vessel from Quebec. (Goods packed in 24 casks flour.)

December 10.—The *Aide de Famille* and 370 pounds tobacco, seized at Alderney. (Goods for illegal exportation to France.)

The largest seizure that we find in 1849 is that made by the *Vigilant* revenue cruiser in Sea Reach (Thames), on December 13. The *Vigilant's* crew boarded an ordinary sailing-barge, the *Charlotte*, took off her hatches, and found in the hold a number of casks, containing in all 14,402 pounds tobacco. This seizure was returned as ' made without information,' but we think it strange that a boy who was employed on the barge, and who was exempted from proceedings because he was under sixteen, bore the same Christian and surname as the mariner on the *Vigilant* who suggested that the barge should be searched. The following awards were made to the seizers : To the master of the *Vigilant*, £431 ; gunner, boatswain, carpenter, and steward, £86 each ; five mariners, £30 each ; seven boys, £21 each ; and £6 to the ship's company as ' head-money.'

The seizure report from Falmouth for the period extending from November 12 to 30, 1849, is quite remarkable, and bears testimony to the industry and skill of the rummaging officers. We reproduce it :

Two pounds tobacco seized ashore from a seaman ; 50 pounds tobacco and 1 pound tea, seized on board the *Alchemist* (vessel detained and fined) ; 13 pounds tobacco, seized on board the *Aghios Spiridion* (vessel detained and fined) ; 22 pounds cigars and 9 pounds tobacco, seized on board the *Peppina* (vessel detained and fined) ; 8 pounds cigars on a further search of the *Peppina ;* 2 pounds cigars and 3 pounds tobacco on board the *Susan ;* 9 pounds cigars, seized on board the *Vasilachi ;* 4 pounds cigars, seized on board the *Parraghia Evangelistica ;* 46 pounds cigars and 162 pounds tobacco on a further search (vessel detained and fined) ; 82 pounds tobacco seized on board the *Alexandra* (vessel detained and fined). Five of the above were Greek vessels.

The gradual transference of Customs control to the various colonial Governments is made apparent in the seizure records of the time by a tendency on the part of the London Customs lawyers to ' unload ' many of their

responsibilities. Thus, when a seizure of sixteen cases
tobacco was made at Quebec on November 8, 1849, on
board the schooner *Niger*, from Cape Breton, the case was
dealt with by the provincial Government, the goods being
restored on condition that the defendant paid the duty
and costs, and 10 dollars as a ' satisfaction ' to the seizing
officer. When an account of the case was sent to Thames
Street, the Solicitor remarked upon the papers that it
was no longer necessary to report Canadian seizures to
the Board. (He meant ' revenue seizures ': cases under
the Navigation and Fishery laws were still reported.)

Seizure notes continued to flow in from the Antipodean
colonies. Below is the list from Port Adelaide, October 24,
1849, to May 1, 1850 : 160 pounds tobacco, concealed in
an imported case of crockery ; 168 pounds tobacco, concealed in an imported cask of soda ; a quantity of rings
and fancy wares, and two trunks of boots, not reported ;
2,500 cigars, seized at a wharf ; 60 pounds cigars, seized
in a shop ; 20 pounds cigars, seized on board the *Amicas ;*
181 pounds cigars, concealed in imported packages of
hops.

The regulations as to boats, etc., were remodelled by
Board's circular of April 26, 1850 (in consequence of the
provisions of Secs. 16 and 17, Cap. 90, 12 and 13 Vict.).
In their new form they stood thus :

CLASS.	SCOPE OF TRAFFIC.
Open boats and vessels under 15 tons.	Only 4 leagues seaward between Beachy Head and North Foreland. On the rest of the coast, 8 leagues seaward. Along the coast, 50 leagues.
Open or half-decked boats above 15 tons.	Only 4 leagues seaward between Beachy Head and North Foreland. On other coasts, 12 leagues seaward. Along the coast, 80 leagues.
Decked vessels under 40 tons, and *all* vessels less than 170 tons, whose length is to the breadth greater than 3 feet 6 inches to 1 foot (except steam vessels).	Only 4 leagues seaward between Beachy Head and North Foreland. On other coasts, except in the Irish Sea, only 12 leagues.

No vessel less than 170 tons might carry arms for resistance in excess of two muskets to every five men. (Any vessel might have one carriage gun, without shot, for signalling.) The maximum number of men and boys as crew was stipulated.

Below are a few remarkable seizures made in the United Kingdom during 1850 :

January 24.—The cutter *Mary*, seized off Shields with 7,187 pounds tobacco-stalks and 323 pounds tobacco.

February 14.—70 tubs spirits, seized ashore at Babbicombe, Devon.

February 23.—A large quantity of adulterants, seized on a tobacco manufacturer's premises at Bristol.

March 21.—A French cutter, captured off Lulworth, after she had thrown her cargo overboard during chase.

March 29.—The *Rob Roy* cutter, seized off Shields with 8,210 pounds tobacco.

April 2.—589 pounds tobacco, found in a cave near Marsden Rock, in the Shields district.

May 14. — 412 pounds tobacco, seized at Leeds. (The goods had been imported in cases of glass at Goole.)

May 23, 25, and various subsequent dates. — About 8,000 pounds tobacco-stalks, seized at Bristol and Aberthaw. (Run by the schooner *Wave*, and afterwards captured by search. Probably only part of the consignment).

July 12 *and* 13.—An immense quantity of coffee and sugar, seized at Liverpool for having been tampered with while in bond. (Connected with the famous ' Duncan Stewart ' case.)

August 3.—The French lugger *Georges*, captured in the English Channel after she had run her cargo. (Crew convicted.)

August 8.—The smack *Zoe*, with 3,098 pounds tobacco-stalks, seized in Dartmouth Harbour.

August 27.—170 gallons spirits, seized in an outhouse at Goldhanger, Essex.

October 1.—The oyster-smack *Rival*, seized in Chichester harbour, while towing 13 tubs spirits.

November 1.—160 pounds cigars, seized by excise officers at Monkwearmouth railway station.

Several seizures were made in Scotland of smuggled silks which were being hawked by pedlars, and at Deal no less than three important seizures of tobacco which had been brought on board Belgian pilot-cutters. The largest seizure we find in the 1850 file is that made on September 13, on board the sloop *Sarah and Susannah*, at Goole. This vessel arrived with a cargo of flints, and the master produced his cargo-book, which showed that he had taken them in at Ramsgate. It was soon manifest that he had since made a trip oversea, for beneath the flints the officers found 15,452 pounds of tobacco and tobacco-stalks. The captain absconded. His wife, who was on board during the voyage, the mate, and the solitary seaman who formed the ' crew,' were arrested. The lady was acquitted, it being held that she had acted under her husband's influence. The mate and sailor were convicted, and while in prison they gave information which led to the arrest of the master, and the financier of the venture, a person living at Yarmouth.

On March 31, 1850, the principal coast officer (Customs) at Brighton saw four tubs floating at some distance from the shore. The weather was so rough that the coast-guardsmen refused to launch their boat, but the plucky officer induced four fishermen to get a boat out, put to sea, with a tide-waiter as coxswain, and secured the tubs, which contained spirits. He then asked the Board that the fishermen might be paid for the risk and trouble, and concerning this request there was almost as much discussion and circumlocution, between the Solicitor and the Accountant-General, as though demand had been made for the whole of the contents of the Treasury. In the end the fishermen got 10s. each for risking their boat and lives.

The case of Mr. Hyams furnishes proof of the extraordinary persistency of the Jewish race in cases where money's worth is concerned. Hyams landed at Folkestone on October 20, 1850, and omitted to declare certain new articles of apparel which were distributed in his baggage. The officers detained them, and Hyams proceeded to bombard the Board with explanations and petitions. Then he applied to Baron Lionel de Rothschild, who was good enough to refer the matter to Mr. Spring Rice at the Treasury. An exhaustive investigation was held by the Board, and the seizure was confirmed. Mr. Hyams, when the inquiry was concluded, expressed himself satisfied. A few days after he fired a parting shot in the shape of a letter, charging the officers with misrepresentation.

It is possible that the Folkestone officers may have been extremely strict, for just previous to the detection of Mr. Hyams the following letter had reached the Board :

'FOLKESTONE, KENT,
'September, 1850.

'MY LORDS AND GENTLEMEN,
'I beg most earnestly to call your Lordships' attention to the character, cast, disposition, and deportment of the men engaged here by the Customs as tide-waiters, rummagers, and boatmen ; the latter are black-guardly, insolent, and abusive, and the former appear to be the very refuse of God's creation—uncultivated, unclean, and obscene, both in their conduct, address, and manner ; indeed, they are the very scum of the community, a perfect disgrace to your Lordships, as well as to Her Majesty's Service.

'These men assume and take upon themselves more than they are either authorized or entitled to do in their capacity as underlings, and to this there appears to be neither bounds nor check, as they continue in the daily practice of heaping abuse and calumny on all those whose lot or business calls them to travel between this country and the Continent ; they are also meddling, offensive,

23

and atrociously wicked, and are each and every one of
them addicted to the vile practice of smoking while on
duty, etc., etc.

    ' Your Lordships' most obedient servant,
       ' A TRAVELLER AND SOJOURNER
           IN HER MAJESTY'S SERVICE.'

Sad to state, this stirring appeal, fortified as it was by
a choice ' derangement of epitaphs,' failed to secure the
dismissal of the Customs staff.

Among many curious items in the various seizure lists
for 1850 we observe one at Dover of seventeen turkeys
seized for not being reported, appraised value £5 4s.,
duty 5s. 2d., and a petition by a seaman of the *Washington
Irving*, an American vessel lying at Liverpool. 150 pounds
tobacco had been found on board, and the ship's officers
put the blame upon the petitioner, who was fined £100,
and imprisoned in default. He stated that the charge
against him was the result of conspiracy, he being the
only Britisher in the crew. He asked the Board to
release him, stating that if this were granted he would
' in future years pray for the welfare of this Great Realm
and its Sovereign.'

Whenever a native of Deal was convicted of smuggling
it was the practice of the inhabitants of that town to
sign a huge memorial to the Treasury, describing him as
a respectable citizen, a devoted husband, a tender father,
and, so far as the smuggling was concerned, a victim of
delusive appearances. It may be mentioned also that
it was the invariable custom of the Treasury to refuse to
release him, but it does not appear that this in any way
discouraged the worthy burgesses. One of these futile
petitions was forwarded in 1850 on behalf of the crew
of the galley *Lucy Long*, who had been in the habit of
using cigars as ballast. It was backed up by Lord
Clarence Paget, who stated that he had been instigated
by ' a large and respectable portion of his constituents,
of all shades of political opinion.'

In August, 1850, the tide-surveyor at Bristol received information of an intended run. He impressed a yawl and two fishermen, went afloat, and seized the *Henri*, a French cutter, with 6,632 pounds tobacco and stalks on board. The Board awarded £456 for this seizure, £228 of which went to the tide-surveyor, and £9 for division between the yawl-owner and the two fishermen. The fishermen complained to the Rev. Mirehouse, vicar of St. George's, and he reported the facts of the case to the Treasury, making it evident that the men had rendered most valuable assistance. The Board directed the officers to pay the men an additional £20.

On December 12, 1850, certain excise officers found under a hedge in front of a house near Penypistill, Pembrokeshire, two cellars, containing in all sixteen bales of tobacco-stalks. Later they searched a farmer's premises, and found a cellar in the garden, beneath a bed of leeks, and another beneath the stable. These contained twenty-two bales. Total quantity seized, 2,153 pounds. The officers stated these seizures were made without information, but on inquiry it became apparent that this was false. The magistrates refused to convict, stating that there was no proof that the party charged had put the goods in the cellars.

During the same year two excise officers found a tub of spirits in a fishmonger's shop in Lower Thames Street, London, and a letter from Lymington, Hants, sent as invoice. They wrote under a feigned name to the sender, and ordered five tubs more, then proceeded to Lymington, watched his premises, and found that he was being supplied by 'the ——s,' a notorious family of smugglers. After watching for some time they made a search, and found the five tubs they had ordered. They then summoned to their assistance the excise supervisor of the district, the men of the coastguard, and a constable, and proceeded to search the houses occupied by the ——s. The search was fruitless as regarded contraband, but the officers persevered until they reached the cottage occupied

by ' Old ——,' a well-known desperado.   Here they
were richly rewarded indeed.   They forced an entrance,
one of the London excisemen, armed with a naked sword,
leading the charge.   Old —— was at the top of the stair-
case, provided with several utensils full of filth, which he
discharged upon the heads of the revenue men.   Undaunted by this unsavoury fusillade, the leading excisemen rushed up the stair and gained the landing.   Then
—— graciously permitted the search to proceed.   ' The
scene indoors,' stated the chief officer of coastguard in
his report, ' was too disgusting to be described.'   Old
—— was exchequered for his complicity in the smuggling,
and imprisoned, but speedily released by Treasury Order.
This clemency may have been the result of a memorial
sent to the Board of Excise, signed by the mayor of
Lymington and several justices of the peace, in which the
officers were stigmatized as *agents provocateurs*, who had
' inveigled and tricked ' —— and others into defrauding
the revenue.   The smuggler's note to the London fishmonger may be found interesting :

' SIR,
        ' 12 pr. of Soles—if Cod is very cheap send.   I
have not received any orders this week we have got so
many Herring boats heare.   I have ' [sent one] ' as a
sampal the price is £3 10s.   You must mix it in this way.
A large pan put 4 quarts and a pint of nice clean water.
Tipe out about half the spirits and mix it well and then put
4 quarts and 1 pint more of water and ad the other spirits
you will find it quite strong enough.   Should you like
2 more I can send them.   It will make altogether 22
quarts of Hollands the longer kept the better it gets you
may look out for it tomorrow morning.'

(The tub was sent in a hamper, packed with fish.)
    Extraordinary tactics on the part of seizing officers,
both at home and in the colonies, were frequently brought
to the notice of the Board.   A case in which Mr. Munro,

the collector of Tortola, was implicated, cannot well be passed over ; it displays so fully the crooked dealings of some of the colonial officials.   The collector had informed the Board that wrecks frequently occurred on the shores of Anegada, and that the Anegadians made a practice of laying hands upon the goods that came ashore, and smuggling them into the foreign islands adjacent.   On January 26, 1850, an American brig, with a valuable cargo, went on the shoals, and although all the cargo was salved, only a part of it reached the Tortola Custom-house.   The collector informed the Board that this was due to the obstinacy of the captain, who had refused to pay for a customs officer to guard the wreck.

It should be mentioned that Munro had previously given the Board much trouble.   In 1846 he had been charged by one of his subordinates with buying two wrecked ships, and then repairing and selling them, with importing goods without paying duty, and with infringing the rules which prohibited customs officers from inter-fering in elections.   The President of the island, Mr. Hay, had censured him, and the Board had concurred.   But Munro had in a way got even with the President, by proving that the latter had illegally exempted himself from paying provincial tonnage dues, and by detecting him in a smuggling transaction, and making him pay the duty on the goods.   The President had thereupon sum-moned Munro before the Privy Council of the island, but Munro stuck to his guns and to the duty, although one of the members of the Council accused him openly of having condoned a smuggling transaction in which he (the member) had taken part.   After much mud had been thrown on both sides the matter was allowed to drop, and it might be thought that Mr. Munro would be more care-ful in future.   But a study of the Anegada wreck case reveals that he could not refrain from meddling.

The most convincing and amusing portion of the Anegada report was the American captain's statement. He deposed that after the goods salved had been put in the

Tortola Custom-house he took up his quarters at an hotel. He had not been there long ere ' a stout loquacious individual ' called on him, and ' in a soft and insinuating manner ' warned him against putting his affairs in charge of one of the ordinary shipping agents, stating that the said agents would render but ' a Flemish account ' of the wrecked goods, and leave him with scarcely enough money to pay his passage home. The stranger also suggested that Munro should be made agent, as he would do the work free of charge. All this, the oily interviewer explained, in the way of Christian charity. ' I tell you what it is, sir,' replied Captain Jacob A. Cobb, ' your advice is too disinterested for me,' and with that escorted him to the door. There the captain observed a gentleman waiting outside, undoubtedly Munro. Captain Cobb also accused Munro of allowing the inhabitants of Tortola to plunder the wrecked goods after they had been put in the Queen's Warehouse. ' For the first two or three days,' he stated, ' there was a grand jubilee at Tortola.' It was admitted that a considerable quantity of wine had been consumed, but the agent chosen by the skipper came to Munro's rescue, and stated that the wine was distributed as samples, to induce bidding at the sale. The President of the island sent the captain's complaint to the Treasury, but could not refrain from displaying some little vindictiveness, which probably assisted in securing Munro's partial exoneration. The matter fizzled out in the end, after discrediting everyone concerned except the unfortunate captain, who, it seems, had merely escaped the winds and waves to fall into peril from the fangs of a nest of harpies.

Two Mauritius merchants cleared 48 hogsheads of brandy duty-free from bond, for exportation from Port Louis to Madagascar. The goods were shipped, and during the night the parties concerned emptied twenty-three of the casks, removed the contents ashore, and filled the casks with water. The officers heard of this too late to capture the run goods, but they went on board and seized the balance. Action was entered against the merchants in the Vice-Admiralty Court of the island, and the bond entered into for due exportation of the goods was adjudged forfeited, but it does not appear that the merchants were made liable to any other penalty. The sureties were unable to pay, and the Customs lawyers in London made severe remarks upon the collector's neglect to inquire into the sufficiency of the sureties before accepting the bond.

Below are a few of the important seizures made in the United Kingdom during 1851 :

January 6.—2,643 pounds tobacco seized at Liverpool, concealed behind false bulkheads in master's state-room, on board the *Warrior* from New York.

March 6.—The *Linnet* (coaster), seized at Southampton, with 6,165 pounds tobacco-stalks.

March.—A large quantity of tobacco and snuff seized at Jersey and Shoreham, concealed in hollow chimbs of casks of cider.

May 9.—468 pounds tobacco and 9 gallons spirits, seized at Yarmouth, concealed on board a foreign trader.

May 29.—The hatch-boat *Fanny*, with 7,395 pounds tobacco, seized near the Galloper Light.

June 4.—200 pounds tobacco, seized by the police at Dublin.

June 29.—An open boat and 621 pounds tobacco-stalks, seized off Salcombe. (Pepperell's wife implicated.)

July 3.—Horse, van, and 649 pounds tobacco-stalks. seized at St. Budeaux.

July 4.—654 pounds tobacco, seized by excise officers in a wood near Eggbuckland, Devon.

July.—98 bales tobacco-stalks (say about 5,000 pounds), seized near Tamerton Folliott, Devon. (Seizing officer censured for suppressing the fact that he had received information.)

September 24.—The smack *Defiance*, seized at the Nore by the revenue cruiser *Fly*, with 6,152 pounds tobacco.

September 27.—A galley and 79 tubs spirits, seized off Selsea.

November 30.—124 tubs spirits, found floating off Langstone harbour.

December 16.—4,488 pounds tobacco, seized at ' Fox's Barn,' Nacton, Suffolk. (A run of more than twice that quantity had been made previously at Trimley.)

December 26.—A French ' tub-boat,' seized off Portland, with 75 tubs and 1 flagon spirits.

A huge run of tobacco-stalks took place early in the year in the vicinity of Brixham. The customs officer stationed at that cosy port came to hear of the transaction, and instituted a search. He found fifty-nine bales in a carrier's stable, thirty-nine buried in a garden belonging to a local shipwright, and twenty-nine in a hayloft and stable at a farm in the neighbourhood. Total quantity seized = 6,619 pounds.

On March 13 the coastguard at Deal seized twenty-four stone bottles of spirits, which a boatman was trying to run. The boatman drew a knife, and made desperate attempts to stab the chief coastguard officer. He was overpowered, and then his mother and sisters attempted to rescue him. They behaved like veritable Amazons, seizing the officers by the hair, throwing them down, and violently assaulting them. The boatman was convicted, and imprisoned for six months. One of the women was acquitted ; the others were sent to gaol for six months each, without hard labour.

On April 3 the *Stag* revenue cutter observed the *Duck* of Portsmouth (a vessel supposed to be exclusively in the coasting trade) cruising off the French coast. After a long and exciting chase she was captured, and her master was found to be one Crasweller, of Hayling Island, a notorious smuggler, who had been convicted in 1845 and 1848. ' During chase,' the *Stag's* commander reported, ' her manœuvres indicated the time of throwing overboard her cargo, although the distance was too great for occular (*sic*) demonstration.' He brought the *Duck* into

Cowes, and laid her ashore.   Then something peculiar was
detected in the conformation of the lower timbers, and a
close search revealed that she had a false bottom, in
which were thirty-six tubs brandy.

The case of *La Cométe*, which ' came to a head ' in 1851,
is worth special notice.   During 1848 the vice-consul at
Zeeland had sent news of this vessel.   She had been on
a smuggling trip to the north of Scotland, cleared £1,000
by the run, and was lying at Flushing ready to depart
for the same bourne with 6,000 pounds leaf tobacco.   It
is likely that she was an English vessel, for her original
name had been *Helena Maria*, afterwards altered to *Venus*,
then to *Phénix*.

The Board apprised the officers on the east coast, and
on the north coasts of Scotland and Ireland.   The vessel
left Flushing, but soon returned with part of her cargo,
the rest having been seized during the operation of running.   She filled up and left again, this time under the
name *La Cométe*, with a bogus clearance for Sweden.   On
February 13, 1849, she was driven dismasted into Whitby,
and at once reported her cargo as for Sweden.   The
packages were of legal size, so nothing could be done.
After refitting she returned to Flushing, apparently for
orders, for she soon sailed again under the name *Planet*.
She continued her voyages during 1849 and 1850, till, on
April 27, 1851, she was sighted within the limits off St.
Abb's Head, and captured by a revenue cruiser.   On this
occasion she was *La Cométe*.   All her crew were convicted
at Leith.   A ' bill of suspension and liberation ' was put
in by the defendants, but the Court of Justiciary refused
it on a bare formality, for not being entered in the Court
of Exchequer.   It appears that had the bill been properly
entered two of its objections to conviction would have
been valid : (1) That the evidence against the prisoners
had not been reduced to writing ; (2) that though counsel
put in a special written statement of certain evidence for
the defence, the justices wrongfully rejected it.   The
vessel was condemned with her cargo (5,868 pounds leaf

and 1,468 pounds stalks). The informer received as reward £303.

On September 29 the revenue cruiser *Adder* detained a French lugger off the Isle of Wight. The lugger had thirty-three bales of tobacco on board, and several empty wrappers similar to those surrounding the bales were found, and this was regarded as evidence that she had disposed of part of her cargo. She had a manifest for the tobacco, and a clearance from Dunkirk for Morlaix. She was taken into Cowes, and then released, it being found that the packages of tobacco were of the weight specified as ' legal ' by the Customs laws. Her master applied for compensation through the French consul at London, and his request was referred to the Board by the Foreign Office, with an order that the preventive officers were to be directed to refrain from seizing ' on unfounded sus- picion ' vessels belonging to a friendly power. The Customs lawyer stated in reply that there could be no doubt that the vessel had been engaged in smuggling, and that her French clearance had been obtained, and the goods packed legally, with a view to defence by quibble if seized. He insisted that the captain of the *Adder* had full right to detain her and examine her cargo, but should not have taken her to Cowes for that purpose. Still, the master of the lugger was not entitled to com- pensation.

The conduct of Edward Smith, a coastguardsman stationed at Felpham, Devon, was made the subject of an inquiry during 1851. It appears that on the morning of August 30 Smith informed his superior officer that whilst on duty on the coast he found several tubs of spirits at low-water-mark, and that as he was approaching them several men sprang upon him, wrenched his loaded pistol from him, bound him hand and foot, and then carried off the tubs ; that he wriggled himself partially free, and then cut his bonds with a knife. The inspecting com- mander placed him under arrest, but on September 4 allowed him to go for a walk on parole. It appears Smith

provided himself with a loaded pistol, and on his return
exhibited it empty, stating that he had met one of the
men who assaulted him, and had chased the fellow some
distance and fired after him.   The offender was actually
arrested soon after, and imprisoned for six months, notwithstanding which the inspecting commander persisted
in charging Smith with connivance, and pursued the
charge with venomous bitterness ; but a Court of Inquiry
acquitted the poor fellow, and cleared his character most
effectively.

Seizure records continued to arrive from certain
colonies during 1850-1852. Among many others may be
noted the following :

May 28, 1850.—459 pounds tobacco, seized at Hawke's
Bay, New Zealand, on premises occupied by ' Yankee
Smith.' Defendant absconded. The collector stated in
his report that the principal portion of the coast was
entirely unprotected, and that there were many facilities
for smuggling.*

July 20, 1850.—659 pounds tobacco and 16,000 cigars,
seized at Port Adelaide, in a tavern kept by Salvador
Guadici. The goods had been cleared duty-free from
bond for exportation to Swansea by a vessel belonging to
Aberdeen, Scotland, and then run ' on the coast below
the harbour mouth,' and removed to Guadici's premises.
Master, mate, and receiver, each fined £100. Ship
released on proof of owners' innocence, but it appears
that her detention cost them £232.

September 19, 1851.—860 pounds tobacco, seized at
Abercrombie Battery, Fort George, Mauritius, ' hid among
aloe-trees.'

October 1, 1852.—(A ' mixed ' venture) 3 cases wine,
1 case tinned salmon, 1 case cocoa paste, 14 pounds
tobacco, 24 shirts, a suit of clothes, and a box of arrowroot,
seized ' on the shore at Hobson's Bay,' Melbourne.

* During 1851 Mr. Carkeek, collector of Wellington, New
Zealand, reported to the governor that the master of a vessel
from Havana landed a full cargo on the coast without Customs
cognizance, and then came to Wellington and tendered the duty !

October 13, 1852.—298 pounds tobacco, seized at Geelong, concealed on board a vessel from Liverpool.

Same Date.—326 pounds tobacco, also concealed on a vessel from Liverpool.

November 10.—351 pounds tobacco, seized at Melbourne, concealed in 19 imported casks of oranges.

Early in 1852 a large seizure of tobacco was made at London, on a vessel loaded with granite from Guernsey. The tobacco had been packed in tins containing about 20 pounds each, and stowed amid the cargo.

Another ingenious fraud was detected in the same port. Casks and circular tins had been imported, containing rape-oil, and it was found that the sides of the packages were double, and that the spaces thus created were packed with tobacco-stalk flour.

Three trunks containing effects, which had been put on board ship at Guernsey for conveyance to London, were found by the Guernsey officers to have double sides, the spaces containing cigars.

A ship which had discharged her foreign cargo, and been cleared by the Customs at Limerick, was found by the officers at Kilrush to be fitted up with large and ingeniously contrived places of concealment. She was seized and condemned. From the investigations afterwards held it appeared probable that immense smuggling had been carried on from this vessel.

Below are a few other cases in 1852 :

May 14 *and* 15.—Two horses, a waggon, 1,512 pounds tobacco, 577 pounds stalks, 138 pounds snuff, and 47 pounds cigars, seized at Ross, Herefordshire, by excise officers ; 29 pounds tobacco, seized at Swansea, in a house occupied by one of the parties concerned in the above.

May 20.—A smack and 494 pounds tobacco, seized off Southwold.

June 5.—The lugger *Earl Grey*, with 300 pounds tobacco and 900 pounds stalks, seized at Deal.

June 18.—250 pounds tobacco, seized at Sunderland, concealed in a ship's hold.

June 22.—The smack *Mary*, seized off Hayling Island, with 14 tubs of spirits concealed in lining of hold.

September 2.—1,290 pounds tobacco-stalks, seized in an inn-yard at Southampton.

September 8.—10 tubs spirits, seized at Brixham, after being hauled ashore and then drawn up a sewer.

The following cases appear remarkable :

On the night of January 11, 1852, a Glasgow tide-waiter, whilst going on duty, observed a man carrying a heavy package from the quay and up Finnerton Street. He followed, but lost sight of his quarry. Returning, he stumbled over two sacks of tobacco lying in the street near a public-house. He procured assistance, searched the public-house, and found two other sacks of tobacco. A further search revealed another sack in a coal-bunker near the door, and seven packages more in a press—in all 704 pounds. A shopkeeper who lived near, and the publican's servant, were prosecuted for ' being concerned ' (they had tried to conceal the goods from the officers during search). The servant was acquitted, and the shopkeeper convicted, the magistrates recommending him strongly to the mercy of the Board. The public-house keeper, a woman, was then prosecuted, but the magistrates held the case ' not proven,' and ' assoilzied ' her. Mr. Muirhead, the local lawyer employed by the collector, reported : ' There is scarcely a chance for the Crown's ever carrying a conviction before the justices here.'

On August 19, 1852, two well-dressed men visited the police-station at Margate, and stated that they were excise officers from London in chase of ' two ruffians who were escaping from the country,' that they had reason to believe the ' ruffians ' had got on board a smack that was hovering off the Margate coast, that they had engaged a boat and four watermen to pursue her, and required a policeman to go with them. A policeman was provided, and away the party went, and picked up the smack beyond the limits of Ramsgate port, seven miles from land. The strangers jumped aboard, and one of them took off the hatches. A pungent smell arose from the hold, and the Margate boatmen at once perceived, to their disgust, that they had been deluded into assisting in the capture of a cargo of contraband. The vessel was the *Marie* of Dunkirk, with 6,000 pounds of tobacco on board. She had a French crew, but in the forecastle were two stalwart Englishmen, who spoke the true Deal dialect. The Margate boatmen refused to assist in navigating the vessel into port, whereupon the two stout Deal men offered to do so, and became at once most friendly with their captors. To such an extent did cordiality prevail that, a small public-house on the coast coming in sight, the excise officers asked the boatmen to pull ashore and obtain a gallon or two of beer. Off came the beer, and the seizing officers passed it round and round, till the sunburnt faces of the French crew, the Deal ' spotsmen,' and the Margate boatmen, grew red as the sun on a frosty evening, and even the rubicund countenance of the policeman acquired a deeper tinge. And thus they proceeded merrily into Ramsgate harbour, where the two seizers placed smack, cargo, and prisoners under the charge of the customs collector, announcing themselves respectively as Mr. R——, excise officer of Rochester, and Mr. S——, excise officer of Stepney. The prisoners were charged, and the magistrates, not being quite certain as to their powers, communicated through the collector with the Thames Street lawyer, who instructed them that the goods were liable to forfeiture, and so was the vessel, but the Frenchmen must be released, the seizure having been made beyond the three-mile limit. The two Deal men were liable, being English, and the seizure being made within four leagues of the land. But there was a quibble as to the vessel. By a recent case of the kind it had been shown that the aspect of international law should be studied in connection with seizures afloat. Therefore the *Marie* must be deemed liable to forfeiture so as to legalize prosecution of the two Deal men, and after they had been prosecuted forfeiture might be waived. The Deal men were convicted accordingly.

Soon afterwards a notorious Margate smuggler called on the Customs solicitor at Thames Street, and told him he had an idea this was a collusive seizure. The solicitor was impressed, and began to look into the matter, and several corroborating suspicions at once entered his mind. First, the tobacco seized was of wretched quality. Second, R——, the chief seizer, was a native of that stronghold of smuggling, Deal, and connected by marriage with several well-known receivers. Third, R—— had stated that he had never seen either of the two Deal men before, yet it turned out that he had kept a tavern in Beach Street, Deal, prior to entering the Excise, and one of the ' spotsmen ' had been his potboy. And it was well known that there were many hardy longshoremen in Deal who, if their wives and families were looked after, would think nought of doing six months in gaol for a bribe of £20. Fourth, the *Marie* had been fooling about many hours off Margate, as though to invite seizure. Fifth, R—— and S—— admitted they had received information, but refused to furnish the informer's name. They alleged that he lived near West Malling, and they implied that he was so extremely sensitive and timorous that the slightest suggestion of publicity would destroy his efficacy as an informer for ever. So the Customs lawyer induced the Board of Excise to look into the matter. The Excise Commissioners were inclined to support their officers. They thought it possible the informer might have acted collusively in luring the smack over to be seized, or might even have financed the venture, it appearing that the expense of hiring the vessel, buying the almost worthless tobacco, and bribing the two Deal men to go to gaol, would amount to but £210, and the informer's share of the seizure-money to £300.* But they would not admit that the officers acted collusively.

* This shows the amount of forethought expended in framing the revenue laws of the period, and the regulations as to seizure awards.

The Customs lawyer merely kept the papers by him, knowing well that the knaves concerned would soon begin to show their hands. First came an application from R—— that the awards might be made as early as possible, for he had already advanced his informer £53, and had spent £11 in expenses (including, no doubt, the amount disbursed off the North Foreland for beer). The lawyer asked for the informer's name. R—— stated the man was one Woodward, generally living at Malling. The lawyer sent for the old Margate smuggler who had first enlightened him, and that hoary rascal intimated an opinion that a dummy informer would be put up if things grew desperate, and that he wouldn't be surprised if that there dummy turned out to be his old pal D—— of Deal, well known as a smuggler, and of old well acquainted with R——.

Meantime the four Margate boatmen who had rowed R—— off to the smack, having incurred some depreciation of self-esteem by being tricked into assisting in the execution of the law, thought they might as well have a share in the profits, and sent in an urgent petition. So did the policeman. The seizing officers protested against these claims, but the Customs Board gave the policeman £5, and the four boatmen £2 10s. each—*these amounts to be deducted from the officers' shares when the latter were paid.*

Soon the pretended informer wrote, signing himself ' Woodward,' and asking for his reward. He stated that people were beginning to suspect him, and that it was not safe for him to show himself in the street. The lawyer asked him to call at his office in Thames Street, and placed the old Margate smuggler in concealment. Just as the informer finished his tale, and reiterated his claim as ' Woodward,' he received a heavy slap from behind, and, turning round, found himself confronted by a grinning ancient, who exclaimed in husky tones : ' Wot cheer, D——, old boy ! How is things headin' just now ?' It does not appear that the informer was at all discomposed, or that any hint was made of proceedings against him. It may be safely assumed that he at once ' owned up,' and that Deal and Margate went from the Custom-house arm-in-arm, and straight into the most convenient tavern.

It might be thought that R—— would hear of this, and cease his solicitations, but it is likely that D—— merely told him a string of lies, for he continued to pester the Customs Board with requests for compensation and awards. The Board made no reply. The papers connected with this extraordinary case conclude with a note by the lawyer in June, 1854, thus :

' The difficulty I have had in dealing with these papers is at an end by a circumstance which confirms my view of the case. I find that R—— has defrauded the Excise and decamped.'*

(Nothing appears as to what became of S——. Probably he was quite unaware that R—— had taken him into an arranged case.)

During 1852 information reached the Board that a Grimsby oyster-boat called the *Lord Rivers* had run across to the French coast. Her captain was one Mimmack, a desperate smuggler belonging to Saltfleet, Lincolnshire. Orders were sent to the eastern and southern ports, and revenue cruisers went in search of her. She was found off Dunkirk, with nothing on board except a number of empty cigar-boxes. During the rest of the year she was closely watched and repeatedly searched, and nothing discovered that would justify her detention, yet it seems she must have been smuggling all the time. On January 28, 1853, she was searched off Dover, and found to have what the officers deemed ' a false stem,' the

---

* We have seen a good many sets of papers in which some of the reports suggest collusion in seizures, but none quite so remarkable as this case. It is clear that the distances from the shore, etc., were studied out by R——, so that the Frenchmen should escape and the ship be released ; that he bribed two of his old acquaintances to suffer imprisonment, and another to personate the informer if necessary ; and that he expected to secure his own promotion, and a tolerable surplus after expenses were paid.

interior of which smelt strongly of spirits. She was detained, but it appearing that such peculiarities of structure were common in vessels of the kind, and there being no actual proof that she had been smuggling, release was granted. In February, however, a person concerned gave startling information as to the doings of Captain Mimmack and his crew, from which it appeared that this little craft, though scarcely ever out of the hands of the revenue men, had carried on a steady traffic in contraband. She was therefore seized, but the crew were not prosecuted.

Early on the morning of March 10, 1853, a policeman detained three horses and two carts near Woodbridge for conveying 1,231 pounds tobacco and 2,541 pounds stalks. Inquiries were made, and it was found that the goods had been landed on the bank of the Orwell from a small vessel called the *Susan*. The vessel was captured with her master and crew, and several persons residing near Bungay were arrested on suspicion of being concerned. One of the crew made a statement, describing the whole of the proceedings, the departure from England, the taking-in of the goods at Flushing, the run, etc. The rest of the crew and the driver of the carts were convicted. After release from gaol the crew made statements still further implicating the Bungay receivers, but the Customs solicitor was indisposed to take proceedings, and recommended that certain moderate sums which had been offered by the accused as compositions should be accepted. ' Perhaps drawing their capital would do more to cripple their smuggling operations than incarceration.' He thought a conviction might be obtained, but it would be by contaminated evidence, which would ' subject the Crown to the usual observations on such occasions.' (It is apparent that Mr. Hamel had been rendered more cautious by the proceedings of the Parliamentary and Charlotte Row Committees. See pp. 324-325 and 329.) The Board concurred.

The proceedings of the police in this case were not exactly creditable, neither were those of the collector of

Woodbridge. The police returned the seizure as made without information, whereas the seizing constable's attention had been called to the conveyances by a local post-office clerk who was going to work. The police appear to have done their best to 'bluff' him out of participation, but the Board, deeply experienced in the ways of seizing officers, refused to be hoodwinked, and compensated the clerk liberally. The Woodbridge customs men, no doubt annoyed that the police handed the seized goods over to the Excise, did their best to squeeze themselves into the seizure, but without avail.

On March 12, 1853, the smack *Ariel* was searched off Ramsgate, and 2 pounds tobacco and seven packs of playing-cards seized. A petty seizure, it may be thought, and little did the revenue men deem that she had just discharged a cargo into the Deal lugger *Mary*, which vessel was making for London river. An hour later the *Mary* was sailing past the Reculvers, when she was boarded by the coastguard, who found that she was carrying 1,615 pounds tobacco-stalks.

Information was given to the authorities that the *John and Susannah* of Lowestoft had gone oversea for a cargo of tobacco. On April 30, 1853, the coastguard seized her off Whitby with 5,165 pounds tobacco. 'Immediately on the discovery being made,' wrote the seizing officer, 'the master, James Blasey, jumped overboard and tried to drown himself, but was rescued by my men. He was very refractory and troublesome.' Quite a remarkable number of people tried to squeeze themselves into this case, some professing to have given information, others to have assisted the seizing officers. The excise officer at Ipswich claimed on the former ground, but was rapped over the knuckles. The real informer pestered the Board with complaints and begging letters. This miserable traitor's appeals for money remind us of the methods of Rogue Riderhood. After receiving £5 as 'pecuniary relief,' £11 8s. as 'share of forfeiture,' £50 3s. 2d. as 'subsistence,' £1 as 'railway expenses,'

and £50 as ' gratuity,' he wrote to say that his life was
in danger from the smugglers. The Board offered to
pay his expenses if he would emigrate, but it seems that
was not in his line. He replied thus :

' HONOURABLE GENTLEMEN in writing to your Honourable board I beg to state that my wishes are in all respects
willing to do the best that ever lay in my power to give
any information to your Honourable board that may
come in my way and I do Flatter myself that by exerting
my powers to do so that I can be of greater service than
perhaps Gentlemen you really think I know a great many
smuggling parties all along the west coast and can do
more than you are aware of providing I had the means to
set me up in the world and I think either Portsmouth or
Southampton the most suitable places for me to do anything in as I am in danger here with thanks for the
suggestion cannot at my age and with a sick wife think of
emigrating but should be happy if I could provide a
Liveing by industry in any place,' etc., etc.

(Imagine him ' flattering ' himself upon the possession
of such accomplishments !)

During September, 1853, the suspicions of the coastguard at Lowestoft were excited by the sudden absence
of a noted smuggler. A look-out was kept. The absentee
returned as suddenly as he had left, and it was suspected that he had been oversea to arrange a run. On
September 16 a lugger was observed hovering off the
coast. The inspecting commander of the Coastguard
hired a steam tug, went in chase, and captured the lugger
about twelve miles from shore. She was *L'Abondance*
of Dunkirk, laden with 7,380 pounds tobacco. The
captain stated that he took the tobacco in at Flushing,
the shipment being supervised by an Englishman, and
that the Englishman had come over in the lugger, and
been landed on the previous night. Five hundred francs
were to be paid for the trip. Two boys, one aged fifteen
and the other twelve, who were on board, were released by

the Customs as 'under age.' The captain and the rest
of the crew were convicted and imprisoned.

The French consul at once approached the Board,
pointing out that three of the men imprisoned were under
eighteen, and ' poor, uneducated fishermen, without any
will of their own.' The Board declined to intervene, and
then the French ambassador memorialized Lord Clarendon
on the men's behalf, who moved the Treasury to refer
the matter to the Board. The Customs solicitor then
stated that it was a common practice to ' man these
vessels, as they term it, with boys,' so as to minimize the
number of convictions, and that there was every reason
to believe that the French fishermen had understood fully
that they were embarking in a contraband transaction.
He also pointed out that the English spotsman was still
at large, and that if he were arrested after the crew had
been released it would be difficult to secure identification.
Later the consul petitioned afresh, urging that the
captain had been made ' the dupe of some designing
Englishman,' but the Board stood firm.

The spotsman, whose name, curiously enough, was
Mantrip, was arrested and convicted. The inspecting
commander had returned the seizure as made without
information, but he soon had to amend his report, for a
letter reached the Board, furnishing proof that the seizure
was entirely due to information furnished by the writer.
The informer was rewarded with a grant of £300.*

It is likely that there were other informers in the
locality, for on the night of October 14, 1853, the yawl
Sophia was seized in Lowestoft harbour, with 5,170 pounds
tobacco.

Information reached Dublin on March 2, 1854, that
the *Mutiné* of Cherbourg would attempt a run. The

---

* Undoubtedly 70 per cent. of the larger seizures made in the
old days were due to information. Many officers, despite the
Board's orders to the contrary, made secret arrangements with
their informers, and it was only when the latter found themselves
likely to be defrauded of the wages of infamy that they appealed
to the Board.

coastguard and police were put on the alert, and on the night of March 8 two policemen observed a brace of suspicious-lookingmen lurking on the coast near Baldoyle. They interrogated the lurkers, and, finding nothing to warrant arrest, allowed them to depart. Soon afterwards the policemen fell across seventeen bales of tobacco. Later a Dublin customs officer was informed that tobacco-stalks had been landed at Rocky Island. Search was made, and 105 bales were found. This made the total quantity seized 6,681 pounds.

On May 21, 1854, a boat belonging to the Queenborough Oyster Company was searched in the Medway by the coastguard, and 2,481 pounds tobacco found on her.

On the night of May 25 the tide-surveyor of Ramsgate observed two suspicious characters on a mud-lighter in the harbour. He went on board, and found in the hold forty-two bales of tobacco, weighing in all 2,123 pounds, which had been run during the evening by a French lugger, and put in charge of the lightermen for transmission to the receiver. The lighter belonged to the Harbour Trustees, and they were directed to enter into a bond of £200 pending investigation of the case. The lighter was afterwards released and the bond cancelled, it appearing that the Harbour Trustees had no cognizance of the attempted fraud.

On November 10 a Norwegian barque arrived at Shields from Drammen, and the customs rummagers found 459 pounds tobacco concealed amid the battens that formed her cargo. Several of the seamen were convicted, and the ship was released on a fine of £5 only. The captain, in applying for her release, furnished a copy of an agreement entered into in Norway between himself and each member of the crew. Below is an extract :

' I, Andrew Hansen, promise to conduct myself as a brave and honest Norwegian sailor . . . and to act in accordance with the Norwegian laws, most especially the law of 28th July, 1824, respecting smuggling and fraud, not taking anything on shore or on board without the captain's knowledge and consent.'

To show the extent to which smuggling had been carried on in the creeks and rivers of East Anglia,* we must travel a few months beyond the announced scope of our treatise. Early in 1855 the excise officers seized 1,400 pounds tobacco at Wenhaston, near Halesworth, on premises occupied by a well-known smuggler. The occupier was convicted and imprisoned, and while in gaol implicated two other persons residing in the neighbourhood of Halesworth, but requested that their arrest might be delayed till he had induced one of them to pay him £60, the amount of a loan for which he held a promissory note. He failed to obtain payment, so the men were arrested and convicted. Then a clergyman living near forwarded to the Board the following letter, received from a parishioner :

' Rev. Sir,
    ' Smuggling has been carried on within the parish of Wenhaston—and Mr. —— at its head—I should say for about twenty-five years, during which period he has done well. The duties of the excise officers and those of the coastguard are unknown to me ; I cannot say much thereon—I do wonder how it can have lasted so long— runs have been made time after time, landed, conveyed about night and day, for a long period, and a fortune saved, and his race unbroken now.
    ' —— has ships, a wherry, the public-house at the harbour mouth of Southwold, horses, carts, and his own men by his side—in fact, every facility to accomplish his object.
    ' We have had the goods by Southwold up the river to the bridge, unloaded there, taken to several places (not a few to Dunwich) sent off by the carrier to Ipswich,

* It is evident from the records that the bulk of the smuggling was transferred from Kent and Sussex to the Eastern Counties in 1831.

then by train to London, while another portion has been
driven by his own man and horses to Mr. ——, draper,
Norwich, who is his brother-in-law.

'I believe all the goods of late have been landed
between Lowestoft and Gorleston—something far from
being right there, that is, I think so—and from information I can obtain much has gone away without coming to
Wenhaston—the last lot came home, a portion of which
was taken by the Excise at ——s, but the quantity left,
I think, on the Monday night before the seizure, and I
have but little doubt was driven by his brother-in-law
to London, and I expect left at Mr. ——s. This man
was once with —— at Wenhaston, and his father now
lives at Dunwich.

'When you arrive in London, I do hope you will refuse
to give in my name. —— has said he shall have it in
three months, and he should like him to be shot in the
road. His man —— says they have obtained it before,
and shall have it again by payment of a fee.* Should the
gentleman demand my name, I must decline giving any
further information. Should, however, it be left in your
hands quietly I will try to put down that disgraceful
traffic which I consider has long been a pest to the parish,
and the existing officers under Government have not been
able to extinguish it.'

The worst that can be said of high tariffs, severe
preventive regulations, and the disbursement of 'blood-
money,' is that they encourage the inherent meannesses
of hypocritical people. It would be safe to assert that
the person who sat quiet for twenty-five years while
contraband traffic was rampant all round him refrained
from joining in the traffic merely because he had not
sufficient courage, and blossomed out as an anonymous
informer when he knew that the law was on his enemy's

* The old smuggler king had circulated a report that informers' names might be obtained on payment of a fee at the
Custom-house, and had hinted that discovery would be followed
by vindictive retribution.

track. The study of smuggling literature forces one to
the grim conclusion that the average man is not by any
means more likely than the average woman to shut his
mouth and mind his own business when his neighbour
is in trouble.

The aim of this treatise has been mainly annalistic, but
the incidental research has unearthed much that may
be informative to the student of fiscal doctrine. Many
thinkers hold that fiscal science occupies too much of
the average man's attention, and that the spectacle of a
group of ordinary citizens, equipped with journals and
statistics, discussing a second-hand proposal of tariffs,
is not particularly cheering. It has been pungently said
that there is nothing so easy as imposing taxes ; that
the fools and madmen of all ages have been adepts at
that disastrous exercise, and that the really wise man—
the man who deserves a golden statue and the worship
of posterity—is he who abolishes a tax. Yet, while
national expenditure continues, many taxes must be
imposed and collected, and a few workday hints on origin
and system may be useful.

The public is now divided into two parties, and, to
describe the position in a broad way, it will be sufficient
to state that they differ as to the system of collection.
The Tariff Reformers desire to revert to the old method
under which most foreign articles were taxed, and it
must be admitted that most of the arguments used to
support their idea are as ancient as the method recommended. The Free Traders also use many well-worn
formulæ, under which they claim for their system every
virtue under Heaven. It is not wise to intervene
abruptly, for it is becoming apparent that many of the
disputants do not desire to be told the naked truth ; they
prefer listening to platitudes that support 'The Pro-
gramme.' Yet the truth is the truth, whether it be

welcome or no, and what is termed 'far-fetched and iconoclastic reasoning' to-day may furnish maxims for the school-children of a hundred years hence.

It follows that a few bald remarks upon method, etc., may be of more immediate service than the most profound reasoning. 'Such were the favoured tactics at such a date ; mark their result,' may go far, when the most symmetrical arguments fail. As contentious stuff will now and then creep in, it may be wise to preface the matter with a closer definition of the attitudes of the two antagonistic parties.

The Free Trader pleads that his system, as exemplified in Great Britain and nowhere else, confines the Customs levies to a few productive articles—articles which he contends are not absolute necessaries. He goes on to state that the revenue is by this method collected accurately and cheaply, and that the mere means of existance are not in any way curtailed. He announces that his system compares favourably with all that differ— viz., with the systems used everywhere except in the United Kingdom—that it is of all systems least oppressive of the poor, and that it does not in any way injure the home producer, but rather stimulates production, and increases the sale of British goods in foreign markets. He points triumphantly around him, indicating in succession the British baker distributing cheap bread, the sporadic evidences of great wealth, and the standard of living (admittedly higher in some respects than under the old system of Protection). These, he states, are the results of Free Trade, and of Free Trade only.

The Tariff Reformer protests that under Free Trade the United Kingdom has been made a 'dumping ground' for low-priced foreign goods ; that we open our markets to the foreigner and he shuts us out from his ; that in consequence most of the articles used in the United Kingdom are of foreign production ; that many once flourishing British lines of business have thus been destroyed, and that others are tottering to a fall. He claims that Tariff Reform, by shutting out many of the articles now imported, would stimulate production in the United Kingdom, and reduce the present ghastly list of unemployed.

It may be easy to show that both of the disputing parties are partially wrong, without proving each to be misled past redemption. Every system, except Thuggee and Sweating, has its advantages as well as its defects. If the misstatements of the advocates of each party be brought under observation, the residue may be left alone, for Truth should need no bolstering up.

QUESTIONS TO BE CONSIDERED.

1. Does the history of Customs duties show that they are necessarily oppressive ?

Perhaps the best way of finding an answer will be to look into the question of the rich man's contribution to Customs revenue. If it be found that he pays, or has paid in the past, his just proportion, it may be admitted that Customs duties are no more oppressive than other forms of taxation. What is the proportion that the rich man should in justice pay ? According to reason, according to practice with regard to the impost on incomes, most of the poor should be exempt or lightly taxed. Few rich men will venture to dispute this publicly. He who inherits wealth inherits its just responsibilities. He who makes money by speculation or business enterprise may be allowed perhaps to ascribe one-tenth of his success to personal excellence—the rest is the result of luck, or of the labour of others. Luck is an acknowledged factor, for every successful speculator or business man knows at least a dozen quite as skilful and energetic as he who have either made little or lost much. Earnest, moderately-paid clerks and salesmen are the ministering angels of fortune, while its very foundation is cheap labour. This being acknowledged, the old and new methods of collection may be examined with profit.

Previous to 1303 the Customs levies were ' The Ancient Custom ' on exported wool, ' Prisage,' and ' The Maltolte.' The first was light, and could not to any extent have oppressed even the English agriculturist, except that the regulations of enforcement were rather irksome. There was an insatiable foreign demand for English wool, and when such is the case the last buyer pays all. (There is at present an insatiable demand for tea and tobacco in the United Kingdom, and, as neither article can be produced here at a profit—as, to put it another way, there is no home-produced supply to compete with the foreign, the consumer in the United Kingdom pays all the duties on those articles. Were we dependent upon the United States for supplies of a peculiar kind of corn which we could not do without, and the United States levied an arbitrary export tax on all such corn shipped to Great Britain, undoubtedly the British consumer would pay the tax.) As to Prisage, which was on imported wine, the poor drank ale, except during those amazing periods when the Gascon vintners flooded the south of England with cheap wine. The Maltolte was an occasional heavy tax, usually levied on exported wool. When, as may have happened on rare occasions, this was applied to imported food-stuffs, the poor suffered, for it appears that food-stuffs were not imported extensively except in times of stress.

From 1303 to the commencement of Edward III.'s *actual* sway the following changes were introduced and maintained : (1) a slight increase in the duty on exported wool ; (2) Butlerage, as a substitute for Prisage, on aliens' wines only ; (3) a slight tax (protective) on imported cloth ; (4) 3d. in the pound on goods imported by aliens (protective).

From the beginning of Edward III.'s actual domination, to the inception of Tunnage and Poundage during the same reign, there were repeated heavy imposts on exported wool, enforced in a way that must have plagued producers. A duty was levied on exported cloth, and, as the English cloth industry was at the time in a struggling condition, it is likely that the producer paid this tax.

From the institution of Tunnage and Poundage to the end of Elizabeth's reign the additional levies were : Tunnage, on imported wine ; Poundage, on denizens' merchandise. (Thus nearly all merchandise was taxed.) The Maltolte on wool became the permanent ' Subsidy.' Arbitrary imposts were laid upon wine by the Tudors.

From the accession of the Stuarts to the revolt of the Long Parliament there was much corrupt farming of Customs, and many monopolistic licences to import, export, etc., were granted. The added burdens were : many additions to the ' official values ' of poundage goods, taxes on exported ale, and tremendous occasional impositions upon tobacco. The growth of the English cloth industry, combined with the heavy and complicated restrictions, had well-nigh stopped the legal exportation of wool.

From 1641 to the end of the Protectorate certain increases were made in the official values of imported goods, and the import-excise was instituted. Customs farming was abolished, and Customs collection purified. The Navigation Act was imposed, and the exportation of wool prohibited. (The Puritans were bitter Protectionists.)

During the period from the Restoration to the beginning of William III.'s reign the Navigation Act, and the Act prohibiting the exportation of wool, were recast and reaffirmed. The Customs duties were farmed till 1671. Tunnage was collected on wines, and Poundage levied at 5 per cent. on the official values of nearly all import and export goods, under what was called ' The Old Subsidy.' The Coinage Duty was instituted. Several imposts were levied, including the tonnage rates on French vessels, an extra tunnage on wine, and an extra rate of poundage on certain imported goods. Duties on a ' sliding scale ' were put on imported corn. Yet it is unlikely that up to

1688 the poor suffered to any noteworthy extent by Customs duties, and it appears that bread and provisions were cheap.

From 1688 to 1791 the Customs duties became heavier and heavier, the most startling increases being made during the reigns of William and Anne, when there appeared in rapid succession ' The second 25 per cent. on French goods,' ' The New Subsidy,' ' The fifteen per cent. on Muslins,' the abominable special duties on salt, ' The one-third Subsidy,' ' The two-thirds Subsidy,' and many other ' permanent ' taxes. The sliding scale upon corn was maintained. The Customs tariff became tremendously complicated, till to some extent rectified by the Consolidating Act of 1787. Bread and other food-stuffs did not become permanently dear till near the end of the century.

After 1791 the combined effects of immense increases in the corn duties, of war and the reckless subsidizing of foreign allies, of the growth of urban population, and the enclosure of common lands, were made terribly manifest. How the poor contrived to exist may to many folk of the present day appear a riddle. Yet there were certain ameliorating circumstances. Although for a long period the importation of cattle, etc., had been prohibited, meat was not dear. Fish was sold at a price which at the present day would be considered amazingly cheap. So was fruit, especially in the rural districts. Beer was cheap, and tolerably pure. The duties on tea, tobacco, and many kinds of spirits were enormous, but at least one-third of the trade in those articles was duty-free (witness the smuggling records). The duties were not collected as now with deadly accuracy. The rich paid more in proportion than the poor. The most oppressive Customs duties of old were those on corn, salt, and sugar, and the corn duties were not oppressive except from 1795 to 1845. Even during those sad fifty years most other absolute necessaries (meat, fish, vegetables, fruit, ale, milk, and the rougher wearing stuffs) were sold at reasonable prices. Tea and tobacco were not esteemed absolute necessaries. Many thousands, especially among

the rural folk, drank ale at breakfast *from pure choice.*
Smoking was not a universal habit.   The foreign spirit
consumed by the lower classes was Plantation rum, usually
a sound and wholesome article, that thoroughly deserved
its nickname ' Nelson's blood,' and this was admitted *at
highly preferential rates.*   Many of the articles, both raw
and manufactured, scheduled as dutiable in the old
tariff lists, produced next to nothing in the way of
Customs, the taxes operating as prohibitions, yet the
home-raised or home-made goods identical were not dear.
(One striking instance may be quoted — the almost
prohibitive apple duty.   Apples were exceedingly cheap
in the south of England.)   The high silk and lace duties
were taxes on luxury, and, when not evaded, were paid
by the rich.   The great evil of most of the old duties
(leaving out of consideration those on salt and sugar and
the later duties on corn) lay in complicated and erratic
collection, and in the smuggling generated.   The dishonest trader was given too many chances, compared with
his more honest neighbour.

If we refer to the present Customs tariff, we shall find
that the poor pay out of all fair proportion.   The
principal producing factors are tea, tobacco, spirits, and
sugar.   Many a working man's wife consumes more tea
than a duchess.   The duty on tea is not graded in proportion to value.   Many a working man smokes more
tobacco than a duke.   (The duke's *disbursements* for
tobacco must not be taken into account ; his personal
consumption is the true item of comparison.)   All tobacco
is rated alike so far as quality goes ; the primest product
of Virginia pays no more in leaf than the worst of German
growth.   Belgian cigars pay the same duty as the choicest
Havanas.   Many a working man consumes more spirits
than the average millionaire.   The duty on the com-
monest Egyptian spirit is the same per proof gallon as
that on the finest French cognac.*   And it is idle to

* Except that the better kinds of spirit are more frequently
imported in bottle, and bottled spirits are liable to a slight surtax.

urge that the working man should not smoke or drink. Merely *high* taxation will not keep the poor from drinking and smoking, and if taxation were made prohibitive in this respect smuggling or illicit distillation would at once be resorted to, and the tariff would have to be remodelled. And no class should have the power to tax the *tastes* of others. Nothing is so profoundly immoral as to save one's pocket by taxing a neighbour's so-called vices, for the world is made up of fallible beings, and the true mission of the fiscal reformer is to understand this, and legislate accordingly.

It follows that the Customs tariff of the present day oppresses the poor, for we are in this so much inferior to our fathers, that the nerve-shaking herbs, tobacco and tea, have become absolute necessaries. The sugar tax is directed at the very hearts of the poor, for the children of the poor are inveterate sugar-consumers. Tea, tobacco, and sugar are all purely foreign articles ; there is no home competition in initial production, and the poor pay on those articles disproportionately to their means. The Customs tariff of to-day is the offspring of the early Victorian desire for cheapness of collection. There is no justice in it. It shuts out next to nothing that Patriotism would wish to be manufactured at home, and, as regards its being paid by the consumer, one might think Adam Smith had devised it, merely to justify his own doctrinal flounderings—merely to be able to say : ' I told you that all import taxes were paid by the consumer, and I have provided you with a tariff that will support my argument.'

2. Is it unwise to ' tinker ' with Customs duties ?

Undoubtedly. A tax may be antagonistic to pure justice and reason, yet have a kind of merit because people have become used to it, and therefore pay it without much reluctance. It has always been a peculiar trait of the English to pay cheerfully moderate indirect taxes, and this because such taxes are not brought home

with startling effect to the payer's mental consciousness.
'Tinkering' with Customs taxes, by making slight
additions, irritates the public, for the goods are usually
bought in small quantities at short intervals, and every
purchase of an ounce of tobacco, a dram of spirits, or a
parcel of tea or sugar, reminds the buyer of that which
he would willingly forget. This is especially the case
when the goods have been previously overtaxed, and the
addition actually limits consumption, thus inspiring
annoyance and producing no additional revenue, and also
when the additional duty is so arranged that the consumer
is charged an extra halfpenny on every small purchase,
of which but one farthing goes to the revenue and the
other to the dealer.

Another objectionable product of 'tinkering' is the
dislocation of trade that ensues. For months prior to
the annual announcement merchants are fretting and
fuming over probabilities. Many an order is delayed,
and many a parcel, purchased on mere speculation,
remains long upon the dealer's hands. But, while speculators are thus occasionally injured, the bulk of the loss
falls upon the consumer. Enterprising firms have been
known to net many thousands of pounds by well-judged
ventures on Budget possibilities. Till within recent
years, it was actually a Customs practice to make special
provision as to staff and hours of attendance, in order to
enable merchants to indulge to the full their mania for
speculation ! It is bad enough for the public to be fleeced
by keen-witted adventurers, but the matter becomes
maddening when the public has to pay overtime to its
own servants, that they may assist the process.

3. Are *ad valorem* duties preferable to specific ?

Were it possible to infect the mercantile world with
sincerity, and to enrol as customs officers none but conspicuously self-sacrificing and efficient persons, an *ad
valorem* tariff would be eminently preferable. It would
ease the poor, who consume the cheaper articles, and sur-

tax the luxuries imported by the rich.   Its chief fault
lies in the uncertainties of collection.   If we are to believe
the Tariff Reformers, the United Kingdom depends more
upon imports than any other country in the world.   A
' reformed ' tariff would not *instantly* check importation,
and it is not contended, even by the most violent de-
claimer, that a reformed tariff would shut out more than a
portion of foreign articles.   Therefore the present customs
men, who have no deep training in the estimation of values,
would be suddenly called upon to check a multitude of
declarations, or the department would have to employ
many highly-paid ' experts.'   (Men of insight and common sense would probably prefer the ordinary customs
man, whom contact has endowed with a *rough* knowledge
of merchandise, to the average conceited and pedantic
' expert.')   In either case it is conceivable that many
difficulties would arise.   Merchants would import goods
and declare them at lower than the actual values, much
delay and many detentions would occur, and be it known
that there are ways of indirectly intimidating overworked
officials.   As to the danger of corruption, it is certain
that the customs officers of the United Kingdom are the
most incorruptible in the world, and this is due to—
(1) the competitive test for admission into the lower
grades , (2) permanence of employment ; (3) the absence
of *ad valorem* duties.   There could be no blacker history
than that of the British landing-officers of the early part
of the nineteenth century, were it possible, by merely
inspecting records, to gauge the extremities of official
depravity.   It is undeniable that, even with the present
staff and under the improved modern methods, a system
of *ad valorem* duties would produce a plentiful stock of
temptations.

At the same time *ad valorem* duties would assist towards
one consummation—a consummation which every Tariff
Reformer* avows is next his heart—the shutting out of

* It is to be hoped that the avowal is sincere.   The tactics of
some of the noisiest of the Tariff Reformers tend to show that
the end aimed at is an all-round rise in the price of goods.

some of the 'cheaper and nastier' foreign goods, the
flimsy and often putrid rubbish which at present is cast
so plentifully upon our shores, to the utter degradation of
many British handicrafts and industries. (Even unscrupulous dealing would assist in this, as it did of old,
when the aim of the ordinary merchant was to import
goods of the highest possible value, and enter them at the
lowest rate that the Customs would allow.) Perhaps this
may explain why most of the articles made by our
ancestors were so much more worthy and enduring than
those constructed at present, why paper of 1710 is still
as good as new and ink of the same date as brilliant as
ever, why ancient furniture is so majestic and substantial
and ancient cutlery so perfect in material and finish,
and why grandfather's clock ticks so musically and keeps
so firm a grip upon the flying seconds. It might even be
held to explain the continuance during bygone centuries—
due, perhaps, to the self-reliant 'Englishness' engendered
—of a certain rough idea of picturesque beauty. Why
was it that the early Victorian period teemed with
dowdyism ? Why does a peasant's cottage of a hundred
years back, though steeped in ruin and decay, convey a
certain charm to the artistic eye ? Will age, or ivy, or
sweet natural surroundings, ever thus endow a cottage
of the sixties ? Will the pork-pie hat and crinoline
of the sixties ever be reproduced on canvas, as artists
of the present day reproduce the trappings of the
Georgian era ? It is to be hoped, if we are to have
Tariff Reform, that, if it fails in everything else that it
has promised, it may make us a little more genuinely
English than we have been during the past seventy
years.

4. May Customs duties be adjusted so as to genuinely
foster certain home manufactures ?

Undoubtedly this was done in the past. The English
woollen industry was simply built upon Protection. As
soon as the old export wool duties reached the dignity of a

'Subsidy,' they began to protect the English cloth manufacturer. English, and later Irish, agriculture suffered
by the system, but the cloth manufacturer, probably the
greatest commercial tyrant that ever existed, prospered
exceedingly. The extent to which the duties acted
protectively towards the manufacturers is shown by their
becoming almost unproductive, years before the exportation of wool was prohibited, and by the vast increase in
the exportation of English cloth in the latter end of
Elizabeth's reign and the beginning of James I. (Prohibition of the exportation of wool was a device to check
'owling,' which practice was encouraged by the French
and Flemings in their desire to hamper the English cloth
manufacturers.) The high duties on foreign woollens
were also protective. The old 'aliens' duties'—surtaxes
on goods imported by foreigners—and the extra levies on
goods brought in foreign ships, combined with the
Navigation laws in building up the British merchant navy,
a distinctive kind of protection, of which the third factor
might be existing in a modified form at the present day,
but for the clumsiness of the pedants who drafted the
Acts incidental, and the innate rascality of some of the
administering officials. The preferences given of old
to fish, oil, and blubber of British taking, and the privileges granted to the Newfoundland fisheries, were of
immense benefit to the industries concerned. It is useless
to argue that some of the concerns alluded to prosper now
without protection. Difficulty lies as much in the way
of establishing as of maintaining a trade. Certain
industries now followed in the United Kingdom would
not have attained importance but for protection. Of
course, the protective idea was often enforced to the
extent of absurdity, but freaks of that kind occur in connection with every system. Fools occasionally obtain
powers of administration, but that does not utterly
invalidate. It may be repeated that many commercial
enterprises were stimulated and preserved of old by
means of Customs enactments. Whether this was good

or no for other ventures, or for the public generally, is outside the present consideration.

Another striking instance of the effect of Protection is the immense and disproportionate growth of London as a centre of shipping. It cannot be shown that London possesses many natural advantages as a port. In the old days the whole of the East India Company's trade was confined to London, and the great city was thus artificially made, not only a hive of British and colonial traffic, but a vast centre of transhipment. Many other kinds of valuable goods were only allowed to be imported into London. As soon as the privileges were abolished the trade of London began to lose its extraordinary eminence. It is likely that most of the modern schemes for the restoration of London's commercial prosperity may prove abortive, merely because the planners have not sufficiently borne this in mind.

It may be pointed out that even the modern tariff contains certain protective items. The surtax on wines and spirits imported in bottle has doubled the bottling of wines and spirits in the United Kingdom. A higher duty is levied on cigars than on tobacco, on manufactured tobacco than on leaf, on manufactured cocoa and coffee than on raw. If these were not intended to act protectively, why were they thus arranged ? It is certain that they *do* act in that way.

5. Is there any weight in the objection to a comprehensive Customs tariff, that it would multiply officials ?

It is likely that we are already overdone with bureaucratism. The average official, after all, is but an average man, with a few extra limitations and a certain dexterity in routine. It must not be thought that the customs men of the present day are worse than other civil servants ; indeed, there is a kind of maritime freshness in the work performed by some of them that has a highly redemptive tendency. As in the days of Adam Smith, they are the most adaptive of revenue officials. There is little that is

hidebound in their methods. They do not possess that
mechanical hardness that distinguishes the 'inland
revenue men,' nor have they much of the astounding
priggishness that exists here and there in 'the West End
departments.' Yet an army of them would scarcely be a
desirable institution. It cannot be too often repeated
that we have already far too many officials and institutions, far too many smug people who worry the world
from behind desks. It is possible that the genuine
English spirit, the subtle essence which has done everything that has bestowed credit on the national name,
does not traverse extensively the atmosphere of
officialdom. Somehow, we have not done particularly
well since the Germanizing of England set in. One thing
is certain, the effective supervision of *ad valorem* transactions could not be achieved by purely clerical means.
The man would have to be 'on the spot'—to handle the
goods. Much would have to be left to the judgment of
the 'waterside officer,' or things would soon go wrong.
Strong-minded and clever men would be needed in plenty,
to do the actual landing work.

6. Can anything be urged in extenuation of the present
craze for statistics ?

Little. Faith in statistics appears to be but a form of
superstition. It is likely that most of the statistics of
commerce, gathered prior to the last ten years, were quite
incorrect. This statement will not particularly dis-
concert such people as hold that incorrect figures are
better than none ; therefore it may be best not to embellish
the page with many specimens, but to mention casually
that even accredited statements of payments into the
Exchequer frequently differ, now to the extent of a
million or two, then to the tune of seventeen shillings and
sixpence ha'penny ; that some of the old statements of
tonnage, imports, exports, etc., though quoted in Parliamentary speeches and perpetuated in tables, will not
bear common-sense consideration ; that for many, many

years our import trade with various countries was estimated according to *ports of shipment instead of places of
production ;* that the values furnished often depend on
the whim of a mere office-boy ; that one huge item was
left out of the export return for many years, and when
this was pointed out by a layman the omission was not
by any means immediately rectified ; that—but space is
limited, and there are folk to whom cold fact is uncomfortable. All old statistics should be dealt with
cautiously. It has been suggested that statistics should
not be collected *continuously* as now, but at long intervals,
as the Census is taken, and then thoroughly. Accurate
collection is next to impossible when the uncountable
mercantile army is always being pestered for returns, but
if statistics were taken every seven years proper arrangements could be made. It is to be assumed that there
are men in the country who could make interesting and
instructive speeches, and assist in governing the nation,
without long lists of figures in front of them.

7. Would Tariff Reform cause a considerable rise in
the price of commodities ?

Hard to say. To be effective, according to the plea
of its advocates, it should shut out many foreign manufactures, and stimulate British production. It appears
likely that in its early stage it would increase prices by
raising the reward of labour. People with fixed incomes
would then suffer. The price of imported raw material
might not be particularly affected, especially such raw
material as foreigners compete to supply us with. The
trade of a nation is much like individual trade. When a
manufacturer is pestered by bagmen who sell raw material,
he is usually able to dictate his own terms, but if many
manufacturers have to resort to one centre of supply the
position is reversed. Broad theories may not with
success be applied to commercial ma†ters.

One circumstance deserves reference—the amazing
insincerity at present displayed in argument. It is not

at all uncommon to hear an ardent ' Reformer ' applaud
his system as a means of obviating unemployment, and
almost in the same breath assert that the unemployed
are unemployable. The mercantile man—and Tariff
Reform is essentially a mercantile idea—is avowedly
opportunistic, and every agitation that he pioneers
should be regarded with profound caution. It is for that
vast body of people who possess fixed incomes to consider
at once whether they are actually willing to pay for a
period more money for certain articles than they have
done in the past. If patriotism will carry them through
the ordeal, no more need be said upon this point. But
they should think deeply upon the matter, and weigh
carefully the ' bagman ' portion of the Tariff Reform
arguments.

The apparently ' blunt ' style of the foregoing remarks
may require explanation. It is due merely to lack of
space, and the consequent necessity of curtness. Be it
understood that the statements are founded upon long
and arduous study of almost every kind of record connected with the older British Customs practice. There
are few branches of research more dry and complicated,
at the same time fuller of pitfalls into which even the
most careful may stumble, than this particular one.
Therefore all idea of being dogmatic must be disclaimed.
The above deductions may be proved to be wrong. Still,
they have been formed cautiously, and should at the
present juncture be found interesting. Above all, the
' prophetic ' position must be disclaimed. The old
records relating to Customs legislation and debate teem
with prophecies, yet it would be difficult to quote one
prophecy in twenty that was fulfilled. Few subjects are
so poorly understood as this of Customs tariffs—this upon
which men argue from morn to dewy eve. Hard is the
task to form a decision upon any of its vital points—at
least, a decision that will stand the test of close thought

and common sense.   This may be because the subject itself is so repellent to naturally intelligent men, for after all there is a touch of spoliation in every kind of impost. This opinion, coming as it does from customs officers, may seem strange, yet there is something in it.   If men would devote as much mental effort to the reduction of national expenditure as they do to the creation of taxes, the world would be all the better for the change.

LIST OF AUTHORITIES.

Revenue legislation : The various Acts quoted in text.

Incidence of duties, etc. : The various Customs handbooks.

Colonial revenue and smuggling : Australia, Tasmania, and New Zealand, Quebec, Mauritius, Newfoundland and New Brunswick, St. Kitts, Jamaica, 'Promiscuous,' Cape of Good Hope, and Nova Scotia Files ; General Letters, 1848.

Departmental regulations : General Letters, 1847, 1848, 1850 ; General Orders, 1853.

Ships' Registry : Privy Council Letter, 1847.

Commercial reciprocity : General Orders, 1852.

First Importation of Semolina : General Orders, 1852.

Chichester : General Orders, 1852.

Parliamentary proceedings : Hansard, April 21, 1853 (Commons).

British smuggling : General Letters, 1845, 1848, 1849, 1850 ; General Orders, 1852 ; ' Remarkable Seizures,' 1848, 1849, 1850, 1851, 1852, 1853, 1854, 1855.

CHAPTER IV

CUSTOMS LITERATI : PEACH ; DOYLE ; ALLINGHAM

Peach.

CHARLES WILLIAM PEACH was born in 1800 at Wansford, Northamptonshire. It appears that he was appointed to the Revenue Coastguard in 1824 through the influence of Lord Westmoreland. After several removals he was stationed at Gorran Haven, near Mevagissey, Cornwall, and remained there till 1845, when, at the intercession of Dr. Buckland, Sir Robert Peel appointed him to the Customs at Fowey. It is evident that he had been in the ' Mounted Guard ' during his stay at Gorran Haven, for the notice of his appointment stands thus in the Establishment Book : ' Charles Wm. Peach, Mounted Guard, appointed Searcher, etc., Treasury Warrant 10th February, 1845.' He was removed to Peterhead as sub-controller in 1849, under Treasury Warrant 16th November. In 1853, by Treasury Warrant of 27th August, he was made controller at Wick, and remained in that office at a salary of £150 a year till 1861, when he was ' retired ' with several other officers, on account of reductions rendered necessary by the Commercial Treaty with France. The Board's Minute of August 15, 1861, authorizing this proceeding, gives his age as sixty, his years of service as thirty-seven and seven-twelfths, and his retiring allowance as £130 a year.

An idea of his attainments may be best gleaned from the following extracts from the *Athenæum's* obituary notice (No. 3,046, pp. 362, 363) :

'Peach's taste for collecting was first awakened while on the coasts of Dorsetshire and Devonshire, where he soon acquired an intimate knowledge of the marine fauna of the south of England. His frequent shiftings were in many respects of considerable advantage to him. They gave him a wider range for his observations, and brought him into contact with scientific enthusiasts, from whom he obtained much useful knowledge and the loan of books. In return Peach was able to provide specimens which helped to clear up many points in natural history. Amongst others he was enabled to supply the Rev. Mr. Layton, of Catfield, Norfolk, with the bones required to complete the elephant found in the well-known "Forest Bed" of Norfolk, which is now in the British Museum. While at Gorran Haven Peach began to direct his observations to geological phenomena, and to cultivate his powers of observation. It was not long before he detected fossils in rocks previously regarded as destitute of organic remains. He at this time made one of the chief discoveries of his life in finding lower Silurian fossils in the rocks of Cornwall, which before that time were considered to be azoic. This discovery was of great value to Sir Henry de la Beche, who was then engaged on the Government Geological Survey, as it furnished him with a basis for mapping the rocks of south-western England.

'The British Association met at Plymouth in 1841, and to that meeting Peach communicated his first scientific paper, "On the Organic Remains of Cornwall." He became a member of the British Association, of the Devon and Cornwall Natural History Society, and of the Royal Cornwall Polytechnic Society. In 1843 he furnished to the Polytechnic Society a "Synopsis of the land and fresh-water shells, starfishes, sea-urchins, coralines, alcyonites, sponges, and marine algæ," which was printed in the "Transactions" for that year. This paper bore testimony to his industry, his habits of observation, and to his excellent self-training. After the

Plymouth meeting most of the eminent geologists and many of the naturalists who attended it proceeded into Cornwall. The Polytechnic Society at Falmouth was the centre of this gathering, and Charles Peach became their guide to many of the points of geological interest in the west of Cornwall. Peach thus formed an acquaintance with several men of eminence, which became, by his genial nature, a lifelong friendship. For many years he was a regular contributor to each of the three county societies of Cornwall, and his zeal received in many ways substantial recognition.

' All this time * this remarkable man never received more than £75 a year, and £30 for the keep of a horse. When it is remembered that Peach married in 1829, and had a family of seven sons and two daughters, it will be matter of surprise how he was enabled to maintain his intellectual pursuits amid the struggles of his everyday life.

' Peach was promoted to Peterhead in 1849, and to Wick in 1853. Here his duties were onerous ; he had to measure large quantities of timber imported for the herring trade, and he was appointed Receiver of Wreck, which gave him the charge of 180 miles of coast. It was while on one of these journeys that he made the discovery of fossils in the altered rocks of the Highlands, which in Sir Roderick Murchison's hands afforded the key to the elucidation of the structure of that region.

' Mr. Peach formed a friendship with Robert Dick, and worked with him in the Old Red Sandstone fossils, and a living geologist has said of his labours in this field that Peach has done " more, indeed, than all other geologists put together." . . . It is pleasant to find that he was not without rewards which were gratifying to so simple-minded a man, who ever worked for the love of truth. The Prince Consort presented him with Professor Macgillivray's " Natural History of Deeside and Bræmar." The Council of the Geological Society of London in 1859

* During his stay at Gorran Haven.

awarded him the Wollaston fund for his discoveries in the
rocks of Devonshire and Cornwall.   In 1875 the Royal
Society of Edinburgh gave him the Neill prize for excellence in natural history.   The Royal Cornwall Polytechnic
Society at two of their annual meetings gave him their
silver medal for the arrangement and collection of zoo-
phytes from the Cornish coast, and a bronze medal for a
collection of algæ.   Besides the above, Peach received
numerous presents of books from natural history societies,
and some small grants of money to enable him to pursue
his investigations.

' Mr. Peach died in Edinburgh, on the 28th of February,
in the 86th year of his age, respected by a large circle of
scientific friends.'

Doyle.

Sir Francis Hastings Charles Doyle was born at
Tadcaster, Yorkshire, in 1810.   He was descended from
an ancient Irish family, which had produced several
military officers, all highly distinguished for personal
courage.

He acquitted himself well at Eton and Oxford, and
among his college intimates were many who afterwards
became illustrious (Mr. Gladstone may be mentioned
conspicuously).   He was called to the Bar in 1837, but
it is evident that he was unsuccessful, or that the occupation was not congenial, for in 1845 Sir Robert Peel made
him Assistant-Solicitor of Excise.   In 1846 he was appointed Receiver-General of Customs.   A circular sent
by the Customs Secretary to the collectors and controllers
at various ports, and worded as follows, appears among
the Customs records :

' July 25th, 1846.

' GENTLEMEN,

' Sir Francis Hastings Doyle, Bart., having been
appointed Receiver-General and Cashier of Her Majesty's
Customs in the room of William Boothby, Bart., deceased,
I have it in command to acquaint you therewith, in order

that your letters and remittances may be addressed and made payable to Sir Francis Hastings Doyle, in like manner as they were to his predecessor.'

Sir Francis, in his ' Reminiscences,' deals humorously with the matter of his Customs appointment. He writes : ' I was kind enough to accept it. I need hardly say that by so doing I gave up all hopes of legal or Parliamentary distinction, resting content with a safe and respectable mediocrity.' He had scarcely taken over the office ere one of the clerks absconded with £270, which sum the new Receiver-General had at once to make up out of his own pocket.*

Sir Francis was made Commissioner of Customs in 1870, in place of R. W. Grey, Esq., deceased. His fellow-Commissioners were Sir T. F. Fremantle, F. Goulburn, G. C. L. Berkeley, and F. Romilly, Esqs. He vacated office in 1883, being succeeded by Viscount Sudley, and died in 1888.

He was well known in his day as a poet, his chief productions being ' Miscellaneous Poems ' (1834), ' The Two Destinies ' (1844), ' Œdipus, King of Thebes ' (1849), and ' The Return of the Guards, and other Poems ' (1866). He succeeded Matthew Arnold as Professor of Poetry at Oxford in 1867, and published ' Lectures on Poetry ' in 1869. He was re-elected in 1872, and received the distinction of D.C.L. when he resigned the Professorship in 1877.

Much of his verse deals with military incidents. He appears to have held as exalted an opinion of the British Army as Mr. Kipling does at the present day. He translated much verse, and his ' Lectures ' display great powers of appreciation and much poetic enthusiasm. Yet it cannot be maintained that he was a great or even a skilful poet. He had an unfortunate knack of breaking down in the last line of a stanza, and many of his best efforts are marred by curious slips into bathos. These

* Later the Treasury refunded the money.

lapses are quite inexplicable, for he had been highly educated. If it be borne in mind that he was a life-long dabbler in the Castalian spring, and a Professor of Poetry at Oxford, they will appear unpardonable.

Below are a few specimens. The first is from ' The Return of the Guards, etc.,' and it should be pointed out that in his preface Sir Francis admitted that his object in publishing the verses was to obtain the vacant Professorship.

> ' Yes, they return ; but who return ?
>   The many or the few ?
> Clothed with a name, in vain the same,
>   Face after face is new.'

Take the first stanza of ' The Doncaster St. Leger ' ·

> ' The sun is bright, the sky is clear,
>   Above the crowded course,
> As the mighty moment draweth near
>   Whose issue shows the horse.'

From ' The Private of the Buffs ' :

> ' Last night among his fellow-roughs
>   He jested, quaffed, and swore—
> A drunken private of the Buffs,
>   *Who never looked before.*'

The following extraordinary verse occurs in ' The Foster-Brother ' :

> ' No fairer maid throughout the land than Gwennolak was seen,
> The daughter of a noble house, a maiden of eighteen.
> Dead the old lord, her father ; dead two sisters, and her mother.
> Her father's wife was left, but of her own blood breathed no other.'

Yet he wrote ' The Loss of the Birkenhead,' which contains really fine lines :

> ' The brave who died,
> Died without flinching, in the bloody surf ;
> They sleep as well beneath that purple tide
>   As others under turf.

> ' They sleep as well, and, roused from their wild grave,
> *Wearing their wounds like stars*, shall rise again,
> Joint-heirs with Christ, because they bled to save
>   His weak ones, not in vain.'

Even in this, his best poem, he could not eliminate the
fatal bathotic termination :

> ' That those whom God's high grace there saved from ill,
> Those also, left His martyrs in the bay,
> Though not by siege, though not in battle, still
> *Full well had earned their pay !!!*'

It is all very strange, especially when one reads his
appreciative notice of Newman's ' Dream of Gerontius.'

His ' Reminiscences ' are interesting. They are the
reminiscences of a fine old Tory, a man hot-blooded,
observant, and humorous. It appears that he entertained an unbounded regard for Gladstone until the latter
went over to the Liberal camp. When in 1880 Gladstone
reassumed office at the head of a large majority, his old
college friend sent him a blunt and characteristic letter,
openly taunting the statesman with his change of
principles. Thus wrote the then Commissioner of
Customs :

' You are about to become the strongest Prime Minister
that has been seen for many years. You are now an
advanced and ever-advancing Liberal. Do you recollect,
forty years ago and more, speaking to me thus : " A Scotch
Tory is worse than an English Whig, a Scotch Whig is
worse than an English Radical, and a Scotch Radical
worse than the Devil himself !" And now, because Scotland has surrendered herself to that sulphureous element,
you quote poor Lady Nairne's verses only to misapply
them, and make her call this infernal region of yours
" The Land o' the Leal !" '

Even Dr. Johnson was not a more strenuous upholder
of what may with justice be called the heroic old English
Toryism. Sir Francis's hatred of the average official
political economist was remarkable, and distinctly
laudable. ' Misplaced thrift,' said he—' the thrift, for
instance, of that narrow-minded skinflint Joseph Hume,
upon whom Mr. Gladstone showered his praises the other

day, to flatter the people of Aberdeen—is simply the worst form of extravagance.'

Sir Francis, like Johnson and Borrow, had an unaccountable antipathy to Scotsmen, and an ardent admiration of English institutions, sports, and rural life. The average man finds little difference between Lowland Scots and Yorkshiremen, yet Sir Francis loved the latter race as much as he disliked the former. There can be no doubt that he was highly eccentric. Many anecdotes that prove this survive in the department, but it appears that he was extremely popular in the Service, both with subordinates and fellow-Commissioners.

His account of an interview with Gladstone just before the passing of one of the Reform Bills illustrates the great statesman's profound distrust of civil servants. ' I say,' said Sir Francis, ' among other roughs, are you going to let me have a vote now ?'* Gladstone replied with great vehemence : ' Never, until universal suffrage is reached ; never, with my consent, shall a civil servant go to the poll !'

Allingham.

William Allingham was born at Ballyshannon, Donegal, in 1824, and appointed to the Customs in 1846. His official record runs thus :

Appointed principal coast officer, Donegal, March 16, 1846.
Appointed sub-collector, Ramsay, Isle of Man, July 3, 1849.
Appointed sub-collector, Ballyshannon, October 28, 1849.
Appointed controller, Coleraine, September 14, 1853.
Resigned, February, 1854.
Reappointed as controller, New Ross, June 19, 1854.
Appointed sub-collector, Ballyshannon, June 3, 1855.
Appointed clerk, fifth class, Examiner's office, London, October 1, 1862.
Appointed principal coast officer, Lymington, May 8, 1863.
Final resignation accepted under Board's Order of June 18, 1870.

It appears he had written some verse, and contributed to the London magazines, prior to his appointment, and he states in his diary that when he went to Belfast in

* Civil servants were at that time disabled from voting.

1846 to be instructed in Customs work he ' talked to the clerks about literature and poetry in a way that excited some astonishment.'

He continued to write, and found little difficulty in attracting the attention of the leading literary men of the day. He visited London on several occasions, and interviewed Leigh Hunt, Carlyle, Thackeray, Coventry Patmore, Rossetti, and other ' lions.' Later he became acquainted with Tennyson, and the intimacy was only severed by death.

He published ' Poems ' in 1850, and ' Day and Night Songs ' in 1854. His first resignation of office was a step towards taking up literature as a profession, but the attempt was not successful. It is stated that he received a grant of £60 a year in 1864 in acknowledgment of his literary merits, and that this was afterwards made £100. He published ' Laurence Bloomfield in Ireland '—his longest piece of verse—in 1864, and ' Fifty Modern Poems ' in 1865. He edited one or two anthologies, and contributed much, both in prose and verse, to the magazines. After his final resignation he became subeditor of *Fraser's Magazine*, and editor in 1874, retaining the office till 1879. He died in 1889.

Allingham must have been a man of engaging manners and amiable disposition, to attract as he did the friendship of so many distinguished men, for his literary powers, especially in verse, were extremely meagre. More tiresome poetry than his would be difficult to find, even among the verse produced by his contemporaries, Eliza Cook and Miller the basket-maker. His work is quite destitute of invention, and often extremely bathotic, and his constructive faculty may with justice be described as contemptible. Some of his verses are altogether absurd, almost rivalling the inimitable banality produced by that older Customs official Congreve :

> ' Speak, speak your desire ;
> I'm all over fire ;
> Say what you require.
> I'll grant it. Now let us retire.'

A few quotations from Allingham's verse should be highly convincing :

> ' Autumnal sunshine spread on Irish hills,
> Imagination's brightening mirror fills,
> Wherein a horseman on a handsome grey
> Along the high road takes his easy way.'

> ' My Lady Harvey comes of Shropshire blood :
> Stately, with finished manners, cold of mood.
> Her eldest son is in the Guards ; her next
> At Eton.   Her two daughters—I'm perplext
> To specify young ladies—they are tall,
> Dark-haired, and smile in speaking.   That is all.'

> ' Along the winding road to Lisnamoy
> The drover trudges and the country boy.'

> ' Flee from London, good my Walter ! boundless jail of bricks
>   and gas,
> Care not if your Exhibition swarm with portrait and Gil Blas.'

The following, from ' The Abbot of Innisfallen,' reveals Allingham at his most bathotic :

> ' Low kneeled that blessed Abbot,
>   When the dawn was waxing bright ;
> He prayed a great prayer for Ireland,
>   He prayed with all his might.

> ' Low kneeled that good old Father,
>   When the sun *began to dart ;*
> He prayed a prayer for all mankind,
>   He prayed it from his heart.'

The utter deeps of deadly dulness are sounded in the following :

> ' Peasant cots with humble haggarts, mansions with obsequious
>   groves :
> A spire, a steeple, rival standards which the liberal distance loves
> To set in union : There the dear but dirty little town abides :
> And you and I come home to dinner after all our walks and rides.'

> ' Learning can nourish Wisdom, when good food
>   Is quietly digested, but too oft
> Unfit, ill-cook'd, or overloaded meals
> Lie crude, and swell the belly with wind, or breed
> Dull fat, mistook for portliness and strength.'

From ' Blackberries ' :

> ' I never write from personal spite
>   So much as a single word ;
> When hot I feel 'tis public zeal,
>   Which may seem to you absurd.'

And :

> ' I heard the dogs howl in the moonlight night,
> And I went to the window to see the sight :
> All the dead that ever I knew
> Going one by one and two by two.'

How such preposterous stuff ever attained publication, how it passed the reviewers, how it went into several editions, and why in the British Museum Catalogue the title ' Poet ' distinguishes William Allingham of Bally-shannon from William Allingham who wrote a treatise on fistula, must be left to our readers' merciful consideration. A more vital matter of debate intrudes. William Allingham, ' Poet,' was sub-editor of *Fraser's* for five years, and editor for another five. No doubt reams of verse were submitted for his inspection. It is unlikely that he was fitted to judge poetry, who deliberately wrote and published the drivel quoted. The decay of English liking for verse, and the suicidal leanings of some of our real modern poets, may be easily accounted for, if within the last thirty years there have been many such editors and sub-editors.

The most interesting thing done by Allingham is his ' Diary,' a mass of jottings, principally about his distinguished friends. It is evident that he was not destitute of humour, though his verse in a way implies that he was. He wrote : ' I have been an official all my life without the least turn for it. I never could attain a true official manner, which is highly artificial, and handles trifles with ludicrously disproportionate gravity.' He uttered another capital ' aside ' upon the futility of the Victorian methods of ' improving ' the working classes. ' Cloudy, but warm. Institution. Take the chair at Penny Reading. Any use ?' He quoted with evident relish Leigh Hunt's remark upon Robert the Obscurantist : ' Shakspere and Milton wrote plainly, the Sun and Moon write plainly : why can't Browning ?' He told of Edward Fitzgerald, that gin-soaked, tobacco-scented, shabbily-dressed bundle of genius and humour, that he kept a rough book in which he recorded all the ' howlers ' he came across.   The book was labelled ' Half-hours with the Worst Authors,' and Allingham was surprised that it was never published. It is likely that he would have found himself figuring in it, to an extent that would have surprised him still more.

APPENDIX

ILLUSTRATIVE DOCUMENTS

No. I. Certified copy, made in 1671, of the report made in 1559, by Amadas and Trevanion, of their survey of Plymouth, Looe, Fowey, Truro, Penryn, Mount's Bay, St. Ives, and Padstow.

' TO THE RIGHT HON^{BLE} LORDS AND BARONS OF OUR SOVRAIGNE LADY THE QUEEN'S ^{TIES} EXCH^{QR} THEIR MOST HUMBLE WILLIAM AMADAS CUSTOMER OF THE PORTS OF PLYMOUTH AND FOWEY IN THE COUNTYS OF DEVON AND CORNWALL AND JOHN TREVANYON COMPTROLL' THERE WITH ALL REV'RENT SUBMISSION AND DOE MAKE OUR SUITE TO YOUR HONO^{RS} AS FOLL^S ON, ETC.

' Whereas our said most dread Soveraigne Lady the Queen by her Letters patents hath assigned and appoynted us with divers others in the said Lres patents nominated to veiw and p^ruse* Limit and appoynt all such Places and Creekes to the said Ports belonging where a Customer Comptroll' and Searcher or their Deputys have been Resident by the space of tenne yeares before the Act in that behalfe made at the Parliament begun at Westminster the three and twentieth of January in the first yeare of the Raigne of our said Soveraigne Lady Elizabeth by the Grace of God of England France and Ireland Queen Defender of the Faith &c., and there Prorogued till the five and twentieth of the same month and then and there holden kept and continued untill the Disolution of the same being the eight of May then next ensueing as in the same Act with the same Lres Patents hereunto annexed more at large appeareth. By virtue whereof wee the said William Amadas and John Trevanyon named in the said Comičon†

---

* View and peruse.   † Commission.

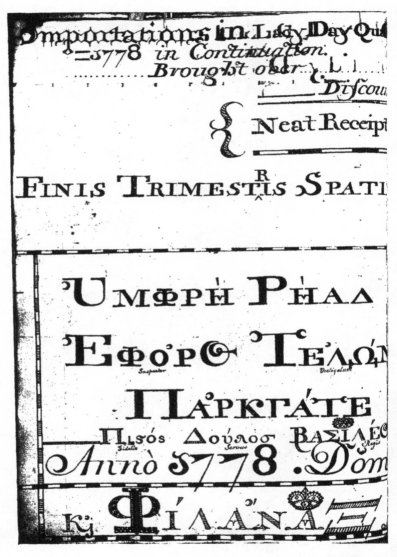

Subſidy .... 3747 3759 3692 Duty

6 128 158 __ 86¼ 171½ 158 ____ 1 13¾   Groſs Total Poundage Goods

__ 13¼ __ 13¼ __ 5¼ __ 10 ___ 13¼

6 114¼ 144⅛ _ 81¼ _ 163½ 158 ___ 1 __ ¼   Σύμπαν Ὁλόκληρο

Summa Totalis

Humphrey Read D. Controller

Parkgate

Vivat Rex et Regina

Vivat Rex

Felicissimè

Ætātĕmquĕ

Χίλιοι ἐπτακόσιοι ἑβδομήκοντα Ὀκτώ.

Mille Septenti Septuaginti Octo .... 1778.

ΤΕΛΟΣ

Ὁλόκληρο Κεφάλαιον .... Summa

		L	S	D
Subsidy Inwards on Poundage Goods		6	11	4
Subsidy on Portugal Wine		—	11	9
Additional Duty on D°.		—	10	9
Total Customs		7	13	11
New Subsidy		1	16	2
⅓ Subsidy		—	12	—
⅔ Subsidy		1	4	1
Subsidy 3747		1	6	2
Subsidy 3759		—	6	—
Impost 3692		1	—	—
Impost on Wine		2	4	6
Coynage on Wine		—	2	2
Duty on Wine .. 3745		—	17	5
Duty on Wine .. 3763		—	17	5
Subsidy on Spirits		—	1	6
Coynage on Spirits		—	1	—
Subsidy Outwards		—	10	10
Hum'.. Read 9ber 78		—	28	—

THE Controller's Abstract For Lady Day Quarter Ending 5th of April 1778.

y READ, DEPUTY-CONTROLLER, PARKGATE.

(It will be seen that little duty was taken.)

Between pp. 106-7.

have veiwed and p'used the said Ports Places and Creekes and have Limitted and Appoynted heereunder written to bee open Places of Charging and Discharging of wares and M'chandizes as well comeing from the p'tes* of beyond the Seas into the said Ports Places and Creekes as goeing out of the same according to the tenor of the Statute aforesaid in manner and forme following (that is to say)

'Att the Port and Towne of Plymouth the Key† there comonly called Hawkins his Key is appoynted for the only Place of Lading and unlading charging and Discharging of all wares and m'chandizes that hereafter shall be Laden and unladen charged and Discharged within the said Port containing in Length by the waters side seaven score foot and in breadth six score foot.

'Item at the Towne of Lowe the Key there comonly called the Towne Key is appoynted (etc., etc.) containing in Breadth forty foot and in Length three score foot.

'Item at the Towne and Port of Fowey the Key there is appoynted (etc., etc.) containing in Length five hundred foot and in breadth six score foot and bounded on the South side with a key comonly called Burlaces his Key And on the North side with a Key there comonly called Trevarrock's Key.

'Item at the Towne of Truroe the key there comonly called the Towne Key is appoynted (etc., etc.) containing in Length five hundred foot and in breadth one hundred foot.

'Item at the Towne of Penryn the Key there is appoynted (etc., etc.) containing in Length three hundred foot from the North end of the Bridge there comonly called the Colledge Bridge to a Courtlage called Summer Court and in breadth twenty foot. And soe likewise from the South end of the said Bridge unto an Oake directly over against the said Summer Court in Length other three hundred foot and in breadth other twenty foot.

'Item at Mount's Bay the Key of Penzance is appoynted (etc., etc.) containing in Length fower hundred and twenty foot and in breadth sixteen foot.

'Item at the Towne of St. Ives the Key there comonly called the Towne Key is appoynted (etc., etc.) containing in Length two hundred and fower foot and in breadth fourteen foot.

'Item And at the Towne of Paddistowe the Key there commonly called the Towne Key is appoynted (etc., etc.) containing in Length eight hundred foot and in Breadth sixteen foot.

* Parts.   † Quay.

' All which p'misses* wee have here certiffied unto yor Hon^ors according to the tenor of the said Lres Patents of Comic͞on to us amongst others directed. In Witness whereof wee the said William Amadas and John Trevanyon to these p'sents have sett our Seales the last day of August in the first yeare of the Raigne of our said Soveraigne Lady Elizabeth by the Grace of God Queen of England France and Ireland Defender of the Faith,' &c.

No. 2. Extracts from the Book of Rates, 1660 (Old Subsidy), showing the divisions and rating for Customs of foreign cloth, linen, leather, and iron. (The Customs ' values' are shown. Divide by twenty for the duty, the rate being 5 per cent. on the value. N.B.—For linens, add half the duty thus obtained, there being a special impost on them.)

		£	s.	d.
'All manner of woollen cloths imported, per yard		8	10	0†
Cloaks of felt, the piece		2	0	0
Coverlets of Scotland, the piece		0	15	0
Callicoes imp^d, the piece		0	10	0
Flannel, the yard		0	1	8
Frise of Ireland, the yard		0	0	9
Cambricks, the piece (13 ells)		2	0	0
Canvas	Dutch and Hessian (120 ells)	3	10	0
	French (narrow) ,,	6	0	0
	,, (broad) ,,	15	0	0
	Packing ,,	2	10	0
Damask	Holland tabling the yd.	1	0	0
	,, towelling ,,	0	7	0
	Silesia tabling ,,	0	4	0
	,, towelling ,,	0	1	4
Diaper	Holland tabling ,,	0	9	0
	,, towelling ,,	0	3	0
	Silesia tabling ,,	0	3	4
	,, towelling ,,	0	1	4
Lawns	French, the piece	1	10	0
	Silesia ,, (4 to 8 yds.)	0	10	0
Linen cloth of the Netherlands, the ell		0	5	0
Do.	Drilling and duck (120 ells)	2	0	0
Do.	Danish, the ell	0	1	8
Do.	Hambro and Silesia (broad) (120 ells)	10	0	0
Do.	,, ,, (narrow) ,,	8	0	0
Do.	Hinderlands and Russian (narrow) (120 ells)	2	8	4
Do.	Irish (120 ells)	2	0	0
Do.	Dowlas (106 ells)	5	0	0
Do.	Minsters (linens) (1,500 ells)	56	13	4
Do.	Oxenbrigs ,, ,,	60	0	0

---

* Premises.   † Of course utterly prohibitive.

			£	s.	d.
Linen cloth	Polonias, Ulsters, Hanovers, Lubecks, Westphalias, Harfords, and all other narrow cloths of Dutch-land and the East Country*	120 ells	4	0	0
Leather ..	Basils, the dozen ..		20	0	0
	Spanish, the doz skins		5	0	0
	Danish ,,		2	0	0
	Turkish and East India, the doz skins		2	0	0
Iron ..	Amys, Spanish, Danish, Swedish, the ton ..		7	0	0
	Small chimney backs, each ..		0	6	8
	Large ,, ,, ,,		0	13	4
	Kettle bands, the cwt. ..		2	0	0
	Fire irons, the gross ..		0	10	0
Iron Hoops, the cwt. ..			1	6	8'

English cloth paid on exportation a specific duty (3s. 4d. on each short cloth if exported by denizens, 6s. 8d. if by aliens. A short cloth was 28 yards in length and 64 pounds in weight). English leather manufactures paid ½d. a pound, English iron 16s. a ton (value £16), English linen 6d. the 40 ells.

No. 3. Copy of Bill of Entry (No. 5), showing imports and exports, London, June 30, 1660, with ports of shipment and destination, importers' and exporters' names, and lists of ships entered inward and cleared outward.

'LONDON, IMPORTED, JUNE 30, 1660.

Barbados.	Nico. Enos ..	..	25	
	Peter Lear ..	..	33	
	Fran. Raines	..	51	
	Paul Allestry	..	87	
	John Miller ..	..	36	
	Nath. Whitfeild	..	2	
	Hen. Barton	..	9	casks sugar.
	Rich. Alie ..	..	109	
	Rich. Batson	..	15	
	Tho. Crisp ..	..	2	
	Tho. Chevely	..	70	
	George Lock	..	2	
	Hen. Grigg ..	..	20	
	,,	..	4	bags cottons.
	James Watkins	..	11	
	Sam. Osborn	..	28 bags ginger.	
Hambro.	Na. Lownds	..	54 barrels plates.	
	John Claypole	..	4 fats iron wyer.	
	Tho. Tyte ..	..	40 C.† ells Germany linen.	
	Wil. Williams	..	60 ,, oxenbrigs.‡	
	Godf. Lee ..	..	58 ,, ,,	
	Rob. Gore ..	..	20 ,, ,,	
			2400 l§ Dutch yarn.	

* (All German and Dutch linen not above three-quarters and a half broad accounted ' narrow.')

† 40 C.=4,000.   ‡ A kind of linen.   § Pounds.

Virginia.	John Hatch	..	6 hhds tobacco.
	Wil. Hebb ..	..	8 ,, ,,
	Rich. Audley	..	10 ,, :,
	Rob. Skelton	..	7 ,, ,,
	Job Sayer ..	..	10 ,, ,,
Hambro.	Cha. Deering	..	86 C.* steel.
Flushing.	Edw. Dethick	..	570 ells linen.
	Peter Roys ..	..	2000 pantiles.
Rochel.	Hen. Allen	..	21 tuns vinegar.
Amsterdam.	Tho. Dava ..	..	3 tuns linseed oyl, 5 fats iron wyer, 2 barrels anotto.
	Rich. Baker	..	13 tuns trayn oyl.
Burdeaux.	Tho. Fincham	..	6 tuns spirits, 8 tuns vinegar.
Hambro.	Tho. Bellingham	..	30 C. ells minsters, 8 barrels smalts, 30 C. ells inderlens.†
Amsterdam.	Jacob Balde	..	2 fats drest hemp, 20 C. hemp
Galipoly.	Ra. Lee ..	..	6 tuns oyl, 2 tuns argol.
France.	John Lethulier	..	80 quarters barly.
Cane‡	James Corcellis	..	15 C. ells canvas.
	Law. Martel	..	260 reames paper.
Harlem.	Wil. Somers	..	13 dozen incle.§
Rochel.	John Marishal	..	10 tuns French wine.
Yarmouth.	Wil. Perkins	..	7 ,, ,, ,,‖

'SIX SHIPS ENTERED INWARDS.

The Prosperous, John Tomson, @ Dublin.
The Constant Rebecca, Jer. Stilgo, @ Stockholm.
The Orenge Tree, Geo. Agenor, @ Berbadoes.
And three ships from Norway.

'EXPORTED, JUNE 30, 1660.

Amsterdam.	Peter Mathews	..	10 serges.
Hambro.	Gerd. Hockle	..	59 ,,
	,, ,,	..	6 cloth rashes.
Rotterdam.	Wil. Cargel ..	..	25 serges.
	,, ,, ..	..	4 bearskins.
	,, ,, ..	..	14 otterskins.
	(An illegible entry.)		
Deip.¶	Hen. Whitead	..	4 serges.
	Wil. Spiller ..	..	20 ,,
	Edw. Ware ..	..	7 ,,
	,, ,, ..	..	3 dozen calve skins.
	John Remington	..	20 Spanish cloths.
		..	64 double bays.**
	Edw. Barkley	..	109 dozen hose.
	,, ,,		
Genoa.	John Dowse	..	25 ,, ,,
	Dan. Edwards	..	20 minikin bays.
Barbadoes.	Isaac Barrow	..	10 C. wrought iron.
	James Blar ..	..	2 short cloths.
Smirna.	John Rand	..	12 ,, ,,
	,, ,,	..	6 long ,,

---

* Cwt.   † Minsters and Hinderlands, certain kinds of linen.
‡ Canet, or Cannes ?   § Inkle.
‖ Liable to the London surtax when removed from an outport.
¶ Dieppe.   ** A kind of West-country cloth.

Dort.	{ Edw. Tidcomb	..	30 short cloths.
	{ " "	..	4 long "
Legorn.	Tho. Goodyear	..	220 perpetuanos.*
Smirna.	Ralph Lee ..	..	5 fodder lead.
Roan.†	{ James Burton	..	3 " "
	{ Steph. Bolton	..	4. C. verditor.
St. Mallo's.	Hen. Oliver ..	..	120 dozen jumps.‡
Russia.	John Cliffe ..	..	336 lb. cloth shreds.
Burdeaux.	Mich. Clipsham	..	90 firkins butter.
Ireland.	John Wright	..	486 lb. Virginia tobacco.
Guinny.§	{ Tho. Bell ..	..	38 C. copper bars.
	{ ", ", ..	..	17 C. brass rings.

'FOREIGN GOODS EXPORTED BY CERTIFICATE.

Russia.	John Gourney	..	7 C. olibanum.
Legorn.	John Welden	..	10 C. red earth.
	{ " "	..	30 " " "
Hambro.	{ Tho. Sanders	..	43 C. panellis sugar.
	{ Ph. Graxty ..	..	4 " " "
Amsterdam.	{ Nich. Cook ..	..	890 lb. mohair yarn.
	{ Law. Sawcer	..	1117 calicos.
Rotterdam.	Roger Scattergood	..	707 "
Roan.	{ John Dickins	..	7000 lb. cotton wool.‖
	{ ", ",	..	300 " " yarn.
Deip.	Law. Sawcer	..	50 pieces bengal stuffs.
New Eng-	-		
land.	Edw. Mytton	..	52 birding-pieces.¶
Barbadoes.	Isaac Barton	..	200 ells canvas.

'SHIPS CLEARED OUT.

The Peter, Wil. Buckley, for St. Vallery.
The Hope, And^r Lehot, for Roan.
The Gift of God, Rob. Deneale, for Deip.'

No. 4. Order of Embargo upon vessels carrying naval stores (during war with Holland, 1665). From Letter-Book of Wells.

' Whereas dureing the present warr wth the Dutch his Maties service doth necessarily require extraordnary supply of Navall p'vitions for the timely p'viding whereof all good & lawfull meanes are to bee made use of : these are therefore in pursuance of a warr^t from his Royall Highnesse James Duke of Yorke Ld High Admirall of England &c to will & require you y^t when any shipps or vessells wherein there shall bee any p'vitions or stores necessary for his Maties Navy shall bee sent

* A kind of cloth or linen ?   † Rouen.   ‡ Query.
§ Guinea.   ‖ Raw cotton.   ¶ Fowling-pieces.

into any Port or Creek within the limits of yor Port of Lynn
& its memb^{rs} by any private man of warre you take espetiall
care to send notice of the same to me by the first opportunity
to the end y^t care may bee taken for the buying of the same
of the true proprietor at the Markett price : And you are not
to suffer the said p'vitions or stores to be carried out of such
port or creek or to bee any waies disposed of untill you shall
receive direccons concerning the same from me & in case by
accident any other shipp or vessell shall be brought or come
into any port or Creek within yor said limits or jurisdiccon
whose lading or any considerable pt thereof shall consist of
Navall p'vitions you are to cause the same to be stoppt and
detained untill further order and to give notice thereof to me
and for so doeing this shall be yor Warr^t. Given under my
hand and seale at Raigneham this 3^d day of Jan^y, 1665.

                                            ' TOWNSHEND.

' To the Mayor of the towne of Lynn
    Regis & to the offic^{rs} of his Maties
    Customs there.'

*No. 5. Form of Master's declaration at report inward of an
English ship from Malaga, 1678. From the Letter-Book
of Wells.*

' You doe affirme and sweare that you are the person whose
name is subscribed hereunto, that you are Master of the shipp
whereof you now make entry, and that there hath been no
other Master dureing this voyage, that the said shipp is
English-built, and that all the owners of the said shipp are
English, that the number of the Marriners of the said shipp's
Company are 18 Englishmen and 4 forreigners, that shee took
in her present lading in the Port of Malaga, that the entry
now tendered by you containes a just accompt of the Burthen,
contents, and ladeing of the said shipp with the particular
marks, numbers, quantities, and contents of every parcell of
goods therein laden, as also of the names of the merchants to
the best of your knowledge : And that you have not broken
bulke nor delivered any goods out of the said shipp, since her
ladeing in the said Port of Malaga : And in cause you finde
any other goods not menconed in this entry you will give the
Principall Officer notice thereof before the delivery thereof
out of the said shipp.'

No. 6. Order in Council issued at accession of James II., reaffirming the repeal of aliens' duties on goods the product of the English realm (January 22, 1685-86). From the Letter-Book of Wells.

BY THE KING'S MOST EXCELLENT MAJ^{TIE} & THE LORDS OF HIS MAJ^{TIE'S} MOST HONOR^{BLE} PRIVY COUNCELL.

' Uppon reading ye Peticõn of Sr Peter Vandeputt & others on behalfe of themselves & severall other merchants of the City of London, setting forth that whereas by an Act in the twelfth yeere of the Raigne of his late Maj^{tie}, entituled, a Subsidy granted to the King of Tonnage & Poundage & other sumes of money payable uppon merchandise exported & imported it was enacted among other things y^t of every £ value of any of the native comodities of this Realme, or Manufacture wrought of such Native Comodities, to bee carried out of this Realme by any Merchant Aliens, according to the value of the Booke of Rates therein mentioned and referred unto, there should be paid unto his said Matie the sum of two shillings, being double as much as any natives paid, wch said Act the Parliam^t afterwards uppon mature deliberation finding to bee p'judicially to hinder the exportation of the native woollen manufactures, leade, tinn, & fish, did by an Act for taking off Aliens' Dutys uppon Comodities of the growth p'duct & Manufacture of the Nation, repeal so much thereof as did concerne any Custome or Subsidy uppon any of the native Comodities of this kingdome, to bee exported out of this Realme, payable by any Merchant Alien made Denisen, or other stranger or Alien, over and above the Custome & Subsidie payable by his Maj^{ties} naturall-born Subjects : Ever since the making of wch said Act merchant Aliens & strangers & theire factors have paid no more Custome for any of the Native Comodities exported by them out of this Realme (Coales excepted) than his Maties naturall-borne Subjects have done, by which the Petitioners conceived y^t that the Trade of the woollen Manufacture & of the Native Comodities had beene much encouraged & the Revenue of the Crowne not thereby lessened.

' Further (by their said Peticon) humbly representing, y^t of late the Comission^{rs} & Offic^{rs} of his Maj^{ties} Customes, uppon the grant of the Customes as they were settled the twelfth yeere of his Maties Reigne, require from all Merchant strangers and Aliens the double duty in the said Act menc̃oned, which if continued would p'bably lessen the exportation of the native goods of the growth of this kingdome, and most certeinely remove part of the trade from the hands of the faire trading Merchants, his Maties good subjects who justly pay his Maj^{ties} Customes (not onely for themselves but as factors) into the hands of slight persons & unfaire traders, who make little scruple of Defrauding his Maj^{ty} and colouring Strangers goods, to the great p'judice of the Petitioners' trade : Praying y^{t} his Maj^{ty} would give direcc̄on to take no other Customes from Merchant Aliens & Strangers or their factors, for goods exported of the native p'duct of this kingdome, then were payable by the Statute of the twenty-fifth of his late Maj^{ties} Reign. And upon heareing the Comissioners of his Maj^{ties} Customes thereuppon, his Maj^{ty} was pleased to declare his Royall pleasure in favour of the Petitioners,' &c., &c.

(The Order proceeds to state that the king will take no more of aliens than of denizens upon such goods exported, as in the latter part of his predecessor's reign, and this although his Subsidy was granted at the rates laid down in the early part of said reign.) 'And if his Maj^{ty} shall hereafter finde cause to alter his Royall pleasure, he will give timely notice thereof, to the end that noe person may be surprised.

'Whitehall, Treasury Chambers, 28th January, 1685. Lett the Comissioners for his Maj^{tie} take care y^{t} the Order of Councell whereof the within written is a true coppie bee duly complied with according to his Maj^{ties} Royall Pleasure therein declared.

'ROCHESTER.'

No. 7. Collector and controller of Yarmouth to Board, June 3, 1689.

'HON^{BLE} SIRS,

'There is brought into this port by Capt. Fitzpatrick, Comander of their Ma^{tys} Frigott the *Lark*, a privatere belonging to Dunkirk. The Sayles and Runing Rigging we have taken into Custody, and the men, being 21 in number, he put on shore on Satturday last. Our Towne Goale being not capable of receiving soe many p'sons wee were forced to desire the assistance of a Justice of the Peace in the County to comitt them to the County Goale at Norwich, w^{ch}, according to yor order of the 30th Aprill last, wee give you accompt thereof.

'Wee have given order for the men to have twopence a day allowance for ye p'sent & if yor Hon^{rs} shall think fitt to abate of that, or allow more, shall observe yor orders.

'Wee find ye Majistrates of this port verry ready to assist us as farr as lies in their powre, but canot comit any p'son to ye County Goale wthout the assistance of a Justice of ye Peass in ye Country, soe that it will be the more charge to theire Ma^{tys}. If yor Hon^{rs} shall think fitt to allow thereof, wee shall p'ceed as wee have done.

'Three of ye p'sons in ye privatere above menc̃oned being Sweeds,* formerly taken by the French, & were forced to goe into the s^d privatere, the Capt has taken into theire Ma^{ts} Service y^e 2nd Inst.'

No. 8. Seizure Note (Irish Customs), 1699.

'July 17th, 1699. Seised by Alexand^r Erwin, in a passeng^{rs} bundle, on board the *Seafarer* of Livp^{le},† Henry Ballintin M_r, one pce of Black Sarge,‡ and sent to the Store the 18 of July, 1699, the Ship being Outward Bound, and it not Entred.

'A^x ERWIN.'

No. 9. Board to Surveyor of Wells, demanding explanation as to a certificate of English taking of fish, irregularly granted. From the Letter-Book of Wells.

'MR. GOODWIN,

'We have before us a p'mitt dated in y^r Port ye 6th Novemb' last signed by y^r selfe ye Custo^r and Collr & by Mr. Isaackston ye Comp^t for 5900 English Caught fish in ye Truelove of Wells Robt Pin for Newcastle, wch wee are informed was sent after ye vessell to Scarborough when ye fish was under ye hands & examination by ye officers of y^t Port, which wee take to bee a very irregular proceeding of yrs, & expect you give us satisfaction how you came to grant the said Permitt, what ground you had for soe doeing, & what knowledge you had of the takeing and loading y^e said fish, & give us an Acc^t of all circumstances of y^e case that might induce you to y^r granting y^e said Permitt, for that wee are credibly informed y^e said fish was never in y_r Port : Wee rest,

'Y^r loveing friends,

T. NEWPORT.
C. GODOLPHIN.
SAM. CLARKE.
ROB^T HENLY.

'Cust° Ho. London
24th *Decr* 1700.'

---

* Swedes.   † Liverpool.   ‡ Serge.

No. 10. *Statement of the average prices of middling wheat from 1697 to 1820, of the duties actually leviable under the 'sliding scale,' when wheat was at the prices shown, and of the balance of imports and exports of corn food-stuffs, from 1697 to 1794. Compiled by the Authors from official returns and the various Books of Rates.*

Periods.	Prices of wheat per statute quarter.	Duty actually leviable on imported wheat.	Excess in quarters of imports of corn food-stuffs over exports.	Explanatory remarks.
	£ s. d.	£ s. d.		
5 years ending— 1701	2 2 8	0 18 0	139,866	This included the duty under the 'New Subsidy.'
6 years ending— 1707	1 5 11	0 19 9	289,304	This included the duties leviable under the '⅓ and ⅔ Subsidies' (discount deducted).
4 years ending— 1711	2 9 9	0 16 7	299,367	The duty less because the price exceeded 44s.
1715	1 17 8	0 19 9	453,986	
1719	1 13 1	,,	485,852	
5 years ending— 1724	1 8 10	,,	532,732	
1729	1 17 7	,,	216,643	
1734	1 5 9	,,	468,244	
1739	1 10 10	,,	597,462	
1744	1 8 7	,,	446,378	
1749	1 7 9	19s. 9d. till 1747; £1 1s. 9d. 1747-49	932,593	Duty higher in and after 1747. Increased by the '1747 Subsidy.'
1754	1 10 5	1 1 9	1,080,077	
1759	1 16 2	,,	273,805	
1764	1 10 7	,,	696,117	

Periods.	Prices of wheat per statute quarter.			Duty actually leviable on imported wheat.	Excess in quarters of imports of corn food-stuffs over exports.	Explanatory remarks.
	£	s.	d.			
5 years ending— 1769	2	3	2	Duty free under temporary Acts of relief.	223,184	
1774	2	7	9	Do. till 1773. In 1773-74, 16s. 11d.	276,206	1773-74, duty less because price exceeded 44s.
1779	2	0	9	1774-78, £1 1s. 9d. 1779, £1 2s. 10d.	290,595	1779, duty higher because increased by an impost of 5 per cent. on proceeds.
1784	2	5	9	1779-81, 17s. 10d. 1782-84, 18s. 8d.	185,906	Price exceeded 44s.
1789	2	3	3	£ s. d. 1 4 3	198,716	Duty increased in 1782 by another impost of 5 per cent. on proceeds. (Discounts abolished in 1781.) Price low. The duty is as levied on cheap wheat before 1779=£1 1s. 9d. plus two imposts of 5 per cent. and the amount previously allowed as discount. (N.B.—Consolidation Act of 1787 raised the limit price from 44s. to 48s.)
1794	2	7	2	1 4 3	1,145,584	The sliding scale altered in 1791. Limit price raised from 48s. to 50s.

Periods.	Prices of wheat per statute quarter. (£ s. d.)	Duties actually leviable on imported wheat. From foreign countries. (£ s. d.)	From British Plantations. (£ s. d.)	Explanatory remarks.
1795	3 14 2	0 0 6	0 0 6	'The second low duty.' Price above 54s. a quarter for foreign and above 52s. for Plantation wheat.
1796	3 17 1	,, 2 9	,, ,, 6	Two temporary imposts of 5 per cent. each on proceeds during 1797. Not added here to duty on Plantation wheat because result fractional. Duty 'first low duty' for foreign. Price between 50s. and 54s. (foreign), but above 52s. (Plantation). 'First low duty' for both. Plantation limit 48s. to 52s. 'Second low duty' for both.
1797	2 13 1			
1798	2 10 3	0 2 9	0 2 9	
1799	3 7 6	0 0 6	0 0 6	
1800	5 13 7	0 0 6	0 0 6	
1801	5 18 3	,, ,,	,, ,,	
1802	3 7 5	,, ,,	,, ,,	
1803	2 16 6	,, ,,	,, ,,	Sliding scale altered. High duty chargeable on foreign wheat when under 63s.; on Plantation when under 53s.
1804	3 0 1	1 4 3	,, ,,	
1805	4 17 10	0 0 6	,, ,,	N.B.—From 1803 to 1814 the 'temporary war duties' were levied, as well as the duties shown, at gradually increasing rates. These would make the 1804 duty on foreign corn about £1 7s. 4d. and the 6d. duty leviable at other periods from 7d. to 8d.
1806	3 19 0	,, ,,	,, ,,	
1807	3 13 3	,, ,,	,, ,,	
1808	3 19 0	,, ,,	,, ,,	
1809	4 15 7	,, ,,	,, ,,	
1810	5 6 2	,, ,,	,, ,,	
1811	4 14 6	,, ,,	,, ,,	
1812	6 5 5	,, ,,	,, ,,	
1813	5 8 9	,, ,,	,, ,,	
1814	5 13 11	Prohibited	Prohibited	
1815	3 4 4	Prohibited	Duty free	By the Act of 1815 foreign wheat was prohibited from use for home consumption when the price was under £4 a quarter, and Plantation wheat when the price was under 67s. (The goods might be imported and warehoused, but not delivered for home use.) If wheat were at the prices quoted or above, it was duty free.
1816	3 15 10	Duty free	,,	
1817	4 14 9	,,	,,	
1818	4 4 1	Prohibited	Prohibited	
1819	3 13 0	,,		
1820	3 5 7	,,		

Of course, the duties in this return are made to fit the average prices shown, and the same rule applies to the prohibitions, etc. For instance, it does not follow that *none* except the ' first low duty ' was paid in 1798, or that imported corn was prohibited from home use through *the whole* of 1820. The scale is merely illustrative, not absolute, as to the particular periods covered.

The reader should refer to pp. 1 to 8. He will perceive that high corn prices did not obtain till nearly the end of the eighteenth century, and that when they were firmly established only nominal duties were actually *collected*. Undoubtedly the alterations in the sliding scale in 1791 and 1804 helped to raise prices, and the wicked prohibitions under the Act of 1815 helped to keep them high. But from 1795 to 1815 high prices were more the result of an increase in population, the crowding of towns, war, and the incidental hampering of oversea traffic, etc., than of high duties. It will be observed that when the strain of actual war was removed the deadly contrivance of occasional prohibition was effected. This was purely a device to keep up rents.

No. 11. Extracts from ' Instructions to Scottish Collectors, 1707.' (*This book contains the whole scheme of Customs as performed in England, and applied to Scotland after the Union, with specimens of all the documents used by collectors.*)

' 1. You are to behave your self in a sober and discreet Manner, so as to give no occasion of Scandal or just Complaint.

' 2. You are not for your Self, nor for any other Person, directly nor indirectly to be concerned in Trade, Merchandise, or Shipping.

' 3. You are not to keep any Ale-House, Tavern, or House of Entertainment to divert you from the performance of your Duty and the Attendances of Her Majesties Service, in the Imployment wherewith you are intrusted, as the Law directs.

' 4. You are to keep your Residence in the Port where you are appointed Collector, and not to leave the same and your District.

' 7. In every Thing and Matter relating to the Duty of a Collector, you are to behave yourself with Prudence and

Circumspection, that Her Majesties Revenue may not suffer any Diminution, nor any Law relating to the Import and Export of Goods be violated or infringed.

' 27. That you may have a clear Idea and perfect Knowledge of the several Branches of Her Majesties Revenue committed to the Management of the Commissioners of Her Customs, and which consequently fall within your Collection, you are to consider the following Scheme, wherein you will find the Duties and Impositions, the Acts of Parliament, and the Pages in the Book of Rates thereto relating ranged in their proper Classes as follows :

Branches of the Revenue.	Acts of Parliament.	Page in the Book of Rates.
Customs { Subsidy outwards .. / ,, inwards .. / Petty-Custom .. / Additional Duty .. / Composition on Petty Seizures .. }	12 Charles 2ᵈ commencing	1
New or further Subsidy ..	9 and 10 William and Mary	514
One-Third Subsidy	2 and 3 Anne, since the Book of Rates	
Two-Thirds ,, ...	3 and 4 Anne, since the Book of Rates	
Impost on Wines and Vinegar	1ˢᵗ James 2ᵈ	334
Impost on Tobacco	1ˢᵗ James 2ᵈ	338
Impositions, 1690	2 William and Mary	366
Impositions, 1692	4 and 5 William and Mary	379
New Duty on Whale-Finns ..	9 and 10 William 3	572
New Duty on Coffee, &c. ..	3 and 4 Anne, since the Book of Rates	
New Additional Duty on Coffee, &c., and drugs ..	3 and 4 Anne, since the Book of Rates	
Second 25 per Cent. on French goods	} 7 and 8 William 3	442
Coynage ..	18 Charles 2ᵈ	292
Prysage ..	12 ,,	1
Butlerage ..	,, ,,	205
Excise on Salt { Inwards .. / Outwards .. }	} 5 Anne, by the Act for the Union	

THIS IS THE FOUNDATION AND RULE OF YOUR BUSINESS.

' 31. You are to observe an Act 5ᵗʰ Anne, Cap 27, Intituled, An Act for continuing several Subsidies, and for ascertaining the Wine Measure, &c., whereby the Law directs that a tun of Wine is to contain 252 Gallons, each Gallon consisting of 231 cubical Inches, so that for collecting the duties on Wines you and the Officers imployed about the Customs are to study the Art of Gaging, wherein the Officers of the Excise will give you some Information when desired, with their Conveniency.*

' 33. With these Gentlemen who have the Inspection of your District, you may concert the Signals which they are to give to your Waiters and Tydesmen, and which the latter are to return for conveying speedy Information of any Ship or Vessel hovering on the Coast, or for the discovery of any other illegal Design.'

' The instructions conclude thus :

' You are to take Notice that the Laws which are now the Standard of Trade and Duties have been constructed with very great Tenderness towards the fair Trading Merchants, with great Encouragements to Industry, and that the severities intended are for the prevention of Frauds, which can only be committed by Men of bad Principles, and destructive to the Common good, who by eluding the Law would render the Supplies Ineffectual, &c.

' By these Laws you are entrusted with the Administration of Oaths, which you are to Execute with Reverence, in a decent manner, that the people who Swear may consider the Consequence of an Oath, in Attesting the Omniscient God to be the Judge of their Deposition.

' **** You have an Essential Encouragement from the

---

* Defoe, in his ' History of the Union of Great Britain,' states as follows : 'Considering the Ignorance for the most part of their officers ' (of the Scottish Excise) 'in the Art of Gauging, and in the new methods of taking the Worts and making a Charge, considering the Difficulty of satisfying and convincing the People who were to pay the Duty, that they had no wrong done them, no Duty' (this in reference to the excise duty on ale) ' was ever settled with so little Noise.'

(It would seem from this that the Scottish customs men would not gain much assistance from the excisemen during the first few years after the Union.)

He also states thus : ' At the beginning the People thought every Seizure of prohibited Goods a Violence upon their Properties, and clamoured at the English and the Union, as if the Union had been made not to bring them under good Government, but to leave them without Government. Upon this Notion they fell to running of Brandy in particular at that prodigious Rate that some thousands of small Casks of Brandy was in Spight of all the Vigilance of Officers secretly supposed to be put on Shore out of the first Dutch Fleet that came to Scotland after the Union, and when the Officers made Seizure of several Parcels the Rabbles by violence rescued them again.' (See also ' The King's Customs,' vol. i., pp. 163, 164.)

Reasonable Hopes of such further Advancement as you shall be found capable of, upon the Representation of your Behaviour to the Lord High Treasurer of Great Britain, who is a Lover of Method and an Encourager of Virtue,' &c.

Specimens from the Instructions. 1. An entry for Plantation tobacco—20,000 lbs. (The duty is 1^d a lb under the Old Subsidy, with a discount of 5 per cent. for prompt payment : under the New Subsidy the same less discount, with another discount of $2\frac{1}{2}$ per cent. : under the $\frac{1}{3}$ Subsidy, $\frac{1}{3}$ of the New Subsidy charge minus the discount, with another discount of $4\frac{1}{2}$ per cent. : under the Additional Duty branch the Old Subsidy less the discount, with another discount of $7\frac{1}{2}$ per cent. : under the Impost 3^d a lb. with a discount of 8 per cent. and another discount of 10 per cent. on the net. Complicated as this document may appear it is as nothing compared with entries during the early part of Geo. 3 reign.)

'LEITH. 25 *June*, 1707.

'In the *William* of Leith, George Smith Master, from Virginia, John Stuart Merchant.

	£ s. d.
Fifty Hogsheads of Tobacco containing Twenty Thousand Pounds Weight	83 06 08
(Signed) John Stuart Discompt 5 per cent. ...	04 03 04

	£ s. d.	£ s. d.		£ s. d.
			Old Subsidy ..	79 03 04
New Subsidy ..	79 03 04 ⎫			
Disct 2½ p Cent.	01 19 07 ⎭ 77 03 09		New Subsidy ..	77 03 09
⅓ Subsidy ..	25 14 07 ⎫			
Disct. 4½ p. Cent.				
for prompt	⎬ 24 11 06		⅓ Subsidy ..	24 11 06
payment ..	01 03 01 ⎭			
Additional Duty	79 03 04 ⎫			
Disct. 7½ p. Cent.	05 18 09 ⎭ 73 04 07		Additional Duty	73 04 07
Impost ..	250 00 00 ⎫			
Disct. 8 p. C. ..	20 00 00 ⎭		Impost ..	207 00 00
	230 00 00 ⎫			*£461 3 2'
Disct. 10 p. c. for				
prompt pay-	⎬ 207 00 00			
ment	23 00 00 ⎭			

* If the goods were bonded the payments would be: O.S., £79 3s. 4d. ; N.S., the same ; ⅓ Subsidy, £26 7s. 9d. ; A.D., £79 3s. 4d. ; Impost, £250 ; Total, £513 17s. 9d. Only one discount would be allowed, that on the Old Subsidy, which branch would be paid before the goods were put in bond. (The bonding would be in the merchant's own warehouse.)

Entry for Deals, Tar, and Sables.

'Leith.   25th *June*, 1707.

'In the *Thomas* of Leith, John Gibson Master, from Drammen ; Thomas Stirling, Merchant.

		£	s.	d.
TS. Sixty Hundred Norway Deals		15	00	00
Twenty Lasts Tar		2	10	00
T S. Ten Timber Sables containing forty skins each Timber		15	00	00
		32	10	00
Discount at 5 per cent. ..		01	12	06

	£	s.	d.
Old Subsidy ..	30	17	06
New Subsidy ..	30	17	06
⅓ Subsidy ..	10	05	10
⅔ ,, ..	20	11	08
Impost 1690 ..	28	02	06
Impost 1692 ..	15	04	08¼

	£	s.	d.
Impost 1690 on Deals	30	00	00
Discount at 6¼ per cent.	1	17	06
	£28	2	06

£135 19 8¼

		s.	d.
Impost 1692 on Tar ..	01	05	00
Sables	15	00	00
	16	05	00
Discount at 6¼ per cent.	01	00	03¾
	£15	04	08¼

Thomas Stirling.'

(Note that in the above the system of discounting differs. From 1707 to 1780 the methods gradually grew more complicated, till few officers could be found able to deal with the whole of the varying duties chargeable on goods.)

No. 12. *Board to collector and controller of Blackney, as to the new Quarantine Act applying to pilots. From the Letter-Book of Blackney.*

'Gentlemen,
'The Rt Hon the Lords Commrs of her Maties Treasy a Lettr from my Lord Dartmouth with one of his Lordp from the Lords of the Admty wherein they propose that Pilots goeing on board Ships that come from Places infected should perform Quarantain in the said ships, because the little boats they usually sail in cannot bear ye sea in bad weather, and my Lord Dartmouth having signified her Maties pleasure to have this method observed, you are in pursuance of their Lordps Directions to take care that her

Maties pleasure therein signified be duly complyed with accordingly : And you are further to take notice that it is her Maties pleasure (as their Lord^ps have acquainted us) that the officers of the Customs and ye command^rs and other Officers of her Maties ships should be assisting to each other in ye due performance of ye Quarantain

'YOUR LOVING FRIENDS.

'Custom H°, London.
    19th December 1710.'

No. 13. *Extracts from Scottish Board's Minutes.*

' 16th Jan^y, 1723/4.

'The Moderator of the Presbytery of Stranraer having made a complaint to ye Board by his letter of ye 13th inst. against James Welsh, Tidesman, in that district, who for ill deportment had been excommunicated & afterwards imprisoned by ye Civill magistrate, from whence he had made his Escape & thereby render'd himself incapable of doing duty for the future : the Commissioners direct that he be dismist ye Service.'

' 28th Feby, 1723/4

'The Commrs proceeded on ye examination they yesterday began with respect to ye information given by Geo Laverock, and Thomas Grier, tidewaiter at Leith, being accordingly interrogated in relation to a charge that was against him of suffering a considerable quantity of paper to be run out of Fowler's ship from Holland in April last, he confess'd that he had conniv'd at that fraud, for wch he had rec^d of Mr. Marjoribanks, Merch^t, a Guinea, and some shillings in silver.

'Thomas Morehouse, also tidewaiter at Leith, was also charg'd with having, in concert with James Phelean, Wm Moncrieff, & ye said Laverock, suffer'd 14 hhds of wine to be run from on board ye *Neptune*, John Nairn master, from Bilbao, in Feby, 1718-9 : as reward for which Laverock said he got 4 guineas for his share & supposes ye others receiv'd as much.

'That Morehouse, Phelean, & he ye said Laverock, finding a box of Hungary water bottles in ye same ship, under ye cabin sole, they bargain'd wth ye Master to carry it on shore, wch they did accordingly in their pockets to James Lundie's

No. 14. *Statement illustrating the method of dividing the proceeds of Customs seizures in the early part of the eighteenth century.*

Goods.	*Cause of Forfeiture.*	*Distribution of Proceeds.*
Tobacco	For being planted in Great Britain	$\frac{1}{3}$ to Crown ; $\frac{1}{3}$ to seizer ; $\frac{1}{3}$ to the poor.
,, ...	,, ,, imported in illegal packages	$\frac{2}{3}$,, $\frac{1}{3}$,,
Cattle	,, ,, imported (importation prohibited)	$\frac{1}{2}$ to seizer (hide and tallow) ; $\frac{1}{2}$ to the poor (rest of carcase).
Ships	For importing cattle	$\frac{1}{2}$ to seizer ; $\frac{1}{2}$ to the poor.
Plantation goods	For being landed prior to deposit of duty	$\frac{3}{4}$ to Crown ; $\frac{1}{4}$ to seizer.
African goods	For irregularities as to ships or trade	$\frac{1}{3}$,, $\frac{1}{3}$,, $\frac{1}{3}$ to the African Co.
Alamodes or lustrings ..	For being imported otherwise than into London	$\frac{2}{3}$,, $\frac{1}{3}$,,
East India goods ..	For being imported by unlicensed persons	$\frac{1}{4}$ to seizer ; $\frac{3}{4}$ to the East India Co.
,, ,, ,, ...	For being landed without directors' warrant	$\frac{2}{3}$ to Crown ; $\frac{1}{3}$ to seizer.
Popish books	For being imported (prohibited)	$\frac{1}{3}$,, $\frac{1}{3}$,, $\frac{1}{3}$ to the poor.
Fish (other than stock-fish or live eels)	,, ,, ,, by aliens	$\frac{1}{2}$ to seizer ; $\frac{1}{2}$ to the poor.
Wool	,, ,, exported	$\frac{1}{3}$ to Crown ; $\frac{2}{3}$ to seizer.
,, ...	,, ,, imported from Ireland	$\frac{1}{2}$ to seizer ; $\frac{1}{2}$ to encouragement of Irish linen industry.
All goods seized by men-of-war		$\frac{1}{4}$ to Crown ; $\frac{1}{4}$ to commander ; $\frac{1}{4}$ to the officers ; $\frac{1}{4}$ to the crew.
All other goods seized ..		$\frac{1}{2}$ to Crown ; $\frac{1}{2}$ to seizer.

house, where they deliver'd them, and rec^d about twenty shillings for that service.

'That on board ye same ship ye abovenam'd officers, finding a parcell of french gloves & playing cards, they deliver'd ye same back to ye Master for a piece of money, but ye informant Laverock does not remember ye sume : but ye said Morehouse firmly insisting upon his innocency and ignorance of ye whole, notwithstanding Laverock, who was present, mention'd severall other circumstances to enforce his assertion & bring ye other to confession : yet as it was to no purpose, & ye board having good grounds from all ye concurring circumstances to look upon him as a person deeply guilty, and unfitt to be trusted for ye future, they resolved to dismiss him from ye Service.'

'Tuesday, 7th July, 1724.

'James Phelean, late tidewaiter at Leith, having made severall discoveries to ye Board of considerable frauds committed at that port, ye Soll^r is to pay him a guinea now & subsist him at ye rate of five shillings a week from this date till further order.

'George Laverock, late tidewaiter at Leith, having made a complaint to ye Board that John Jack & John Alexander, weighing porters at Leith, had abused and assaulted him, by reason of his having discovered severall frauds committed by ye officers at that port : the Comm^{rs} direct that the said two officers be dismist.'

'Wednesday, 10th February, 1724/5.

'The Board having rec^d advice from ye officers at Stranraer by their letter dated ye 6th inst that a ship of about 60 tons burthen was come in there, having on board of her one John Somervil of Glasgow & Ben- Cross of London, two masters of ships, together with 4 Sailors & 2 boys, wch said Somervil & Cross had at different times been taken by a Pyrate of 22 guns, who about a month ago gave them this ship, chiefly laden with oyle and fruit, wch vessel, by ye arms on her stern, appears to be a French one : The Commrs thereupon direct that my Lord Townshend have ye copy of ye said letter sent him, and that in ye mean time ye officers at Stranraer be directed to keep trusty tidesmen on board said ship, & to suffer no goods whatsoever to be taken on shore without first receiving ye Board's directions.'

'*Wednesday, 3ʳᵈ March, 1724/5.*

' The Commʳˢ having recᵈ letters from ye officers in Orkney & Caithness, relating to ye pyrate ship lately taken in ye Orkneys, and it appearing by yᵉ affidavits therein contain'd that severall merchants and others have been concern'd in trading with ye said pyrate & supplying her with necessaries and some ammunition : The Board immediately communicated ye contents of ye said letters to Mr. Grahame ye Judge Admirall & Mr. Sinclair his Majesty's Sollicitor, & it being a matter that immediately concerns ye former's office, such orders were dispatch'd by him as were found necessary upon that occasion, & sent under cover of ye Board's letter to ye officers at Inverness, to be by them forwarded by Express to ye respective places the Judge Admirall's severall warrants were directed to.'

No. 15. Scottish Board's Minutes on various acts of resistance of the revenue authorities, 1735-36.

'*Friday, 13ᵗʰ June, 1735.*

' Ordered : That Mr. Armour : Assistant Sollicitor, do without loss of time make up an account of his disbursements upon any matters under his direction & lay the same before the Board without any further delay & particularly the charges incurred on a prosecution before the Baillie of Cuningham agᵗ sundry persons for breaking open the Custom House of Irvine in July 1733.

' The Surveyor-Genˡ and collector of Inverness to be directed forthwith to send up copys of the severall warrants of commitment of the Officers of the Customs & three Soldiers who are imprisoned in Relation to the deceas'd Hugh Fraser, merchᵗ there, who was killed by one of the soldiers when out in the King's boat to protect the officers, and Letters being to go from my Lord Advocate & the Sherriff to admit them all to bail except McAdam, one of the soldiers who is charged with having killed Fraser. The Surveyʳ Genl and Collector is to become surety for them and to defray the charge thereof, & likewise agreeable to the Sheriff's letter to get McAdam liberated from the Stocks or Irons, so that he may only Remain in prison in an open & free manner till he is tryed by due Course of Law, and the said Surveyʳ Genl & collector are in the mean time to furnish him with comfortable Subsistance, & to acquaint the Commander of the Troops that the Board will protect him.'

(It appears that Fraser was killed in attempting a rescue, and the magistrates committed the Customs men and soldiers concerned to prison pending trial, and loaded McAdam with irons. Both he and the others received the royal pardon. It is evident that the troops had been sent to Inverness in consequence of the collector's complaint, quoted at pp. 230, 231, vol. i., ' The King's Customs.')

' Thursday, 2ⁿᵈ Octobʳ, 1735.

' Mr. Armour having acquainted the Board that there will be occasion for Mr. Townson, land-wr, and the boatmen of Inverness (now here) to attend again to give evidence in the Court of Admiralty in the Cause against McKinnen and others, for assaulting them, &c., and they being apprehensive that in case of their return to Inverness, they may be hindred from being here in time to give their evidence, the Commrs direct,' &c.

(It is likely that the officers feared they would be prevented by force if they returned to Inverness, so they were put on duty at Aberdeen, and the Aberdeen boatmen sent to Inverness.)

' Friday, 3ʳᵈ Octobʳ.

' The collector of Dundee having acquainted the Board that James Young and James Laird, tidesmen, who had been boarded on ye ship *Good Intention* from Norway, were in the night time deforc'd by the mate & ship's crew, & a considerable quantity of goods run out of her, a prosecution,' &c., &c.

' Monday, 6ᵗ Octobʳ.

' The Board being acquainted that Robert Bryson, Shipmaᵗʳ, is pursuing Mr. McGill, Tide Surveyor at Kirkaldy, for the Subsistence of a party of Soldiers station'd on board the said Bryson's ship, Mr. Armour is to take care to defend Mr. McGill at the Crown's Expence.'

(The soldiers had been quartered on the ship, and the captain brought an action to recover the cost of their keep.)

' Wednesday, 26ᵗʰ Novembʳ, 1735.

' The collector of Kirkaldy has leave to come hither (to Edinburgh) for six days, and John William Cosens, Tidesman there, for Twelve days.'

(The Custom House at Kirkaldy had been broken into, and a sum of money stolen. Cosens was suspected of connivance.)

'Thursday, 22ⁿᵈ Jan. 1735/6.

'Mr. Armour having this day reported : That from the examination of the severall persons who were Guilty or accessory to the breaking open and stealing a sum of money out of the Custom House at Kirkaldy, & particularly one Wilson, that there is good ground to believe John William Cosens, Tidesman, has been in the knowledge of the Robbery, and discovered the place where the money was lodged, but that there is not sufficient evidence for proseeuting him criminally, in which his Maj^{tys} Soll^r Genl, Mr Areskine ' (Erskine) ' concurring, the Board agreed to his being forth-with dismist the Service, &c. The precognitions taken at Kirkaldy, and by his Maj^{tys} said Sollr Genl were put into Mr Armour,s hands, for him to proceed against Millar and Hunter.'

(It is just possible that the generally-accepted account of Wilson's theft of Customs money from the Kirkaldy collector at Pittenweem may be incorrect. It is evident that Wilson— whose execution caused the Porteous riots—was charged with robbing the Kirkaldy Custom-house.)

'Friday, 9ᵗʰ March, 1735/6.

'A Petition of Robert Hay, collector of Kirkaldy, to the Lords Comm^{rs} of the Treasury, praying Relief touching the Loss of £96 12s. 7½d. Stole out of the Custom House, was this day delivered in at the Board, and read together with their Ldps. reference thereupon.'

No. 16. *Board's Letter to the collector and controller of Hull, apprising them of a smuggling vessel's arrival on the coast,* 1735-36. *From the Letter-Book of Hull.*

' GENTLEMEN,
    ' Inclosed you will receive Extract of a letter from Mr. Southgate, Commander of a vessell in the service of Wells, dated 11th inst : Representing that a Brigantine belonging to Berwick, William Wilkinson, master, from Burdeaux, laden with Wine and Brandy, being hovering upon that Coast, and that it appears to him the said Cargoe is intended to be run in this Kingdom, and as the said vessell sailed for the Yorkshire Coast with a design to run her cargoe : We direct

you to give Notice thereof with a description of the Vessell to the severall officers belonging to your Port, with directions to keep a careful look out for the said Vessell and to use their utmost endeavours to prevent her running any Goods, giving us an acco^t of your Proceedings.

'Your loving Friends,

'J. STANLEY, J. EVELYN, B. FAIRFAX, R. CORBET.

'16th March, 1735/6.'

No. 17. Order sent by the Customs Secretary to all English ports.

'17th, Jany, 1740.

'Mr. Thomas Cartwell, an Officer at the port of Rye, having been lately murdered, and a Corporal and three Dragoons, whom he took to his assistance, very much wounded by the Smuglers, and a Considerable Quantity of Tea, which had been seized, rescued from them :

'You are to acquaint all the Officers at your Port that when ever they shall go out to make seizures they are to take care to have a sufficient Military force wth them, in case there are any forces quartred in y^r Parts, for which purpose they are to wait upon the Commanding Officer and acquaint him with the nature of the Service, & consult him as to the force necessary for their assistance, that the Service may not suffer in the manner it has done on the late occasion, which I have in Command to signify to you.'

No. 18. Extracts from the 'Coast Cocket Book' of Dartmouth, 1745, showing coastwise traffic from various ports.

[Cover.]   'The Port of Exeter.

'A Blank Book containing six leaves for the Customers and Comptrollers within Dartmouth, a member thereof.* Of all goods and merchandises to be carried between port and port and for certificates from the Feast of the Nat^y of our Lord God Anno 18 Regni Regis Georgii Secundi untill the Feast of St. John the Baptist then next following that is to say for the space of half a year.

'DARTMOUTH.'

* A member of Exeter.

[Within.] 'In the *Alexander* of Dartm^h, David Reeves Mr., pr. Cocq^t, 29th November last.   Dan Caudewell & Co.

' 4 trusses c^t 1540 ells German & Russia & 45 yards Brit^h Linnen.
20 casks ct 760 galls spirits.
6 hhds 3 casks 1 truss 2 boxes sugar.
2 pipes with staves.
2 dozen empty rundletts.
6 empty Pipes.
1 hhd glass and earthenware.
2 tons lead & shott.
3 bags & 1 pocket Hops.
43½ sacks Seeds.
3 butts 2 puncheons 3 barr^ls oil.
3 boxes 1 bottle 2 parcells 1 cake 4 bags 2 bask^ts 3 barr^ls oilmen's ware.

4 trusses 1 bundle haberdashery.
3 tons hemp.
30 cases Hard sope.
1 box 1 pottmanteau apparell.
2 barr^ls 1 bask^ett 1 box tin-monger's ware.
1 truss household goods.
2 half hhds 1 barrell porter.
3 topmasts, 3 yards, 4 tons cordage.
40 empty casks.
½ ton Cheese.
3 casks ct 80 galls Spirits.
12 quarters beans.
20 barrells Tarr.
2800 pipe-staves (From London).'

' 4th *March*, 1744/5.

'In the *Postboy* of Cowes Mich^s Grigg Mr., pr. Cocq^t 11th ultimo.   Turnpenny & Co.

' 2 Tons Barr Iron.
3 hampers, 1 bundle Ironware.
43 casks ct 1400 galls British Brandy.
1 cask ct 108 galls Rum.
1 caskett Snuff.
27 Crates Earthenware.
10 hhds 1 tierce refined Sugar.
½ butt Currants.
2 hhds Musco^do Sugar.
½ ton Barr Iron.
6 Boxes Tyn plates.
37 dozen Bottles.
1 box 4 Crates Glass & Earthen ware.

23 bags, 22 half bags Nails.
5 cwt. Shearmoulds.*
½ ,,   Steel.
40 barr^ls Tarr.

landed at Plymouth :

2 hhds musco^do Sugar.
10 hhds lump Sugar
35 bags Nails.
2 hampers Ironware.
½ butt Currants.
1 baskett Ironware.
2 pkges Glass (From Bristol).'

(Only six vessels arrived during the half-year with general cargo. Five of these were from London, one from Bristol. Three vessels arrived from Newcastle with coals, three from Sunderland, two from Swansea, and one from Llanelly. Ten vessels arrived from Milford with culm. One vessel left for Exeter carrying 14 puncheons duty-paid rum, with 2 casks brandy, 4 casks geneva, and 22 casks of rum. These last were seized goods, condemned in the Exchequer, and sent to Exeter for sale. She carried also 7 hogsheads cider, 2 chests lemons and oranges, and 3 casks blubber. Seven vessels left for London, the total of

* Planks used in shipbuilding.

their cargoes being 30 'pack-cloths' wool, which equals
97½ hundredweight; 1 pipe, 798 hogsheads, 3 puncheons, and
85 half-hogsheads cider; 35 quarters malt; 48 quintals dry
Newfoundland codfish, 16 bales serges; 842 quarters oats;
100 quarters barley; and 3 sailors' chests.)

Copy of cocket for 10 packages wool carried coastwise from Dartmouth to London.

'Know all Men by these Presents that we, *John Andrews of
Dover in the County of Kent, Marriner, and Saml Windeatt, of
Berry Pomroy in the County of Devon, Fellmonger,* are firmly
bound unto our Sovereign Lord *George the Second* in the Sum
of *Five Hundred and Forty-six Pounds* of good and lawful
money of Great Britain, to be paid to our said Lord the King,
his heirs and successors, to which certain Payment well and
truly to be made We bind ourselves and every of us jointly
and severally for and in the whole our Heirs, Executors,
Administrators, and Assigns, and every of them by these
Presents: Sealed with our Seals dated the *twenty-fifth* day of
January in the *eighteenth* year of the Reign of our Sovereign
Lord *George the Second,* by the Grace of God, &c.

'The Condition of this Obligation is such. That if *Ten
pack-cloths at Thirty-two hundred and two quarters of a hundred
w^t Raw British Wooll Consigned to Samuel Ruggles of Bocking
in Essex* mentioned in an Entry made in the Custom House
in the Port of *Dartmouth* the Day of the date above written
in the name of *Saml Windeatt* and laden in the Ship or Vessel
called the *Endeavour of Dov^r Jno Andrews Mr for Lond^n*
be discharged and laid on land in the aforesaid Port of *London,*
or in some Port or Creek within Great Britain, or any of the
Dominions thereof, and in no other Place, and if the aforesaid
John Andrews shall within six months next after the day of
the date hereof bring a true Certificate from the Officers of
His Majesty's Customs of the Port, Creek, or Place, where
he shall happen to discharge or land the said Goods, certifying
that the said Goods are there discharged and laid on the Land,
unto the Officers of His Majesty's Customs in the said Port
of *Dartmouth*: That then this present obligation to be void,
or else to remain and be in full Force and Virtue.

'Sealed and Delivered in the presence of

'WM. COWELL.   JOHN ANDREWS.
THOS. SKINNER.   SAM^L WINDEATT.'

Certificate of Landing of the above Goods.

'London. Know ye that Samuel Windeatt hath landed in this port ten Cloaths raw wool marked numbered and weighing as on the back hereof. Containing Thirty-three hundred three quarters and seven pounds weight,

Coast. out of the *Endeavour,* Mr. John Andrews, from Dartmouth, as by Cocq^t thence, dated 25th Jany 1744: What security you have taken in that behalf you may release: Given by the officers of the Great Customs, dated 20th February, 1744. Eighteenth year King George the Second.

'H. Lewis, Cust^{mr}. T. Player, D. Compt^r.'

(Document endorsed with coastwaiters' account of reweighing. This document went to Dartmouth with the cocket. The Dartmouth officers then endorsed the cocket, and cancelled the bond.)

No. 19. Scottish Board's Minute on a 'relanding' of dutiable goods, which had been shipped for foreign parts (a kind of smuggling prevalent in Scotland).

'*Wednesday, 10th April,* 1745.

'The Collector and Comptroller of Anstruther having transmitted to the Board a copy of a report made there the 19th of last month by James Redlay, master of the ship *Ann & Cathrine,* of Leith, for Hamburgh in Germany : viz. :

Goods loaded at Leith.
40 tons coals.

Loaded at Anstruther.
103 Ankers containing 988 gallons of brandy.
2 ,, ,, 19 ,, ,, geneva.
1 box ,, 74 lbs Bohea tea.
2 cannisters ,, 20 ,, ,,

*Reported at Leith for foreign Parts.
1 Anker & 3 half-ankers of foreign spirits.
2 Casks of sugar.
5 bundles of tea.
2 ,, coffee berries.*

---

* The master had entered Leith with foreign spirits, sugar, tea, and coffee, probably shipped in England. He then loaded coals at Leith, and went to Anstruther, where he took in brandy, geneva, and tea. He cleared out for foreign, and two days later the ship was found at Burntisland, with nothing on board but coals.

' And acquainted them the said Master sailed from thence the same day he made the above report, and Mr. James Patterson, tide surveyor at Leith, having informed the Board that the said ship came into Burntisland harbour on the 21st of the said month at 12 o'clock at noon, having only coals on board, and the Sollicitor having reported that the master should be prosecuted for treble the value of the goods run, upon the statute 8th Ann : Resolved, that the Sollicitor do proceed accordingly.'

No. 20. *Scottish Board's Minute upon conduct of one Porteous, a tidewaiter (possibly a relative of the subject of the Porteous Riots).*

' *Tuesday, 30th April,* 1745.

' The Commissioners having considered the charge given by their order to Francis Porteous, Tidewaiter at Leith, founded upon a complaint signed by Mr. James Patterson, tide-surveyor at Leith, John* Anderson & Thomas Vernon, Land-carriage waiters at the City gates of Edinb^r, then acting as tidewaiters at Leith, that the said Francis Porteous, being stationed on the 24th instant upon the *Janet* of Leith, John Watt Master, loaded with wine, he left his duty and went on shoar with the Master and several of the Sailors to drink with them, and returned the worse for Liquor.

' That he Spirited up the Sailors against the said Anderson & Vernon, who were joined with him on Duty on board the said Vessel, and threatened to throw them over Board : And having likewise considered the said Porteous's answers to the said Charge, the observations of the Collector and Comptroller of Leith thereupon, and he having advanced nothing Satisfactory in his Vindication, and the Collector and Comptroller having reported that he is a dangerous Officer, and further, he having been formerly guilty of Sundry Misdemeanours in the Execution of his Duty, and excused upon promises to be exact and diligent in doing his duty for the future : Resolved, that he be dismissed, and his Deputation called in to be cancelled.'

* Anderson and Vernon had previously complained of one John Cunningham, that he had repeatedly beaten and assaulted them.

No. 21. Various Minutes by the Scottish Board, exemplifying the effect on Customs business, etc., of the rebellion in 1745.

'*Monday, 9th September, 1745.*

'Mansfeldt Cardonnel, Esq., in the Chair.

'The Secretary laid before the Board a letter from Mr. Lowe with the warrant of the Lords of the Treasury for—
'Alexander Shank, Surveyor of the Customs at Kirkaldy.'

(The report breaks off here, and no further record appears till November 29, 1745. Gardiner was defeated at Collbrig on September 16. The Pretender occupied Holyrood on the 18th, and left early in November. It appears that the Commissioners of Customs left off work some time before the city was captured, and did not resume till some time after the Pretender was across the Border and well on his way to Derby.)

'*Friday, 29th November, 1745.*

'Richard Somers, Esq., in the Chair.

'Received several letters and directed answers thereto.

'*Monday, 2nd December, 1745.*

'John Campbell, Esq., in the Chair.

'The Commissioners considered the several letters received during the Interuption of Business by the Rebels Entering the Town, and directed answers to such Ports as the Rebels are not in possession of.

'*Tuesday, 3rd December, 1745.*

'John Campbell, Esq., in the Chair.

'The Commissioners received a letter from Mr. Scrope, with a copy of one from the Duke of Newcastle, signifying his Majesty's pleasure that Directions should be sent to the officers of the Customs in the several ports to stop and search all Soldiers which shall arrive from Holland, whether they have passes or discharges from the respective regiments in the service of the States-General, to which they may have belonged, or not, and to detain them in safe custody till further orders, there being reason to apprehend that many of them have deserted with a design to pass into this kingdom in order to join the Rebels.

'Thursday, 19th December, 1745.

' Richard Somers, Esq., in the Chair.

' Received the establishments for the officers employed in the Customs and Salt Duty for Michaelmas quarter, 1745, warranted by the Lords Commissioners of the Treasury.

' The Rebels having retreated back into Scotland, and being within a few days' march of this Town, and Business thereby interrupted ; The books and papers belonging to the Custom House, formerly lodged in the Castle, and brought down from thence after the Rebels evacuated this town, are again to be carried up for Security.'

(No further entry appears till February 12, 1745-46.)

' Lord Rosse in the Chair ' (none else present except Somers).

' Ordered that the several officers have notice to bring from the Castle the Books and Papers belonging to their respective offices, deposited there for Security during the Rebellion.

' That a Circular letter be sent to the several ports, requiring the principal officers to enquire in the most expeditious, particular, full, and impartial manner, into the Conduct and Behaviour of the Inferiour Officers, during the Unnatural and Horrid Rebellion, and to report the same to the Board without delay.'

(Work went on as usual. The Battle of Culloden was fought on April 16.)

'Wednesday, 9th April, 1746.

' Alexander Arbuthnot, Esq., in the Chair.

' The Supervisor of the Salt Duty at Prestonpans having transmitted to the Board an account of the Officers and Watchmen in that collection who continued to act under the Rebels, the same was returned for the Collector and Supervisor to give the matter in Charge to the respective Officers, and to send it back with the Officers' answers, and their observations, for the Consideration of the Board.

'Tuesday, 6th May, 1746.

' John Campbell, Esq., in the Chair.

' The Lord Justice Clerk having transmitted to the Board a Memorial and paper, a part containing sundry regulations and directions for discovering such persons as have been

concerned in the Rebellion, and desired them to give direc-
tions accordingly to all the officers under their management :
Resolved : That a copy of the said Memorial and separate
Paper be sent to all the ports.

' Thursday, 15th May, 1746.

' Alexander Arbuthnot, Esq., in the Chair.

' The Commissioners having received sundry affidavits
against James Rannie, King's Couper at Leith, that he was
aiding and assisting to the Rebels, particularly by Pressing
Persons, by virtue of an order from the Young Pretender's
Secretary, to drive their Baggage, and it further appearing
that he has not produced a certificate of his qualifying to the
Government according to law, though frequently required
so to do, and he having been formerly suspended for neglect
of duty : Resolved, that the said James Rannie, for the
above reasons, be dismissed till he clears himself before proper
judges, to the satisfaction of the Board, &c.'

(On June 18, 1746, the Board resolved that proceedings
should be taken against certain persons who acted as sellers
of the goods in the King's Warehouse, and others who received
money for the said sales and handed it over to the rebels.
On July 10 they dismissed thirteen officers at Prestonpans
for having acted under the rebels. Many other officers were
charged.)

' Monday, 28th July, 1746.

' Mansfeldt Cardonnel, Esq., in the Chair.

' The Lord Justice Clerk having by a letter of this date
signified to the Board that he has received intelligence that
the Pretender's Son has left the Highlands and is come
towards the Coast in order to make his escape, and desired
the Board to give orders to the officers at all the ports, except
those north of Dundee, to lay an embargo on all shipping,
&c. &c.'

(On August 11 the Board allowed James Robertson
£2 10s. ' for entering in a Book lists of Persons concerned in
the Rebellion.')

' Monday, 4ᵗʰ August, 1746.

' Richard Somers, Esq., in the Chair.

' The Lord Justice Clerk having signified to the Board that the Information that the Pretender's Son had left the Highlands and was come towards the Coast to make his Escape by Shipping proves uncertain, and desired that the Embargo laid in consequence of the said Information may be taken off : Resolved, that directions be immediately sent to the several Ports accordingly.

' Wednesday, 8ᵗʰ October, 1746.

' John Campbell, Esq., in the Chair.

' The Right Honorable the Earle of Albemarle Commander in Chief of his Majesty's Forces in Scotland having signified that he has received Information that many of the Rebels of the first Rank are still lurking upon the East Coast of Scotland waiting the opportunity of Escaping in some Vessel from the Ports on the said Coast, and desired the Board to give directions to the several officers of the Customs stationed at those ports in the strictest manner to search all Outward Bound vessels of whatever Size, least any Rebels should be concealed on them, and also to make Inquiry where such Rebels may be lurking in order to their being apprehended, &c.

' Thursday, 18ᵗʰ December, 1746.

' Lord Rosse in the Chair.

' Considered the Petition of Mr. James Patersone, Tide Surveyor at Leith, setting forth his Services during the late Rebellion, and Copys of the certificates annexed of the Generals, Sir John Cope, Handasyde, and Guest, Admiral Byng, and his Majesty's late Advocate and Sollicitor General. of those Services to the Government. The Board are of opinion it is not in their Power to Reward him out of the Revenue, but resolve to Present Mr. Patersone to the Lords of the Treasury for the first suitable Vacancy.

' Thursday, 29ᵗʰ January, 1746-7.

' Richard Somers, Esq., in the Chair.

' The Collector and Comptroller of Borrowstoness having in their letter of the 23ʳᵈ instant given the Board an Account of some Rebels being apprehended on board a Ship bound for Holland, the same was laid before the Justice Clerk the 25ᵗʰ instant.'

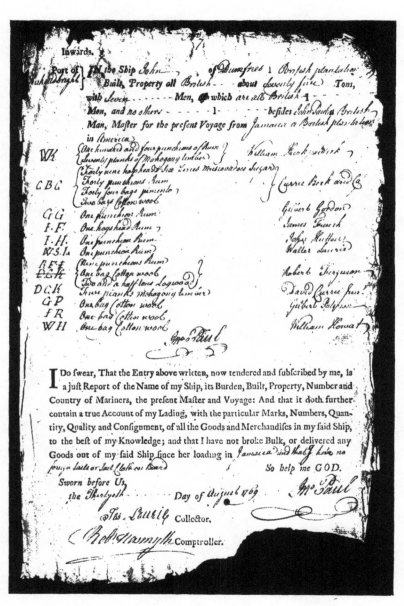

FACSIMILE OF REPORT OF THE 'JOHN,' OF DUMFRIES. JOHN PAUL
('PAUL JONES'), MASTER (1769).

To face p. 439.

'*7th April,* 1909.

'The signatures which appear on the reports of the *John*, of Dumfries, are those of a person much celebrated in naval history. John Paul was born at Kirkbean in 1747. His father, John Paul, had three other sons, one of whom, William Paul, was adopted by an elderly Scotsman named Jones, who had settled in Virginia. John Paul, senior, died in 1767, and was buried in Kirkbean churchyard, his son John erecting a tombstone to his memory.

'John Paul, junior, went to sea at an early age, and eventually became captain of the *John*, of Dumfries (by Buell erroneously called the *John* of Kirkcudbright). This vessel belonged to Currie, Beck, and Co., a Scottish firm of ship-owners located at Whitehaven. (Buell gives the title of the firm as " Donald Currie, Beck, and Co.," and makes reference to a vessel named the *Grantully Castle*, of which John Paul eventually became master. It must not, however, be thought that this was the source of the firm of to-day that bears the name of " Donald Currie," and has recently had a ship called the *Grantully Castle*. Inquiries have elicited that the firm of Donald Currie and Co. is quite modern.)

'On one of the voyages indicated in the accompanying reports, John Paul had occasion to strike a mutinous sailor. On arrival at the Plantations the man died, and John Paul was tried at Tortola for the offence and acquitted. On his arrival at Whitehaven he was again put upon trial and acquitted. One of the reports (1769) bears endorsement to the effect that the *John* went on to Whitehaven to complete discharge. (Buell states that she was at Whitehaven in 1770 ; and the reports show that after the 1770 trip John Paul was no longer master. Therefore, it may have been that the vessel, *in 1770*, after discharging her cargo at Kirkcudbright, went to Whitehaven to load or to complete loading.)

'The accounts of John Paul's career in 1771 differ. Buell states that he became captain of the *Grantully Castle*, trading to Lisbon, Madeira, East Indies, and the Plantations, but in the " National Dictionary of Biography " it is stated that he spent a considerable period of that time in smuggling between the Isle of Man and the Solway Firth. It appears he was in Virginia in 1773, and found that his brother William had but a few hours to live. William had succeeded to the estate left by Jones, and in the will was a provision that John should succeed to the estate at William's death, on condition that he assumed the name of Jones. Thus he became a Virginian planter, and thenceforth signed himself " Paul Jones."

' When the War of Independence broke out, " Paul Jones " joined the American Navy, and eventually became captain of the *Ranger*. His exploits as a naval commander are well known and quite extraordinary. There can be no doubt that he possessed talent, courage, and sincerity in their highest and most original forms, but he is stated to have been exceedingly hasty and irritable, and much disposed to quarrel. When he left the American Navy he secured a command in the Russian, which he had to resign, evidently through the jealousy and undermining tactics of other Russian commanders.

' He had, for some reason or other, a deadly hatred of the British, whom he repeatedly stigmatizes in his letters as an arrogant and faithless race ; and it is noticeable that most of his depredations were committed near the scenes of his boyhood. But he was ardently attached to the French, and they repaid his attachment by many favours and much " lionizing." He died in Paris, of dropsy of the heart, in 1792, and was buried in Père la Chaise, " in a shroud, without uniform or trappings of any kind." Principally through the instrumentality of President Roosevelt, his remains were removed to America in 1905, and interred in the crypt of the chapel of the Naval Academy at Annapolis.

' He is described as about 5 feet 7 inches in height, exceedingly swarthy, but with handsome features, and remarkably well built.'

(The above has been extracted from the Customs Library Memoranda.)

No. 22. Extracts from ' The Annual Register ' (1782 *to* 1802).

' *Feb.* 15*th*, 1782.

' Yesterday was tried, before the Earl of Mansfield in the Court of King's Bench at Guildhall, a cause of general concern. A merchant of Flushing brought an action against a merchant of this city for the recovery of the amount of three bills of exchange given by the defendant for tea sold to the plaintiff, and delivered at Ostend to the defendant's order : the defence was that the tea never came to the defendant's hand, but was seized as run goods, therefore the plaintiff was liable to the loss : the defendant went upon two other points of law, namely, that the plaintiff could not apply for justice, as the act of selling the tea was a fraud upon the revenue : also that if the tea had actually been delivered the plaintiff was not entitled to recover. The noble judge in his charge to the jury remarked that Flushing and Ostend were the most famous ports for smuggling. If the jury considered the tea to be sold for the purpose of being smuggled to England they would find for the defendant. He observed that the East India ships were the only bottoms of conveyance of tea to England* : besides it was proved that the plaintiff kept boats and horses to convey tea to the coast of England. The jury found for the defendant, and thereby made the notes void.

' *Jany.* 10*th*, 1785.

' The following facts relative to the seizing and burning of the smugglers' boats may be depended on : advice was sent to Mr. Pitt that the severity of the season had occasioned the smugglers to lay up their craft, and a fine opportunity offered for the destroying them if sufficient force could be procured to intimidate the smugglers from attempting a rescue. Mr. Pitt sent to the War Office, and required a regiment of soldiers to be at Deal on a certain day. He was told it could not be complied with. His answer was it must, and a regiment was immediately marched. But the commanding officer found on his arrival that the people of the town, having some intimation of the business, had advised the publicans to pull down their signs, in order that the soldiers might have no quarters. They took the advice, and no quarters were to be had. A large barn at a small distance presented itself as an eligible place, and the quartermaster rode off to the landlord, who refused to let it on any other terms than for two years certain. The officer took it, marched the men in, and then with very much difficulty procured them some provisions. The next day Lieut. Bray received orders to prepare some cutters to hover off the beach, and the soldiers were all drawn out. The inhabitants, not imagining what was going to be done, thought the cutters were to embark

---

* The East India Company, and persons licensed by them, were the only parties allowed by law to land tea. It is evident from the context that the plaintiff was an Englishman living at Ostend, who undertook to illegally land tea, and to convey it to the warehouses of London merchants.

the soldiers in, but to their surprise orders were given to the men to burn the boats, and, the force being so great, the inhabitants were obliged to remain silent spectators, and dared not attempt a rescue.

'*Sept.* 4*th*, 1787.

'*Leeds.*—The captain of the Swedish ship seized at Hull a few days ago for having a quantity of wool on board* has now made an open confession, and impeached several people in that neighbourhood, who it seems have carried on a large trade in this iniquitous practice for some time past. The mate of the ship has declared upon oath that he believes every Swede or Danish vessel that comes into the port of Hull smuggles wool abroad every voyage, both captain and crew being concerned in this business, and although the quantity in each ship is but trifling yet when it comes to be considered that there are twenty or thirty ships of those two nations which make three or four voyages to Hull annually, the wool smuggled even from the above port becomes considerable. Two other ships were also seized on Saturday last at Hull, with wool.'

(Most of the ' owling ' was done with the produce of Lincolnshire, Kent, and Sussex.)

'*June*, 1788.

' Mr. Tankard, a king's officer at Dartford, in consequence of an information, stopped the mail coach from Dover, and demanded from the guard the key of the trunk on which he sat. Being refused, he broke the trunk open, and two letter bags, with the brass labels ' Dover bags,' were found filled with lace. The coach and horses were seized.

'*Novr.* 29*th*, 1802.

' It may be recollected that about four years ago Johnson, the notorious smuggler, and another, were apprehended for obstructing and ill-using some revenue officers on the Sussex coast, and were committed to the New Gaol in the Borough to take their trial, but effected their escape in the most daring way, and remained at large notwithstanding £500 reward was offered for their apprehension. The first time Johnson

* For exportation (prohibited). It is apparent that English wool commanded a much higher price abroad than in England (see pp. 380, 387, 388).

was heard of after his escape was at the time the expedition to the Helder was meditated by Government, when he made an offer of his services to accompany the expedition, as from his smuggling connexions he had gained a complete knowledge of the Dutch coast : Government accepted of his services, and granted him a full pardon on his promise never to be again concerned in the smuggling trade. Johnson acquitted himself in this undertaking so much that he became a great favourite with several of the ex-ministers, and with the late Sir Ralph Abercrombie in particular. He afterwards contracted debts to the amount of £11,000, was arrested, and lodged in the Fleet prison nearly six months ago, where he remained. It appears before he became an inhabitant of the Fleet that in his pecuniary difficulties he again had recourse to smuggling, and he was capitally indicted on very strong grounds. Johnson, aware of these circumstances, turned his thoughts once more to making his escape, which he effected, notwithstanding he was confined in a strong room with two doors, or rather a double door, such as are generally fixed to the chambers in Inns of Court. At the top of each door was a panel instead of glass. It was by forcing out these two panels and creeping through the holes of them that Johnson was enabled to reach the gallery, and from thence the high wall that surrounds the prison, which it was impossible for him to have done without accomplices, as the panel of the outer door, it appears, had been forced from without. On his coming to that part of the wall next to Fleet Street, he found a rope ladder, which his friends on the outside had provided for him, and placed there agreeable to their plan. In the evening he arrived in a chaise and four on the coast of Brighton, where a lugger was in waiting for him in which he embarked, and arrived at Calais on his way to Flushing, after landing at Dieppe. He had a severe wound in the thigh, which he related to have received in the following manner : He had got on the top of the last wall that separated him from the street, 70 feet from the ground : a lamp was placed in the wall at some distance beneath the place where he was. He let himself down the wall exactly over the iron bar, and when he was forced to give up his hold he stretched his legs so as to fall astride. He had taken every precaution, and fell across the bar without overturning or hurting himself, but as he could not guard against an additional piece of iron it caught his thigh above the knee, and ripped it up almost to the top. At this moment he heard the watchman crying the hour, and had so much fortitude as to remain astride in that situation, bleeding most abundantly, till the watchman had gone his round without perceiving him. Immediately after he had the resolution to let himself down at all hazards.'

No. 23. *Statement of Net Produce of Plantation Customs in 1784.*

(New Brunswick, Port Roseway in Nova Scotia, and Cape Breton, had only been provided with Customs establishments during the current year. Therefore their accounts do not appear in the statement. Return from Tortola also not forthcoming.)

Colony.	Net after charges of management paid.	Deficit.	Remarks.
	£ s. d.	£ s. d.	
Jamaica		504 18 6	
Barbados ..	553 11 4		
Antigua	145 6 11¾		
St. Kitts ..	387 8 2		
Montserrat ..	81 17 3		
Nevis	33 6 8		
Newfoundland ..		354 4 8¼	
Grenada		208 9 7¾	
St. Vincent's ..		86 9 6¾	
Dominica ..		56 1 1¾	
Bahamas ..	81 16 6		
Bermuda ..	272 11 1¾		
Nova Scotia ..	36 18 11		
St. John's Islands		67 8 11	
Quebec		310 16 9¾	
		1,588 9 3¼	
		4 7 8¼	Balance accruing to the imperial revenue
	1,592 16 11½	1,592 16 11½	

(The above statement signed by ' J. Mills, for the Receiver-General: Joshua Powell, for the Controller-General: and J. Dalley, Supervisor of Payments.')

No. 24. Extracts from statement of the charges upon coal bought coastwise to the port of London during the latter part of the eighteenth century.

' This examinant saith: That he is one of the two clerks to the 15 sea-coal meters for the City of London, and has been so for 24 years ; he and the other clerk are appointed by them, and do all the official business except that all the warrants and duplicates are signed by one coal meter, and they hold a Board once every month, January excepted. He understands the appointment of the sea-coal meters is vested in the Corporation of the City of London, and the office, when vacant, is sold for the term of 21 years, by public auction, in the Chamber of London, for the benefit of the City : they have sold for upwards ot £6000, and the last was sold for about £5300, besides which every coal meter pays an annual sum of £100 to the Chamber of London.   The purchaser must be a freeman of London, and in case of his demise the term is vested in his representatives.

' EDWARD MILLSOM.

' *Nov. 1st and 2nd, 1784.*'

(The charges were : 1s. 2d. per chaldron (36 bushels, weighing, say, 30 hundredweight). This sum was paid at the meter's office ; 10d. of it went to the City as ' Orphans' Duty,' 3d. was divided among the meters, who were sinecurists, and the other 1d. went to their deputies, who did the actual measuring. Then the following duties were payable at the Custom House: 3s. and 2s. a chaldron as ' Coast Duties,' and further sums under the ' Church-building Duty,' only payable in the port of London, and the imposts of 1779 and 1782. Thus the total charges per chaldron were about 9s. 4d.)

No. 25. Extracts from a statement made by the official who acted as deputy to the London Collector outwards during the latter part of the eighteenth century.

' This examinant saith : That he is *chief* deputy to the duke of Manchester, who is the collector of the Customs outwards in the port of London.   The collector holds his office by patent, for life : he executes no part of the business.

' The collector is paid by a salary and fees : his salary is

£276 13s. 4d. a year, inserted in his patent : the fees are received by the deputy and paid over to the chief deputy, for the use of the collector : they amounted last year to about £1855.

'This examinant also saith : That he himself has no salary, but is paid by the deputy, out of the fees he receives from merchants,* £360 a year, and by the deputy of the Coast business, out of the like fees, £88 4s. od. a year, and from the Receiver of the Trinity Lights £9 9s. od.

'J. MELLER.'

'*June* 16, 1785.

No. 26. *Specimens of documents used in the payment of Customs duties just prior to the Consolidation of* 1787.

ENTRY FOR SIXTY PAIRS BELLOWS.

Branches.	Value of Parcel.			Duty.		
	£	s.	d.	£	s.	d.
Old Subsidy	10	0	0	0	10	0
New ,, ...	10	0	0	0	10	0
⅓ ,, ...	3	6	8	0	3	4
⅔ ,, ...	6	13	4	0	6	8
Subsidy 1747	10	0	0	0	10	0
Duty on Hides, &c.	45	0	0	2	5	0
Additional Duty on Hides, &c.	45	0	0	2	5	0
	130	0	0			
Impost, 1779	6	10	0	0	6	6
,, 1782	6	10	0	0	6	6
	143	0	0	7	3	0

(Explanation : The Old Subsidy value is the value as set in 1660. The duty on the old, new, ⅓, and ⅔ subsidies, and the Subsidy 1747 is at the rate of 5 per cent. on the value. The Duty on Hides, etc., is at the rate of 15 per cent. on the *genuine value* (£15) as declared by the importer. So is the Additional Duty on Hides, etc. The Imposts, 1779 and 1782, are at the rate of 5 per cent. on the total duties payable previous

* It is stated that the Collector's office was a sinecure, and evident that the chief deputy's was one as well.

to 1779. N.B.—The discounts for prompt payment had been abolished in 1781. Otherwise this document would have been almost unexplainable.)

STATEMENT OF DUTY PAYABLE ON TWENTY REAMS FRENCH ROYAL PAPER.

Branches.	Value of Parcel (Document).			Duty.		
	£	s.	d.	£	s.	d.
Old Subsidy	20	0	0	1	0	0
New ,, ...	20	0	0	1	0	0
⅓ ,, ...	6	13	4	0	6	8
⅔ ,, ...	13	6	8	0	13	4
Subsidy 1747	20	0	0	1	0	0
,, 1759	20	0	0	1	0	0
Impost 1692	100	0	0	5	0	0
French Duty	100	0	0	5	0	0
Duty on Soap, Paper, &c. ..	280	0	0	14	0	0
Add¹ Duty ,, ..	140	0	0	7	0	0
Duty on Paper, 1784 ..	140	0	0	7	0	0
	860	0	0			
Impost 1779	43	0	0	2	3	0
,, 1782	43	0	0	2	3	0
	£946	0	0	£47	6	0

(Explanation : The duty under the old, new, ⅓, ⅔, 1747, and 1749 subsidies is at the rate of 5 per cent. on the value as set in 1660. The Impost, 1692, is at the special rate of 25 per cent., the goods being French. The French Duty is the same. The Duty on Soap, Paper, &c., is a specific rate per ream according to quality = 10 reams atlas at 16ˢ, and 10 reams super royal at 12ˢ = in all £14. The Additional Duty is half this. The Duty on Paper, 1784, is a specific rate per ream = 10 Atlas at 10ˢ, and 10 super royal at 4ˢ = £7 in all. The imposts are at the rate of 5 per cent. on the produce of all duties previous to 1779.)

No. 27. *An account of the quantities of tobacco and snuff seized in England, Ireland, and Scotland in each year from 1789 to 1825 inclusive.* *

Year.	England—		Scotland—		Ireland—	
	Lbs. to- bacco.	Snuff.	Lbs. to- bacco.	Snuff.	Lbs. to- bacco.	Snuff.
1789	401,710	36,909	128,980	4,297	153,838	154
1790	149,964	19,943	79,426	2,303	209,981	328
1791	177,449	20,310	291,812	4,260	306,292	715
1792	144,563	8,937	89,408	2,168	233,054	247
1793	156,528	1,489	81,806	2,009	80,092	369
1794	137,868	4,896	50,922	2,231	39,216	18
1795	96,073	5,935	66,284	2,272	20,596	
1796	164,295	9,989	114,565	747	44,066	
1797	112,178	3,618	15,091	410	606	
1798	86,584	2,836	5,277	19	7,763	6
1799	92,182	4,702	4,091	101	31,542	83
1800	121,685	1,557	283,276	1,046	95,879	90
1801	133,752	3,235	5,254	130	62,138	
1802	108,134	10,016	24,167	28	83,907	147
1803	134,846	1,341	7,060	1,246	239,955	141
1804	117,597	1,527	2,276	1,860	237,987	46
1805	181,209	947	13,786	908	115,358	146
1806	43,601	606	3,928	1,969	195,267	407
1807	102,955	738	31,592	629	112,109	259
1808	21,607	2,867	3,422	621	120,119	140
1809	6,466	1,086	2,752	1,270	15,196	147
1810	21,862	360	2,136	462	50,640	73
1811	39,964	170	1,850	387	17,741	77
1812	99,871	383	1,312	759	52,905	154
1813	3,313	519	534	454	5,222	126
1814	4,331	855	723	270	6,099	77
1815	18,026	578	1,039	125	32,723	9
1816	18,005	2,941	930	248	22,314	35
1817	51,985	1,254	1,195	148	59,219	77
1818	64,295	521	6,007	352	43,884	93
1819	28,461	760	3,481	531	201,239	165
1820	73,247	1,445	35,415	1,850	883,971	179
1821	73,298	548	22,418	2,219	424,823	138
1822	72,378	3,338	80,914	5,026	525,466	12
1823	98,748	11,633	14,113	189	254,991	31
1824	97,969	12,509	1,884	579	282,035	60
1825	100,970	6,287	1,373	13	234,119	39

* This is not a complete account, yet it is the only one available. From 1789 to 1814 the English account does not include the London Customs seizures, the records previous to 1814 being destroyed by fire. From 1789 to 1797 the Irish account does not include the Excise seizures in Ireland, the records having disappeared.

(Remarks : The Irish record for 1797 and 1798 was affected by the rebellion. Undoubtedly the whole record for 1813 and 1814 was rendered imperfect by the burning of the London Custom-house. The immense increase in the seizure records of Ireland in 1819 and 1820 marks the establishment of the Coastguard. For the previous ten years smuggling on the south and west coasts of Ireland, by Americans especially, had been vast and unchecked. Note also the increase in the English and Scottish records in 1820-22. The English Coast Blockade was established in 1817, and the Scottish Coast-guard in 1819-20. *The rewards to seizing officers were increased* in 1820. All these new arrangements appear to have left their mark upon the seizure records.)

No. 28. Comparison from two accredited authorities of separate statements of Customs payments into Exchequer (Great Britain, 1802-06 ; United Kingdom, 1822-26).

(' No. 1 ' is accompanied by elaborate explanations as to the various disbursements from the gross receipts. ' No. 2 ' is quoted from a Parliamentary Return. The quoter heads it as a statement of ' Customs yield to the Exchequer,' which, if it means anything, must signify the actual payments into the Exchequer. Yet he states that the expenses of collection have not been deducted ! We have therefore deducted the said expenses from his account. It will be seen that if his statement had been accepted as a return of actual payments, the discrepancies would have been still more pronounced. It should also be stated that the account from which we have extracted ' No. 2 ' goes back to 1692, yet states that the returns for 1692-1706 are for Great Britain. It is to be assumed that ' England ' was meant.)

Year ending January 5 in—	No. 1.	No. 2.	
1802	£		£ 8,758,184
		Deduct charges of collection	523,588
	5,871,200		8,234,596
1803			7,698,958
		Deduct ..	549,614
	6,058,626		7,149,344

Year ending January 5 in—	No. 1.	No. 2.	
1804	£		£
		Deduct ..	8,158,494 555,965
	7,179,620		7,602,529
1805			9,424,711
		Deduct ..	566,999
	8,357,871		8,857,712
1806			10,129,634
		Deduct ..	614,913
	9,084,458		9,514,721
1822			12,734,560
		Deduct ..	1,479,587
	10,582,762		11,254,973
1823			12,958,101
		Deduct ..	1,547,486
	10,663,616		11,410,615
1824			13,854,536
		Deduct ..	1,567,779
	11,498,762		12,286,757
1825			13,519,151
		Deduct ..	1,462,096
	11,327,741		12,057,055
1826			18,749,076
		Deduct ..	1,504,703
	16,541,524		17,244,373

No. 29. Copy of Scottish Board's Minute of February 1, 1813, showing material for indictment of smugglers.

'Ordered that the Solicitor do prosecute the Persons concerned in these transactions, as proposed by Mr. Menzies, viz. :
'John Miller, Master of the *Hercules* of Glasgow, upon the Act 8th Ann, Cap. 7, Sec. 17, for the penalty of treble the value of 80 gallons of Rum, for having been assisting or otherwise concerned in unshipping the same without payment of

No. 30.—Comparative statement of duties levied on brandy and rum, tobacco, tea, and wine: 1803 to 1854.

Articles.	1803.	1826.	1834.	1845.	1854.	Explanatory Remarks.
Brandy and Rum (The rates on most other spirits were higher.)	Brandy, single, per gallon, 13s. 10d. Rum, single, 11s. 1d.	Brandy, per proof gallon, £1 2s. 6d. Rum, 8s. 6d.	Brandy, per proof gallon, £1 2s. 6d. Rum, 9s.	Brandy, per proof gallon, £1 2s. 10d. Rum, 9s. 4d.	Brandy, per proof gallon, 15s. Rum, into England, 8s. 2d. Rum, into Scotland, 8s. Rum, into Ireland, 4s. 4d.	'Single' means underproof. Overproof spirits were called 'double.' The rates from 1826 onward are per proof gallon. The rum rate is that levied on Plantation rum, which was preferentially treated.
Tobacco	British possessions: leaf, per pound, 1s. 7d. Spanish, 4s. 8d. Cigars (not shown).	British possessions: in America, leaf, per pound, 3s. 9d. Russia, Turkey, E. I. Co.'s possessions, 4s. Any other place, 6s. Cigars, 18s.	British possessions in America: leaf, per pound, 2s. 9d. Any other place, 3s. Cigars, 9s.	All kinds of leaf, per pound, 3s. 1d. Cigars, 9s. 5d.	All kinds of leaf, per pound, 3s. 1d. Cigars, 9s. 5d.	
Tea	Under 2s. 6d. a pound, 60 per cent. ad val. 2s. 6d. and above, 90 per cent.	At or under 2s. a pound, 96 per cent. Above 2s., 100 per cent.	Bohea, per pound, 1s. 6d. Congou, etc., 2s. 2d. Souchong, etc., 3s.	All kinds, per pound, 2s. 2d.	All kinds, per pound, 1s. 6d.	
Wine	French, per gallon, 10s. 4d. Spanish and Portuguese, 6s. 10d.	French, per gallon, 7s. 3d. Cape, 2s. 5d. All other wines, 4s. 10d.	Cape, per gallon, 2s. 9d. All other wines, 5s. 6d.	Cape, per gallon, 2s. 10d. All other 5s. 9d.	British possessions, per gallon, 2s. 10d. All other wines, 5s. 9d.	

Fractions of a penny disregarded. Readers who desire to authenticate these figures must bear in mind that the duties for 1803 include the 'temporary war duties,' but not the 'Convoy duty.' Whenever there was a privilege granted to goods brought in British ships, the preferential rate has been used. When an Excise duty was levied as well as a Customs duty, the two rates have been totalled. The rates shown for tobacco and wine in 1845 and 1854, and for tea in 1845, include the 'additional 5 per cent. duty.'

duties : on the Act 9th Geo. 2*, Cap. 25, Sec. 23, for the like penalty, in respect the said Rum was put out of the said vessel within the distance of 4 leagues of the coast of this kingdom : on the Act 26th, Geo. 3, Cap. 40, Sec. 8, for the penalty of £200 for breaking bulk within the said distance from the coast : and on his bond granted pursuant to the Act 26th Geo. 3, Cap 40, Sec 15. †

'The Mate of the said vessel upon the Act 26th, Geo. 3, Cap. 40, Sec. 8, for the penalty of £200 for breaking bulk : and on his smuggling bond given pursuant to the 15th Section of the said Act.

' Robert Russel, weaver, in Kilbride, who brought the Rum in his boat to Little Cumbrae, and afterwards conveyed the same to Kilbride, on the Act 8th Ann, Cap. 7, Sec. 17, for the penalty of treble the value of the Rum, for having been assisting or otherwise concerned in the unshipping thereof without payment of duties : for the like penalty in respect the Rum knowingly came into his hands, after being so unshipped : under the Act 9th, Geo. 2, Cap. 25, Sec. 23, for the like penalty of treble value for having been aiding and assisting or otherwise concerned in receiving the said Rum after being so unshipped within 4 leagues of the coast.

' Robert Barbour, farmer, in Yonderfield, in the lands of Arniel, and his sons Humphry and William Barbour, on the Act 38th, Geo. 3‡, Cap. 89, Sec. 8, for the penalty of treble the value of the 50 bolls of Irish salt, for being concerned or employed in unshipping, landing, removing, or putting the same on shore, without payment of duties : and for the like penalty in respect the said salt knowingly came to their hands after being so unshipped.'

No. 31. Copy of a certificate of registry (de novo) as granted to a ship built in the British Plantations. Date, March 15, 1815.

' In pursuance of an Act passed in the twenty-sixth year of the reign of King George the Third, intituled : an Act for the further Increase and Encouragement of Shipping and Navigation :

'*William Fryer of Wimborne in the County of Dorset, and*

* Known as the ' First Act of Indemnity.' See vol. i., p. 212.
† Known as the ' Manifest Act.' See vol. i. p. 326.
‡ See vol. i., p. 404.

Robert Pack of the town and County of Poole, Merchants,
having taken and subscribed the Oath required by this Act
and having sworn that *they are* sole owners of the Ship or
Vessel called *Eagle* of *Poole* whereof *William Stickens* is at
present Master, and that the said Ship or Vessel was *built at
Barrington in Nova Scotia in the year* 1801, *as appears by a
certificate of a former Register granted at St. John's, Newfoundland,* 22ⁿᵈ *Octʳ* 1814: *No.* 69 *now delivered up, and cancelled
and the said vessel registered* de novo *at this Port, in pursuance
of the Act of 27 Geo.* 3, *Cap.* 19: and *John Stansmore, tide-
surveyor,* having certified to us that the said vessel is *British
Plantation built* has *one* Deck and *two* Masts ; that her length
from the Fore Part of the Main Stem to the After-part of the
Sternpost aloft is 56 *feet* her breadth at the broadest part,
above the Main Wales 17 *feet* her height *in the hold* 8 *feet,* and
admeasures 64$\frac{63}{94}$ Tons : that she is a *square-sterned Schooner
with rise quarter-deck,* has no Gallery, and *no figure*-Head, and
the said subscribing owner having consented and agreed to
the above Description and Admeasurement, and having
caused sufficient Security to be given, as is required by the
said Act, the said *Schooner Eagle* has been duly registered at
the Port of *Poole.*

' Given under our hands and seals of office, at the Custom
House in the said Port of *Poole,* &c., &c.'

No. 32. *Copy of ' Libel ' exhibited in the Vice-Admiralty Court,
Jamaica, by the naval officer who seized the American
brigantine ' Union ' for trading in the Plantations contrary
to the Navigation laws.*

' JAMAICA.

' Malcolm *qui tam vˢ* The brigantine *Union.*

' In the Court of Vice-Admiralty.

' Charles Malcolm, Esquire, late Commander of His Majesty's
Ship *Sybelle* as well for and on behalf of our Sovereign Lord
the King as for and on behalf of himself the said Charles
Malcolm and his Officers, Seamen, Marines, and Mariners.

against

A certain Brigantine or Vessel called the *Union* whereof one
Allen Putnam late was or pretended to be Master her Tackle
Furniture and Apparel and certain Goods, Wares, and

APPENDIX

Merchandize. To wit : Twenty-six hogsheads and seventy-two boxes of Fish, eighty boxes of Soap, fifty boxes of Candles, forty-nine barrels of Beef, three hundred barrels of Flour, seven bales of Sheeting, a quantity of Lumber, twenty-two barrels of Potatoes, 5 boxes of Nails, one hundred and thirty Shooks, and three thousand Hoops, laden in and on board her.

'Be it remembered that on the twenty-second day of February in the fifty-ninth year of the Reign of our Sovereign Lord George the Third, by the Grace of God of the United Kingdom of Great Britain and Ireland King and of Jamaica Lord Defender of the Faith and so forth (&c.), came Charles Malcolm Esquire (&c.) by John Lynch one of the Proctors of this Honourable Court and the true and lawful Procurator and Proctor of him the said Charles Malcolm (&c.) in this behalf prosecutor against a certain Brigantine called the *Union* (recapitulation of cargo, etc.) To wit, at the Parish of Port Royal in the County of Surry and said island of Jamaica and within the jurisdiction of this Honourable Court the said island of Jamaica then and now being an island plantation or colony in America belonging to and in possession of His Majesty and the said Charles Malcolm late Commander as aforesaid on the behalf aforesaid by his Proctor aforesaid doth article allege and propound and say that after the making and passing of a certain Act of Parliament made and passed in the twelfth year of the Reign of His late Majesty King Charles the Second intitled ' An Act for the Encouraging and Increasing of Shipping and Navigation ' and also after the making and passing of a certain other Act of Parliament made and passed in the seventh and eighth years of the Reign of His late Majesty King William the Third intitled ' An Act for preventing Frauds and regulating Abuses in the Plantation Trade ' and before the day of exhibiting this Libel To wit on the fifteenth day of February in the year of Our Lord One Thousand Eight Hundred and Nineteen and whilst the said Charles Malcolm was Commander of His Majesty's ship *Sybelle* he the said Charles Malcolm as such Commander as aforesaid did seize as forfeited to and for the use of our said Sovereign Lord the King and of himself the said Charles Malcolm his officers (&c.) the said Brigantine or Vessel called the *Union* (recapitulation of cargo, etc.). For this, To wit that whereas after the making and passing of the Acts of Parliament aforesaid and before the day of exhibiting this Libel (&c.) certain goods wares and merchandizes To wit (recapitulation) were imported in the said Brigantine or Vessel called the *Union* into the island of Jamaica To wit into the port of Port Royal in the parish of (&c.) and within the jurisdiction (&c.) the said Brigantine or Vessel called the *Union* not being of the Built* of England or of the Built of Ireland or the said Colonies or Plantations and wholly owned by the People thereof or any of them and Navigated with the Master and three-fourths of the Mariners of the said places only and the said Brigantine or Vessel not having been taken as Prize and Condemnation thereof made in one of the Courts of Admiralty in England Ireland or the said Colonies or Plantations and not being navigated by the Master and three-fourths of the Mariners English or of the said Plantations as aforesaid and whereof the property did belong to Englishmen contrary to Law and to the form and effect of the aforesaid Statutes in such case made and provided whereby and by force of the said several Statutes or one of them the said Brigantine or Vessel called the *Union* (recapitulation) became and were and are forfeited and lost One Moiety thereof to the use of our said Sovereign Lord the King and the other Moiety thereof to the use of the said Charles Malcolm his Officers Seamen Marines and Mariners.

'Whereupon and upon all and singular the premises the said Charles Malcolm (&c.) by his Proctor aforesaid humbly prays that the said Brigantine or vessel called the *Union* (&c.) may be confiscated and adjudged forfeited and lost one half thereof (&c.) and that this libel may be received.

'WILLIAM BURGE (Attorney-General).
LYNCH (Proctor).'

N.B.—Many irritating repetitions have been left out in our copy (see the parentheses).

No. 33. *Extract from a petition furnished by Tortola merchants,* 1815.

(Forty-five of the principal merchants of St. Thomas, West Indies, petitioned the British Rear-Admiral, Sir P. C. Durham, that St. Thomas might still be the place of rendezvous for West Indiamen waiting to be convoyed to

---

* Build, invariably expressed as 'Built' in the old Statutes.

Great Britain, although the island had ceased to be a British possession. On hearing of this the merchants of Tortola put forward a counter-petition, as below :)

' SIR,

' On the restoration of the Danish islands, St. Thomas becoming thereby a foreign colony, we were firmly persuaded that Tortola would again be the place of rendézvous. Our hopes were kept alive notwithstanding that merchants of St. Thomas addressed your Excellency. We had not the slightest apprehension that a foreign port would be preferred to Tortola, where from 300 to 400 sail have frequently been accommodated, but we cannot conceal the astonishment and regret we have felt on reading a copy of your answer to the merchants of St. Thomas, and this day seeing a part of the fleet pass this port on their way to that island. We had relied on one paragraph in which your Excellency had assured the Gentlemen of St. Thomas that you would do everything in your power to grant their request, ' if the planters of the different islands should start no objection.'

' As another fleet will be collected before the Double Insurance takes place, we cannot, without forgetting our duty as British subjects to be jealous of our privileges, refrain from submitting remarks on the injurious effect likely to be produced to the British revenue, trade, and subjects. First, as to the revenue : we will suppose a fleet of 200 sail anchor in the roads and harbour of St. Thomas, with a boat from every second ship on shore every day, being little short of 400 sailors, who will furnish themselves with East India goods, gin, tobacco, and other contraband articles, to be smuggled into England.'

(The petitioners then assume that one or more of the merchantmen may be run ashore at St. Thomas.)

' —and discharge and repair damages. The expense must be paid for by the sale at that foreign port of part of her sugars, the duties whereon are lost to his Majesty, whereas no such loss would accrue if the rendezvous was at a British port. We refer your Excellency to the Act of 12 Chas. 2nd.

' The provision trade from Ireland and our North American colonies would receive material injury. Captains of vessels and passengers, from Demerara down to Tortola, knowing that St. Thomas is to be the rendezvous, and that they can there purchase provisions of the American States from 30 to

50 per cent. less than Irish or British-American, would take in their stores at that port, thereby carrying an alarming influx into a foreign island.

'There are many situations in which vessels may be placed, if suffered to rendezvous there, calculated to affect their policies of insurance. And, should any sudden change take place in the politics of Europe while a British fleet was lying in a Danish port, consequences might be serious.

'It may be asserted that the flesh and vegetable markets at Tortola do not equal those at St. Thomas. This is not absolutely the case : beef, mutton, pork, poultry, and vegetables are produced here in great abundance, and a notice of one or two days of the expectation of a Convoy is quite sufficient. These islands contain a great number of poor but industrious inhabitants. As British subjects they certainly have superior claims over foreigners. Many of them have supplied themselves with articles they expected to sell to the fleet.

'We trust that your Excellency will direct the next fleet to assemble at and sail from the Harbour of Tortola. Our utmost and united exertions will be used to render every service and accommodation to the ships, which we trust will be found to equal what they have ever experienced at St. Thomas.'

(The above proves that the art of mercantile advertisement was almost as well understood a hundred years ago as now. Below is an extract from the Rear-Admiral's reply :)

' GENTLEMEN,
        ' I am in receipt of your petition, with your admirable calculation, which nothing can equal but the exorbitant charges, &c., which I know from experience the Squadron has met with in many instances at Tortola.

' I consider the anchorage of St. Thomas far superior to that of Tortola, which port I shall never make the rendezvous when it can be avoided.'

The indomitable merchants of Tortola sent the correspondence to the Board of Customs.* Board's Minute thereon :

' The parties to be acquainted that this is not a matter that comes under the cognisance of this Board.'

* Evidently thinking that the Board might put the Navigation laws into operation against the Rear-Admiral.

No. 34. *Extract from a petition against customs officers'*
fees (1816).

' VIRGIN ISLANDS, TORTOLA.

' TO THE RIGHT HONOURABLE THE COMM^{RS} OF CUSTOMS.

' The humble petition and memorial of sundry inhabitants
of the Virgin Islands, who are owners of small boats and
vessels under tonnage : Sheweth : That, by the docket of fees
established by the Commissioners sent out from England in
the year 1812 or thereabouts, small boats from ten to twelve
tons burthen are required to pay to the different officers of the
Customs the sum of six dollars, equal to the sum of two pounds
nine shillings and sixpence Tortola currency, for a non-
objection note in ballast, and a further sum of two shillings
at the Revenue fort.

' That the owners of the boats of the description aforesaid
are persons possessing very little or no property, and many of
them with large families to support, and that to be done
through no other channel than by the employment of their
said boats.

' That this description of boats are most commonly employed to carry passengers and letters through the Virgin
Islands, and to and from the adjacent Danish islands : That
many of the said boats, being decked for safety from the high
seas that run between these islands, are compelled to take
registers, and to pay at the Custom-house thirteen-and-a-
half dollars, and to his honor the President four dollars . . . .

' That one of your memorialists is the owner of a small
boat of ten tons burthen, which boat is employed by the
deputy postmaster at St. Croix* to convey the letters which
come through the English post-office to this island, and from
hence to St. Croix : That at St. Croix he does not pay one
farthing for Custom-house fees, but at this port is compelled
to pay six dollars, which is nearly a moiety of the sum which
your memorialist receives for the voyage, out of which sum
three persons are paid wages as seamen, exclusive of providing
them with provisions.

' Your petitioners therefore humbly pray your Honors to
take their situation into your serious consideration ' (etc., etc.).

(Eleven signatures.)

(No relief afforded.)

* Danish colony.

No. 35. Précis of a petition sent to the King by Trinidad merchants, praying relief on account of the forfeiture of their goods for duties and law costs, the said merchants having objected to pay duties, levied according to Spanish law as operating in the island before it became a British colony. (Probable date, 1820.)

' TO THE KING'S MOST EXCELLENT MAJESTY IN COUNCIL.

' The humble petition and appeal of Messrs Edgar, Lyon, and Fleming of the island of Trinidad, merchants, Messrs Walrond, Edmonstone, and Co. of the same place, merchants, and Messrs Clarke and Co. of the same place, merchants : most humbly sheweth :

' That in the month of December, 1814, your petitioners were severally concerned in the importation into Trinidad, in British vessels navigated accordii g to law, of certain manufactured goods from Scotland, upon which a duty of 3½ per cent. *ad valorem* was charged by the officers of the Customs in that colony, and in order to procure entry of the same your petitioners were obliged to give their several promissory notes for the amount of the duty on the said articles in which they were interested : your petitioners Messrs. Edgar, Lyon, and Fleming, and Walrond, Edmonstone, and Co. two several notes for the sum of 1712 dollars and for the sum of £785 10s. currency respectively, your petitioners Messrs. Duncanson, Clarke, and Co. for the sum of £350 currency.

' That your petitioners, being advised that the demand of the said duties was unwarranted and illegal, respectively refused to pay the said promissory notes when they became due, whereupon Henry Fuller, Esq., H.M. Attorney Genl of the said island, upon the 3rd Feb. 1815, commenced proceedings against your petitioners in the Tribunal of the Intendant according to the forms of Spanish law. Your petitioners were cited to appear before the Escribano of the said Court. An order was issued to seize the goods of your petitioners to the value of the said sums and costs.

' That execution was levied upon the goods of your petitioners, and the same remained sequestered, after which your petitioners were cited to shew cause why final judgment should not be pronounced against them.

' That your petitioners prayed to be allowed copies of certain ordinances of 1783, 1786, 1794, and 1796, relating to the payment of duties, issued by the Spanish Government, which were in force at the time of the surrender of the colony to the British arms in February, 1797.

'That copies of the Ordinances of 1783 and 1786, and certain Ordinances of 1795 and 1796, were furnished to your petitioners, but they were unable to obtain copies of certain other Ordinances of 1796, regulating by whom and under what circumstances the said duty was to be payable, and they prayed permission to prove by oral testimony the manner in which the duty had been levied : viz., upon foreign goods imported in foreign bottoms at the time when the colony remained in possession of the Spaniards.

'That H.E. the Governor, exercising the office of Intendant, gave judgment, allowing the said Ordinances to be received in evidence, but rejecting the prayer of the petition for leave to adduce the other evidence tendered as above.

'That your petitioners, conceiving themselves aggrieved, presented a petition to the Governor, praying leave to appeal to your most gracious Majesty in Council.

'That the said Attorney Gen¹ presented a petition to the said Court, in opposition, in which he insisted on the legality of the said demands.

'That H.E. the Governor gave judgment, directing execution to be carried into effect against the goods seized, that the same should be sold, and that the Attorney Gen¹ should enter into bond on behalf of the Crown to make restitution in case the said judgment should be reversed, and admitting the appeal upon the usual securities.

'That the goods were sold for the payment of the said promissory notes, amounting to £1991 10s. currency, with taxed costs amounting to £1066 19s. 6d., the amount of which was received by the Treasurer of the said island of Trinidad.

'Your petitioners pray that the said decree may be reversed and annulled, and that a day may be appointed to hear the said appeals, and that Henry Fuller, Attorney Gen¹ for the island of Trinidad, do appear and attend the hearing thereof, and that your Majesty will be pleased to grant to your petitioners such other relief as to your Majesty shall seem meet.'

(Unfortunately there is no information as to how the colonial Hampdens fared, for the Board disowned connection with the case, pointing out that the 3½ per cent. duty was purely colonial. The 3½ per cent. duty had been abolished, so far as British *linen and cotton goods* were concerned, by a Privy Council Order of November 27, 1815. It would be interesting to know whether there was really any legal authority for the continuance of a Spanish duty, after the date of British occupation, and also whether the original duty was levied on *all* kinds of goods, or, as the appellants claimed, merely on foreign goods in foreign ships. It is apparent that the legal costs, as usual, were monstrous, and that the Crown lawyer was determined to secure them.)

No. 36. Documents connected with the clearance of a British vessel (foreign-built, evidently taken as prize and then given a British Register) with a cargo of spirits and molasses from one British colony to another. Date 1820.

(1. Licence. 2. Entry of goods outwards. 3. Certificate of clearance. 4. Certificate that 4½ per cent. duties paid. 5. Master's bond that goods shall not be landed contrary to Navigation laws. 6. Certificate of origin of goods. 7. Master's bond that such part of cargo as consists of spirits shall not be landed in the Isle of Man. 8. List of crew [missing from file].)

NO. I.

' Saint Christopher.

' Whereas it has been represented to us by Roger Woodburne of the said island Merchant that it is his wish to export from the same direct to the islands of Malta and Gibraltar on board the brig *Superior* Andrew Cook master the following articles being of the growth produce and manufacture of the said island That is to say eighty puncheons of rum fifty puncheons of molasses thirty puncheons of rum shrub eight hogsheads and seven tierces of muscovado sugar amounting in value to the total sum of two thousand one hundred and forty-seven pounds ten shillings sterling money of Great Britain. And whereas he has therefore requested us to grant him a Licence for that purpose we do hereby grant him the said Roger Woodburne a permission or Licence to load the said articles on board the said brig *Superior* bound direct to the island of Malta and Gibraltar aforesaid. He with the said Andrew Cook master of the said brig having given the security required by law.

' Given under our hands and seals of office at the Custom House, Basseterre, this 13th day of November, 1820, in the first year of His Majesty's reign.

' C. WOODLEY, Collector.
W. H. MALE, Controller.'

No. 2.

'St. Christopher, 16ᵗʰ *Novem.*, 1820.

'On Board the *Brig Superior*, *Andrew Cook*, Master, for *Gibraltar*.

Roger Woodburne.

' *Marks.*

W Nos 1/15 { 8 Hogsheads Sugar at 1400 is 11200
7 Tierces —do— at 800 is 5600
16800 lbs.

W 1/80   80 puncheons Rum at 90 is 7200 *gallons.*
W 1/50   50 puncheons Molasses at 90 is 4500 *gallons.*
W 101/130 30 puncheons Shrub at 90 is 2700 *gallons.*

    Sugar duty 756 lbs.
   Rum and Shrub duty 445½ *galls.* @ 2s. 9d. .. £61   5   1½
   Molasses duty   202½   ,,   ,, 2s.   20   5   0
              £81 10   1½

' *Jno Hasell, Junʳ*
  Actᵍ Searcher
To the Waiters and Searcher.

      ' *C. Woodley*, Collector.
      W. H. Male, Controller.'

(Authors' Note.—The duties were the ' 4½ per cent.' The sugar duty was taken in kind; the rum and molasses duties were commuted. The searcher's examination is shown on the back of the document.)

No. 3.

' *Saint Christopher.*

' These are to certify all whom it may concern that *Andrew Cook* master or Commander of the *brig Superior* burthen *246* tons, mounted with *no* guns, navigated with *12* men, *foreign* built, and bound for *Gibraltar*, having on board '

(Here follows recapitulation of cargo)

' hath here entered and cleared his said vessel according to law.

' Given under our hands and seals (etc.).
      ' *C. Woodley, Collr.*
      W. H. Male, Contr.'

No. 4.

'Saint Christopher.

CUSTOM HOUSE, *Basseterre.*

' These are to certify, That the *brig Superior, Andrew Cook* master, for *Gibraltar* hath here loaden and taken on board '

(Recapitulation of cargo)

' for which his Majesty's Duty of Four-and-Half per Cent. hath been here fully answered and paid.
' Given under (etc.).

' *C. Woodley, Collr.*
W. H. Male, Contr.'

No. 5.

'Saint Christopher.

' These are to certify all whom it doth concern, that '

(Recapitulation as to master, vessel, destination, and cargo)

' and hath here given bond with *one* sufficient surety in the sum of *Two Thousand Pounds* with condition That all Rum which shall be laden on board the said ship shall not be landed at any part of Europe to the northward of Cape Finisterre, except Great Britain or Ireland, and that all other non-enumerated goods (except Rum) so laden on board thereof shall not be landed at any port of Europe to the northward of Cape Finisterre, except in Great Britain, Ireland, Jersey, or Guernsey. And these are further to certify that it appears by the original Register now produced to us that the above-mentioned ship was registered at *Liverpool* the *11*th day of *August 1816.*
' Given under (etc.).

' *C. Woodley, Collr.*
W. H. Male, Contr.'

(AUTHORS' NOTE.—Readers may be referred to Sec. 30, Cap. 52, 6 Geo. 3 ; Cap. 2, 7 Geo. 3 ; and Sec. 3, Cap. 28, 9 Geo. 3.)

No. 6.

'Saint Christopher.

' These are to certify that proof has been produced to us by affidavits, agreeable to the Act 4 Geo. 3, Cap. 15, that the undermentioned goods and merchandize, now shipped on board the *brig Superior, Andrew Cook* master, bound for

Gibraltar, are of the growth, produce, or manufacture of the British Colonies :'

(Recapitulation of cargo and details of registry.)

' Given under (etc.).

' *C. Woodley, Collr.*
W. H. Male, Contr.'

No. 7.

' *Saint Christopher.*

' These are to certify '

(Details as to master, ship, cargo, etc.)

' and hath also here given Bond with *one* sufficient surety in the sum of *Two Thousand Pounds* with condition that the said *Rum, Shrub*, or any part thereof, shall not be carried to or landed in the Isle of Man.

' Given under (etc.).

C. Woodley, Collr.
W. M. Male, Contr.'

(AUTHORS' NOTE.—See Cap. 39, 5 Geo. 3 for the above. One document is missing from the file—the list of men, furnishing names, station, ages, stature, etc. This was issued so that the collector at port of arrival could satisfy himself that the proper number of ' King's subjects ' were employed.)

No. 37. List of Fees charged on Customs transactions by the officers at Kingston, Jamaica, up to 1821.

By the Collector.

	£	s.	d.
On entering a vessel with cargo from Europe	10	1	3
,, endorsing a British consul's manifest (for wine carried as cargo)	2	15	0
,, clearing vessel outwards for Europe (with cargo)	15	16	3
,, granting a new register (if required)	5	6	8
,, endorsing as to change of master or owner (if required)	1	15	0
,, Certificate to cancel bonds	0	12	6
,, Licence and bond if negro slaves carried as passengers	1	6	8
,, Certificate if carrying liberated negroes	1	6	8
,, Special manifest if tobacco carried as cargo	1	15	0
,, ' Sea Letter ' for one voyage (if required)	1	15	0
Collector's total charges	42	10	0
Controller's charges (at ⅓ the collector's rate)	14	3	4
Tide-surveyor's charges on entry and clearance	2	13	4
Landing-surveyor's do.	2	13	4
Waiters and searchers (usually four in number) each £2 13s. 4d.	10	13	4
	£72	13	4

N.B.—The above is the *maximum* amount, leviable by the officers for their own emolument, on the kind of vessel that yielded most profit, when every impostable transaction possible took place.   It will be seen, however, that if a vessel merely entered and cleared from Europe, the collector could charge £25 17s. 6d., the controller £8 12s. 6d., and six other officers £2 13s. 4d. each.   Total, £50 10s.

The entry and clearance fees chargeable on vessels with cargo from a British colony (without any special transaction) were : collectors, £8 5s. 10d. ; controllers, £2 15s. 3d. ; other officers, £16.   Total, £27 11s. 1d.   Coasting drogers paid 7s. 6d. to the collector and 2s. 6d. to the controller for entry and clearance, and no more.   If a vessel arrived with a cargo of goods taken as prize (a frequent occurrence), she had to pay special fees of £2 15s. to the collector and 15s. to the controller for a ' permit to land cargo.'

No. 38. Gross receipt of Customs, 1823 to 1838 inclusive, with cost of collection (departmental statistics).

Date.	England.		Scotland.		Ireland.	
	Gross.	Cost per cent.	Gross.	Cost per cent.	Gross.	Cost per cent.
	£		£		£	
1823	12,695,004	$7\frac{5}{8}$	891,409	$16\frac{1}{20}$	1,918,455	$23\frac{1}{8}$
1824	12,689,690	$7\frac{1}{2}$	953,837	$14\frac{7}{8}$	1,847,630	$19\frac{7}{8}$
1825	16,713,756	$5\frac{5}{8}$	1,512,960	$10\frac{1}{4}$	2,140,934	$17\frac{1}{8}$
1826	17,252,350	$5\frac{19}{20}$	1,299,351	$11\frac{5}{8}$	2,031,222	$17\frac{2}{3}$
1827	17,627,949	$5\frac{3}{4}$	1,376,044	$10\frac{5}{8}$	2,005,057	$16\frac{1}{2}$
1828	17,642,362	$5\frac{13}{20}$	1,376,001	$10\frac{1}{20}$	1,590,347	$19\frac{5}{8}$
1829	17,524,138	$5\frac{7}{20}$	1,372,089	$9\frac{3}{4}$	1,675,609	$18\frac{1}{8}$
1830	17,984,549	5	1,520,791	$8\frac{1}{4}$	1,579,183	$17\frac{1}{8}$
1831	16,688,586	$5\frac{5}{8}$	1,479,904	$7\frac{1}{2}$	1,477,448	$17\frac{7}{8}$
1832	16,689,751	$6\frac{1}{10}$	1,477,913	$7\frac{2}{5}$	1,516,908	$16\frac{5}{8}$
1833	15,724,967	$6\frac{1}{10}$	1,338,513	8	1,511,701	$16\frac{3}{10}$
1834	17,922,158	$5\frac{1}{2}$	1,441,393	$7\frac{1}{5}$	1,755,368	$13\frac{4}{5}$
1835	19,602,726	$5\frac{1}{8}$	1,529,996	$6\frac{5}{8}$	2,016,176	$12\frac{1}{4}$
1836	20,334,650	$4\frac{4}{5}$	1,587,648	$6\frac{1}{10}$	2,036,738	$11\frac{4}{5}$
1837	19,335,474	$4\frac{15}{16}$	1,626,291	$6\frac{3}{10}$	1,945,849	$12\frac{1}{4}$
1838	19,592,846	$4\frac{15}{16}$	1,666,398	$6\frac{1}{10}$	1,951,636	12

No. 39. Scottish Board's Minute of August 20, 1821.

' Read the report of the Solicitor on letter from Rear-Admiral Otway, with copy of one from Capt. Melville of the

Earl Moira cruiser, stating an unsuccessful attack by a boat's crew upon a smuggling lugger, in which one of the mariners was killed and two severely wounded.

' Ordered: Copies to be transmitted to Lerwick and Kirkwall, with directions to the officers to use every means in their power for obtaining information respecting the crew of the smuggling lugger, the port to which she belongs, and such other particulars as may lead to the discovery of the persons on board of her who were concerned in the attacking, killing, and wounding the mariners belonging to the *Earl Moira.*'

No. 40. Irish Customs Board's advertisement of seized tobacco for sale in May, 1824. (The Cork record probably includes the goods seized in 1822 on the ' Peru,' at Kinsale, see pp. 118-120). Only the sound tobacco was sold ; therefore the advertisement does not enlighten as to the full amount of tobacco seized. (Much of the ' Peru's ' cargo was damaged.)

Notice to Importers of Tobacco.

' The Commissioners of Customs hereby give Notice that it is their intention to offer for sale, to Importers of Tobacco *only*, all Seized Tobaccoes in Store worth the duties, and which may have been legally condemned at the Ports of

Dublin	about 9,200 lbs.	Londonderry	about 15,000 lbs.
Cork	,, 185,000 ,,	Sligo	,, 600 ,,
Belfast	,, 100,000 ,,	Strangford ..	,, 12,000 ,,
Galway	,, 40,000 ,,	Waterford ..	,, 8,400 ,,
Limerick	,, 147,000 ,,		*

and to receive Tenders for the purchase of the same, on or before the first day of July next.

' And they further give Notice that the Sampling will commence on the 20th May, at which time every facility will be given the Merchants to view the same, as no claim will be admitted on account of the Tobaccoes being considered inferior to the Samples.

' Purchasers must either warehouse the Tobaccoes so purchased, according to law, or take them away in ten days after they shall be declared, paying down the purchase money, or† purchase money and duty as the case may be,

---

* Total between 230 and 231 tons.

† (Purchase money if the goods were to be warehoused; purchase money and duty if they were for immediate clearance.—Authors.)

at the same time, otherwise the Board's agreement to the proposal to be null and void.

' As the Tobacco that may be purchased under the conditions of this Advertisement will be considered exactly in the same situation as if it had that day been regularly imported by the Merchant who makes the purchase, the purchasers must bear the expense attending removing, unwarehousing, warehousing, cooperage, and porterage.

' No proposal will be taken into consideration if the price offered be less than two pence per lb. exclusive of the Duties, and the proposal must have reference to each specific lot, as well as the marks and numbers of the several casks of which it is composed.

' Sealed proposals, with the words " Tenders for Tobacco " endorsed thereon, to be sent addressed under cover to the Secretary of the Board of Customs, Custom House, Dublin, on or before Twelve o'clock at noon on Thursday, the first July, after which time no tender will be received.

' By order of the Commissioners,

' C. I. A. MACLEAN,
' Secretary.'

' CUSTOM HOUSE, DUBLIN.'

No. 41. Specimen of Colonial reports of seizure and subsequent proceedings, 1824.

' CUSTOM HOUSE, ST. VINCENT.

' HONOURABLE SIRS,

' We have the honour to acquaint you that a seizure was made on the 2nd inst. by Messrs. Hodder and Billinghurst, of the sloop *Dandy* belonging to this port, and her cargo, consisting of 40 firkins and 4 ½-firkins butter, 69 boxes candles, and 18 cases oil, the whole being French property and prohibited.

' Information was received by the above officers that the *Dandy* (a suspected vessel) was in the Bay of Barmuallie, about 12 miles leeward of Kingstown, and that two or three persons were on shore endeavouring to effect a sale of her cargo. The officers proceeded (about sunset) in their boat, and fell in with the sloop one mile and a half from the shore, apparently beating to windward.

' The Attorney-General had no doubt as to the legality of their having so acted. The information was filed on the

16th. The goods have been appraised and sold under an order from the Court of Vice-Admiralty as perishable articles, and also the vessel.

' On the part of the prosecution the evidence will be respectable, and positive as to the intention to smuggle ; it will also, we presume, be positive that they did come to an anchor that evening in violation of S. 18, Cap. 44, 3 Geo. IV.

' We beg to state that the goods belonged to two Frenchmen, passengers on board, who will probably be induced to enter a claim, under the impression that as nothing was landed the going into a port does not constitute importation. Their only excuse was to get a supply of water (having left Martinique only 36 hours) and that their destination was the Gulph of Paria.

'GEO. HUSKISSON, *Coll[r]*.
RICH[D] ARRINDALE, *Cont[r]*.

		Appraised value in currency.	Amount sold for.
		£ s. d.	£ s. d.
Sloop	.. ..	82 10 0	97 0 0
Butter	.. ..	168 0 0	261 4 9
Candles	.. ..	138 0 0	156 6 6
Oil ..	.. ..	22 10 0	31 9 9
		411 0 0	546 1 0

' Since the above was written we have been informed that a Mr. Lamotte, one of the passengers, having procured security, intends to put in a claim. He is a native and resident of Grenada, whose connexions are French, at Martinique.'

(Later report.)
' We have now to inform you that the Claimant (Etienne Lamotte) clandestinely withdrew from this island, and has not since been heard of. The sureties, becoming responsible in the sum of £60 sterling, were called on for payment. A monition was served, which has had the effect of bringing them to a promise of payment at an early day.

'From the heavy charges attending the prosecution of seizures in this colony, we submit the expediency of a revision of the colonial docket under which such charges are made.

'The present system cannot but operate as a discouragement to the officers, and severely indeed would it have been felt by them in the above case, had it been otherwise decided.'

No. 42. Notice offering reward for discovery of certain smugglers who had resisted and assaulted the customs men at Swanage.

'*13th November, 1827.*

'Whereas it has been humbly represented to the King that in the Evening of Wednesday the 19th of September last an outrageous assault was committed at Swanage, in the County of Dorset, upon the Persons of the Chief Officer and Crew while employed at their Duty in the said place in the Prevention of Smuggling, by a gang of about 70 Smugglers, most of whom were armed with Fire Arms, Swords, and Swingles, and that the said Chief Officer and Several of the Crew were severely wounded :

'His Majesty, for the better discovering of the Offenders concerned in the commission of this Outrage, is hereby pleased to offer His most gracious pardon to any one or more of them, present at and aiding in such Outrage (save and except those who actually assaulted and beat the Chief Officer and his Crew) who shall discover his or their accomplice or accomplices therein so that he or they may be apprehended and brought to justice.

'LANDSDOWNE.

'And the Commissioners of His Majesty's Customs do hereby offer a Reward of

£200

'to any Person or Persons who shall make such discovery (save and except as aforesaid), the same to be paid by the Collector of His Majesty's Customs, at the said port of Poole, on the Conviction of the Offenders or any of them.

'T. WHITMORE,
'*Secretary to the Commissioners of Customs.*'

No. 43. Statement of the average annual emoluments of Planta-tion customs collectors (salaries and fees) during the five years ending January 5, 1826 (the date at which fees were abolished).

Port.	Amount per year of salaries and fees (salaries nominal).
	£ s. d.
Kingston, Jamaica*	6,525 11 4
Morant Bay ,, ...	881 10 6
Port Antonio ,, ...	823 6 2
Annatto Bay ,, ...	700 0 0
Port Maria ,, ...	758 2 9
St. Anne's ,, ...	459 18 10
Falmouth ,, ...	1,329 15 0
St. Lucea ,, ...	589 3 2
Montego Bay ,, ...	1,980 12 7
Savannah-la-Mar ,, ...	853 8 10
Bridgetown, Barbados	2,343 8 10
Oistens ,, ...	152 10 0
Speights ,, ...	417 8 11
Hole Town ,, ...	157 11 8
Antigua	1,835 17 7
St. Kitts	1,011 1 6
Nevis	504 4 6
Montserrat	352 0 0
Tortola	493 15 2
Grenada	1,839 1 0
St. Vincent	1,603 9 3
Dominica	1,057 14 0
Trinidad	2,392 5 9
Tobago	1,481 10 0
St. Lucia	1,291 4 4
Demerara†	5,219 8 7
Berbice	940 0 0
Nassau	789 13 4
Turk's Island	745 10 0
Exuma	103 9 4
Crooked Island	114 4 2
Bermuda	906 15 1
Newfoundland	1,928 1 11
Nova Scotia	2,013 15 0
Cape Breton	383 8 7
St. John, New Brunswick	3,210 9 11
St. Andrew's ,, ...	732 0 7
Prince Edward's Island	386 7 10
Quebec‡	4,261 15 1

* The Kingston controller made £2,551 7s. 5d. ; the tide-surveyor, £1,067 19s. 7d.

† The Demerara controller made £1,766 9s. 5d. ; the first clerk, £400 ; the second clerk, £366 13s. 4d. ; the third clerk, £250 ; the three landing-waiters £1,021 4s. 11d. each.

‡ The Quebec controller made £2,098 14s. 10d. ; the two landing-waiters £1,015 1s. 5d. each.

The total annual amount of the Plantation Customs emoluments

No. 44. Licence granted by the Customs Board to a vessel (armed) to trade as a whaler (Southern Fishery), 1828.

' Licence (No. 56513.)

' By the Commissioners for managing and causing to be levied and collected His Majesty's Customs.

' Value. *Three Thousand Pounds.*

' Suffer the *Ship* or vessel called the *Coronet* of *London John Kenney* master *Carvel* built *ninety-four* feet *eleven* inches long *twenty-five* feet *six* inches broad *two hundred and seventy-five* 3/94 tons, with a *standing* bowsprit *Armed with eight guns, six nine and twelve-pounders, thirty muskets, thirty pistols, thirty cutlasses, thirty rounds of powder and ball* whereof *Francis Deacon of Russell St. Bermondsey and others, are* owners, intended to be employed in *the Southern Whale Fishery*, to pass without any Lett, Hindrance, Seizure, or Molestation, provided it shall appear by certificate on the back hereof from the collector, controller, or other proper officer of the Customs that the said Owners have given security to their satisfaction as required by law. Given under our hands, &c.'

No. 45. Customs officers at Montego Bay, Jamaica, to London Board, announcing negro insurrection, 1831-32.

' *Jan.* 13th, 1832.

' HONOURABLE SIRS,

' It is our painful duty to inform your Honors of the rebellion of the negroes of this parish, the destruction of the greater number of its country-houses and their properties by fire, much loss of life in several skirmishes between the military and the insurgents, as also by the execution of many of the leaders of the rebellion, martial law having been duly proclaimed on the last day of the year.

' It appears that some insurrections have taken place in other parishes, but the principal seat of the rebellion is in this, where the insurgents first commenced by firing several country-houses about 10 or 12 miles to leeward of this town, on the night of the 27th ult.

---

was £115,990 19s. 8d., divided amongst 243 officials. The total net amount remitted to the imperial Exchequer for the year ending January 5, 1826, was £15,032 15s. 6d. Thus, for every £1 gained by the Exchequer nearly £7 15s. was paid in salaries and fees to officials.

'We have reserved this letter to send by the Export Packet Post, that we might communicate the latest intelligence to your Honors, and we rejoice to state that the present appearances are much more favorable, several estates' negroes having returned quietly to work, many having surrendered, fires comparatively of rare occurrence, and hopes (but not very sanguine) are entertained of a speedy and entire suppression of the revolt.

'The headquarters of the Commander-in-Chief, Sir Willoughby Cotton, are in this town, and three vessels of war, under Commodore Farquhar, are in the harbour. No reasonable apprehension is entertained of an attack, but the utmost vigilance is required to guard against the prowling incendiary, as most of our servants are negro slaves, and our houses are principally built of wood.

'It is not, however, our province to enter into the general detail of this unhappy rebellion, but we beg leave to narrate such circumstances as relate more particularly to this office. On the first appearance of revolt your officers wrote to the Custos and Magistracy, dispensing with the legal exemption from the civil and military employment, and offering their services in whatever situation they might be thought most useful, out of office hours. We have accordingly been appointed Storekeepers of provisions for the troops, and the Magistracy having guaranteed the payment or satisfaction of duty on flour in bond, we have suffered delivery to the Commissariat in some instances without payment to the colonial Receiver General. In other cases, that officer being at an outport with his company of militia, we have rec^d the duties ourselves, which we shall hand over to him on his return. We have also been required not to clear any vessel from this port, as they would afford a refuge for women and children in the event of emergency (and indeed most nights till lately they have been completely crowded), but this restriction has been dispensed with as regards droging vessels, and we now clear out large vessels on special order to that effect from the Commander of the Forces or the Commodore. When the danger of fire was more imminent, the regular troops not having arrived, we selected the more valuable documents of this office, and deposited them in a case for immediate removal to a vessel in the harbour in the event of alarm, and after the business of the day they are again deposited in the same case, and as the collector's clerk sleeps in a room adjoining the office, they would instantly be conveyed on board a sloop lying off the Custom House wharf.

' The above are the principal occurrences relating more especially to this department, to which we may be permitted to add that all your officers are at their posts, and we trust that the official duties have been correctly performed.

' We have the honor to be,

' Your most obedient Servants,

' JOHN ROBY, *Collector.*

N. ASHBY, *Controller.*'

Board's minute, 10th March, 1832 :

' The Board approve.'

No. 46. Extract from a statement as to obstruction of customs officers, 1834 (illustrative of the state of popular feeling in Tortola).

' VIRGIN ISLANDS,

' TORTOLA.

' Augustus McCleverty, customs boatman, sworn, declares :

' Between 5 and 6 last evening Mr. Richardson, searcher, ordered the Customs boat to take him to Sea Cow Bay. We went towards " Jimmy Duff's Bottom "; there was nothing there. Mr. Richardson said " Pull towards Mr. Littsom's place "; we pulled off there but could see nothing. Mr. Richardson said " We'll go back "; while we were in the act of turning the boat one of the hands sung out that there was a boat just coming in. Mr. Richardson said " Boys, we will board, and see what she is." Boat still stood into the bay, and we pulled up to her. Mr. Richardson hailed and directed them to heave to; they immediately jibed and stood before the wind. We pulled alongside. Mr. Richardson said " Augustus, get on board." I went on board, and Eneas Pickering jumped out of the hold and said " ——— ——— you, you have no business here; I'll put you overboard," and did attempt it. I told him I was ordered to come on board; he said he did not care a ———, he would put himself out of the way, and hauled his wind and stood to the southward. He then said " ——— ——— it, put her about, put Augustus on board his boat." I said " Luff, or you'll run our boat down "; he said " ——— ——— it, draw her away." The hands in the Custom-house boat pulled her quickly and just crossed our bow. He then luffed up again, apparently with the intention of running the Custom-house boat down, so much so that the jib boom obliged Mr. Richardson to stoop to avoid it.   Our boat managed to get alongside.   Eneas said, " Augustus, I order you to get into your boat," which I immediately did. Dunbo, one of the hands in our boat, still held on to the vessel, and Edward Lloyd, one of the hands on board the said vessel, said " There is a bill forward : chop his —— hands off."   A man came forward and took up something and made a chop at Dunbo which struck the boat.   We tried to get alongside the second and third time, but the force opposed was too great : every time we went alongside they chopp'd at us.'

(Prosecution was instituted against Lloyd.   The judge summed up in favour of a conviction, but the jury acquitted the prisoner.   Crown costs, £23 5s. 9d. currency.)

No. 47. Official statement of life-saving services rendered by the Coastguard on the east coasts of England and Scotland (8th December, 1835, to April, 1836).   Summarised.

8th December, 1835. — John Gregory, coastguardsman, stationed at St. Andrews, Fifeshire, leaped into the sea and saved the life of a local pilot.   The Humane Society presented Gregory with an acknowledgment on vellum.

17th January, 1836. — The *Janet* of St. Andrews drove ashore at the mouth of Elie Harbour, Fifeshire.   Lieut. Randall of the Coastguard and his men boarded her through a tremendous surf, saved the crew, and afterwards by extraordinary exertions saved the vessel and cargo.   Thanked by the Board and the Admiralty.   (Randall had frequently been thanked for daring conduct, having personally rescued over 30 people.)

17th February, 1836.—The *Janet and Agnes* wrecked off Scarborough.   The coastguard saved four of the crew.   The rest were drowned.

18th Feby, 1836.—The *Janet* of Scotland drove ashore near Pakefield, Suffolk.   Coastguard rescued the crew. Vessel broke up directly afterwards.

Same date.—The same coastguardsmen rescued the crew of the *Venus* of Weymouth, getting a hawser on her and bringing the men off by repeated trips in a small boat.   (At this time 15 vessels were ashore ' within a short distance.'   The crews of all were saved by the coastguardsmen and fishermen.)

Silver medal to Coastguard Lieutenant Joachim, and a money reward to his crew.

Same date.—The *William Parker* of North Shields dashed to pieces against a cliff near Bridlington. The Coastguard saved the crew, hauling them up the cliff by ropes.

5th March, 1836.—The *London Packet* of Aberdeen went on the rocks off Peterhead. The Coastguard rescued crew and passengers just before the vessel broke up.

8th April, 1836.—The *Tyne* of Newcastle went ashore on a reef in Spey Bay. The Coastguard rescued the crew and saved ship and cargo.

No. 48. Form of receipt given to the Dominican collector of customs by persons who received from him as apprentices negroes captured on slavers.

' Received from the Hon'ble Symonds Bridgwater, collector of the Customs' (number) 'African apprentices, which I promise to feed and provide for agreeably to the Orders in Council, and for whom I promise to enter into any Indenture or Security required. I further promise to furnish the collector, in the course of ten days, with the particulars below mentioned of each apprentice, and I shall consider such promise as binding as if such Indenture or Security had actually been signed or given.

' 1. His or her African name.
  2. The name by which to be called in future.
  3. The sex.
  4. Age.
  5. Height or stature.
  6. Marks or peculiarities of feature.
  7. Place of nativity.
  8. Colour.

' ROSEAU, *May,* 1837.'

(The indenture alluded to was made between the collector and the person to whom the negro was apprenticed. It stated the term of apprenticeship, and the trade to which the negro was to be put, and that such negro should be properly fed, clothed, and doctored, baptized, and instructed in the Christian faith. The collector to have power to visit and interrogate the apprentice, nor was the latter to be removed by sea without Customs licence, or to be put to field labour if a female. If the master died before expiration of term the indenture became void. The penalty on the master for infraction was double the amount for which the negro would sell if a slave.)

No. 49. Memorial presented to the Controller-General of Coastguard in 1838 *by John Hatch, chief officer of Coastguard, St. Margaret's Bay.*

' HUMBLY SHEWETH,

' That your memorialist has served upwards of six years in the Royal Navy, as volunteer of the first class, midshipman, and master's mate, on board H.M. ships *Apelles, Barfleur, Nemure,* and *Ferret,* for which he encloses copies of certificates and testimonials.

' He was twice stranded (near Margate in December, 1808, and on the coast of France near Boulogne in May, 1812, when the *Apelles* was captured by the enemy). He at the Flushing expedition served as orderly to Sir Richard Keats, and was intrusted by him with despatches to General Hope. He was capsized in the *Apelles* jolly-boat off Dungeness in November, 1810, when the master, surgeon, and one seaman were drowned. He has been maimed twice (in the *Barfleur* near Toulon in 1813, and in the *Ferret* near Brest in 1815), the last time severely, at the capture of a fort, a man-of-war brig, cutter, and seven sail of merchant vessels, when your memorialist had charge of a boat.

' He has served nearly eighteen years as chief officer in the Coast Guard Service. He has made some seizures, and has had full charge of four vessels in distress, which were conveyed to places of safety by the coastguard : viz. the brig *Hugh* of Belfast, from Denmark, with a cargo of sugar—she was boarded between Portnessoch and the Mull of Galloway—she had two feet of water in her hold, and her rudder unshipped—all the crew left except the mate and two men : the sloop *Firth of Forth,* with a cargo of herring, on shore in the bay of Luce, totally abandoned by her crew : a sloop belonging to Limekilns with a cargo of lime, on fire near Burgh Head : and the Russian ship *Fathers Landa,* on shore near St. Margaret's Bay, and your memorialist does humbly hope that his servitude in the navy may entitle him to the same pay as mates of the navy of the present day are now to receive when appointed chief officers in the Coastguard Service.

' And your memorialist as in duty bound will ever pray.'

(Hatch encloses laudatory statements from naval officers Oliver, Dougal, Sir Edward Berry, Maitland, Stirling, Campbell, Prosser, Hellard, and Parry, also from the owner of

the brig *Hugh*, the customs collector of Stranraer, the late
M.P. for Galloway, the ' proprietor of Burghead,' and the
Cromarty magistrates. It is to be trusted that this formidable
backing secured him the extra pay desired.)

*No. 50. Application by James Brooke, afterwards Rajah of
Sarawak, that his yacht ' Royalist,' lying at Table Bay
on her way to the Indian Archipelago, should enjoy the
' exemption from report and clearance ' usually granted to
vessels of the Royal Yacht Squadron, 1839.**

' THE HONORABLE THE COMMISSIONERS OF HER
MAJESTY'S CUSTOMS.

' SIRS,
' Mr. Field, the collector of customs of this colony,
having thought it his duty to enter my vessel at the Custom
House, I have to beg the exemption from the dues, usually
granted to yachts under similar circumstances. I have been
given to understand likewise that no orders respecting yachts
belonging to the Yacht Squadron have been received at the
Custom House, and that in consequence all yachts arriving
here must be considered in the light of merchant vessels.
May I further request you will take the subject under your
consideration and forward the necessary orders, should you
be of opinion that the privileges of yachts of the Squadron
extend to this colony as well as to our colonial possessions
in the Mediterranean.
' I have the honor to be, Sirs,
' Your obedient Servant,
' J. BROOKE.'

' YACHT ' ROYALIST,' R.Y.S.,
TABLE BAY, CAPE OF GOOD HOPE,
20th March, 1839.'

Board's minute, June 14, 1839 :
' Applicant to be informed that the collector of the Cape
would appear to have acted correctly on the occasion in
question, and that the Board cannot comply with this request.'

* Brooke was bound for Borneo, on his celebrated expedition against
the Dyak pirates.

No. 51. Customs notice, posted at Sydney, New South Wales, 1841.

' NOTICE.

' Whereas

SMUGGLING

to a considerable extent is known to have been carried on in the Harbour of Port Jackson, and at other places along the Coast of this Colony, both by Persons commanding vessels and Persons residing on shore, who in other respects are considered respectable : And whereas it would appear, from the circumstance of no information having ever been given of such transactions, that it is not generally known that the Person giving information is entitled to a Reward, without having his Name divulged :

' Notice is hereby given, that any Person giving information to the Collector or other officer of Customs of any Spirits, Tobacco, or other dutiable goods being concealed on board any vessel, or having been put into any other vessel (either within or without the Harbour) or having been landed without payment of Duty, so as to lead to the seizure of such Goods, he or she will be entitled to one-third of whatever sum may accrue to the seizing officer from the sale of such Goods, however large it may be : and the name of the Party will not be suffered to transpire.

' J. GIBBES, *Collector.*'

'CUSTOM HOUSE, *August 6th*, 1841.'

No. 52. Jersey smuggler's confession.

' ISLAND OF JERSEY.

' The Deponent, ——, late master of the *Eliza* of this port, declareth that on the morning of the 8th June last, instead of proceeding to St. Germains (France) for whence she had cleared on the 6th proceeding, she went to Bonne-nuit Bay in this Island, the owner, ——, being on board, as well as —— of Bembridge, Isle of Wight, and ——, residing here, the two latter forming with myself the crew, and there took in from a boat which came alongside several times about two & a half tons of tobacco stems, spirits in casks, segars,

and snuff, which Deponent had agreed with the above ——
and a Mr. ——, tobacconist, of this place, to take to Wales,
at the rate of fifty pounds per ton, but not to be paid for
above two tons, two shares of which as master I was to
receive, one-third each to the crew ; and the other one-third
for the vessel* ; that we sailed the said night, —— remaining
on board, and arrived at a bay to the eastward of that of
Fishguard, near Cardigan, the afternoon of the 5th day, that
—— proceeded on shore, with ——, and found that we had
gone too far to the eastward, we then proceeded to Fishguard
Bay, where —— landed at daybreak, and after some time
requested us to keep off until the evening, which we did,
running in at about 11 o'clock that evening, when he came
off with five or six men in a boat, and took the goods in four
or five trips on shore, he remaining on shore after the first
trip, as also —— and ——, to assist in conveying the goods
to a store close by, early the following afternoon we left,
leaving him at Fishguard, and went to St. Germain, where
we took in thirty-two sheep, and returned to this Island on
the 29th following, accounting to the officers here for her
long absence that we had been benipped at St. Germain.
That we were not boarded or spoken by any English revenue
officer, cutter, or boat, during our absence.   That since that
return five pounds were paid to myself and five to my wife,
by Mr. ——, who has also paid five to —— (on account)
being the whole that I have as yet received.

'That at about 3 a.m. of the 22nd Sept. last, when I left
St. Helier's New Harbour without a clearance, we, being the
aforenamed —— and —— in lieu of ——, on board as crew,
proceeded to or near Grève de Lecq, and there found a large
boat at anchor waiting for us, with goods which we took on
board, being about five tons (some being obliged to be put
in the cabin of our vessel) of leaf tobacco in bales from
thirty-six to forty pounds each, snuff in bales and segars
in boxes, and several bags of tea and cases of spirits.   ——
had left this island by *Sir Francis Drake*, Plymouth steamer,
the same morning, on his way to Fishguard Bay, where I
was instructed to meet him.   We sailed the same morning,
viz. the 22nd, and landed in our boat, manned by ——, the
night of the 25th, at Fishguard, the boatmen returning on

---

* This is rather confusing, but it is likely that he was to get
£66 13s. 4d., each of the crew one-third of the remainder, and the
remaining £11 odd was to defray expenses of vessel.

board. I found that —— had not yet arrived there: after some time I found one of the men concerned in former transaction and returned on board with him and five or six others in a shore boat, and they or some of them in seven or eight trips to the shore landed all the tobacco, &c. Early next morning we got under weigh and proceeded to an adjacent bay to the westward, and there took in some stones for ballast, the vessel being too light for working, and returned to this Island on the evening of the 29th following; on our way home, say the 28th, we were boarded in Mount's Bay by a boat belonging, the Deponent believes, to the *Sylvia* revenue cutter, to the officer of which Deponent stated, to account for his being there without papers, that he had piloted a vessel down Channel. That for this trip, which Deponent had agreed with the aforenamed —— was to be paid at the rate of former trips, but not for more than four tons, he has as yet received nothing, and that in consequence thereof, as well as for other misunderstandings between Deponent and the above parties, he has considered it a duty which he owes himself to make the present declaration.

'Signed and declared before us at Custom House, Jersey, this 30th day of Novr. 1848.

'(Signed)   —— ——

'G. B. RADFORD, *Pl Offr.*
JAs RIDER, *Contr.*'

No. 53. *Report made by the actual seizer of the Charlotte*, 1849.

'I am Mariner of the *Vigilant* revenue cruiser. On the evening of the 13th December instant I was one of the hands sent in a boat from the cutter to board a vessel seen coming up the river Thames. When we got near her I perceived her to be a barge. When the boat got alongside I with the rest of the boat's crew went on board. She had a quantity of straw on deck. I helped to remove some of the straw abaft the mast, and got to the main hatch, which was lifted up. I, with one hand, got into her hold, and by the light of the lanthorn saw there were some casks in it. I heard the gunner, who was on deck, ask what was in the casks, and heard somebody answer Tallow

' I then heard the gunner say he must see what was in them, and also heard someone answer, " You have got a good Prize."

' The gunner then came into the hold, and ' (I) ' saw him take off a piece of tin which was nailed over a hole in one of the casks, there was a piece of wood under it.

' I then came on deck and with William Matson went into the barge's cabin, one of the men belonging to the barge followed us into the cabin, and he said " It's no use." I observed " How is that ?" He said, " What is our loss is your gain."

' I asked him what they had got in the casks, he answered Leaf Tobacco, I then asked him how much there was, he said between nine and ten tons as far as he knew.

' I went on deck after that.

' The gunner then ordered me and three other hands to go into the boat and acquaint Captain Gowlland.

' Signed in my presence this 17th day of December, I. Moore Hodder, Collr (Rochester).

' FREDERICK FRENCH.'

No. 54. Précis of papers connected with a large seizure, made ' on rummage,' at Liverpool, in 1850.

' (To the Collector and Controller, Liverpool) :

' RIVER INSPECTOR'S OFFICE.

' GENTLEMEN,

' I beg to report that yesterday afternoon, on rummaging the barque *Warrior* from New York, we discovered beneath the master's stateroom, behind a false bulkhead, 11 bales of leaf tobacco, weighing net 1380 lbs, and also a quantity of lumps of foreign manufd tobacco, weighing net 1263 lbs : total, 2643 lbs net.'

(Proceeds that master, both mates, and an apprentice, arrested.)

' They were charged before Edward Rushton, Esq., this day, when the master, first mate, and apprentice were remanded, to await the directions of the Honble Board. The magistrate being satisfied that the second mate had no guilty knowledge of the transaction, he was discharged.

' WILLIAM JAGO.'

(London Customs Solicitor's report on above) :

' The vessel and tobacco are liable to forfeiture, and the parties to detention and prosecution before the justices for the penalty of £100 each, under Sections 3, 53, and 88, Cap. 87, 8/9 Vict.'

(Board's minute) :

' Retain the goods as a seizure : proceed against the parties : keep hands on the vessel.'

(Master and mate imprisoned, the apprentice acquitted, it being thought he was coerced into assisting. Collector and controller call on Jago to state whether the master is able to maintain himself while in prison.)

' GENTLEMEN,
' I beg to report that I have to-day seen the above-named individual. He informs me that the whole of his property consists in an eighth part of the *Warrior*, and that his pay as master of that vessel has ceased, and that he is therefore not in circumstances to support himself in prison.

'WILLIAM JAGO.'

(Maintenance allowance accordingly. Six other part owners, natives of Drogheda, apply to Board, asking for release of their vessel.)

(Board's minute) :

' Adverting to the quantity of tobacco seized, the Board do not see fit to release the vessel from seizure, and direct that she be returned into the Court of Exchequer for condemnation.'

(Owners apply to Treasury, quoting cases of two vessels owned by others, seized and afterwards released. Board state that in one case quoted the owners gave information leading to seizure : in the other only 980 pounds were found, and the vessel released on payment by owners of £100. They suggest release of *Warrior* on payment of £400. Owners fail to pay. Vessel condemned, and sold for £625.)

No. 55. Advertisement offering reward for apprehension of a smuggler, 1851 (see p. 352).

'TEN POUNDS
REWARD.

Whereas

SAMUEL NORTON,

late Master of the

Sloop *Samuel & Susannah* of Goole,

who stands charged with

SMUGGLING

Absconded from Goole on the 13th of September last. He is about 5 feet 5 inches high, dark eyes, rather roundshouldered, and a little bowlegged. He is about 35 years of age.

' All reasonable expenses, independent of the above Reward, will be paid on his apprehension, by immediately communicating with Mr. George Cordukes, Superintendent Constable, Goole, who holds a warrant against him.

' There cannot be a doubt of his conviction, as the *Vessel and Goods were condemned in the Exchequer in Michaelmas Term last.*

'GOOLE, 19*th day of May*, 1851.'

No. 56. Suffolk smuggler's confession, 1852.

(A large quantity of tobacco had been seized in a barn. Supposed to be only part of a quantity run. The ' spotsman ' deposed as below) :

' About the month of September, 1851, I met a person named —— at the *Lion* publichouse in Ipswich. I had been engaged with him in a smuggling transaction about May in the same year. He said to me that he wished I could get a vessel that would carry 5 or 6 tons, and he would give me £1 a bale, meaning that that was the sum he would pay me for every bale of tobacco I could smuggle into this kingdom. I told him I thought I could. In consequence of this conversation I saw a man named —— who owned a vessel called the *Neptune*, and having ascertained from him that I could

have his vessel I again saw —— in the month of October
following, at the *Mulberry Tree* publichouse in Ipswich,
when I told him that I could get a vessel that was going to
Lowestoft, and would return with empty cement barrels and
sacks, and would then go over to Nieuport. He then gave
me a letter directed to Mr. —— a tobacco merchant (English)
at Nieuport. The *Neptune* cleared out for Lowestoft, myself
acting as pilot. On arriving there I went to the *Suffolk
Arms*, where I met —— who asked me when I should be
able to start. I answered " tomorrow," and he then said,
" Well, make the best of your way." I sailed from Lowestoft
on a Friday, and arrived at Nieuport in the course of the
next day, when I handed Mr. —— the letter from ——.
When he opened it he said that he could not pay me £100
(as desired) but he would guarantee that it should be paid
as soon as the tobacco was on the walls—meaning the em-
bankment or river wall of the Orwell—as soon as we were
there. And in the course of that day the *Neptune* received
200 bales into her (one or two of which I cut open for the
purpose of procuring samples for —— to sell by), which I
and the crew assisted in loading, and sailed the same night
for the river Orwell. It was agreed between myself and
—— that the cargo was to be landed at a place in that river
called Trimley Sluice (where I and he assisted in landing
a similar cargo of 80 bales in the May preceding). I arrived
in the Orwell in the course of the following Sunday afternoon,
and sailed till we came abreast of Trimley Sluice, when two
of the *Neptune's* crew rowed me ashore in the boat, and the
vessel went up as far as Collinor' (?) ' Point. I went on to the
Ship inn at Levington, kept by —— to get assistance to
remove the bales when landed. In my way thither I met
Lord Alfred Paget and his gamekeeper, the latter of whom
bid me good-day. From the *Ship* I went to ——'s mill, and
there I found —— in company with the occupier, to whom
I gave the samples, and with whom we sat and smoked,
the conversation between us being generally the best time
and under what circumstances we should remove the bales,
and the miller said he would go down with his horse and cart
and assist, and I then left for that purpose, leaving —— in
——'s house. On arriving at the marsh I saw the bales laid
out in scores. I saw horses and carts, belonging to ——
——, ——, ——, ——, and —— : four of these carts with
100 bales altogether, with which they drove away. Two of

the said carts, viz. ——'s, and another, returned twice, and were loaded with the remainder of the bales. I accompanied them to a farm belonging to a person named —— at Bucklesham, where I assisted in unloading the bales into the loft of a stable belonging to him. The miller told me that he had received 100 of the bales. I and —— went to the miller's house and slept there that night, and —— asked me whether the goods were all right and I told him they were, and he desired me at breakfast-time to meet him at the *Mulberry Tree* in Ipswich in a day or two. I accordingly went there on the Wednesday evening following, and received from him a £50 Bank of England note, which I changed at the Yellow Bank at Ipswich, first endorsing my name thereon.

' In the course of two or three days afterwards I received from him at the *Mulberry Tree* another £50 note, which I changed at the Yellow Bank, endorsing my name as before.

' On each of these occasions I paid the master of the *Neptune* £40 at the *Union Jack* publichouse, on account of the services of his vessel, himself, and crew.

' In the course of a few days afterwards I saw —— at the *Victoria Arms* publichouse in Ipswich, on which occasion the master of the *Neptune* was in company with us, and I saw —— pay him two £50 notes.

' Within a month afterwards I received from —— 50s. at the *Mulberry Tree* for my share in bringing over the bales.

' The vessel *Neptune* was seized at Emsworth in Sussex, and I received a letter from —— to a Mr. ——, an innkeeper and butcher at Southwick, Sussex, on the subject, and —— gave me £3 or £4 to defray my expenses in going there.'

(This has been selected as remarkable, on account of the deadly particularization and conclusiveness of the narrative. It will be seen that for bringing over about 12,000 pounds of tobacco the receivers paid as below :

	£	s.	d.
To the spotsman	22	10	0
To the master and crew	180	0	0
To the owners of the carts, etc.—say ..	25	0	0
	227	10	0

The goods would cost in Nieuport—say, 1s. a pound = £600. Roughly, other expenses included, £850 for the cargo. At 3s.

a pound—a very moderate price, duty-paid—the goods would fetch £1,800. It is likely the spotsman thought himself underpaid, whence the information.)

No. 57. *Précis of papers connected with a seizure in the Medway, 1854.*

Statement of William Coulls, chief Customs boatman at Standgate Creek :

' I was afloat on duty in the river Medway on the morning of Sunday the 21st May instant, about ½ past 3 o'clock in the morning, when I observed a half-decked boat ½ a mile north-east of Standgate Creek. I was then boarding several vessels passing up the Medway, and I let the boat I had just observed get up the river some distance before I made towards her, when she had made about a mile further up the river, and made towards her for about 10 minutes, when I came along-side her. At this time Charles Jennings, a boatman, and James West, also a boatman, were with me. On coming along-side the suspicious-looking boat I found ——— and ——— on board, and asked them what they had got in their boat, when they answered, "Oysters for Chatham." I went on board and examined her, and on going under the hatches I found that she had no oysters on board, but there were one or two old sails and several coils of rope, on removing which I found several canvas bales, with the number "40" on each, and suspecting that they contained tobacco I called my boatman on board. I detained the boat, which is named the *Charity*, and proceeded with her to the coastguard station at Standgate Creek. On finding the bales I said to the prisoners, "You have very good oysters in." ——— asked me if I was satisfied. I told him I was, when he said "Take her, for I have had enough trouble with her," and in the course of a few minutes afterwards he told me he had come over Nieuport Bar with a reef in her mainsail. On examining the contents of the boat I found 62 bales in her, 61 of which contained unmanfd leaf tobacco, and 1 bale, that had been opened, containing manufd shag tobacco, the whole of which I conveyed with the boat *Charity* to the Custom House at Rochester, and delivered the same to the controller. The prisoners I placed on board the *Shamrock* revenue cutter.'

(Both smugglers committed for six months in default of paying a fine of £100 each.)

Their memorial, sent from prison, to the Board :

'The Humble Petition of —— and ——, inhabitants of Queenborough, now confined in Maidstone jail, sheweth :

'That your petitioners very imprudently violated the Law of the Land, in being guilty of smuggling, which step they not only exceedingly regret, but promise in future not to be guilty of a like offence.

'Your petitioners will feel very grateful to your Honourable Board if you will extend to them a similar act of clemency as to others who have been placed in a like position.

'Your petitioners humbly represent to your Honourable Board that they have already been in prison for three months, and that their present distressing position is aggravated by the fact that their wives and children are entirely dependent upon them for support. The case of your petitioner ——'s wife is of a very affecting character, inasmuch as she is greatly afflicted.

'Trusting that your Honourable Board will take your petitioners' case into your merciful consideration, &c.

'We, the undersigned inhabitants of Queenborough, beg cordially to support the prayer of the above petitioners.'

(Here follow the signatures of the mayor, the incumbent, the churchwardens, and many others.)

(Board's minute) :

'The request cannot be complied with.'

(Then the incumbent addresses the Board privately) :

'GENTLEMEN,

'I have taken pains to inquire of several influential persons in this place regarding the former character and conduct of —— and —— the petitioners who seek at your hands remission of part of their sentence of imprisonment for smuggling, and I find that previous to their being guilty of that act they were regarded as respectable and industrious men. I have been incumbent of this place for only three months, and therefore am unable of my own knowledge to speak of them, but the above testimony is that of persons whom I can trust, and who are of known integrity in my parish. I can therefore conscientiously express a hope that you will kindly listen to the prayer of their petition.

'I am, Gentlemen, yours faithfully,
'GEORGE D. THOMSON, B.A.'

(Board's minute) :

'The applicant to be informed that, adverting to the magnitude of the offence of which the parties were guilty, the Board cannot direct their release.'

No. 58. Précis of papers connected with a seizure in Ireland (Co. Donegal), showing method of charging expenses, subsistence, etc.

'13th March, 1855.

'SIR,

'I beg leave to acquaint you that on the night of the 10th instant a seizure of 8 cwt of tobacco, with the man, horse, and cart by which it was being conveyed, was made by the Revenue Police stationed at Church Hill, in the Letterkenny road, 24 miles inland. It appears that the man ——, apprehended in charge of it, is from the neighbourhood of Derrybeg, and I have every reason to conclude that this seizure is the remaining portion of the tobacco landed from the *Betsy* and *Nora Creina*, as reported in my letter of the 11th Novr last, enclosing the deposition of James ——, and which tobacco, having been concealed in the adjacent mountains, escaped the strict search made by the Coastguard and Revenue Police at the time. It evidently follows from this and the three previous seizures made by the Coastguard and Constabulary that the smugglers have been baffled in all their attempts to secure the tobacco after it was landed, the whole of which I am credibly informed has now been seized, &c, &c.

'FRANCIS COLLINS,
'*Inspecting Lieutenant.*

'TO THE COMPTROLLER OF COASTGUARD
    LONDON.'

(Board's minute) :

'Retain the goods, horse, and cart, as a seizure : Proceed against the party for the penalty of £100.'

(Below is the return invariably made at the time in such cases, both in Ireland and Great Britain) :

'Name, residence, and occupation of the Party .. .. .. —— —— of Derrybeg, carman.

Offence committed, description and quantity of goods .. Carrying 867 lbs. tobacco.

Date when offence committed .. 9th March, 1855.

Place where .. .. .. Drumlurga parish, Kilmainham, Co. Donegal.

When, and by whom, arrested .. 9th March, 1855. Lieut. Robert Newcomen, 9th Revenue Police.

When, and before whom, convicted — T. Patterson, J. M. Beers, J. Chambers, and J. Fleming, Esqs., J.Ps at petty sessions in Letterkenny, 28th March, 1855.

Amount of Penalty, &c. .. £100. Imprisonment for 9 months, unless he shall sooner pay same.

Where sent, or in what custody — Lifford Gaol.

Of what Country, &c. .. .. Subject of her Majesty.

Apparent age .. .. .. 50.

Apparent state of bodily health — Good.

Whether married or single .. He will not state.

Number of children depending on him .. .. Do.

General Character .. .. Not known.

Whether convicted of Smuggling before — No information as to this has been obtained.'

(It is likely that the prisoner gave a wrong name.)

PRÉCIS OF PROCEEDS, EXPENSES, ETC.

	£	s.	d.		£	s.	d.
'Horse and cart sold for	7	17	6	Prosecuting solicitor's charges	5	4	0
(Tobacco destroyed)				Justices' clerk ..	1	3	6
Loss to Crown by				Messengers	0	3	6
seizure	26	13	0*	Keep of detained horse (14 days) ..	0	17	6
				Customs officers' travelling charges ..	3	1	0
				Support of prisoner while in jail, 134 days at 6d. a day ..	3	7	0
				Paid to officers as reward	19	14	0
				Paid to officers as headmoney ..	1	0	0
	34	10	6		34	10	6'

(In connection with this case there was much amusing discussion as to whether the grant of 6d. a day was payable in the case of an Irish prisoner. Most of the official experts thought that it was only payable in Great Britain, and that the Irish rate was 4½d. a day, but, a precedent being furnished, the charge was passed. N.B.—In other records the *English* rate is shown as 7d.)

* This is quite a moderate item. The larger the seizures, of course the larger the grants of reward.

ADDENDA

(ILLUSTRATIVE DOCUMENTS, see pp. 439-440.)

No. 21A. *Extract from Scottish Board's Memoranda, September 20, 1779, containing deposition made by captain of revenue cruiser, as to movements of squadron commanded by Paul Jones.*

(The account states that on September 16, 1779, the Board were informed that the squadron, which had been viewed off Dunbar on the 14th, appeared off the Isle of May. Captain Brown, of the *Princess Royal* cutter, was ordered to reconnoitre, and, if the ships belonged to the enemy, he was to ' fire three guns, quick,' as a signal to an armed King's ship then lying in Leith Roads, also to fly a jack at his masthead as an additional signal.)

' And Mr. Brown having proceeded agreeably thereto and returned to Leith at half-an-hour after eleven o'clock on Friday morning ' (the 17th) ' his declaration was taken in the Presence of the Honble Capt. Napier, Regulating Officer, and George Clerk Maxwell & Adam Smith, Esqrs, Commissioners of the Customs, which is as follows :

' " Mr. Brown, commander of one of the Customhouse Cutters, having received orders from the Commissioners of the Customs to reconnoitre the Ships coming up the Firth, made sail this morning, and at Daybreak found himself within Pistol Shot of a fifty Gun French Ship,* upon which he tacked about, and afterwards retook a prize they had taken in the Mouth of the Firth, but a French twenty-four Gun Frigate immediately made up, and obliged him to abandon

---

* Undoubtedly *Le Bon Homme Richard.*

the Prize : they brought on Shore a Boy from the Prize, who says they put four soldiers, four Men, & two Officers on board him. The French Squadron consists of a fifty Gun Ship, a twenty four Gun Frigate, and a Brig mounting ten Guns. The Ships sail ill, and they say they are determined to come up to Leith Road. The Commander of the fifty Gun Ship is said to be acquainted with the Coast. Both the fifty Gun Ship and Frigate are painted Black. The fifty Gun Ship has a White Bottom and very clumsy mast head. The Boy says seven sail of them sailed in Company * : they went north † the length of Shetland, and returned separated in a Gale of Wind, some Days ago, from the rest of the Squadron. 17th September, 1779.'' '

(The Memoranda proceed that Adam Smith and Clerk Maxwell transmitted this deposition by express at 2.15 p.m., September 17, to the Treasury, London, and ordered the three revenue sloops on the east coast to be placed under the direction of the Commander-in-Chief. It is evident from the Memoranda that the British Government had been informed promptly of Jones's previous movements, even of his setting out from France, and that the revenue cruisers all round the British coast were on the look-out, manned and armed ' to the fullest extent,' and ready to assist the British fleet. It is quite evident, too, that Captain Brown was a smart and reliable sailorman, and that the Scottish Customs Commissioners were alive to their responsibilities.)

* Probably including prizes.
† Along the west coast of Ireland, and around the north of Scotland ?

INDEX

ALLINGHAM, William, 401
America, trade with, 145, 312, 319
  American tobacco ships, 26
  smuggling, 36, 62, 68, 96, 118, 148, 213, 234, 248, 249, 255, 257, 276, 277, 281, 339, 346, 347
  encroachments, 62, 180, 189, 293
  captures of British ships, 68
  violence, 147
  grievances, 174, 357
  form part syndicate, 190
  fisheries bountied, 222
  wreck, 223
  cheese peculiarly marked, 223
  Vice-Consul wrongfully accused, 261
  infringements of copyright, 282, 338
  disputes with Colonial officers, 313
Anti-Corn Law League, 205
Antigua. See West Indies
Arms, export of, 44
  running, to France, 105
  running (Cape Colony), 317
Artificers, decoying, 87
  emigration permitted, 93
Assay, 210
Athol family, Isle of Man, 94
Aulnage. See Cloth

Australia :
  early trade, 25
  warehousing privileges, 182
  and New Zealand, preference, 215
  an elusive smuggler, 260
  Customs staff, 297
  hired convicts, 300
  Botany Bay, 182, 300
  Melbourne, official salaries, 317
  smuggling, 363
  New South Wales :
    trade of, 192, 197
    Sydney, collector appointed, 151, 156
    smuggling statistics, 253, 257
    separation from Victoria, 317
    smuggling tobacco, 279
    an illegal seizure, 260
    forged banknotes, 304
    emigrant ship arrested, 316
    copyright evasion, 338
    reward offered, 478
  South Australia :
    defective Ordinance, 301

Australia (*continued*) :
　South Australia :
　　revenue, 314
　　Port Adelaide, illegal
　　　seizure, 200
　　trade of, 225
　　list of seizures,
　　　350, 363
　Tasmania :
　　unique warehouse,185
　　Launceston, trade and
　　　revenue, 203, 225
　　questionable duties,
　　　205
　　smuggling spirits, 279
　　favoured tide-waiter,
　　　289
　　rum for troops, 301
　　defective laws, 304
　　salaries, tariffs, and
　　　gold, 325
　　cancelled Customs
　　　commissions, 326
　Victoria :
　　tariff revised, 325
　　trade of, 1853, 336
　　Geelong, trade of, 314
　　separation from New
　　　South Wales, 317

Baltimore, 30
Bank of England, 29
Barbadoes. See West Indies
Beaufort, duke of, 23
Bermuda, slave-trade case, 152
Bideford, 316
Billingsgate, 24
Bill of store, 154
Board of Customs, 10
　library destroyed, 47
　wine store, 47
　power to restore
　　seizures, 58
　English, Irish, and
　　Scotch consolidated,
　　88, 90
　duties of Commis-
　　sioners, 90
　Sir Thomas Fre-
　　mantle, 120
　inspection and report
　　by, 121
　constitution, 135

Board of Customs (*continued*) :
　control of Colonial
　　Customs, 139,
　　288
　ceases, 292, 298,
　　326
　Mr. Dean, 203, 279
　judicial functions, 336
　Sir F. Doyle, 397
Boats of illegal build, 100
　regulations for open, 256,
　　350
　See also Ships, and Preven-
　　tive laws
Bognor, 252
Bonding system. See Ware-
　housing
Bonds, fees for, 80
　abolished, 84
Brighton, 108, 122, 352
Bristol, 57, 117
Bute, Marquis of, 23
Butlerage. See Prisage and
　Butlerage

Canada :
　exports, 42.
　fisheries question, 62, 149,
　　180, 188, 204, 292-5
　official incidents, 174
　official friction, 179, 291
　evasion of Navigation Act,
　　185
　timber from, deck cargoes,
　　190
　tea restrictions, 192
　first preference granted to
　　Britain, 214
　seizures, 248, 350
　smuggled books, 281
　emigrants to, 290
　an anonymous complaint,
　　291
　Customs staff, 297
　Labrador, Customs agent,
　　148
　collector for, 196
　officers, 221
　included in New-
　　foundland, 221
　New Brunswick, 36, 37, 162
　　extensive smuggling,
　　67

Canada (*continued*) :
  New Brunswick, fees, 93
    officials attacked, 117,
      147
    salaries unpaid, 157
    imported tokens, 188
    smuggling, 260, 339,
      340
    Navigation Laws
      questions, 312
    copyright evasion, 343
  Newfoundland, 196
    fisheries, 62, 149, 180,
      188, 204, 292-5
    free ports, etc., 180-2
    smuggling, 124, 340
    Labrador difficulties,
      148-9, 221
  Nova Scotia, 37, 62
    coal-mines, 78
    Customs fees, 85
    free ports, 147
    cost of Customs estab-
      lishment, 152
    friction, 158
    criticism of Customs
      department, 195
    Navigation Laws, 298
    Imperial and Colonial
      collector, 299
    importunate official,
      338
  Quebec, 39, 146, 290
Cape Colony :
  early trade, 219
  smuggling arms into, 318
Cardiff, 24
Carlists, arms for, 194
Casks, fraudulent, 240, 254
Ceylon. See India
Cloth, 87
Coast blockage, 113, 114, 116,
  121-2, 133, 235, 241
Coastguard, 184, 231, 242-3,
  246, 394
  supersede Coast Blockade,
    240-1
  officers promoted, 244-5
  strength of, 278
  men for navy, 337
  officer bound by smugglers,
    362
  life-saving services, 474

Coastwise duties, 76
  traffic, 92, 305
    general transires, 252
    intercolonial, 288
    opened to foreign
      ships, 336
    in 1754, 430-34
    coal charges,1784, 445
Cocoa, manufactured, importation permitted, 90
Coin, exportation of, 34, 70
  for West Indies, 181
  tokens, 188
Chartism, 206
Channel Islands, 104, 210,
  253, 277, 311, 339, 364, 478
Chichester, 116, 234, 320
Church, concessions to, 49, 151,
  161, 196, 211, 217
Colonies :
  passenger traffic regulated,
    20
  abuses in, 36
  smuggling, 36
  salaries and receipts, 36-41
  frauds in, 39
  officers to obey governors,
    57
  superannuated, 60
  warehousing in, 94, 171
  laws revised, 138
  official friction, 141-3
  dual duties, 211
  oil from, 215
  foreign trade with, 289
  powers of local legislatures,
    291
  home Customs control,
    292, 326, 349
  list of, in 1847, 297
  imperial duties abolished
    in, 298
  Navigation Laws in, 299
  preference diminished, 315
  collector's emoluments in
    1826, 444, 470
Comptroller-General, 177
Consular privileges, 315
Copyright, 19, 58, 208, 210,
  215, 219
  Act, evasions, 182, 212,
    256, 338
  international, 217

Copyright case, Mr. Murray's opinion, 283
Cork, 32, 315
Corn :
  duties on, the ancient (1660-1800), 1-8
    revised, 27, 59
    in 1828, 150-1
    in 1842, 207
    in 1845, 290
    in 1849, 291
    suspended, 295, 296
    to be paid at importation, 306
  prices, 1696-1793, 4-5
    1792-1800, 8
    1801-12, 28
  prices, duty, and imports, 1701-1820, 416-18
  Anti-Corn Law League, 205
  bounties on imported, 28
    on exported, 3
  exports and imports, 7, 8
  Irish, 8, 29
  Manx legislation, 77
  early Canadian preference on, 214
Cornwall, survey of ports in, 405
Cruisers, 14, 113, 127
  officers' uniform, 27
  medicine chests for, 105
  repairs, 255
Custom House :
  land for, 42
  burnt down, 45
  rebuilding of, 48, 79
  thefts from, 175
Customs :
  Union of Great Britain and Ireland, 15
  purchase of appointments in, 19
  consolidation of laws, 33, 74-5, 135-40, 168-72, 285
  review of, in 1820, 78-84
  Board of, and Commissioners. See Board
  to collect all import duties, 91
  and Excise compared, 92

Customs (continued) :
  powers of search, 105, 286
  bounties and drawbacks, 171
  amendment of laws, 209, 306, 310
  revenue of ports, 1844, 226
  huge frauds, 261
  Committee of Inquiry, 264-9
  hours, 320
  Committee of Inquiry into, 323-5
  debate in Commons on, 327
  taxes reviewed, 380-3
  ad valorem duties, 385-6
  entry (1787), 446
  duties, 452
  revenue 1823-1838, 465
Customs officers. See Officers of Customs

Dartmouth, coast traffic, 1744, 432
Deal, 99, 102, 109, 110, 250, 255, 354, 441
Dean. See Board of Customs
Deck cargoes, 190
Demerara :
  smuggling in, 116
    and collusion, 184
Devon, survey of ports, 408
Docks, East India, 25
  Commercial, 36
  in London, 23, 80
  London, frauds in, 261, 321-3
Dominica. See West Indies
Dover, 124, 238-40, 253
Doyle, Sir Francis. See Board of Customs
Drawbacks, 171
Duties, aliens', 1685-86, 413
  ad valorem, 15
  butter and cheese, 62
  war, 64
  books, 107
  various, 138
  coal (export), 288

East India Company, 21, 58, 61, 168, 285, 337
  privileges, 84, 145

East India Company, certain
  privileges abolished,
  171
  St. Helena withdrawn
    from, 171
  ports of importation,
    177
  time limit extended,
    329
  troops for, 329
Emigrant ships :
  supervision of, 20, 190
  regulations for, 68,
    139
  duration of voyages,
    164
  Passenger Act, 193-4,
    290
  overcrowding, 303
  borrowed boats, 316
  breaking detention,
    316
Emigrants, Canadian, 290
Enclosure Acts, 4
Excise, 23
  duties on tea, 21
  prosecution, 26
  duty on tobacco, 44
  Board of, 88
  officers transferred to
    Customs, 91
  duties transferred to Cus-
    toms, 91
  and Customs, 92
  seizures, 97, 345, 352, 355,
    359, 375
  officers attacked, 98, 355
  powers of search, 105,
    286
  commissions issued, 184
  drawback frauds, 191
  survey of tobacco manu-
    facturers, 210
  collusive seizure, 365-8
  letter from informer, 375
Exeter, coastwise trade (1745),
  430
Exportation, time of, defined,
  169
Export duties, 75, 288
  prohibitions, 168
    of money, 176
  bounty, 171, 138

Falmouth, 49-55, 349
Fees, Irish Customs, 10, 31
  abolished, 18, 29, 31
  revised, 38, 84, 161
  colonial, 85, 93, 140, 158
  Vice-Admiralty Court, 163
  ' odd pence,' 187
  colonial petition against,
    458
  list of Jamaican, 464
Fisheries Convention, Canadian,
  62, 149, 180, 188,
  292-5
  home, 214
Fishing-boats, 218
  smuggling by, 272
Flags, pendants seized, 195
Flotsam, duty on, 42
Folkestone, 243, 353
Four and a half per cent. duties:
  pensioners and pro-
    ceeds, 29, 162
  repealed, 187
Fowey, 346
France, importance of trade,
  230
Franklin, Sir John, 302
Frauds, hop, 74
  export, 82
  London Dock, 261-9, 321-3
Free ports, 302
Free trade and Protection, 377-
  393
  duties abolished, 285
Fremantle, Sir Thomas. See
  Board of Customs
French goods, duties on, 44
  prisoners, 414
Frewin. See Jickling
Fuller, Henry, 70
Fund, Customs, Annuity and
  Benevolent, 65-6

Gauger, London, 71
Gibraltar, rock from, 45
Glasgow, 365
Grafton, duke of, 24, 28
Graham, Lieutenant, 133
Greenock, 123, 194
Greenwich Hospital for seamen,
  178
Gregson's (Mother) gang, 274
Grey, Earl, 318

Gold Coast :
    Customs staff and
        duties, 309
Guano, 200

Hamel, Solicitor, 329
Holidays, Customs, 28
Hours, Customs, 70
Hull, trade of, 162, 276, 328,
    442
Hume, J. D., 229, 328
Hydrometer, Sikes', 65
    Clarke's, 65

Illustrative documents. See at
    end of Index
Importation, time of, defined,
    169
    restricted goods, 285
Import duties, all transferred to
        Customs, 91
    waived, 151, 161
    many abolished, 286-8
Import statistics, 78
Imposts, temporary, 21
India :
    oil from, 194
    Surinam claim, 217
    East India Company's
        territory, 337
    Ceylon :
        trade of, 193, 225
        illegal trading, 250-1
        smuggling, 225, 258
        Customs staff, 298
        trade question, 253
Inquiry into Customs, 264-9,
    323-4
Ireland :
    price of corn, 8
    Customs under Act of
        Union, 9-15
    seizures, 9
    Commissioners for, 10
    fees, 10, 11, 12
        abolished, 31
    official defaulters, 11
    laxity, 11-14
    hours, 14
    Union with Great Britain,
        15-17
    offices   abolished,   18,
        30

Ireland (continued) :
    Customs revenue, 30
        pensioners, 32
    prisage and butlerage, 35
    Baltimore, 83
    duties   assimilated   to
        British, 92
    smuggling, 96, 118, 129,
        243, 259, 276, 364
    pikes for, 117
    illicit distillation, 184
    Repeal Associations, 215
    arms seized, 255
    wreck and riot, 312
    base coin, 315
    illustrative documents, 415,
        448, 466, 488

Jamaica. See West Indies
Jickling's ' Digest ' of Customs
    Laws, 60
Jones, Paul, 439, 490

Kelly, Miss, housekeeper, 45

Laing, David, architect, 48
Leeward   Islands.   See   West
    Indies
Lewes, 114
Literati, Customs :
    Peach, 394
    Doyle, 397
    Allingham, 401
Liverpool, 58, 82, 173, 187, 191,
    199, 320, 328, 339, 481
    serious trouble at, 172
London, 22, 36, 80, 81, 232
    city gauger, 71
    smuggling, 97, 102, 272,
        339, 274-5
    dock frauds, 321
    trade of, 328
    illustrative   documents,
        409, 445

Machinery :
    export prohibition, 64, 176
        repealed, 215
Maidstone, 85
Malta, 155
Man, Isle of :
    corn legislation, 77
    Customs duties, 94, 13

Man, Isle of (*continued*):
    restricted importa-
      tions, 171, 218, 289
    smuggling, 250
    restricted trade, 286
      laws repealed,
       331
Marks on merchandise, 187, 223
Mauritius :
    tariff complications, 146
    trouble at Port Louis, 164,
      183
    a Navigation Act case, 174
    lists of seizures, 248, 363
    drug prohibition, 256
    opium smuggling, 280,
      341-3
    evasion of Navigation laws,
      289
    brandy export fraud, 358
Measures, standard, 93
Ministers, foreign, packages for,
    191
Mint, erection of, in U.S.A., 64
Montserrat. See West Indies
Murray, John, 344
Murray, Sir Geo., 158

Naval stores, embargo on, 411
Nevis. See West Indies
Navigation laws, 286, 381
    Jamaican case, 32
    Trinidad case, 71, 85
    relaxed, 69, 92
    illegal seizures, 71, 200
    suspended locally, 77,
      179
    amended, 84
    complaint against, 85
    consolidated and re-
      laxed, 137, 170
    evasion of, 185, 289
    official decisions under,
      189, 190
    a limitation of the, 198
    seizures under, 203,
      250, 255
    controller of, ap-
      pointed, 298
    emasculated, 304-5
    questions relating to,
      312, 314
    terse summary, 314

Navigation laws, memorial
    against repeal of, 325
    repeal of, 336
Navy officer's seizure, 113
    recruits wanted for, 194
Newcastle, 67
Newhaven, 124, 246
New Zealand :
    shipbuilding in, 160
    trade of, 160
    settlements and trade,
      181
    created a colony, 200
    contraband traffic, 213
    preference for Aus-
      tralia, 215
    fiscal experiments, 223
    illegal seizure, 261
    Customs staff, 298
    exports, 314
    sheep-wash, 319
    barter and smuggling,
      346
    smuggling, 363

Oaths, revised, 84
    abolished, 161
Officers of Customs :
    holidays, 28, 135
    hours, 28, 135
    Superannuation Fund
      abolished, 37
    collector's seizures
      (Pellew), 49
    Annuity and Benevo-
      lent Fund, 66
    offices abolished, 81
    Violent officials, 86,
      133
    attacked, 99
    limits of service ex-
      tended, 89
    and Oath of Suprem-
      acy, 93
    widows' pensions, 101
    illegal search by, 102
    concerned in smug-
      gling, 108
    accommodation when
      boarded, 112
    attempts to bribe, 115
    trouble at Liverpool,
      172

Officers of Customs (*continued*) :
	official safe plundered
		by, 175
	socialistic tendencies,
		199
	to conduct law cases,
		291
	soliciting promotion,
		296
	murder of O'Connor,
		gauger, 306
	boarding	hardships,
		311
	census, return of, 315
	' satisfactions ' abol-
		ished, 336
	disputes with mer-
		chants, 336
	collusive seizures, 115,
		344
	gentle abuse of, 353
	illustrative documents,
		419, 424-5, 426, 430
Offices, sale of, prohibited, 33
Oysters, duty on, 66

Parry, Lieutenant, 243
Passenger traffic. See Emi-
		gration
	Act, 193, 298
Passengers' baggage, 154, 311
Peach, Chas. Wm., 394
Pellew (Collector), 49
Pepperell, Richard, 336, 346,
		359
Pilotage conditions, 93
Piracy, 427
Plantations.   See Colonies
Plate, assay of, 210
Plymouth, 311, 339
Ports and creeks, list of, 332-5
Portsmouth, 253, 255
Poundage, 381
Preference, colonial, abolished,
		315
Preventive laws and regula-
		tions :
	a prosecution, 25
	' hovering ' limits ex-
		tended, 96, 100, 350
	forfeiture of ships, 96,
		100
	licensing ships, 100

Preventive laws and regula-
		tions (*continued*) :
	preventive	officers'
		widows, 101
	throwing goods over-
		board, 101
	Isle of Man, 101
	landguard, 101
	ships of illegal build,
		100, 107
	warning	smugglers,
		115
	system, 113, 125
	consolidation of laws,
		136, 169, 286
	laws revised, 241, 250
	penalties revised, 282
	restrictions on ships,
		350
Prisage and butlerage, 23, 380
	purchased by Treas-
		ury, 28
	in Ireland, 35
	in County Palatine,
		164
Prisoners, Customs, support of,
		43
Prohibitions :
	import, corn, 27
	export, evaded, 176
	of machinery repealed,
		215
	export, 286
	import, 208, 285-6
	removed some import, 209

Quarantine Act, 18
	evasion of, 68
	' Limerick	Trader '
		case, 86
	cholera, 161, 164
	smallpox on slaver,
		185
	infected sheep, 302
	pilots and, 423
Quarter days, financial, 337
Quays, legal, scheme to pur-
		chase, 24

Rates, Book of, 1660, 408-9
Ramsgate, 240
Receiver-General, 29
Reciprocity laws, 319

Registry of Shipping, 137, 154, 160, 190, 286, 305
   foreign shareholders, 138, 296
   specimen certificate, 452
Regrating, 33
Report, ship's, 412
Revenue :
   Irish, 1781-1816, 30
     1819, 79
     1802-1806, 449
   British, 1819, 79
   Scottish, 1819, 79
   Great Britain and Ireland, consolidated, 64, 226
   Committee of Inquiry into, 228
Russia, war with, shipping arrangements, 337

St. Kitts. See West Indies
St. Vincent. See West Indies
Salaries, public, 35
Scotland :
   sinecurists, 9
   revenue from ports, 83
   Board censured, 83
   smuggling, 123, 254
   report on preventive system, 126-9
   duty on colonial spirits, 337
   smugglers improperly acquitted, 365
   illustrative documents, 419, 427-9, 433, 435, 448, 450, 474
Seamen's Act, Merchant, 298
Seizures, Treasury protest against, 56
   division of rewards, 425
Shields, North, 67
Ships :
   captured by French, 45
   with simulated licences, 49
   captured by Americans, 68
   passenger. See Emigration
   preventive regulations. See Preventive
   registry. See Registry of Shipping
   trading limits, 350

Ships (continued) :
   illustrative documents, 452, 461, 471, 477
Sierra Leone :
   collector's defalcations, 145
Sight entries, 12, 214, 255
Silk, duties on, 44
Sinecures, Scottish, 9
   Irish, 9
   Irish offices abolished, 30
   abolished, 38, 69
   offices abolished, 81, 177
   patent collector's fees (London), 445
Slave laws :
   slave trade abolished, 30
   subsequent troubles, 141, 142, 152
   slavery abolished in colonies, 171
Slaves, infected slave ships, 185
   captured, 186
Smith, Adam, 33, 490
Smuggling :
   laws revised, 251, 282
   letters, 74
   seizures, 1816-1818, 80
   1801-1825, 95-134
   vanishing rewards, 99, 233
   fighting at Deal, 99
   seizure rewards, 100, 118, 233
   illegal search, 101
   silk, 102, 237
   distinguished culprits, 103-4, 108, 220, 249
   undefended suits, 104
   continental depots, 104
   devices for, ships', 106, 107, 111-112, 121, 123, 124-5, 130, 231, 233-4, 252, 258, 347, 364, 370
   goods, 107, 111, 112, 116, 123, 124, 125, 130-1, 234, 240, 245, 247, 250, 254, 270, 339, 347, 364
   caves, 107
   by officials, 108
   contemplated, 109, 130

Smuggling (*continued*) :
tea, penalties for, 110
by military, 110
officers assaulted, 111-13,
116, 360
coastguard officer's diary,
114
in Ireland, remarkable, 118
reports upon, 122
in Scotland, 123, 126-9
returns relating to, 126
informers' rewards, 131
signalling to smugglers,
231-2
coral, 232
successful runs, 234-5
books, 237, 256
statistics of, 253, 271
armed conflicts, 234, 242-4
promotions for suppressing,
244-5
mounted guard, 245
rafted tubs of spirits, 247
concealment on the person,
250
spirits in fraudulent casks,
254
by fishing-boats, 255, 256,
272
Le Courier, diagram of, 258
tobacco as boot-soles and
rope, 270
tobacco manufacturers'
methods, 271, 272
by coasting vessels, 273,
275
Mother Gregson's gang,
274
wholesale, 273-7
account, 277
dogs used in, 278
in passengers' baggage,
340, 353
collusive seizures, 344
a Jersey boat's record, 344
the *Charlotte*, 349
specimen rewards, 349, 355
seizures, lists of, 345-6,
348, 349, 351, 359,
364-5
accounts of, 352, 354-
6, 360-2, 369-77
Excise seizures, 355

Smuggling (*continued*) :
many cargoes, 361
coastguardsman's adven-
ture, 362
smugglers improperly ac-
quitted, 365
Excise seizure and collu-
sion, 365-9
French vessel seized, 372
Norwegian seamen's agree-
ment, 374
in East Anglia, informer's
letter, 375
illustrative documents,
429, 440, 441-2, 448,
469, 478, 480-1, 483, 486,
488
Society Islands, 160
Solicitor, Customs, pay of, 82
Southampton, 315
Spirits, testing, 65
duties on, 170, 451
merchants' free samples,
184, 296
measurement in bottle, 218
minimum size of packages
of, 251
fraudulent casks for, 254
colonial, duties on, 295,
337
foreign, to be warehoused
before removal, 296
Staple Acts repealed, 87
Stockton, 164, 271, 273
Stores, ships', duty free, 163,
164
Sugar, tests for, 151
duties reduced, 302
increased, 337
refining in bond, 337
Superannuation allowances, 35,
161
fund abolished, 37

Tariff, Customs :
consolidated, 21
extra duties, 31
duties, 1819, 74-5
revised, 1823, 90
1826, 138
1833, 170
1842, 210
1845, 285

Tariff, Customs (*continued*):
  simplified, 286
  reductions and abolitions,
    286-8, 291, 302
  ad valorem duties, 1853,
    329
  specific duties, 1853, 330
  varied, 337
  review of, from 1300 A.D.,
    380,
  its incidence, 383-4
  reviewed, 228-231
Tariff Reform and Free Trade,
  377-393.
Tea, Excise duty on, 21, 75
  duties, 170
  duty transferred to Cus-
    toms, 172
  restricted importations of,
    172
  statistics, 192
Thames police instituted, 19
Timber duty, 210
Tobacco :
  warehousing, 22
  duty on, 44
  cigars, duty on, 90
  Excise supervision of
    manufacturers' premises,
    211
  minimum size of packages,
    251, 306
  manufacturers and smug-
    glers, 271
  adulteration of, 278
  for sheep-wash, 319
  destruction of seized, 320
Tonnage duties, 76
Tortola. See West Indies
Trade marks, commercial conventions, 187
Trade of ports, 328
Treaties, commercial, 319
Trinidad. See West Indies
Turtle, 200

Walden, Lord Howard de,
  300
Warehousing Act, 21, 22-3, 80
  tobacco, rum, rice, coffee,
    cocoa, etc., 22
  removal privileges, 34
  in Liverpool, 82

Warehousing Act revised, 90,
  138, 170, 288
  spirits, allowances on, 163
  bacon, 187
  coffee, and husking, 194
  suggested colonial change,
    204
  warehouse sweepings, 321
  marking packages in bond,
    335
War, imposts, 21
War, foreign ships on declaration of, 337
Weights and measures, stand-
  ards, 94
  Act repealed, 178
Wells, 415
West Indies, 40-1
  Antigua, 39
    slaver captured, 61
    smuggling, 78
    indignant collector,
      140, 143
  Barbados :
    rum and lumber trade,
      39
    emoluments in, 37
    smuggling in, 76, 131
    salary disputes, 167
  Dominica :
    slave trade, 141, 186
    pendants seized, 195
    census troubles, 219
    vessel seized, 232
    officials assaulted, 236
    smuggling, 246, 281
    negro apprentice agree-
      ment, 475
  Grenada, official friction,
    142
  Jamaica :
    Duke of Manchester's
      claim, 59
    defaulting collector, 76
    seizures, 106, 132
    friction, 143, 155, 216
    naval officer's salary,
      155
    Navigation Act, 162,
      314
    slave riots in, 166, 167
    an infected slave ship,
      185

West Indies (*continued*) :
　Jamaica :
　　trade, revenue, and warehouses, 197
　　droit, s. 223
　　trade mark cases, 223
　　seizure of gin, 236
　　copyright works seized, 256, 282
　　Mr. Murray's opinion, 282
　　officers assaulted, 283
　　Lord Howard de Walden, 300
　　an unrecognized Power, 300
　　a frugal official, 304
　　evasion of duties, 309, 313
　　damaged goods and port limits, 310
　　illustrative documents, 453, 464, 471
　Leeward Islands :
　　Navigation laws suspended, 77
　　Bonding changes, 204
　Montserrat, 140
　　Navigation laws seizure, 67
　　landing-waiter's plaint, 220
　　valued negroes, 221
　Nevis :
　　coastwise traffic extension, 213
　　a dual appointment, 299
　St. Kitts, 39
　　slavery questions, 142
　　cost of Customs administration, 154
　　an office squabble, 187

West Indies (*continued*) :
　St. Kitts :
　　coastwise traffic extension, 213
　　officials attacked, 236, 253
　　distinguished smugglers, 249
　　unwarrantable complaint, 302
　St. Vincent :
　　smuggling gin, 282
　　seizure report, 467
　Tortola :
　　wreck and irregularities, 356-8
　　merchants' petition, 455
　　petition against fees, 458
　　obstructing officers, 473
　Trinidad :
　　Navigation laws, cases, 71-4
　　slaves landed, 185
　　merchants' petition, 459
Westminster, Court of, superseded, 178
Weymouth, 242, 258
Wharves, sufferance, 24
Wine, duties on, 1812, 43
　levied per gallon, 95
　duties on, 161, 451
　for Prince Regent, sampled, 58
Wool, 58, 87
　foreign, duty on, 21
　duties, 380
Wreck, duty on salved goods, 42, 179
　Admiralty droits, 187

ILLUSTRATIVE DOCUMENTS

NO.		PAGE
1.	Customers' survey of ports, 1671	406
2.	Extracts from Book of Rates, 1660	408
3.	Bill of Entry, 1660	409
4.	Embargo on vessels carrying naval stores, 1665	411
5.	Master's declaration on ship's report, 1678	412
6.	Order in Council, repeal of aliens' duties, 1685	413
7.	Report of capture of French privateer, 1689	414
8.	Seizure note, 1699	415
9.	Board's inquiry into granting permit for fish, 1700	415
10.	Prices, duties, imports of corn, 1701-1820	416
11.	Instructions to Scottish collectors, 1707	419
12.	Pilots and quarantine, 1710	423
13.	Extracts from Scottish Board's minutes, 1723-1724	424
14.	Regulations for dividing seizure moneys	425
15.	Extracts from Scottish Board's minutes, 1735-1736	427
16.	Advice of smuggling vessel on coast, 1735-1736	429
17.	Ordering military assistance against smugglers, 1740	430
18.	Coastwise traffic, 1745	430
19.	Relanding dutiable goods (Scotland), 1745	433
20.	Minute dismissing Francis Porteous, 1745	434
21.	Board's minute, Scotland, rebellion, 1745	435
	Report signed by John Paul (Paul Jones)	439
22.	Extracts from Annual Register (Smuggling), 1782-1802	440
23.	Net produce of Plantation Customs, 1784	444
24.	Coastwise coal charges (London), 1784	445
25.	Patent Collector's fees (London), 1785	445
26.	Specimen duty warrants, 1787	446
27.	Return showing tobacco and snuff seized, 1789-1825	448
28.	Payments into Exchequer from Customs, 1802-1826	449
29.	Form of indictment of smugglers, 1813	450
30.	Comparison of duties on spirits, tobacco, tea, and wine	451
31.	Copy of Certificate of Registry, 1815	452
32.	' Libel ' exhibited in Vice-Admiralty Court prosecution	453
33.	Petition from Tortola merchants, 1815	455
34.	Petition against Customs fees (Tortola), 1816	458
35.	Trinidad merchant's petition, 1820	459
36.	Colonial clearance documents for British ship, 1820	461
37.	Customs fees charged at Kingston, Jamaica, 1821	464
38.	Customs revenue receipts, 1823-1838	465
39.	Smugglers kill and wound navy men, 1821	465

NO.   PAGE
40. Sale of seized tobacco (Ireland), 1824 -   -   - 466
41. Seizure and sale of French sloop (St. Vincent), 1824 - 467
42. Reward offered for discovery of smugglers, 1827   - 469
43. Plantation collectors' salaries and fees, 1826 -   - 470
44. Licence to a vessel to trade as a whaler, 1828 -   - 471
45. Report on negro insurrection in Jamaica, 1832   - 471
46. Report on obstruction of Customs officers in Tortola,
      1834   -   -   -   -   -   - 473
47. Statement of coastguard service in saving life, 1836 - 474
48. Receipt given for negroes for apprenticing (Dominica),
      1837   -   -   -   -   - 475
49. Coastguard officers' memorial -   -   -   - 476
50. Application for exemption of yacht from report, 1839 - 477
51. Reward offered for discovery of smugglers, 1841   - 478
52. Jersey smugglers, confession, 1848   -   - 480
53. Report made by seizer of *Charlotte*, 1849   -   - 480
54. Report of a seizure at Liverpool, 1850 -   -   - 481
55. Reward offered for discovery of smuggler, 1851   - 483
56. Suffolk smuggler's confession, 1852   -   -   - 484
57. Papers on a seizure in the Medway, 1854   -   - 486
58. Papers on a seizure in Ireland, 1855 -   -   - 488
21a. (Apdenda) Memoranda relating to Paul Jones, 1779 - 490

PRESS NOTICES OF VOLUME I. OF
THE KING'S CUSTOMS
FROM THE EARLIEST TIMES TO THE YEAR 1800.

Demy 8vo. 10s. 6d. *net.*

'Messrs. Atton and Holland must be congratulated on having made the most of their exceptional sources of information in producing an entertaining as well as an historically interesting work.'—*Outlook.*

'The authors have shown great industry and judgment in the collection and utilization of material, the enormous extent of which must have made the task of selection one of considerable difficulty.'—*Morning Post.*

'Every chapter has its list of authorities cited at its close, and where practicable opens with a clear statement of principal Statutes affecting the period under consideration. Thus the general reader will find the course of legislation and procedure made intelligible, stage by stage, as becomes a popular history. . . . Extremely instructive, and often full of entertainment.'—*Westminster Gazette.*

'A popular history of "The King's Customs" was much needed, and Messrs. Henry Atton and Henry Hurst Holland are to be congratulated upon the exhaustive work which they have produced. It provides an extremely interesting "account of maritime revenue and contraband traffic in England, Scotland, and Ireland from the earliest times to the year 1800." . . . The whole volume is of engrossing interest.'—*Dundee Advertiser.*

'It will undoubtedly be a good thing if some of those who argue loudest either for or against Tariff Reform will familiarize themselves with this book—a process that will have the effect of preventing some from wasting their eloquence and of encouraging others to back up intrinsically sound arguments by the evidences of history.'—*Evening Standard.*

'A most interesting account of maritime revenue and contraband traffic in the United Kingdom from the earliest times to the year 1800.'—*Daily Mail.*

'The authors . . . had full access to Departmental materials in its preparation. These materials . . . are, as a rule, dry and bare of the sap and spirit of human interest. Mr. Atton and Mr. Holland have, however, the art of setting the skeleton together, bone and bone, and clothing them with flesh and blood, and even giving them touches of romantic colouring.'—*Scotsman.*

'A book of unique character, well conceived, and ably executed.'—*Birmingham Gazette.*

'All sorts of odd and interesting information can be gleaned from "The King's Customs." . . . It is no mere dry register of facts, but is a lively record which its authors have every reason to describe as "popular."'—*Sunday Times.*